PENGUIN BOOKS

NAPOLEON AS MILITARY COMMANDER

General Sir James Marshall-Cornwall was born in 1887 and educated at Rugby, where he was a contemporary of Rupert Brooke.
He went to the Royal Military Academy, Woolwich, in 1905 and
was commissioned into the Royal Field Artillery in 1907. He served
in Field-Marshall Haig's staff in the First World War and played
an active part in the Second World War, in charge of Western
Command, then spent the rest of the war working with the SOE and
MI6. He retired after the war, but remained active. Between 1948
and 1951 he was editor-in-chief of the Captured German Archives
at the Foreign Office and was President of the Royal Geographical
Society, 1954–8. He was appointed CBE in 1919 and KCB in 1940.
His other books include *Marshal Massena* (1965); *Haig as Military
Commander* (forthcoming in Classic Penguin, 2002); and *Wars and
Rumours of Wars*, an autobiography (1984). He died in 1985.

D0168355

1 *Napoleon at the zenith of his career, 1810 (aged 41)*
After a portrait by Vigneux

NAPOLEON

as Military Commander

General Sir James Marshall-Cornwall
KCB, CBE, DSO, MC

*L'histoire n'est pas une science, c'est un art,
et on n'y réussit que par l'imagination.*

Anatole France

PENGUIN BOOKS

PENGUIN BOOKS

Published by the Penguin Group
Penguin Books Ltd, 80 Strand, London WC2R ORL, England
Penguin Putnam Inc., 375 Hudson Street, New York, New York 10014, USA
Penguin Books Australia Ltd, Ringwood, Victoria, Australia
Penguin Books Canada Ltd, 10 Alcorn Avenue, Toronto, Ontario, Canada M4V 3B2
Penguin Books India (P) Ltd, 11 Community Centre, Panchsheel Park,
New Delhi – 110 017, India
Penguin Books (NZ) Ltd, Cnr Rosedale and Airborne Roads, Albany, Auckland,
New Zealand
Penguin Books (South Africa) (Pty) Ltd, 24 Sturdee Avenue, Rosebank 2196, South Africa

Penguin Books Ltd, Registered Offices: 80 Strand, London WC2R ORL, England

www.penguin.com

First published by B. T. Batsford Ltd 1967
Published as a Classic Penguin 2002
1

Contents

'*Il serait plaisant de voir un jour les philosophes et les apostats suivre Bonaparte à la Messe en grinçant des dents, et les républicains se courber devant lui. Ils avaient pourtant juré de tuer le premier qui ravirait le pouvoir. Il serait plaisant qu'il créât un jour des cordons et qu'il en décorât les rois ; qu'il fît des princes et qu'il s'alliât avec quelque ancienne dynastie . . . . Malheur à lui s'il n'est pas toujours vainqueur !*'

'It would be pleasing to see one day the philosophers and apostates following Bonaparte to Mass, gnashing their teeth, and to see the Republicans bowing and scraping before him, after having sworn to kill the first person who should overthrow the government. It would be pleasing if he should some day institute honours and awards and decorate kings with them; if he should create princes, and ally himself with some ancient dynasty . . . . Woe to him if he is not always a conqueror!'

Antoine Rivarol (1753–1801)
(who died while Bonaparte was still First Consul)

Illustrations

Maps

Acknowledgment

The Author and Publishers wish to thank the following for permission to reproduce the illustrations included in this book:

The Trustees of the British Museum, for figs. 1, 2, 3, 13, 17, 18 and 23; Anna S. K. Brown Military Collection, Providence, Rhode Island, for figs. 15 and 16; The Mansell Collection, for figs. 7, 14, 22 and 28; The Mansell-Bulloz Collection, for figs. 19 and 20; The Musée de l'Armée, Invalides, Paris, for figs. 24, 25 and 26; The Musée National de Versailles, for figs. 9, 11 and 12; The Radio Times Hulton Picture Library, for figs. 8, 10 and 27; The Royal Geographical Society, for fig. 21; The Wellington Museum, Apsley House, London, for fig. 4; The Trustees of the Wallace Collection, for the jacket illustration and for fig. 5; Ernest Weal Esq., Souvenir Napoléonien, for fig. 6.

Fig. 29 is from *Précis de la Guerre entre la France et l'Autriche*, Paris, 1822.

The Author and Publishers would also like to thank the Oxford University Press for permission to reproduce the maps of Northern Italy, Battle of Rivoli, Battle of Aspern-Essling and the Battle of Wagram.

Prologue

It was Goethe who likened the Napoleonic legend to the Revelation of St. John the Divine: 'Everyone feels that there is something in it, but nobody knows quite what it is.' The Napoleonic paean has been hymned by many worshippers, and the countless conscientious historians who have unearthed the facts of his career have left little scope for further spadework. The pieces of the puzzle are at everyone's disposal, in great profusion if not confusion; the difficulty lies in fitting them together to produce the correct picture. Most of Napoleon's better biographers have been abler critics of his statecraft than of his strategy. For English readers the conception of Napoleon as an original thinker in the field of military doctrine has been successfully debunked by Liddell Hart.* Liddell Hart was not the first person to discover this, for it was revealed a generation earlier by Colin,† though perhaps Liddell Hart has argued the point more cogently.‡

The fact is that Napoleon devised no new doctrine in either strategy or tactics; indeed he never claimed to have. Had he done so, he might have avoided the appalling losses which his troops suffered over and over again, right up to the futile carnage of his last battle. But he was a master of the conduct of war; he was the supreme craftsman of his trade, who knew how to make the most effective, though not the most economical use of the tools and techniques which he found ready to his hand.

The aim of this book is to portray Napoleon as a military commander. In Napoleon's career, however, strategy and statecraft were so closely interwoven that it is difficult to treat of one aspect without encroaching on the other. In this respect his career bore a certain resemblance to that of Cromwell, which Napoleon had studied closely. Napoleon, of course, was a greater genius than Cromwell, both as statesman and soldier. In the main, however,

---

* B. H. Liddell Hart, *The Ghost of Napoleon* (Faber & Faber, 1933).

† Capitaine J. Colin, *L'Éducation militaire de Napoléon* (Paris, 1900).

‡ This point of view was also expressed very lucidly by Spenser Wilkinson in his Oxford lectures in 1914 (*The French Army before Napoleon*, Clarendon Press, 1915).

the present volume deals with the military side of Napoleon's career, being written primarily for students of war.

I have based this study on two hypotheses: firstly, as has been indicated above, that Napoleon was no innovator in the art or science of war; secondly, that, to quote Lord Wavell, 'Good generals, unlike poets, are made rather than born' (*Soldiers and Soldiering*). This latter theorem I have tried to prove in the first chapter, which describes Napoleon's early upbringing and training, and particularly his self-education, for there is no doubt that the varied environment and experiences of his early life exerted a marked influence on the development of his character and abilities.

The second chapter describes the legacy of military doctrine and organization which Napoleon inherited from his fore-runners, and on which he based his conduct of war. The subsequent chapters trace his campaigns in chronological order, in order to analyse his methods of conducting them.

It would be futile to attempt a comprehensive bibliography of Napoleonana. I have merely appended a short list of those sources which I have found most useful to consult; among these I should like to pay a special tribute to Frédéric Masson, that fountain-head of research into whose well so many historians have dipped their buckets.

I

The Formative Years
1769-1792

It is by no means axiomatic that great military commanders are moulded or even influenced by their early upbringing and environment. The boyhood, for instance, of Arthur Wellesley, born in the same year as Napoleon, gave little promise of his later achievements: an undistinguished career at Eton, followed by a spell of lax tuition in a Brussels *pension* and, finally, the rather featureless régime of a semi-military French academy in Anjou, which he left at the age of 17 to obtain his purchased Commission as an infantry Ensign. This haphazard training hardly seemed calculated to evoke the military talents which blossomed in the years to come.

With the future Emperor of the French the case was very different. Napoleone Buonaparte was born on 15 August 1769 at Ajaccio in Corsica. Exactly 15 months earlier, the island of Corsica, formerly a possession of the Genoese Republic, was transferred by treaty to the French crown and was occupied by French troops. The Corsicans, an independent and stubborn race, had disliked the Genoese, but they liked their new masters still less. Under the leadership of Pasquale Paoli (1725–1807) they continued against the French occupation the same dogged resistance that they had previously maintained against the Genoese. Carlo Buonaparte, the father of the future Emperor, and his wife Letizia (*née* Ramolino) had joined the resistance movement led by Paoli, and were actually on the run from their family estate when Napoleone was born; he was their second son, the first, Giuseppe, being a year older.

Letizia was a handsome woman of strong character. Though an affectionate mother, she took a firm line in bringing up her children, and had no hesitation in resorting to corporal punishment when she thought it necessary. Her strict training proved an antidote to the indulgent attitude of her easy-going husband, and there is no doubt that her influence moulded to a marked degree the character of the young Napoleone. In future years he retained the greatest affection and respect for *Madame Mère*, who stood staunchly by him during the troubled days at the close of his career.

It may be said too that many of the characteristics of his native Corsica were bred in the bone of the future Emperor. He came of a race of hardy and independent-minded islanders. By tradition the feeling of family clannishness and solidarity was strong among them, and throughout his career Napoleon was obsessed by a sense of duty towards his relations. This family attachment formed a marked feature of the more sentimental side of Napoleon's nature, and was undoubtedly inherited from his Corsican ancestry and upbringing. It was destined to prove a troublesome burden in later years, when he felt obliged to shower crowns and riches on his brothers and sisters despite their frailties and treacheries. His brothers (and brothers-in-law) were unstable in character; they wrecked his policy by their incongruence as kings, and they lost his battles by their incompetence as commanders.

The Corsicans were by nature addicted to mutual suspicion and political intrigue, and this taint certainly showed itself in Napoleon's future behaviour. Not only did it mark his negotiations with enemies and allies, but it also marred his handling of his military subordinates; he never dealt frankly with them, but made a habit of playing off one against the other. Finally, one is forced to recognize that Napoleon inherited a vindictive strain which stemmed from the Corsican tradition of the vendetta. This vengeful spirit found its worst expression in his treacherous kidnapping and execution of the Duc d'Enghien in 1804.

In 1769 the French finally crushed the Corsican *maquisards*, and the insurgent leader, Paoli, fled to England; Carlo Buonaparte, however, made his peace with the conquerors, and he and his wife became great friends of the French Governor, the Comte de Marbeuf. On claiming descent from an old Tuscan noble family, Carlo Buonaparte was in 1770 recognized by the French authorities to be of noble birth, which under the *ancien régime* entitled his family to special privileges. By this means the nine-year-old Napoleone, together with his elder brother, Giuseppe, were found places in a religious school at Autun in Burgundy. Napoleone only spent three months at Autun, but he worked hard and acquired a tolerable knowledge of French, though he spoke it with a marked Corsican accent. Their parents intended that Giuseppe should be trained for the Church and Napoleone for the Army,

2 *Aged 16 : in 1785 From a contemporary sketch by Pontornini*
3 *Aged 31 : in 1800 From a portrait by Louis Bacler d'Albe (1761–1824)*
4 *Aged 36 : about 1805 From a portrait by Robert Le Fèvre (1756–1830)*
5 *Aged 45 : in 1815 From a miniature by Muneret*

6 Bonaparte at Milan, 1797 (aged 28)
After a portrait by Andrea Appiani (1754–1817); engraved by Francesco
Bartolozzi (1727–1815). Reproduced by courtesy of Ernest Weal, Esq.,
'Souvenir Napoléonien'

and in the following year (1779), again through Marbeuf's influence, the younger brother was granted a royal bursary for free education at the cadet school at Brienne in Champagne.

There were 12 of these royal cadet schools, scattered about France, which prepared the sons of noblemen to hold Commissions in the armed forces. Each school had about 100 cadets, half of whom were *pensionnaires*, or paying pupils, the other half being *boursiers*, or King's Scholars, whose board and education was met by the Privy Purse. For the *boursiers* a means test was required, and for both categories a certificate of noble lineage, extending back for two centuries, was obligatory. Nominations were made by the War Minister, but the schools were administered by various religious orders, Brienne being under the care of the Minimes.

The young Buonaparte (or *de Buonaparte*, as he was officially enrolled) entered Brienne before he was ten and remained there until he was 15. It was there that the foundations of his education were laid. He was an industrious and apt pupil, especially in Mathematics, History and Geography. His first inclination was to enter the Navy, but he was apparently dissuaded from that career by his mother, and he then decided to work for a Commission in the royal corps of artillery. He was not popular with his fellow cadets, being reserved and aloof by nature, and naturally felt rather a fish out of water. He soon learnt to speak French well, though still with a Corsican accent, which caused mirth among his comrades, who also made mock of his rather flimsy title to *noblesse*. Napoleone suffered further from the handicap of poverty, for his impecunious and spendthrift father failed to supply him with pocket-money. His strange name, Napoleone, traditional in the Buonaparte family, was also a source of ridicule, and indeed of embarrassment when he came to receive his First Communion, as the officiating prelate objected that it did not appear in the Calendar of Saints. All these handicaps might have crushed the spirit of a less determined boy, but they seem rather to have strengthened his determination to overcome obstacles and to assert his individuality. Instead of developing an inferiority complex, the young Corsican affected to look down on his fellows.

The curriculum at Brienne comprised Writing, French, Latin, German, History, Geography, Mathematics, Drawing, Music, Dancing and Fencing. Some of the teachers were clerics, but most of the technical subjects were taught by lay instructors. Discipline was fairly strict, no leave of absence during the five-year course being granted except on compassionate grounds. At the age of 15 Buonaparte obtained a nomination to the École Militaire, or Royal Military College, on the Champ de Mars in Paris, where he entered on the second stage of his military education, which now became more specialized; Fortification was added to the curriculum, and several hours a week were devoted to Drill, Musketry and Equitation. No attempt was made, however, to teach the cadets Military History or Tactics.

There were 126 gentlemen-cadets at the École Militaire, divided as at Brienne between paying *pensionnaires* and *boursiers*, like Buonaparte, who were educated at the King's expense. They were destined for all arms of the service, including the Navy. Twenty-five of the cadets were working for Commissions in the artillery. Here again Buonaparte encountered the snobbish disdain of the paying cadets; he admits to having waged bitter feuds with the haughtier members of the *haute noblesse*; and, despite the jeers of his comrades, he would always stand up for his beloved Corsica, which he had not seen for five years. However, he was becoming less morose and withdrawn than he had been at Brienne; the young Corsican was gradually getting the chip worn off his shoulder. It took the average cadet at the École Militaire two or three years to qualify for a Commission, but Buonaparte applied himself so assiduously that he took the passing-out examination at the end of his first year, and in September 1785, at the age of 16, he was commissioned with three other cadets, all older than himself, as *lieutenant en second* in the royal corps of artillery. His examiner in the passing-out test was the famous mathematician, Pierre-Simon Laplace (1749–1827).

Two of the artillery cadets who passed out at the same time as Buonaparte deserve a mention: Alexandre des Mazis and Louis-Edmond de Phélipeaux. Both of them resigned their Commissions and emigrated seven years later on the abolition of the monarchy. Des Mazis was Buonaparte's closest friend at the École Militaire and also later when they both joined the same artillery regiment. Phélipeaux, on the other hand, was always at daggers drawn with the young Corsican. After leaving France during the Revolution, he became a Colonel in the British service and, together with Commodore Sidney Smith, was responsible for defeating Buonaparte at the siege of Acre in May 1799.

On leaving the École Militaire, Buonaparte was posted to the La Fère artillery regiment, then stationed at Valence-sur-Rhône. During his first three months with the regiment he had to do sentry duty and other tasks as a private soldier, and it was not until 10 January 1786 that he took his place as a commissioned officer. He is described at this time as being '*timide et sauvage*', and had no private means besides his pay and allowances, which only amounted to £45 (or $126) a year. Buonaparte's first tour of regimental duty was a short one, for in September 1786 he obtained leave of absence on the plea of urgent family affairs, and returned to his native Corsica.

The Buonaparte family had indeed fallen on difficult times. Carlo, the father, had in February 1785 died of cancer in the stomach, leaving his family practically penniless. Encouraged by Marbeuf (1712-1787), the Governor of Corsica, Carlo had planted a large nursery of mulberry trees in the expectation of receiving a government subsidy, as the French authorities were anxious to foster the cultivation of silkworms in the island; this subsidy, however, had never been paid, and Letizia Buonaparte was left in desperate straits, owing a debt of nearly 9000 francs for the mulberry trees, and with the burden of maintaining the six younger children, three boys and three girls. Fortunately she was a woman of strong and determined character.

The eldest son, Giuseppe, had been originally intended for the Church, but developed no inclination to follow that calling and wanted to try for a Commission in the artillery. Unsuccessful in this, he went to the University of Pisa to study law. It fell, therefore, to Napoleone to assist his mother in her difficulties, and from now on he assumed responsibility for managing the family affairs. While on leave in Corsica he decided to go to Paris to extract from the Government the promised subsidy for the mulberry nursery. His long furlough having now expired, he sent his Commanding Officer a medical certificate that he was unfit for duty, and obtained a further extension. On 12 September 1787 he embarked for the Continent and proceeded to Paris. His negotiations there were protracted, but fruitless; they did, however, give him some insight into the dilatory methods of administrative departments and endowed him with a dislike for 'red tape'. It is a curious sidelight on the state of regimental discipline at that time that he managed to obtain nearly two years of furlough during his first four years of regimental service.

Towards the end of 1787 the La Fère artillery regiment, after several changes of station during Buonaparte's absence, moved to Auxonne in the Saône valley. In June 1788 Buonaparte, now nearly 19, at last returned to duty with his regiment. The regiment at Auxonne acted as depot unit to the School of Artillery there, then under command of Major-General Baron Jean-Pierre Duteil (1722-1794), perhaps the most distinguished gunner officer in the French army. Buonaparte thus had the advantage of learning all the latest tactical and technical developments in his arm of the service. He now applied himself seriously to the study of his profession, and no longer displayed the morose and taciturn attitude which had characterized him at Brienne and at the École Militaire. Although he was the youngest subaltern in the regiment, in August 1788 General Duteil nominated him as member of a committee to investigate means for firing explosive shells from long-barrelled guns, previously only fired from mortars, a practice which involved technical difficulties. The young subaltern discharged his duties so

17

intelligently that he attracted the favourable notice of the Commandant, who became his friend and adviser.

Apart from his service duties, Buonaparte plunged into an intensive course of self-education, devouring in particular books on military and political history. In order to train his memory, he wrote out a précis of every book he read, and these voluminous digests still survive; they cover a wide field of subjects and indicate the trend of his thoughts and ambitions. For instance, he studied intensely the lives of Alexander, Hannibal and Caesar. He even made a special study of the history of England from the time of Caesar to the accession of William III, and made a list of the kings of the Saxon Heptarchy with their dates from A.D. 457 to 825. According to his own account, he used to work 15 or 16 hours a day. In the words of Professor Holland Rose:

He was more or less a rebel at school; but when his mind had once awakened, it became a powerful machine, grinding all the materials that came within reach, appropriating them and sorting them in compartments ready for the time of use. All this was done before or after the work of drill, and amidst conditions of health and poverty far from favourable to prolonged study.*

Buonaparte was also deeply interested in political science, and his mind was powerfully influenced by Jean-Jacques Rousseau's *Contrat Social* which had been published in 1786, giving vent to the doctrines which inspired the French Revolution. What had particularly attracted Buonaparte to Rousseau's work was its advocacy of a free and independent Corsica. In the course of the next 12 months the French Revolution broke out and the National Assembly assumed constitutional powers in June 1789. A month later the Bastille was stormed. The Revolution formed a turning-point in Buonaparte's career. Brought up for the past ten years in the company of aristocrats, he had never considered himself as one of them, and he had constantly been subjected to their snobbery and disdain. Although he had been fed, clothed and educated at the expense of His Most Christian Majesty Louis XVI, he felt no allegiance to the monarchy or to the *ancien régime*. Besides, he was still a Corsican, rather than a Frenchman, and hoped that a new order might bestow independence on his native island.

The revolutionary excesses taking place in Paris soon spread to the provinces. On 19 July, five days after the storming of the Bastille, a mob of rioters sounded the *tocsin* from the parish church at Auxonne, sacked the Mairie and destroyed the tax registers. The La Fère regiment stood to arms and for a time order was restored, but the officers found that they could no

* *The Personality of Napoleon*, pp. 13–14.

longer rely on their men. In fact there were not enough officers present to maintain discipline, for half of them were absent on leave. On 16 August (the day after Buonaparte's twentieth birthday) the regiment itself mutinied, seized the funds in the regimental chest and indulged in a drunken orgy.

A month later Buonaparte decided to return to Corsica to take a hand in its liberation, and obtained six months' leave of absence. On reaching the island at the end of September, he at once threw himself into local politics; he took part in organizing a National Guard, as was being done all over France, and he was the author of an Address which was despatched to the National Assembly in Paris. On 30 November the National Assembly, under the influence of Mirabeau, declared that Corsica formed part of France and that Corsicans would enjoy full and equal rights as Frenchmen. This proclamation did not altogether satisfy Corsican national aspirations, and opposing feuds and parties sprang up. In April 1790, his leave having expired, Buonaparte applied for a further extension until 15 October on the grounds of ill-health. He and his brother then joined a popular movement to recall to Corsica their old national champion Paoli, who had been driven from the island 20 years previously by the French and had since been living as an exile in England. Paoli was now summoned to Paris by the National Assembly and sent to Corsica as Governor.

Meanwhile the revolutionary leaven had started a ferment of unrest among the intractable Corsicans. They could not understand why, in this new era of liberty, the fortresses of Ajaccio and Bastia were still garrisoned by a French army of occupation. Trouble broke out in June 1790 between the French troops and the National Guard, resulting in the death of several French officers. Buonaparte sided with the Corsican patriots against his French comrades. So involved did he become in local politics that he again overstayed his leave and did not rejoin his regiment at Auxonne until 10 February 1791. This time he took with him his younger brother Luigi (now rechristened Louis), aged 12, whose education he had undertaken to relieve his mother.

In the summer of 1791 the French artillery was reorganized with the intention of democratizing it, and on 14 June Buonaparte was transferred from the La Fère regiment to the 4th Artillery Regiment at Valence-sur-Rhône. He was also promoted to *premier lieutenant* with effect from 1 April 1791. A week after Buonaparte's transfer to Valence, Louis XVI attempted to escape from Paris but was recaptured on the following day at Varennes. The National Assembly then ordered all officers to sign a pledge of allegiance to its own authority. Two years earlier the officers had taken an oath to serve the nation *and* the King, whose name was now omitted. This raised a conflict of loyalties in the minds of many officers, a large number of whom emigrated rather than take the new oath. For Buonaparte, however, there was no hesitation; as he wrote in his notes at the time:

I have read all the speeches of the pro-monarchist advocates; I only see in them frantic efforts to support a bad cause. . . . If I had ever entertained any doubt on the matter, reading their speeches would have dispelled it.*

In fact Buonaparte was already a convinced Jacobin.

In early 1791 the Academy of Lyon offered a prize of 1200 francs (rather more than Buonaparte's total annual pay and allowances) for the best essay on the subject: 'What truths and sentiments should be taught to men to ensure their happiness?' On his return to Auxonne from Corsica, Buonaparte had decided to compete for this prize. Based on his study of Rousseau's works, he produced a long and sententious political essay, known as '*Le discours de Lyon*'. It failed to impress the examining panel, but it reveals the *Weltanschauung* of the young Buonaparte at this early stage of his career. His ideas were somewhat different to those he would have expressed ten years later, when he was climbing the ladder to autocratic power. A few extracts are instructive:

Where kings hold sovereignty, men no longer exist; there is only the oppressor slave, viler than the oppressed slave.

The French, besotted by kings and their ministers, nobles and their prejudices, priests and their impostures, have at last awoken and have recognized the rights of man.

In his concluding peroration he made a somewhat prophetic statement:

Men of genius are meteors destined to burn out in order to illuminate their era.*

But if Buonaparte's mind was Jacobin, his heart was Corsican, and he decided to return to assist his native island's struggle for independence. Since obtaining his Commission in September 1785, he had already enjoyed two spells of leave, one of 21 months and the other of 17, so that of six years' commissioned service he had spent more than three years on leave. He now applied for another furlough of six months, which his Colonel very naturally refused, since all leave had been stopped owing to the threatening international situation, and units were short of officers owing to the number who had resigned their Commissions and emigrated. Buonaparte, however, refused to accept defeat and appealed to his friend, General Duteil, who had just been appointed Inspector-General of Artillery.† Through Duteil's

* Frédéric Masson, *Napoléon inconnu* (Paris, 1895).

† General Baron Duteil had no love for the Revolution, but was so devoted to his profession that he did not resign his Commission and continued to serve until the end of 1793. He was then condemned to death by a military court as an aristocrat and was guillotined at Lyon on 22 February 1794.

influence in August 1791 he obtained three months' leave on full pay and left France with his brother Louis, reaching Ajaccio early in September.

On 15 October his great-uncle, Archdeacon Lucciano Buonaparte, died, leaving a certain amount of money, which relieved the family from further financial anxiety, and the two elder Buonapartes plunged heavily into local politics. They sided with the Ajaccio party which stood for Paoli and Corsican independence, as opposed to the people of Bastia who favoured French rule. On 1 November 1791 the acting Commander-in-Chief of the troops, a Corsican and a friend of Buonaparte, appointed him as Adjutant (*adjudant-major*) of one of the four Corsican National Guard battalions, with the acting rank of Captain, owing to the great shortage of regular officers. Unfortunately, on 3 February 1792 the War Ministry issued a new order that all regular officers below the rank of Lieutenant-Colonel, serving with volunteer battalions, were to rejoin their units by 1 April. This was a blow to Buonaparte, who had already overstayed his leave, which had expired at the end of November. The only way to escape the regulation and remain in Corsica was to get promoted to the rank of Lieutenant-Colonel. Under the new régime this was a matter of election by ballot in each unit. By dint of unscrupulous intrigue and the forcible abduction of one of the official scrutineers, Lieutenant (acting Captain) Buonaparte was on 1 April elected Lieutenant-Colonel of the 2nd (Ajaccio) Battalion of the Corsican Volunteers. It was a flagrantly dishonest performance, and it foreshadowed many *coups d'état* in the days to come.

Exactly two months earlier another, but older and more experienced Adjutant, Captain André Massena, had been elected Lieutenant-Colonel of the 2nd Battalion of the Var Volunteers. Massena's election, however, was due to merit and not to trickery.

Within a week the youthful Lieutenant-Colonel got himself and his battalion into serious trouble. The National Assembly in Paris had dissolved the religious orders, and consequently the local Directory in Corsica in February 1792 ordered the suppression of the monasteries in Ajaccio, Bastia, Bonifacio and Corte. In Ajaccio, however, the people were strongly attached to their ancient faith and petitioned the local government to let the Capuchins remain in their monastery. On Easter Sunday, 8 April, the priests celebrated Mass in the monastery of St. Francis, and a religious procession was announced for the following day, greatly to Buonaparte's indignation. That evening a brawl took place near the Cathedral between some of Buonaparte's volunteers and the local workmen and sailors. In the ensuing scuffle firearms were discharged and one of Buonaparte's subalterns was shot dead. Buonaparte decided to wreak vengeance on the inhabitants of Ajaccio. The citadel, which dominated the town, was occupied by a French regular battalion commanded by Colonel Maillard. The young Lieutenant-Colonel approached Colonel Maillard and demanded that his volunteers should be admitted to the citadel and supplied with ammunition, as it was not safe for them to remain in their billets in the town. Maillard refused, as this would be contrary to his orders, and he ordered Buonaparte to withdraw his volunteers from the town, which Buonaparte refused to do. The next morning some of his volunteers opened fire on the citizens leaving the Cathedral after attending Mass, several women and children being killed. The volunteers then got out of hand, pillaged shops, seized the cattle coming into market and prevented the citizens from getting access to the fountains. The young Lieutenant-Colonel was unable to control his undisciplined rabble; what was still worse, he attempted to seduce the French soldiers in the citadel from allegiance to the garrison commander.

Buonaparte's folly brought on him the disapproval of Paoli, who controlled the central government from Corte. Commissioners were sent to Ajaccio to investigate the trouble, and Buonaparte's battalion was transferred from Ajaccio to Corte. His first exercise of independent command had proved a disgraceful failure. One can only excuse it by supposing that the strong wine of liberty and equality had intoxicated the mind of the young officer. He doubtless profited by the experience.

The local bickerings in Corsica, however, were a mere side-show in comparison with the portentous drama which was then unfolding in metropolitan France. On 20 April 1792 the Legislative Assembly declared war on Austria, and shortly afterwards on Sardinia. At the end of the month the Revolutionary levies suffered a bad reverse in their first encounter with the disciplined Austrian troops near Lille. The French found themselves handicapped by a serious shortage of officers owing to the wholesale emigration of those of aristocratic birth. Of the 55 cadets of the École Militaire who were commissioned on 1 September 1785 (of whom Buonaparte was one) only six still remained in the service. On 28 May, therefore, Buonaparte hurried back to Paris to make sure that his escapades in Corsica had not prejudiced his chances of promotion. Fortunately they had not, despite the fact that he had overstayed his leave so flagrantly. On 10 July he was promoted to the rank of Captain in the 4th Artillery Regiment, and his promotion was antedated to 6 February with full pay from that date; at the same time he was drawing his emoluments as Lieutenant-Colonel in the Corsican Volunteers.

The Revolutionary frenzy in Paris was now approaching its climax, and on 10 August Buonaparte was an eyewitness of the storming of the Tuileries by the mob and the massacre of the Swiss Guards. Paris was an unhealthy place for officers who might be suspected of being aristocrats; besides he had the duty of escorting back to Corsica his sister, Maria-Anna (now Elisa), aged 15, who was being educated at the seminary for young ladies at St. Cyr, now being broken up. On 15 September he reached Ajaccio and resumed command of his battalion of Volunteers.

We have now reviewed in some detail the first 23 years of Napoleon's career. Those years covered an amazing apprenticeship for the still more astonishing 23 years of active command which lay ahead. From early boyhood he had studied his profession with exceptional zeal and tenacity of purpose. He was, of course, endowed from the start with considerable intellectual gifts; but he had trained his memory and his analytical powers of reasoning and deduction by sheer hard work and determination under the spur of a restless ambition.

Not only did Napoleon embark on his career of military command at the age of 23 with an unusually comprehensive wealth of professional knowledge, but he had also acquired a profound sense of statecraft through the wide field of his reading and from his experience of the budding French Revolution and the subtle intrigues of his Corsican countrymen. Moreover, he had learnt to study men as well as books, and had attained a Machiavellian insight into the mental workings of his fellow-creatures.

Let us compare once more his training with that of his English contemporary and future opponent. At the age of 23 the future Duke of Wellington's military education was limited to what he could pick up at Dublin Castle as A.D.C. to the Lord-Lieutenant of Ireland, while his political experience was confined to his membership of the Irish House of Commons, while representing his family borough of Trim in County Meath.

II

The Military Legacy inherited by Napoleon

It is one of the myths inherent in his legend that Napoleon invented a new system of warfare. This was not the case, and the myth was dispelled 65 years ago by Colin in his *L'Éducation militaire de Napoléon*. For English readers the veil has been lifted more recently by Spenser Wilkinson in 1930 and Liddell Hart in 1933. Napoleon cannot be claimed as the inventor of *Blitzkrieg* any more than Alexander, Hannibal or Caesar, three leaders on whom Napoleon consciously modelled himself. *Blitzkrieg* is no new principle of war; it is merely the ruthless application *à outrance* of the prime factors of mobility, speed and concentration of force; in fact, what the German army did in Poland in 1939 and in France in 1940.

While in exile at St. Helena Napoleon did indeed claim that he had devised a new form of strategy; he is recorded to have said to Gourgaud: 'The great art of battles is to change one's line of operations during the action; it is my own conception, and is quite new.' This was nonsense, and can be discounted, as so many of his attempts at self-justification made while in exile. Napoleon was nearer the mark, also at St. Helena, when he gave the advice:

Wage war offensively, like Alexander, Hannibal, Caesar, Gustavus Adolphus, Turenne, Prince Eugene and Frederick; read and re-read the history of their 83 campaigns; model yourself on them; it is the only way to become a Great Captain and to master the secrets of the art.

But Napoleon was no mere armchair student of the past; his genius lay in his ability to apply in the field with energy and intelligence the lessons of history.

If Napoleon devised no new form of strategy, neither did he evolve any original conception as regards tactics, organization, administration or equipment.

In the field of tactics the French armies of the Consulate and Empire merely continued to practise the methods developed by the Revolutionary forces during the campaigns of the period 1792–1795, which were based on the latest regulations issued to the royal army in 1791. These tactical methods resulted from the experience of the numerous wars waged by France during the eighteenth century. The normal procedure was that the commander launched his main attack in dense assault columns against what he judged to be the key-point of the enemy's position, after shaking the defence with preparatory fire by skirmishers in open order and a concentrated and converging artillery bombardment. Napoleon made no essential change in this basic procedure; being a gunner and conversant with the effect and range of his own arm, he may have increased the proportion of guns to infantry, and may have introduced the practice of retaining a reserve of guns under his own control in order to concentrate their fire at the climax of the battle, but he made no innovation in artillery tactics. As we shall see, he studied his subject very assiduously at the School of Artillery, and took to heart the lessons he was taught there.

As regards 'grand tactics', the envelopment of a flank, particularly with the aid of cavalry, was no new procedure in war; so little was it a normal Napoleonic practice that he made no attempt whatsoever to threaten Wellington's vulnerable flank in the Waterloo campaign. The organization of Napoleon's armies in divisions and army corps, in order to achieve greater flexibility in the approach march and encounter battle, merely followed the practice which was being adopted in other European armies in the light of the experience of the Seven Years' War.

Napoleon's insistence that his armies should live off the country in which they were operating, thus obtaining freedom of manœuvre through not being dependent on supply convoys or magazines, was the normal practice of the Revolutionary armies. It originated from the financial inability and administrative incompetence of the National Convention to feed the armies which it launched beyond the frontiers of France.

Although Napoleon's technical knowledge of artillery and weapons was of a high order, the fact remains that no improvements were made in the equipment of the French armies during his 15 years as Consul and Emperor. The flint-lock muskets of the French infantry at Waterloo were of the same pattern as those used at Marengo, and no different from those carried by the victors of Fleurus and Wattignies. Similarly, the French field-guns remained unchanged in range and calibre throughout the whole period of the Consulate and Empire, and in fact were identical with those designed by Gribeauval a generation earlier.

Napoleon, however, did not shut his mind to new developments in artillery technique. As a young officer at the School of Artillery in 1788 he had written a memorandum for the Commandant on a method of firing explosive shell from guns instead of from mortars. This, of course, was not his own idea, and the practice had been introduced in the British service ten years earlier. A paper is also extant which he wrote at that time on the advantages of rifled cannon over smooth-bore weapons, but this may have been the précis of a lecture which he had heard at the School of Artillery. In any case, rifled cannon were not introduced into the French army until many years after his death. At the same time, Napoleon was always on the look-out for new technical developments. In 1810 we find the Emperor writing repeatedly to his ordnance designers, ordering them to produce long-range rockets for siege operations similar to those that had recently been invented by William Congreve at Woolwich.* His experts, however, failed to produce any. There is no evidence of Napoleon having taken any notice of 'spherical case shot', invented at the beginning of the nineteenth century by Lieutenant-Colonel Henry Shrapnel, and used successfully against the French troops in Portugal in the early stages of the Peninsular War. On the whole, perhaps, we may ascribe the lack of weapon improvements during the Napoleonic period to the difficulties of manufacture and re-armament in a country already strained to the limit of its industrial capacity by the continuous expansion of its armed forces.

We can now examine in more detail the legacy of (a) military doctrine and (b) material equipment which Napoleon inherited from his predecessors.

Military doctrine

During the century in which Napoleon was born the French monarchy waged four major wars:

(a) The Spanish Succession (1702–1713)
(b) The Polish Succession (1733–1738)
(c) The Austrian Succession (1741–1748)
(d) The Seven Years' War (1756–1763)

France also participated to a certain extent in the War of American Independence (1778–1783). These campaigns produced a wealth of military

---

* *J'attache une grande importance aux fusées à la Congrève* (*Corr.* 16333). (References to the *Correspondance de Napoléon Ier*, published in 32 volumes, are listed as *Corr.* . . .). Translations in all cases are by the author.

experience, but, strange to say, only one commander of outstanding genius—
Marshal Count Maurice de Saxe (1696–1750). Marshal Saxe was not only a
great commander in the field, but also an original thinker in strategy,
organization and tactics. Liddell Hart has with some justice called him 'the
military prophet'. Saxe's *Rêveries*, written about 1732, were not published
until seven years after his death; even then they did not receive the attention
they deserved. However, they gradually permeated French military thought
and laid the foundations of the doctrine which prevailed at the close of the
century.

The basic purpose of Marshal Saxe's doctrine was to increase the mobility
and manœuvrability of an army. To achieve this he proposed an army
organized in 'legions', the prototype of the modern 'division', each self-
contained as a homogeneous fighting formation of all arms. The 'legion'
(3580 of all ranks) was composed of four regiments (880), each of four centuries (220), together with a half-century of cavalry for reconnaissance duties.
This reduced the problem of organization to the simplest possible terms. Each
infantry century was to be accompanied by an *amusette*, or light field-gun of
2-inch calibre throwing a half-pound shot, drawn on a two-wheeled hand-
cart. He also wished to arm his infantry with a breech-loading weapon, but
this desirable development was not achieved until more than a century later.
The infantry attack was to be preceded by a swarm of skirmishers, who
would open fire on the enemy at a range of 300 yards, and would then fall
back in the intervals between the assaulting centuries, which under cover of
the fire of the *tirailleurs* would advance in columns eight deep. Another
tactical method practised by Saxe, which worked well at Fontenoy (1745),
was to hold *points d'appui* in front of the main position to break up the
attacker's assault columns.

The principles laid down by Saxe, and followed after his death by Marshal
de Broglie, formed the basis of French battle tactics for the next half-
century. Infantry regiments were formed up in line or in column according as
whether fire-power or assault impetus was required, and when approaching
the enemy groups of skirmishers were thrown out on each flank. As the
result of the Seven Years' War the tendency was for formations to become
more rigid and stereotyped, and under the influence of Frederick the Great
a high standard of drill and fire-discipline was attained. But Frederick's
famous 'oblique order', in which battalions advanced in echelon to outflank
the enemy, a manœuvre which proved so successful against the Austrians at
Leuthen (1757), was not adopted by the French.

The divisional organization foreshadowed by Marshal Saxe was adopted
by Marshal de Broglie in 1759. An army thus organized gained elasticity and

liberty of action, and could operate more freely in outmanœuvring or out-flanking the enemy. Another organizational development of the Seven Years' War was to divide an army into a *corps de bataille*, or main body, preceded by a *corps d'avant-garde* and flanked by *réserves de droite et de gauche*. This again achieved greater flexibility of manœuvre, as the main body could deploy or outflank the enemy while the advanced guard engaged him frontally. It is interesting to note that this was exactly the formation adopted by Bonaparte in 1796 at the opening of his first campaign in Piedmont. The art of handling an army thus divided lay in keeping the various elements under strict control within mutual supporting distance, to avoid any component being defeated in detail, and to concentrate for battle at the decisive moment. The general principle was to march divided in separate columns but to fight united.

There is no evidence to show that Napoleon in his youth ever studied Saxe's *Rêveries*, or analysed the strategy and tactics of Frederick the Great. We know that in 1788 at Auxonne he read a *Vie de Frédéric II*, published at Strasbourg in 1787, but this only gave a general outline of Frederick's campaigns between 1740 and 1763, without any discussion of his tactical methods. On the other hand it is certain that Napoleon's theoretical knowledge of strategy and tactics was derived from a close study of two outstanding military writers of the eighteenth century, Bourcet and Guibert.

In Liddell Hart's view, General Pierre-Joseph de Bourcet (1700–1780) can be considered 'the greatest of chiefs of staff'. Originally an infantry officer, he transferred to the engineers. He gained extensive experience of staff work in the various Piedmont campaigns between 1734 and 1747, and his *Principes de la guerre de montagnes* appeared in 1775. Bourcet's main contribution to the development of strategic practice was to insist on the division of an army into several columns which could advance on parallel or convergent roads and be re-united for battle at the right moment, in fact on the lines proposed by Marshal Saxe.

Bourcet was followed as a military thinker by General Jacques-Antoine-Hippolyte, Comte de Guibert (1743–1790), who obtained early war experience in the Seven Years' War, and in 1772 published his *Essai général de tactique*, which gained a wide circulation and was translated into many languages. His main theme was the necessity for tactical mobility and manœuvrability on the battlefield. One extract from his book sums up his doctrine, which guided the tactical handling of troops in battle till the end of the century:

In former days the movements necessary to bring an army into column or into line of battle were so slow and complicated that it took whole hours to get into position; one had to deploy a long way from the enemy. In future the movements should be simple, rapid and applicable to all kinds of ground; order of battle will be formed as late and as close to the enemy as possible, for columns are much easier to manœuvre than lines; by disclosing one's point of attack at the last moment, the enemy will have no time to counter it.

On arriving within range of the enemy, the General gives the signal to form line of battle. All his troops, drilled to deploy rapidly, will form line of battle instantaneously, and the attack will start before the enemy has time to realize where he is being hit.

Another point made by Guibert was that an army could never be free to manœuvre and deploy rapidly under the old system of magazines with ponderous supply trains and convoys, but must learn to live on the country; he quotes Cato's advice to the Roman Senate: 'War must nourish war.' This principle was adopted by the Revolutionary armies and later continued by Napoleon. Guibert was even more in advance of his time when he perceived that war could not be waged on the grand scale by the small professional armies maintained by European States in the seventeenth century. In his *Essai général de tactique* he pointed out that 'the hegemony of Europe will fall to that nation which . . . becomes possessed of manly virtues and creates a national army'. Thus was born the idea of 'a nation in arms' which the French Revolution was to translate into practice 20 years later.

The theories evolved by Bourcet and Guibert embodied the fundamental conceptions of warfare on which the young Buonaparte was brought up. They inspired the conduct of the Revolutionary campaigns between 1792 and 1795, from which the 'Napoleonic system' of war was clearly derived. Although Napoleon was not the inventor of these principles, he had the genius and skill to put them into practice more boldly and ruthlessly than his predecessors.

When the Republican armies took the field in 1792 against their Austrian, Prussian and Sardinian opponents they perforce took over the tactical methods of the royal army. Under the leadership of Lafayette, Carnot, Dumouriez, Kellermann and other capable officers of the *ancien régime* who declined to emigrate, an *amalgame* was formed of the existing units of the old long-service army merged with the flood of newly raised 'volunteer' levies. In principle a battalion of the old regular army formed the nucleus of a *demi-brigade* in combination with two new volunteer battalions. In 1793 the armies were reinforced by a further call-up of 100,000 conscripts. The new levies made up for their lack of training by immense enthusiasm and *élan*, so that the Revolutionary troops tended to adopt 'horde tactics'. After initial reverses when confronted by the disciplined Austrian volleys, the soldiers of the Republic soon acquired cohesion and combat experience. The weak point

29

was the officer corps, since two-thirds of the infantry and cavalry officers had emigrated after the execution of the King. The proportion of artillery officers who resigned their Commissions was much lower, so that the fire-discipline of the field batteries was of a higher standard than in the infantry battalions. This was largely the cause of the French artillery success against the Prussians at Valmy in September 1792, and later at Jemappes and Wattignies.

In 1791, in the early days of the Revolution, a new tactical manual had been issued to the French army, based on the precepts enunciated by Guibert and on the lessons of the Seven Years' War. The massed *colonne serrée*, preceded by a swarm of skirmishers, was the normal attack formation, and the marching rate was increased to 100 paces a minute from the Frederician 76. An attack in massed column, of course, prevented the full development of a battalion's fire-power, such as it could deliver when drawn up in line, but it gave more sense of confidence and cohesion to hastily trained levies. This attack formation in close column remained unchanged throughout the Napoleonic wars, frequently leading to disastrous results, as at Bussaco and Waterloo.

Napoleon's military education was based, not only on the theoretical precepts of Bourcet and Guibert, but on the more practical lessons which he received at Auxonne in handling his own arm of the service, the artillery. In this respect he was primarily indebted to one of the greatest of French artillerymen, General Jean-Baptiste de Gribeauval (1715-1789). As a Lieutenant-Colonel, Gribeauval had been lent to the Austrian army in 1757, shortly after the outbreak of the Seven Years' War. At that time both the Austrian and Prussian armies were ahead of the French in artillery technique and training, and when Gribeauval returned to France in 1764 as Inspector of Artillery he introduced sweeping reforms. The first thing he did was to rationalize the distribution of the different calibres, separating the heavier weapons more suitable for siege and coast defence duties from the 12-pounders, 6-inch howitzers, 8-pounders and 4-pounders which he allocated to the field batteries. The 4-pounders were frequently attached to infantry and cavalry units to effect closer tactical cooperation. He also increased the mobility of the arm by reducing the weight of the equipment without sacrificing range or shell-power. Gribeauval's ideas were carried on by another outstanding gunner, General Jean-Pierre Duteil, who was appointed Inspector-General of Artillery in 1791. For seven years previously he had been Commandant of the School of Artillery at Auxonne where Buonaparte was his disciple.

Napoleon's artillery education was also greatly influenced by General Duteil's younger brother, General Jean du Teil (1738-1820), under whom he served at the siege of Toulon. The younger du Teil (known during the *ancien régime* as 'le Chevalier du Teil' to distinguish him from his elder brother, who was a Baron) was a well-known writer on the tactical handling of artillery. In 1778 he had written a book on the employment of artillery in the field, entitled *L'usage de l'artillerie nouvelle,* in which he insisted on the concentration of artillery fire on the actual points selected for the infantry attack.

We must concentrate artillery fire on the points of attack which are decisive for victory. The artillery, sustained and reinforced intelligently, will produce decisive results.

Du Teil further advocated intimate cooperation between infantry and gunners:

It is indispensable that the artillery should understand infantry tactics, or at least the object of their movements and manœuvres, . . . in order to judge when to increase their rate of fire or change position.

Frederick the Great had been the first to organize horse artillery to cooperate with cavalry in the Seven Years' War, and du Teil suggested that the French should follow suit:

The 4-pounders will drive into action facing the enemy's guns, not in formal procession as was formerly the practice, with horses harnessed in tandem, . . . but lightened and hooked in to limbers. They will gallop into position and form 'action front' at their battle intervals. By their rapidity of manœuvre and rate of fire these 4-pounders will overpower a battery even of 24-pounders, for they will fire three or four rounds to every one of their opponents.

In 1791 the French adopted the Prussian innovation of horse artillery, with all the gunners mounted.

Material equipment

The Wars of Religion of the seventeenth century had seen the match-lock musket replace the arquebus as the main missile weapon of the infantry in all European armies. The match-lock, however, was a clumsy and inefficient weapon, especially in wet weather, and about the beginning of the eighteenth century it was replaced by the flint-lock. The flint-lock smooth-bore musket, of which the British 'Brown Bess' was perhaps the most efficient pattern, remained the standard infantry firearm of European armies from Fontenoy to Waterloo.

Ring-bayonets, or socket-bayonets, had at the end of the seventeenth century replaced the original plug-bayonet, which fitted into the muzzle of the musket, thereby preventing the latter from being fired after fixing bayonets. Owing to the disapproval of Louis XIV, ring-bayonets were not introduced into the French service until 1703. The musket and bayonet then superseded the pike as the main infantry weapon for close combat. There was little to choose between the infantry weapons of the French, British, Prussian or Austrian armies throughout the eighteenth century.

The American War of Independence (1778–1783) taught the British the value of the rifle, owing to its superiority in range and penetration (though not rate of fire) over the smooth-bore flint-lock musket. The 'Baker rifle' had been introduced into the British service in 1800, but was only issued to special units which acted as sharpshooters. It took twice as long to load a muzzle-loading rifle as it did to load a smooth-bore musket. Its greater costliness and difficulty of manufacture also retarded its general issue as an infantry weapon. The rifle made an early appearance in France, for the body-guard of Louis XIII (1610–1643) was armed with it, but in 1807 Napoleon actually withdrew the rifle from those of his troops to whom it had been issued in the earlier wars of the Republic. In fact, the French army made hardly any use of the rifle until the conquest of Algeria in 1830.

As regards artillery, the standard equipment of French field batteries with 6-inch howitzers, 12-pounders, 8-pounders and 4-pounders, introduced by Gribeauval in the latter half of the eighteenth century, remained unchanged throughout the Napoleonic period. With these weapons Gribeauval had achieved the heaviest weight of metal compatible with adequate mobility across normal country. This was indeed a greater weight of metal than was achieved by the British artillery, whose comparable weapons were 5½-inch howitzers, 9-pounders, 6-pounders and 3-pounders. In spite of throwing a lighter weight of shot, however, the British weapons slightly outranged the comparable French ones, and the British gunners attained a higher standard of mobility thanks to the lighter weights behind their gun-teams.

Although Napoleon, a highly trained gunner, made no improvements in the weapon system which he inherited from Gribeauval, he did effect some novel *ad hoc* improvisations in artillery transport. During the winter fighting in the Maritime Alps in 1794–1795, when commanding the artillery of the Army of Italy, he mounted his guns on sledges, so that they could follow the infantry up the snow-covered mule-tracks. Again, when crossing the Great St. Bernard in 1800, he dragged his guns across the pass on hollowed-out, split tree-trunks, a device which he learnt from the local woodcutters. In order to increase the effect of his artillery bombardments, Napoleon during his later campaigns attached a 12-pounder battery to each army corps.

When the young Buonaparte, at the age of 24, found himself for the first time in command of regular troops in battle, he had inherited a very substantial legacy of tactical training and military organization, as well as a highly developed weapon system. All this was based on the experience of the many campaigns of the eighteenth century. For this legacy he was indebted to a brilliant group of military thinkers and experts: Bourcet, Guibert, Gribeauval and the du Teil brothers. All of them had drawn their theoretical inspiration from the original concepts of Maurice de Saxe. Napoleon was wise enough not to tinker with his legacy; he knew how to exploit it to the full.

III

Baptism of Fire
1793-1795

In the autumn of 1792, at the full height of the French Revolution, Buonaparte was back in his native island, fired with the ambition to restore its
independence on Republican lines. But the Revolution which had split
France had also caused a schism in Corsican politics. In January 1793 Louis
XVI was executed. Paoli, the great champion of Corsican liberty, was no
lover of kings, but he was still less enthusiastic about regicides. His exile of
20 years in England had inclined him to more moderate and liberal views,
and he was now suspected of being a counter-revolutionary by the Jacobin
party in Paris to which young Buonaparte had attached himself. So there now
arose a feud between the Buonaparte family and Paoli, the virtual ruler of
the island. Meanwhile, the Executive Council of the Convention in Paris
was hatching a military and naval project which cut across the local island
controversies.

The Revolutionary Government had since the previous May been at war
with the King of Sardinia, who from his capital at Turin also ruled over the
fertile plains of Piedmont. The Executive Council had for some months been
planning to seize the small island of Maddalena, lying off the northern point
of Sardinia and commanding the important sea-route through the Strait of
Bonifacio. The capture of this island would form a stepping-stone for a landing at Cagliari and the complete conquest of the island of Sardinia. An
expeditionary force was to leave Toulon, escorted by the French Mediterranean fleet under Rear-Admiral Truguet, pick up at Ajaccio a contingent of
Corsican Volunteers contributed by Paoli, and land on Maddalena. On the

34

way they would seize the rocky islet of San Stefano. The Executive Council was at that time preoccupied with the King's trial and there were frequent changes of plan and bickerings with Paoli about the size of the Corsican contingent, so that the expedition did not leave Toulon until 8 January 1793. By that time the French contingent had been reduced to 4000 untrained and ill-disciplined volunteers from Marseille. When the expedition arrived at Ajaccio, fighting accompanied by bloodshed broke out between the French and the Corsicans. A naval demonstration was made against Cagliari on 15/16 February as a feint, but the Marseillais volunteers panicked and the force returned to Ajaccio. Eventually the expedition left Bonifacio on 22 February under command of Colonna-Cesari, an elderly Corsican Colonel of Gendarmerie, with Lieutenant-Colonel Buonaparte as his Second-in-Command. The latter had his Corsican volunteer battalion and also the artillery of the force, consisting of one 6-inch mortar and two 4-pounder guns. The islet of San Stefano was captured without difficulty and the expedition proceeded to Maddalena. Here they sat down to besiege a martello tower, which surrendered to them on the following day. The sailors from Marseille then decided that they had done enough fighting; they mutinied and compelled the impotent Cesari to re-embark the force. This was carried out in great disorder on 25 February, and Buonaparte had the mortification of abandoning his three pieces of artillery on the beach. It was a bad start in the career of a gunner officer, but he had no responsibility for either planning or commanding the expedition. It may have served as a lesson on the necessity for training and good discipline in a combined operation of this nature.

On returning to Ajaccio, Buonaparte once more plunged into local politics. As a result of the failure of the Maddalena expedition, the rift between the French Government and Paoli was widening, and Buonaparte now took the part of the Paris Government. With his volunteers he made an abortive attempt to capture the Ajaccio citadel which was held by the Paolists. His volunteers were defeated and he himself had to go into hiding; eventually the whole Buonaparte family were forced to quit the island; they sailed from Calvi and landed at Toulon on 13 June 1793. The young Corsican now abandoned the cause of his native island and identified his future with Revolutionary France.

Being a refugee from Corsica, it was important for Buonaparte to reinstate himself in the French army. After settling his family at Marseille, he reported himself to the local artillery commander, General Jean du Teil, a well-known military writer and the younger brother of his old Commandant at Auxonne. Buonaparte was now assigned the task of organizing forges in the coast-defence batteries of the Mediterranean coast to prepare red-hot shot for engaging British warships. The Reign of Terror was in full swing, and at the beginning of June the more moderate Girondins in the Paris Assembly were overthrown by the Jacobin party. The South of France, however, was largely in sympathy with the Monarchists, and particularly the important towns of Marseille and Toulon. On 15 July Buonaparte, who was on his way to take command of a field battery in the Army of the Alps, was put in charge of the artillery of a force organized to suppress the local counter-revolutionary movement. This force was commanded by General Jean-François Carteaux, an artist in private life, but he had been for 20 years a trooper in a dragoon regiment and a gendarme. Within a month the insurrectionary movement collapsed throughout most of the Midi. Buonaparte took the opportunity of a few days' leisure to write a remarkable political pamphlet entitled *Le souper de Beaucaire*, intended to persuade the people of Marseille to submit to the winning Jacobin faction in the interest of national unity. This essay showed that its writer possessed a wide knowledge of strategic principles as well as of political affairs.

The Girondin faction, however, was still in control at the naval base of Toulon, then being closely blockaded by a British fleet under Admiral Lord Hood. Under the threat of starvation by blockade the Executive Committee of Toulon decided to hand the base over to the British Admiral on 27 August. The harbour was occupied by a British squadron, and the town and fortifications were garrisoned by 2000 British soldiers and marines, supplemented by an unreliable mixed force of 15,000 Spanish, Sardinian and Neapolitan troops.

The harbour of Toulon (p. 37), one of the best in the Mediterranean, is protected on the seaward side by two rocky headlands jutting out eastwards. The inner one, known as Le Caire, separates the inner roadstead (*petite rade*) from the outer one (*grande rade*) and was defended by two batteries, Fort de l'Éguillette and Fort Balaguier. These batteries could only fire seawards, not inland. To the north of the town and dockyard rises the barrier of Mont Faron, a sharp ridge 1800 feet high and two miles long, running east and west. A chain of detached forts covered the crest of Mont Faron and blocked the landward approaches to the harbour from east and west. The defensive perimeter was 12 miles long, requiring a very considerable garrison.

On the instructions of the Convention in Paris, General Carteaux's force, after capturing Marseille, advanced eastwards at the end of August in order to invest Toulon, in conjunction with another force under General Lapoype, coming from Nice. On 7 September Carteaux's force encountered a Royalist force at Ollioules, four miles west of Toulon, where his artillery commander, Captain Dommartin, was wounded. Captain Buonaparte, who had reverted

36

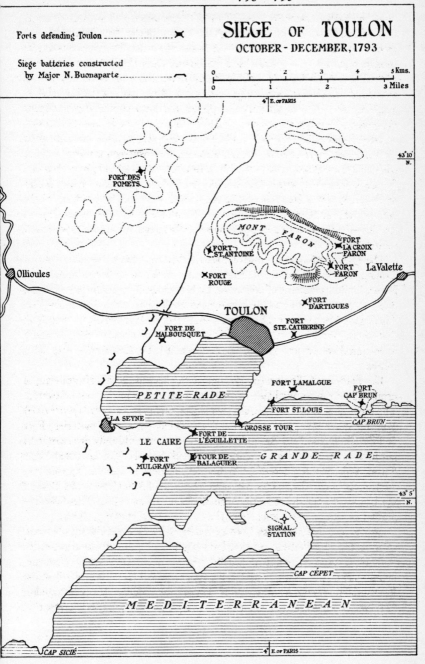

Forts defending Toulon .... ✕

Siege batteries constructed
by Major N. Buonaparte .... ⌐

SIEGE OF TOULON
OCTOBER - DECEMBER, 1793

0   1   2   3   4   5 Kms.
0   1   2   3 Miles

4° E. OF PARIS

43° 10′ N.

FORT DES POMETS

MONT FARON

FORT ST.ANTOINE

FORT LA CROIX FARON

FORT ROUGE

FORT FARON

La Valette

Ollioules

FORT D'ARTIGUES

TOULON

FORT STE.CATHERINE

FORT DE MALBOUSQUET

FORT LAMALGUE

FORT CAP BRUN

PETITE RADE

FORT ST.LOUIS

CAP BRUN

LA SEYNE

GROSSE TOUR

FORT DE L'ÉGUILLETTE

GRANDE RADE

LE CAIRE

TOUR DE BALAGUIER

FORT MULGRAVE

43° 5′ N.

SIGNAL STATION

CAP CÉPET

MEDITERRANEAN

CAP SICIÉ

4° E. OF PARIS

to his assignment with the coast defences, happened on 16 September to be passing through Ollioules on his way to Antibes. It also happened that Antoine-Christophe Saliceti, a Corsican and an old friend of the Buonaparte family, and now an influential politician in the Convention, was the senior *représentant du peuple*, or political commissar, with Carteaux's force. At Saliceti's suggestion Buonaparte was appointed to replace Dommartin in command of Carteaux's artillery. It was a strange combination of circumstances.

Toulon was then invested by the troops of Carteaux and Lapoype. The latter was an officer of the old régime, but as he was a *ci-devant* Marquis, Carteaux was given the over-all command of the besieging force. Napoleon in his memoirs has given us a lengthy account of the siege of Toulon; this narrative is a very *ex parte* one, and far from flattering to his seniors, but there are other sources from which to piece together the real story.

It did not take the bright young artillery commander long to perceive that the key to the fortress was the peninsula of Le Caire, which commanded both the outer and inner harbours. If the French could gain possession of this headland, they could not only command the entrance to the inner harbour, but they could make both harbours untenable by the British warships. As this key-point was inadequately defended on the landward side, the British soon fortified it with a strong redoubt which they called Fort Mulgrave, named by the French *petit Gibraltar*. Buonaparte at once proceeded to construct 13 siege batteries on the western face of the perimeter, six of them sited so that their fire could be concentrated on Fort Mulgrave. From his knowledge of the local coast defences, he was able to find the guns and material required. In all he installed 53 siege pieces, varying from 24-pounders and 44-pounders to 8-inch and 12-inch mortars. As soon as Buonaparte had decided on his plan for the conduct of the siege, he explained it to Carteaux and to the political commissars, Saliceti and Gasparin, who at once approved it and forwarded it on 20 September to the Committee of Public Safety in Paris. Carnot's staff produced a rival plan which envisaged a concentric attack on the whole perimeter by an army of 150,000 men. The Committee eventually accepted a modified form of Buonaparte's plan.

While Buonaparte was erecting his siege batteries during the next few weeks, Saliceti and Gasparin decided that Carteaux was quite incompetent as a commander, and reported unfavourably on him to Paris. In consequence, in the middle of November the Committee of Public Safety appointed an experienced veteran, General Jacques Coquille Dugommier (1738-1794) to command the besieging army, with General du Teil to command his artillery.

This again was a stroke of good fortune for Buonaparte; du Teil was a sick man and had to be carried up to inspect the batteries; he was very impressed with Buonaparte's plan and the way in which he was executing it, and told him to go ahead. Dugommier finally approved Buonaparte's plan of attack on 25 November. By the middle of December the strength of the besieging army had risen to 38,000, more than double that of the besieged, and all was ready. On the 17th, after a bombardment of 48 hours, a converging attack was launched on both flanks of the perimeter, the main assault being directed against Fort Mulgrave with a column of 6000 infantry.

By the following day the key-point of Fort Mulgrave had been captured, together with the batteries of L'Éguillette and Balaguier; Buonaparte himself took part in the infantry assault and was wounded in the thigh by a British bayonet. The Allied vessels in the harbour were now under the direct fire of the French and had to be hastily withdrawn by Commodore Sidney Smith. On the following day the Allied garrison evacuated Toulon in considerable disorder, after setting fire to the arsenal.

The siege of Toulon was the first successful military operation in which Buonaparte had taken part. He certainly made a considerable contribution to the victory, which his own memoirs tend to exaggerate. He was favourably mentioned in Dugommier's despatches to the Convention, and still more warmly in du Teil's report to the War Minister:

> Words fail me to describe Buonaparte's merits. He has great knowledge and as much intelligence and courage; and that is only a faint outline of the qualities of this rare officer.

On 19 October the War Ministry had promoted him to the rank of *chef de bataillon* (Major) at the early age of 24, doubtless on account of the shortage of regular officers due to emigration. Three days after the conclusion of the siege, on the recommendation of the political commissars, he was promoted *général de brigade*. He thus skipped the intermediate ranks of Lieutenant-Colonel and Colonel. Buonaparte had now got his first footing on the ladder of fame. On the whole he had been fortunate. Without wishing to belittle in any way his really meritorious services at Toulon, one cannot help feeling that any ordinarily intelligent officer with his training could have picked the vital point on which the security of the harbour depended. The lack of any rivals in this field caused Buonaparte's abilities to shine the more brightly. Other fortuitous circumstances were in his favour: firstly that he happened to arrive at Ollioules shortly after Carteaux's artillery commander had become a casualty; secondly that his influential supporter Saliceti was there to recommend him for the vacancy; thirdly that du Teil, who knew him well, was appointed as artillery commander to the force and retained Buonaparte as his understudy.

Another piece of good fortune for Buonaparte was the arrival at the end of November of an additional political commissar with the army besieging Toulon. This was Paul Barras (1755-1829), who was later to exert a favourable influence on Buonaparte's career. This able but unscrupulous individual belonged to an aristocratic family of the Midi. He had been an officer in the royal army, and had served in Bengal against the troops of the Honourable East India Company. With considerable astuteness he had joined the Revolutionaries and was already a politician of some standing in the Convention. At Toulon he was quick to note Buonaparte's abilities.

After the capture of Toulon Buonaparte reverted to his previous assignment as inspector of the Mediterranean coast defences. He reorganized the coast batteries at Marseille, Toulon, Antibes and Nice to such good effect that the British were forced to abandon the advanced base which they had established in the islands off Hyères, and which Buonaparte at once refortified. At the beginning of March 1794 Brigadier-General Buonaparte was appointed to command the artillery of the Army of Italy, with headquarters at Nice. He took with him two young gunner officers whom he had picked up during the siege of Toulon, Captain Marmont and Lieutenant Junot.

Also in March, Dugommier handed over command of the Army of Italy to General Pierre Dumerbion (1734-1797), a capable soldier, but elderly and unenterprising. Knowing the fate of many commanders who had opposed the views of the political commissars attached to their headquarters, Dumerbion was perfectly prepared to follow the instructions dictated by his *représentants du peuple en mission*. The Reign of Terror was approaching its climax; military failure, or a mere whisper of suspicion about their *civisme* (revolutionary zeal), had already meant the guillotine for many good Generals, including Custine and Houchard. Only in the previous month the same fate had befallen the kindly and harmless Inspector-General of Artillery, in spite of all that he had done for French gunnery, and of having modified his name to the less aristocratic-looking Duteil.

The most important of the political commissars attached to Dumerbion's army were Augustin Robespierre (younger brother of Maximilien, the dictator of the Convention in Paris) and the Corsican Saliceti, both of whom were friends and admirers of Buonaparte. Two months earlier the Committee of Public Safety, on the advice of Carnot their strategic adviser, had directed the Army of Italy to carry out a spring offensive along the Italian Riviera (Map 1*) to capture the Piedmontese port of Onéglia, 50 miles east of Nice, in order to

* Front endpaper.

relieve the supply situation. Saliceti and Robespierre now asked Buonaparte to draw up a plan for this operation. It was accepted by Dumerbion and put into operation forthwith; the result was completely successful, and Onéglia was captured on 6 April. In spite of deep snow, Massena's * division on the left wing drove the Austro-Sardinians back to the crest of the Maritime Alps, occupying the important features of the Colle Ardente and the Ponte di Nava, as well as the fort of Saorgio in the Roya valley, which opened the way to the important Colle di Tenda on the main watershed. Buonaparte took command of the artillery of the force; he organized his 4-pounders and 8-pounders as mountain batteries with sledge transport, so that the infantry could have artillery support in their forward positions. The success of this operation established Buonaparte's reputation as a tactical planner. In fact, he had applied the lessons of Bourcet, who had planned an operation on identical lines in this same area 50 years previously.

Encouraged by the Onéglia success, Buonaparte on 20 June put forward a plan for a further advance by Dumerbion's Army of Italy, in cooperation with the Army of the Alps on its left, with the object of invading Piedmont by the valley of the Stura. This plan again was almost an exact replica of the plan prepared by Bourcet in 1744 for his chief, Marshal de Maillebois, in the invasion of Piedmont. Buonaparte's Stura plan was accompanied by a remarkable memorandum on the strategic situation of the French armed forces at that time. France was then at war with Austria, Britain, Piedmont and Spain. Maximilien Robespierre was anxious to take the offensive on all fronts, while his more cautious strategist Carnot preferred to remain on the defensive everywhere to conserve the country's strength. Buonaparte's note pointed out that the French had 14 armies strung out along the frontiers; they could not attack with all 14, as they had not enough good N.C.O.s to go round, nor had they sufficient horses, powder or ammunition wagons. Buonaparte pointed out that it would be folly to attempt an invasion of Spain, so the Army of the Pyrenees must remain on the defensive. The Armies of Italy and the Alps should be integrated and should invade Piedmont and force it to make peace. That army could then advance through Lombardy and the Tyrol to threaten Vienna in conjunction with the Army of the Rhine. This was a remarkable appreciation of the strategic situation, and it exactly foreshadowed the Napoleonic strategy of the years 1796–1805.

Robespierre junior proceeded to Paris at the end of June with Buonaparte's plan for the invasion of Piedmont, and also with his politico-strategic

---

* André Massena (1758–1817), one of the ablest of Napoleon's Generals, had been a Warrant Officer in the royal army prior to the Revolution. He was created Marshal (1804), Duke of Rivoli (1808) and Prince of Essling (1809).

memorandum; both were submitted to the Committee of Public Safety, but the moment was inopportune. The political situation in Paris was approaching a crisis; people's minds were reacting against the horrors of the Reign of Terror. The Robespierre dictatorship was overthrown by the *coup d'état* of 9 Thermidor (27 July), and Carnot cancelled the projected offensive in Piedmont.

The Thermidorian *coup d'état* had an unfortunate personal repercussion on Buonaparte. Robespierre junior had been his strong supporter, but now all associates of the Robespierres were politically suspect. On 15 July Ricord, one of the political commissars with Dumerbion's army, had sent Buonaparte on an intelligence mission to the neutral city of Genoa, in company with Haller, a Swiss banker who was trying to raise a financial loan there on behalf of the French Government. The Committee of Public Safety suspected that Buonaparte was involved in some treacherous intrigue and ordered his immediate arrest. He was imprisoned on 9 August in the Fort Carré at Antibes and his papers were searched, but nothing incriminating was found. His friend Saliceti, who had been told to investigate the matter, managed to clear his character, and reported to the Committee that Buonaparte's services were indispensable to the army. He was released from imprisonment on 20 August and returned to duty at Nice.

Saliceti had good reason for securing Buonaparte's release, for he was then urging Dumerbion to undertake an autumn offensive with the object of occupying the Cadibona Pass, the important saddle between the Maritime Alps and the Ligurian Apennines, west of Savona, which offered the easiest approach to the plain of Piedmont. This was also a plan of Buonaparte's, based again on the ideas of Bourcet. Dumerbion's offensive started on 15 September, and Dego in the Bórmida valley was captured on the 21st. Dumerbion reported to the Convention that he owed his success 'to the ability of the General of artillery'.

Dumerbion's offensive was halted at Dego as Carnot was unwilling to become involved in a winter campaign in the mountains. Besides, he was anxious to employ the Army of Italy in a landing on Corsica, where Paoli had allowed the British Navy to establish an advanced base. Buonaparte organized the artillery contingent of the force, but, owing to unfavourable weather and the superior strength of the British fleet, the expedition did not leave Toulon until 11 March 1795. Buonaparte embarked with the expeditionary force. It was his second experience of a combined operation in Corsican waters, and it proved as abortive as the first one. On 14 March the expedition encountered a British squadron under Vice-Admiral Hotham, received rough handling and was forced to return to harbour.

Meanwhile, early in November 1794, General Barthélemy Schérer (1747–1804) had taken over command of the Army of Italy. A confidential report which he wrote on Buonaparte contained the following:

This officer is General of the artillery, in which arm he possesses real knowledge, but he has a little too much ambition, and intrigues for his own advancement.

On 3 March 1795 Schérer was replaced by General François-Christophe Kellermann (1735–1820), a tough and elderly Alsatian, who had helped to defeat the Prussians at Valmy in September 1792. Napoleon in later years commented that 'Kellermann was totally lacking in any qualities necessary in a Commander-in-Chief'.

Early in May Buonaparte quitted his command of the artillery of the Army of Italy and returned to Paris. There he remained for some weeks unemployed, many of the politicians being suspicious of him owing to his connections with the Robespierre clique. In June he was appointed to command an infantry brigade in the west of France, which he refused indignantly, and applied for sick leave.

During Buonaparte's absence from the Army of Italy, the Austro-Sardinians opened an offensive on 24 June and drove Kellermann's troops from the positions which they held on the crest of the Maritime Alps. The French were forced to withdraw to the Borghetto line, south of Loano, and abandon the useful little harbour of Vado.

The summer of 1795 was one of political ferment in Paris, and Buonaparte made a point of keeping in touch with the trend of affairs and in making contact with influential persons, as he realized that a government crisis was approaching. Among the people he got in touch with was the arch-intriguer Paul Barras, who had first met him at the siege of Toulon. In August Buonaparte's fortunes suddenly took a turn for the better, for he was attached to the *bureau topographique*, or plans section, of the Committee of Public Safety, the post previously held by the veteran Carnot. Now he was the military planning officer of the Convention. At the same time he was toying with several other alternative assignments, such as going to Turkey as head of a military mission.

In the following month the political crisis came to a head. Elections were held throughout the country on 21 September to decide the establishment of a new constitution. Political feeling ran high, and the Convention gave Barras full powers to maintain order. The members of the Government barricaded themselves inside the Louvre and the Tuileries, and on 5 October a hostile mob tried to storm them. Barras gave Buonaparte command of the 'Army of the Interior', that is to say, all the troops not with the armies at the front. Buonaparte, who had been authorized by Barras to use force, sent a cavalry officer named Joachim Murat to collect some guns from the nearest artillery depot, and posted them to command the approaches. As the mob approached the barricades in the Rue St. Honoré, he opened fire and dispersed the rioters. It was the *coup d'état* of 13 Vendémiaire.

IV

The Lightning Strikes
1796

As a young officer Buonaparte had carefully studied Marshal de Maillebois's campaign of 1744–1745 and the plans for the invasion of Piedmont drawn up by Bourcet, his Chief of Staff. During the 14 months of his command of the artillery of the Army of Italy, he himself had become intimately acquainted with the geography of the Maritime Alps and of the weather conditions prevalent at different seasons of the year. He had actually planned two of the offensives carried out successfully by Dumerbion, namely the capture of Onéglia in April 1794 and of Dego in September. He had personally reconnoitred all the Alpine passes: the Colle di Tenda (6200 feet), Colle Ardente and Colle di Nava (3000 feet), all captured by Massena in the April offensive. He knew that even the best of these, the Colle di Tenda, was approached by a road too steep and tortuous to be passable by artillery before the melting of the snow in late summer. On 21 September he had actually reached Dego with Dumerbion's staff, and had been impressed with its topographical importance as a stepping-stone in the conquest of Piedmont, for it lay in the lower Bórmida valley, only 15 miles from the fortress of Ceva.

Dego could be reached by crossing the watershed at its lowest point, the Colle di Cadibona, only 1425 feet, whence the main road, passable for all arms, ran north-westwards by Altare and Cárcare to Dego and Ceva. This was the 'Savona Gap', the low saddle across the watershed which separated the Maritime Alps from the Ligurian Apennines. It was the strategic key to the plains of Piedmont.

During the summer of 1795, when he was working at the *bureau topographique* in Paris, he had elaborated his plan for the invasion of Piedmont.

He reckoned that the Sardinians could be easily knocked out of the war before the Austrians came to their assistance, and that the French could then drive the Austrians back to Mantua and the Trentino, opening the way for the Army of the Rhine to advance on Vienna. This indeed was the theme which he had outlined in his still earlier memorandum of 20 June 1794, which Robespierre junior had taken to Paris, but which had been lost sight of in the Thermidorian *coup d'état*.

Besides the geographical features, the operational plan had to take account of the enemy's strength and dispositions. These depended to a certain extent on political factors. The Army of Italy was faced beyond the mountain range by the combined forces of the King of Sardinia and the Austrian army in Lombardy; these together outnumbered the French very considerably. The alliance, however, between the Emperor of Austria and the King of Sardinia was a tenuous one. Indeed, an influential party in the Turin Government would have preferred to come to terms with the French and remain neutral, leaving the Austrians and the French to fight it out between themselves. The elderly King Vittorio-Amadeo III overruled this advice and decided to throw in his lot with the Emperor Francis, suggesting that he himself should be given the supreme command. The Emperor promised to support him with the Austrian army in Lombardy, but sent him an Austrian General, Baron Michael von Colli, to command the Sardinian army, which did not increase the popularity of the Austrians with their Piedmontese allies. The command of the Austrian troops, as well as the supreme command in the theatre of operations, was at the last moment entrusted to General Baron Johann Beaulieu, a 71-year-old veteran of the Seven Years' War, who had orders not to move the Austrian troops further west than the river Tánaro. Thus the prospect of whole-hearted cooperation between Bonaparte's two opponents was slender.

A further international complication was the position of Genoa on the eastern flank of the theatre of operations. The Republic of Genoa was a neutral maritime State interposed between Piedmont and the Grand Duchy of Tuscany. The Genoese had no wish to be involved in the war, nor was it a French interest to drag them in; the neutral harbour of Genoa was a useful source of supplies for them, as Nelson's Mediterranean fleet maintained a close blockade of the French ports. The Austrians, however, suspected that the French might be tempted to seize Genoa, and were most anxious to prevent them doing so.

At the end of September 1795 the elderly Kellermann was replaced in command of the Army of Italy by Schérer and was transferred to the less important Army of the Alps. At the end of November, thanks to a brilliant attack carried out by Massena, Schérer had recovered most of the ground lost by Kellermann in June. The French front line now ran from Savona to the Cadibona Pass, and thence westwards along the Alpine crest. Schérer's headquarters were back at Nice, while Massena deputized for him at Savona, 100 miles to the east. If only Schérer had pushed forward into the plain of Piedmont and occupied Dego after his November success he would have been in a far better position and would have been able to feed his troops in more fertile country; as it was, they spent a miserable winter on the snow-clad crest of the Maritime Alps. From his headquarters at Nice Schérer bombarded the Directory in Paris with demands for provisions, clothing, boots and equipment, all of which were lacking. The Directory took little heed of these requests, for the treasury was empty. At last, worn out and disgusted, Schérer sent in his resignation on 4 February.

Schérer's resignation caused some consternation in the ranks of the Army of Italy, and speculation was rife as to who would be their new chief. In the past two years they had had a succession of elderly and not very competent commanders: first Dugommier, then Dumerbion, then Schérer, then Kellermann, then Schérer again; surely they would now get somebody younger and more vigorous; Massena, 37 years old and an outstanding leader in the field, seemed the obvious choice. But the Directory thought otherwise. They had at their disposal a brilliant young officer, only 26 years old, who had played a leading role in the capture of Toulon. His ruthless handling of the guns in defence of the Tuileries had put the reins of government in their hands. For months past he had been elaborating projects for the invasion of Piedmont; let him now be made responsible for executing these plans. On 27 February the young officer was told that he was to replace Schérer, and on 2 March he was officially appointed to command the Army of Italy.

The Executive Directory, which in October 1795 had replaced the National Convention, soon turned its thoughts to the invasion of Italy. Two of the five Directors were ex-officers of the old royal army, Barras and Carnot, and the latter had been head of the *bureau topographique* which had studied the problem deeply. On the day that Buonaparte was appointed to his new command, the Directory drew up an *Instruction pour le général en chef de l'armée d'Italie*, which was handed to him four days later; it was doubtless based on the plans which he himself had worked out. The directive of 2 March contained the following significant clauses:

An attack on Piedmont only will not achieve the aim that the Executive Directory should set itself, namely, to drive the Austrians out of Italy and to bring about as soon as possible a glorious and lasting peace. . . . The Directory has found it necessary to aim particularly at an offensive campaign directed chiefly against the

47

Austrian forces in Italy, so contrived that by the overthrow of the Piedmontese at the beginning of military operations, the French army in Italy shall be safe from any operations on their part during the rest of the campaign. . . . We must do all in our power to drive the enemy beyond the Po, and to concentrate our greatest efforts in the direction of the Milanese. This however cannot be effected until the French army has taken Ceva. . . . After he has made himself master of Ceva, the Commander-in-Chief shall provision his army as quickly as possible from the resources available in Piedmont. He shall then direct his forces principally against the Austrians; he shall drive the enemy across the Po, finding himself the means of crossing that river. . . . The Directory insists on the necessity of provisioning the Army of Italy both in and by the enemy countries, and of giving it everything it may need to the full extent of the available resources. Heavy contributions are to be raised, of which half shall be paid into the funds for maintaining the various services and half shall be used to pay the troops in cash. (*Debidour*, I. 717)

This directive was clear and to the point; the new Commander-in-Chief was given a free hand as to his routes of advance and tactical methods; he was only given his main strategic objectives in their logical order of priority, namely: to seize the key-point of Ceva and knock the Piedmontese out of the war; then to re-provision his army and drive the Austrians beyond the Po; finally, to advance on Milan. The directive, perhaps wisely, did not outline any ulterior objective. It will be seen how brilliantly these instructions were carried out.

The new Commander-in-Chief had a great deal to attend to, and he wasted no time in getting down to his task, for the administrative services of his army were in a shocking condition. But he found time to think of other things; he altered the spelling of his name, which looked too Italian, and now spelt it 'Bonaparte'. He had also fallen deeply in love with the beautiful widow of a guillotined aristocrat, the Vicomte Alexandre de Beauharnais, and he married her hastily on 9 March, leaving two days later for Marseille.

First of all he collected a small headquarter staff. His choice of a Chief of Staff was a good one; the combination of his own power of leadership with the meticulous industry of Alexandre Berthier (1754–1814) proved an unbroken success for the next 18 years. Berthier was then 42 years old; his early training was as a cartographer; while a young officer he had served on Rochambeau's staff in North America during the War of Independence. He had been Chief of Staff to Kellermann in the previous year, and knew the geography of the Maritime Alps as well as Bonaparte himself. Berthier's soldierly qualities were limited to the conduct of staff duties, but in that field he was unrivalled. Napoleon later summed up his abilities and limitations as follows:

He was very active; he would accompany his Commander-in-Chief on every reconnaissance and every journey, without his office work being ever slowed down.

He had no decision of character and was quite unfitted for command, but possessed all the qualities of a good Chief of Staff. He was a good map-reader, knew everything about reconnaissance, and attended personally to the issue of orders; he was expert at presenting clearly the most complicated movements of an army. (*Corr.* XXIX. 107)

Berthier was indeed the perfect staff officer for a commander who knew how to make up his mind without being prompted; he served his master faithfully throughout all his campaigns until the last one. Strange to say, he deserted Napoleon before Waterloo, when his absence proved disastrous.

Besides Berthier, Bonaparte brought with him as A.D.C.s two young gunners whom he had collected at the siege of Toulon, Captains Marmont and Junot. There was also Lieutenant-Colonel Joachim Murat, the dashing cavalry officer who had galloped off to fetch the guns for the Vendémiaire 'whiff of grapeshot'. Finally, there was his young brother Louis, aged 18, whom he had tutored at Auxonne.

After re-organizing the rearward services of his army, Bonaparte reached his headquarters at Nice on 26 March. Three days later he reviewed some of his troops in the back area and issued an encouraging order of the day. In his Memoirs he claims to have given them quite a different harangue, holding out the promise of rich provinces to conquer. No contemporary record exists of such an address, and it must be discounted as one of the many myths concocted at St. Helena (*Corr.* XXIX. 84).

Before taking over command at the front, there was much to be done to repair Schérer's sloth and the neglect of the departments in Paris. Bonaparte was not one of those commanders who prefer to leave administrative details to their subordinates. He knew that an army must be fed, paid, clothed and provided with transport, as well as trained to fight. In this case the training had been done already by experienced divisional commanders. During the next week he issued a stream of purposeful orders for reinforcing the forward divisions; the cavalry were moved up from the Rhône valley, where they had wintered owing to the lack of forage on the Riviera. The mention of the river Po in his instructions involved the organization of a bridging-train, in those days the responsibility of the artillery, not of the engineers. Gun-teams were shipped up to the port of Vado, to be disembarked at the last minute, so as to maintain secrecy. The meat ration of the troops was doubled, ammunition parks were stocked and transport columns organized. There was no time to be lost; the snow was melting on the Maritime Alps, and the advance must start by the middle of April. On the 4th Bonaparte moved his headquarters up to Albenga and made a tour of his forward troops.

On 9 April 1796 the Army of Italy numbered some 63,000 men. Of this number, two weak divisions under Macquard and Garnier were required to guard the Alpine passes on the left flank, and three coast defence brigades had the task of protecting the still more vulnerable line of communications back along the Riviera coast to Nice, liable at any moment to be raided by Nelson's fleet. That left only 41,000 available for field operations. His field army comprised five divisions, under Massena, Laharpe, Augereau, Serrurier and Meynier, all tough and seasoned veterans, except perhaps Meynier, who was rheumatic. Bonaparte now organized these in a *corps d'avant-garde* (19,000) under Massena and a *corps de bataille* (12,000) under Augereau, with a left flank-guard (10,000) under Serrurier. This was no new idea of Bonaparte's but an echo from Guibert. Massena was to cross the Cadibona Pass and hold Montenotte and Dego to ward off the Austrians, while Augereau from the west and Serrurier from the south would make a converging attack on Ceva. This manœuvre was in exact conformity with Bonaparte's instructions from the Directory that he should first crush the Piedmontese and then deal with the Austrians.

We can now turn to the strength and dispositions of the enemy. The King of Sardinia had about 70,000 Piedmontese troops, but a large proportion of these were required to hold the Alpine passes and to garrison the various fortresses, such as Cúneo, Ceva, Alessándria and Tortona, which covered the river crossings and the approaches to Turin. Only 25,000 were available as a mobile field force, and these were extended, facing south, on a front of about 30 miles on the line Cúneo–Mondovi–Ceva–Millésimo, under command of the Austrian General Colli. Farther to the east the Austrian army under Beaulieu, 28,000 strong, was widely distributed in the triangle Alessándria, Millésimo, the Bocchetta Pass (10 miles north of Genoa). Beaulieu's headquarters were at Acqui, and his right flank approached Colli's left near Millésimo in the upper Bórmida valley. A detached Austrian brigade under Provera was intended to link up with the Piedmontese near Millésimo; the remaining Austrian divisions, from right to left, were commanded by Argenteau, Vukássovich and Pittoni, with Sebottendorf's in reserve in the area Acqui–Alessándria–Tortona.

It was thus obvious that the French army of 41,000 was inferior in numbers to the combined strength of 53,000 Austro-Sardinians, should these be able to unite. Bonaparte's strategic plan, therefore, must depend on a manœuvre on interior lines, with his army concentrated, in order to defeat each of his foes separately before they could unite to crush him. He was, however, at a tactical disadvantage due to the topography of the area, as he had to pass the bulk of his army through the narrow defile of the Cadibona Pass before he could strike at either of his opponents. On the other side of the mountain range his enemies were operating in the lower foot-hills and the plain, where mutual support should have been easier, although this advantage was largely negatived by the fact that all the river valleys ran north and south, impeding lateral communication.

Before operations began, the strategic situation was modified by a curious political development, which at first upset Bonaparte's initial plan, but in the end reacted in his favour.

The French Government, being very short of money, had in the first week of March sent to Genoa Bonaparte's friend Saliceti, who was one of the political commissars attached to the Army of Italy. The object of Saliceti's mission was to raise a loan from the Genoese Senate. In spite of his efforts, backed by those of Faipoult, the French diplomatic representative, the Genoese refused to open their purse-strings. Saliceti then thought that a little intimidation might prove effective, so he persuaded his Government to make a military demonstration. On instructions from the Directory, Massena sent up to Voltri, only seven miles west of Genoa, a *demi-brigade* of Cervoni's brigade which held the coastal sector north-east of Savona; Cervoni's regiment occupied Voltri on 26 March, the very day that Bonaparte assumed command of the Army. The French move merely hardened the hearts of the Genoese, who manned their town defences, but it thoroughly alarmed the Austrians, who thought that the French were advancing to occupy Genoa. This was not Bonaparte's intention, as he was still purchasing supplies in Genoa, and to attack that port might involve its seizure by the British Navy. But he quickly realized that a threat to Genoa might turn to his advantage, so on 6 April he reinforced the regiment at Voltri with the rest of Cervoni's brigade. The Austrian Ambassador at Turin and the Austrian envoy at Genoa were now so alarmed that they both urged Beaulieu to act immediately to stop the French advance on Genoa. Beaulieu fell into the trap and set his army in motion. Pittoni's division was to occupy the Bocchetta Pass leading to Genoa; Vukássovich was to march on Voltri and drive the French vanguard back, while Argenteau was to advance southward to the crest of the Ligurian Apennines, and occupy Montenotte and Monte Negino (2300 feet), which commanded the Cadibona Pass. His intention was to strike at Bonaparte's left flank during his expected march along the Riviera to Genoa. By this false move Beaulieu lost the war.

Beaulieu's advance began on 10 April. Pittoni with seven battalions attacked Cervoni at Voltri, and the French retired in good order to Savona on the 11th. Vukássovich advanced southward to Sassello, and Argenteau on his right moved on Montenotte, but he was late in starting, and Rampon, one of Massena's brigade commanders, occupied Monte Negino before him.

Bonaparte had moved up to Savona on the 10th to see Massena and Laharpe and make final arrangements for his intended advance on the 15th. He now found that the whole Austrian army was in motion towards him, so he had to quickly change his plan and deal with Beaulieu first, instead of attacking Colli. On the 11th he moved up to Santuário, just south of Monte Negino, and found that Rampon, who held a strong position, was being attacked by six Austrian battalions under Argenteau. No further Austrian troops had appeared west of Montenotte. Bonaparte assembled his divisional commanders and dictated his orders. Laharpe was to attack Argenteau frontally on the following morning; Massena during the night was to march his whole division along the Altare ridge west of Montenotte and attack Argenteau's right rear at dawn. The French attack went in as planned and was completely successful. When the morning mist lifted on 12 April, Argenteau found himself nearly surrounded. After a short fight his force melted away and withdrew in some disorder north-eastwards towards Acqui. Bonaparte's first battle at Montenotte really decided the campaign; he had driven a wedge between his two opponents, and there was little chance of their future junction. He was quick to exploit the situation; while Laharpe held the ground won at Montenotte, Massena was ordered to push north to Cáiro and Dego, to deal with any Austrian reinforcements; Augereau's fresh troops were to move up to Cárcare and then turn west to Millésimo, while Serrurier was to advance down the Tánaro valley from Garéssio to threaten Ceva. Bonaparte's headquarters moved up to Cárcare. He considered Meynier unfit to command a division, so gave one of his brigades to Massena and two to Augereau.

On the afternoon of 12 April Bonaparte issued the following order of the day:

Vive la République! Today, 12 April, General Massena's division, together with that of General Laharpe, attacked the Austrians, 13,000 strong, commanded by General Beaulieu in person and Generals d'Argenteau and Roccavina, holding the important position of Montenotte. The Republicans have completely defeated the Austrians and have killed or wounded about 3000. (*Corr.* 139)

Rukavina was one of Argenteau's brigadiers; Beaulieu, however, was not present at the battle, and indeed did not hear of it until two days later, as he was then on his way back from Voltri to his headquarters at Acqui.

It was the first time that the gunner Bonaparte had handled infantry in the field, and the result had been brilliantly successful. That was due to no miraculous stroke of genius or of luck; he had applied faithfully the tactical lessons which he had learnt from Bourcet, Guibert and du Teil; above all, he had applied them with clear perception, quick decision and rapidity of action.

On the morning of the 13th Augereau advanced westwards with three infantry brigades, some 9000 men, to attack the Piedmontese at Millésimo. Here his way was blocked by a detached Austrian brigade under General Provera, together with a Piedmontese grenadier battalion, which was holding the valley of the western Bórmida. On Augereau's approach Provera with the bulk of his brigade took refuge in the ancient castle of Cosseria on the summit of a steep hill. Augereau attempted to storm the castle, but was repulsed with heavy loss. Provera, however, having exhausted his ammunition, food and water, surrendered on the following day. Meanwhile Augereau drove Colli's troops westwards from Millésimo towards Ceva.

Bonaparte, having successfully widened the gap between the Austrians and Piedmontese, now turned back to rejoin Massena, who reported that he was held up by Argenteau's rearguard in a strong position at Dego. On the afternoon of 14 April Bonaparte organized another enveloping attack; Massena attacked frontally, while Laharpe forded the Bórmida below the town and engaged the Austrians from the rear; 2600 Austrians were captured and the remnants of Argenteau's force retreated northward through the Spigno gorges to Acqui.

The battle of Dego, however, was not yet over. Beaulieu had originally given Vukássovich orders to drive back the French brigade at Voltri. This was actually done by Pittoni, on his left, and Vukássovich had advanced westwards along the Apennine ridge with his seven battalions to join Argenteau at Sassello. On the morning of the 14th he received an urgent order to come to Argenteau's rescue at Dego. After marching all night, he suddenly appeared on the morning of the 15th on the flank of the French at Dego, forcing them to evacuate the town in hurried confusion. Massena, however, soon restored the situation and, launching a counter-attack, drove Vukássovich northwards to Acqui.

Beaulieu, having from the start completely lost control of his army, was now trying to collect its scattered remnants in the area between the fortresses of Alessándria and Tortona, in order to defend the crossings of the Po. On 16 April he wrote a pessimistic despatch to the Austrian Emperor:

The army is in a very bad situation. . . . I am now endeavouring to collect the remaining troops at Acqui. . . . I shall then take up the most advantageous position for the safety of the army and to secure the defence of Lombardy. I beg your Majesty to consider what can be hoped for from an army which barely amounts to 16,000 men.

Since he had started the campaign six days earlier with an army of 28,000, the Austrian losses must have been considerable.

Having disposed of his major opponent for the time being, Bonaparte could now turn his attention to, and concentrate his whole force against, the

Sardinians. From his headquarters at Cárcare he issued orders for a converging attack on Colli's entrenched camp at Ceva. Augereau was to attack the position frontally, while Massena made a turning movement on the right and Serrurier on the left. Bonaparte then moved his headquarters up to Millésimo. The French columns advanced on the 18th, but found to their surprise the camp evacuated. During the night Colli had retired to a strong position on the Corsaglia stream between San Michele and Lesegno; he still had 13,000 men under his command, about half what he had started with. A frontal attack by the French on the 19th failed with heavy loss. On the 21st Bonaparte organized a final enveloping attack, re-uniting all his divisions; Serrurier's turning movement round the enemy's right flank proved decisive.

Colli was driven back through Mondovi and retired northwards towards Turin. The French had now reached the plain of Piedmont and the cavalry division under Stengel took up the pursuit of the beaten Sardinian army, though Stengel himself fell, mortally wounded. Plenipotentiaries from the King met Bonaparte at Cherasco, 33 miles south of Turin, and an armistice was signed there on 28 April. On the 26th Bonaparte had issued the following order of the day:

Soldiers, in 15 days you have won six victories, captured 21 colours, 55 guns, several fortresses, and conquered the richest part of Piedmont; you have taken 15,000 prisoners, killed or wounded more than 10,000 men. (*Corr.* 234)

It was no small achievement for a young General. At the age of 26 he had defeated two hostile armies in succession and established his reputation as an outstanding leader of troops.

The conquest of Piedmont was Bonaparte's first campaign as a Commander-in-Chief; it was possibly the most brilliant one of his whole career. It may be argued that he was fortunate in having as his principal opponent the elderly and inefficient Beaulieu, who displayed the most crass ineptitude and was easy game. Leaving that aside, Bonaparte was faced at the outset with very real difficulties. Firstly, the geography of the theatre of operations was unfavourable; it is true that he had a mountain barrier to screen his initial concentration, but in that barrier there was only one narrow defile through which he could pass the bulk of his army, which meant taking a considerable risk. Secondly, his line of communication from Savona back to Nice was 100 miles long; as it ran along the coast, it was liable to interruption at any point by Nelson's fleet; one may wonder indeed why no attempt was made to cut it. Thirdly, his supply system was very inadequate, partly because he had insufficient time to organize it, and partly because the operations started four days earlier than he had anticipated. Bonaparte had originally intended to deal first with the Sardinians, as they were nearer his line of communication, and then to turn on the Austrians, whose forces were more widely dispersed. Argenteau's unexpected advance along the Apennines might have thrown a lesser commander off balance; that Bonaparte could so rapidly re-adjust his plans to meet this unexpected move exemplifies his extraordinary flexibility of mind.

The Piedmont campaign shows that although Bonaparte made no original contribution to the art of war, he displayed extreme dexterity in the application of established first principles, both in his strategic manœuvre and in his tactical operations. On every occasion when he made a purely frontal attack, the result was a failure; whenever he combined a frontal with an enveloping attack, he was successful; but that was no new principle of war.

We should note also the secrecy with which his preliminary concentration was effected. At the beginning of April the Army of Italy was holding the same positions which it had gained the previous November by Schérer's Loano offensive. During the winter months active patrolling had been carried out along the front by Massena and Laharpe, and the enemy's dispositions were well known, thanks to Massena's intelligence service. No additional activity was now displayed, but units were unobtrusively transferred from the coastal sector to reinforce Serrurier's division up at Garéssio. The artillery batteries were short of gun-teams owing to the scarcity of forage in the forward area; at the beginning of April Bonaparte sent up gun-teams by sea to Vado, instructing Massena to disembark them only just prior to the operation. In order to deceive the enemy and divert his attention from the Cadibona Pass, Cervoni's brigade was marched up along the coast to Voltri; this bait was so hastily swallowed by Beaulieu that he imagined Genoa to be the main French objective.

Beaulieu having made the first mistaken move, Bonaparte swiftly profited by it; changing his original plan, he delivered his first blow on the dispersed Austrian divisions before they could unite, firstly at Montenotte and then at Dego. This was a good example of *flexibility of manœuvre*. In these lightning blows, Bonaparte put into practice the theoretical lessons which he had absorbed from his study of previous campaigns: *concentration of force* against the immediately important objective, and *economy of force* in retaining a reserve to deal with further emergencies. Massena's divisions were employed at the start to deal with the Austrians at Montenotte and Dego, while Augereau's fresh troops were launched on the Sardinians at Millésimo. When the Austrians had been finally disposed of, every division was concentrated for the knock-out blow at Mondovi, Serrurier's fresh division being used for the decisive outflanking movement. The whole series of operations was governed by the principle of *maintaining the objective*. *Tactical envelopment* of the most vulnerable flank always proved successful, and at the end, when the level plain had been reached, cavalry were used to *exploit success* and to pursue the beaten enemy. Prior to that, the cavalry could not be employed, even for reconnaissance purposes, owing to the nature of the terrain, as they could not leave the roads in the mountainous area.

The actions in the Piedmont campaign were infantry battles, the artillery playing a minor role, largely owing to the nature of the country. Victory was won mainly by the legs of the soldiers, whose rapidity of marching was quite remarkable, in spite of the fact that the commissariat arrangements frequently broke down, principally because operations began four days earlier than Bonaparte had intended. On one occasion one of Augereau's battalions had to be entirely equipped with muskets captured from the Austrians. The credit for the marching and fighting powers of the troops must largely be ascribed to their divisional commanders, four out of five of whom were tough veterans with long experience of mountain warfare. During the battle of Montenotte Bonaparte removed the rheumatic Meynier from command of his division, but the other four distinguished themselves conspicuously. In spite of his comparative youth, Bonaparte seems to have had no difficulty in asserting his authority over subordinates with much greater fighting experience.

The personality of the young Commander-in-Chief deserves notice. He was short in stature, like Massena, and not very careful of his dress. He still spoke with a harsh Corsican accent. During his period as artillery commander of the Army of Italy, he had not been popular with his fellows, being considered a morose and moody young officer, who was mainly concerned with his own advancement. When his appointment as Army Commander was announced, the senior officers such as Massena and Augereau were horrified at the prospect of serving under such a fledgeling (*blanc-bec*). As soon as he started to dictate his orders, however, there was no question of disputing his personal authority and power of command. Still, one can understand that at first there existed an under-current of jealousy and perhaps hesitation to obey on the part of experienced and independent-minded commanders like Massena and Augereau. Marmont, who was then serving on Bonaparte's staff, has recorded that:

Not only did his orders fail to be met with that confidence, that faith in its leader which magnifies tenfold the resources of an army, but also the very disposition to obey was shaken by the rivalries and pretensions of much older Generals, who had themselves long held commands.

As a result of this first campaign all such hesitations and jealousies were swept away. Four smashing victories in nine days was a record to convince the most hardened *grognard*. From now onward the youthful leader moved from conquest to conquest with the whole-hearted confidence and cooperation of his subordinate commanders.

Perhaps one of the most important lessons learnt by Bonaparte from the Piedmont campaign was the necessity for maintaining strict discipline among his troops. He had previously had bitter experience of the results of bad discipline with his Corsican volunteers. Nor have French troops ever been noted for submissive discipline. When the Army of Italy, after wintering in the snow-clad Alps, descended on the fertile plains and well-stocked villages of Piedmont an orgy of looting broke out. Two particularly glaring incidents had occurred: one was at Dego on 14 April; the Austrians had hastily evacuated the town, abandoning their gun-teams and baggage-mules; the French soldiers appropriated these for their own use, so that Bonaparte had to purchase them for a *louis* each. The other case, which occurred during the heavy fighting at San Michele on the Corsaglia river on the 20th, was even worse. A light infantry regiment of Serrurier's division had captured the village, but at once dispersed to loot it; the Piedmontese counter-attacked and recaptured the village, so that Bonaparte's attack had to be postponed until the following day.

Bonaparte realized that the army which he had taken over had been sadly neglected; the men were ragged, poorly equipped and half-starved; their pay had always been months in arrear. From now on he would ensure that they lived on the fat of the land, but without acting as a scourge on the regions they conquered. There would be pillage on a large scale, but it would be organized pillage, and the men would maintain their self-respect. By this means he soon acquired the confidence and devotion of his troops.

V

The Conquest of Lombardy
1796

The Armistice of Cherasco meant that Bonaparte had successfully gained the first objective assigned to him by the Directors in their *Instruction* of 6 March, namely the conquest of Piedmont. Pending the conclusion of a definite peace treaty between the Directory and the King of Sardinia, Bonaparte had ensured himself a secure spring-board for his next move against the Austrians by insisting in the armistice terms on the surrender as hostages of the fortresses of Cúneo, Alessándria and Tortona. Having paid and re-equipped his troops at the expense of the Piedmontese, he now prepared to move eastwards in order to drive the Austrians out of Lombardy, Milan being the final objective given him by the Directory. But to reach Milan he would have to cross the most formidable river of Italy, the Po; and also its left-hand tributary, the Ticino, and each crossing would be disputed by Beaulieu's army. These rivers were now in full flood with the melting of the Alpine snows, and the French bridging train was still far in the rear. So Bonaparte resorted to a clever *ruse de guerre* to outwit his opponent.

The fourth clause of the Cherasco armistice gave the French army the right to pass through Piedmontese territory and cross the Po at Valenza. To support the illusion that he intended to cross at Valenza, Bonaparte moved Massena's and Serrurier's divisions to that neighbourhood and ordered them to requisition barges and reconnoitre crossing places. These preparations soon came to Beaulieu's ears; he crossed the Po at Valenza with his own army and took up position to prevent the French doing so. By that means he also covered the direct approach to Milan. Beaulieu's army now numbered about 21,000; the French, who had received reinforcements, perhaps twice that number. Bonaparte moved his headquarters up to Tortona on 3 May, and on the following day assembled a picked force of six battalions of grenadiers and fusiliers from the divisions of Massena, Augereau and Laharpe. During 6/7 May this column, under Brigadier-General Dallemagne's orders, made a forced march eastwards to Piacenza, 55 miles down stream from Valenza. Meanwhile Major Andréossy, the gunner officer in charge of Bonaparte's bridging train, moved down the Po, collecting barges on the way, and organized the crossing at Piacenza. The actual crossing operation was entrusted by Bonaparte to a young Colonel, Jean Lannes,* whose conspicuous ability and courage he had noticed on the battlefield of Dego, three weeks earlier. On 7 May Andréossy had assembled a number of barges and a large ferry-boat capable of carrying 500 men at a time. The operation was brilliantly carried out by Lannes, very slight opposition being encountered. On the following day contact was made with the left flank of Beaulieu's army and some desultory fighting took place. In an affair of outposts during the night General Laharpe was shot dead by one of his own pickets.

By 9 May Bonaparte's whole army was across the Po and there was no further water obstacle to bar their road to Milan. The army marched northwestwards, Massena's division again forming the advanced guard. On that day Bonaparte sent a despatch to Carnot:

> We have at last crossed the Po. The second campaign has begun. Beaulieu has been outwitted; he calculates pretty inaccurately and falls into every trap one sets for him. . . . One more victory and we shall be masters of Italy. (*Corr.* 366)

The surprise crossing of the Po was a brilliant strategic achievement, although perhaps not ethically justified. Piacenza at that time was a neutral city, belonging to the Duchy of Parma. Not only did Bonaparte infringe the neutrality of Parma without asking anybody's permission, but he levied on the unfortunate Duke a fine of £80,000 in order to pay the French troops; he also made large requisitions in kind, and confiscated 20 pictures by Michelangelo and Correggio, which he despatched to Paris. One cannot blame Bonaparte for this latter piece of robbery, for he had been ordered by the Directory to carry it out. Bonaparte then proceeded to subject the territory of the Duke of Módena, also neutral, to similar treatment.

As soon as Beaulieu heard that the French had crossed the Po, he realized that he must abandon the Duchy of Milan; so he marched eastwards by

---

* Jean Lannes (1769–1809) was created a Marshal (1804) and Duke of Montebello (1808). He died of wounds received at the battle of Aspern-Essling (May 1809), the first of Napoleon's Marshals to fall in battle.

Crema and Bréscia, heading for the narrow valleys of the Trentino. On crossing the river Adda by the bridge at Lodi, he left a strong rearguard to delay the French at the bridge. This force was 10,000 strong with 14 guns and some cavalry under Sebottendorf, whose division had not been engaged in the Montenotte and Dego battles.

And now occurred one of the most dramatic episodes of the campaign, and indeed of Napoleon's whole career. Massena's advanced guard, on its way from Piacenza to Milan, reached the little town of Lodi shortly after midday on 10 May. The town stood a short distance from the right bank of the river Adda, which was crossed by a wooden bridge 170 yards long; the Austrians had partially destroyed the bridge near the far bank, which was strongly held by Sebottendorf's troops. Bonaparte came up and decided to force a crossing. It is not clear why he made this decision; the Austrians were all on the far bank, and would certainly withdraw during the night. They could hardly have interfered with his immediate objective, which was not to follow Beaulieu but to occupy Milan. Perhaps he felt that this was his last chance of hitting at the Austrians, as their main body had now eluded him.

Under the cover of the town wall Bonaparte and Massena reconnoitred the bridge, which was strongly held and enfiladed by the muzzles of two batteries. Bonaparte brought up a battery, laid the guns himself and called for a storming party. The column formed up behind the town wall, the gates were opened and the assault was launched down the road to the bridge; it was met with a storm of grape-shot, causing the column to waver. Under cover of the smoke the attack was renewed, led by Massena and Berthier; as the sun set, the French stormed the bridge and the Austrian defence melted away.

The storming of the bridge at Lodi had no strategic influence on the campaign, but it did produce a profound psychological effect on the troops taking part in it and also on Bonaparte himself. For the first time he had fought in the front line with his men, and they now hailed him as '*le petit caporal*'. It certainly fortified his own feeling of self-confidence. As he said afterwards at St. Helena:

It was only after Lodi that I got the idea that I might, after all, play a decisive role on our political stage. It was then that the first spark of my high ambition was born. (*Corr.* XXIX. 102 fn.)

A few days later, at Milan, he remarked to his A.D.C. Marmont:

The future holds for us successes greater far than those we have already achieved. . . . In our time no one has conceived anything great; it is for me to set the example.

After Lodi the advance to Milan was resumed without interference from the enemy, and Bonaparte rode into the Lombard capital on 15 May.

At this juncture there arose a conflict of opinion regarding war aims between the young Commander-in-Chief and the Directory in Paris. While Bonaparte was still artillery commander in the Army of Italy, he had sketched out in his mind a general plan for driving the Austrians out of Italy. Later, when employed at the *bureau topographique* in Paris, he had elaborated this idea on a grander scale, envisaging a penetration of the Tyrol by the Army of Italy, combined with an advance on Vienna by the 200,000 men of the French armies deployed on the Rhine frontier, the *Rhin-et-Moselle* under Moreau and the *Sambre-et-Meuse* under Jourdan. This idea of a vast pincer movement was now taking practical shape, for Beaulieu's army was in full flight before him, seeking refuge in the fastnesses of the Trentino Alps.

The strategic aims of the Directory, however, were not so ambitious. The executive government of France had, since the previous November, been vested in five Directors: Le Tourneur, Carnot, Barras, Rewbell and Larevellière-Lépeaux. Carnot, the 'organizer of victory' and cautious planner, was obviously the strategic adviser to the *Directoire Exécutif*. Carnot had always considered Bonaparte's idea of a vast converging movement on Vienna as a wild fantasy. There was no mention of such far-flung objectives in the directive handed to Bonaparte on 6 March. He had been given three tasks: firstly, to eliminate the Piedmontese; secondly, to defeat the Austrians; thirdly, to occupy the Duchy of Milan. What next? Carnot's plan was simple: the Austrians would return reinforced to renew the struggle in Italy; the French treasury was bankrupt; the whole of Italy lay at Bonaparte's feet; Italy was the richest and most fertile country in Europe; France must drain the resources of Italy to the full. On 7 May the Directory ordered Bonaparte to hand over the greater part of his troops to Kellermann, who, with his Army of the Alps, would take over the Milanese province and hold the Austrians in check. Bonaparte then, with a reduced army, was to drive southwards on a predatory foray, to occupy Tuscany and Parma, to force a loan on Genoa, to advance on Rome, compelling the Pope to pay tribute; finally, Naples and Corsica might be 'liberated'.

In this deliberate clipping of the eagle's wings one may sense a touch of professional jealousy on the part of the elderly Carnot. The other Directors too thought that the youthful eagle was soaring a bit too high, and might get out of hand as well as out of sight. Finally, they reminded the Commander-in-Chief that his future military operations must be approved by the political representatives attached to his army, Garran and Saliceti. When Bonaparte received these instructions from the Directory on 14 May, four days after his victory at Lodi, he was furious. He rejected them firmly, though politely.

He was particularly incensed by the proposal that his Army should be split into two and be shared with the elderly Kellermann:

> To arrange the union of Kellermann and myself in Italy is to plan ruin. I cannot serve voluntarily with a man who considers himself the first General in Europe and, besides, I believe it better to have one bad General than two good ones.

Bonaparte was also indignant at the injunction that he must subordinate his troop movements to the approval of the political commissars, even though one of them was his old friend and ally Saliceti. Finally, he offered to resign his command.

The Directors capitulated to their vigorous young commander; on 21 May Carnot wrote again in conciliatory terms, and Kellermann's Army of the Alps continued to act as a draft-finding depot for Bonaparte's Army of Italy.

Bonaparte halted for a week in Milan to rest and re-equip his ragged troops, and paid them in cash from the enormous contribution of £800,000 which he levied on the unfortunate inhabitants. He ruthlessly quelled an insurrection which broke out at Pavia.

The Duchy of Milan, a fief belonging to Austria, was now in his power, so Bonaparte decided to pursue the remnants of Beaulieu's army in its retreat to the Tyrol, to gain which it had to pass through the neutral territory of the Venetian Republic. On 27 May Massena's advanced guard entered Bréscia, crossed the river Mincio at Valéggio on the 30th and established his headquarters at Verona on 1 June. A minor incident which occurred at Valéggio was nearly disastrous for the Commander-in-Chief. The advanced guard under Massena having gone ahead, Bonaparte halted for a midday meal and rest in a country house near the bridge, which had been left unguarded. An Austrian cavalry patrol rode up and entered the village. Shots rang out and Bonaparte and his staff were nearly captured, but the Commander-in-Chief managed to escape, half-dressed, by the back door. As a result of this narrow escape, Bonaparte created for himself a personal bodyguard consisting of two grenadier battalions under the command of Colonel Lannes, with a cavalry troop of *Guides-à-cheval* under Captain Bessières.* This was the embryo from which sprang later the Consular, and still later the Imperial Guard.

By the beginning of June Bonaparte had not only wrested the whole of Lombardy from its Austrian Governor, the Archduke Ferdinand, but he had also infringed the neutrality of the Venetian Republic. He had some excuse for doing so, since Beaulieu, to secure his retreat to the Trentino, had occu-

---

* Jean-Baptiste Bessières (1768–1813) was created a Marshal (1804) and Duke of Istria (1808). He later commanded the Imperial Guard and was killed in the Leipzig campaign.

pied the Venetian fortress of Peschiera. This was one of the famous Quadrilateral of medieval fortresses—Peschiera, Verona, Legnago and Mantua, which covered the western approaches to Venice. Of these the only really defensible one was Mantua, an Austrian fief, which was impregnable against normal siege operations, as it was almost entirely surrounded by the river Mincio, which here swells to the proportion of a lake. These fortresses, particularly Verona and Mantua, were very important in the forthcoming operations as they commanded vital road junctions and river crossings in the marshy flood-plain of the Po. Beaulieu himself, with 14,000 men, took refuge in the fortress of Mantua, the remainder of his army escaping northwards into the Tyrol.

Having blockaded Mantua, and having got rid of the remaining Austrian forces for the time being, Bonaparte established an outpost line in Venetian territory along the right bank of the river Ádige. He then decided to conciliate his masters, the Directors, by carrying out the large-scale predatory expedition which they had enjoined on him in their instructions of 7 May. This would also give his troops the chance of some plunder, without the risk of incurring casualties.

After handing over to Massena the outpost line on the Ádige, north and south of Verona, Bonaparte set out in mid-June on his fiscal foray. First of all he despatched Murat with a flying column to Genoa in order to assert French authority there; then Augereau was sent with another column to Bologna, which formed part of the Papal States. He himself reached Bologna with a third column; after threatening to march on Rome, on 23 June he signed an armistice convention with delegates from Pope Pius VI, obtaining the cession to France of the territories of Bologna, Ferrara and Ancona, together with a huge indemnity and a precious contribution of pictures, statuary and manuscripts from the Vatican treasures. Bonaparte then made a lightning dash across the Apennines to Pistoja, Leghorn and Florence, where he obtained the submission of the Grand Duke of Tuscany. Wherever he encountered resistance, as at Lugo near Ravenna, he crushed it with merciless severity. By mid-July he had returned to his headquarters at Milan.

On 21 June Bonaparte had written to the Directory:

Italy is now all in French hands; but with such a small army we must be ready for anything; . . . We must be strong everywhere. There must, therefore, be a single policy in military, diplomatic and financial matters. In one place we have to burn and shoot to intimidate people and make a striking example; in another place things happen to which we must turn a blind eye and keep quiet about because the time is not ripe. For the moment, here in Italy, diplomacy is a function of the military. (*Corr.* 664)

Here we see the successful soldier developing into the statesman; but it was statesmanship bolstered up by bayonets.

Bonaparte had not undertaken his month's foray southwards only to please the Directors and to keep his army happy. He had bludgeoned the States of central Italy into submission for a definite military purpose, namely, to secure his right flank and rearward communications while he pursued the war into Austrian territory. This was the ultimate object which he never lost sight of, although it was not one assigned to him by his Government. He now turned to the more immediate military task, to meet the Austrian counter-stroke which he knew to be impending.

Before the Austrian onslaught developed, it was important to capture the isolated fortress of Mantua in his rear. This was no easy task, although he was amply supplied with siege artillery, looted from the Italian arsenals. Mantua was immensely strong by nature, as it was surrounded on three sides by the river Mincio, here between 500 and 800 yards wide, the fourth side being protected by a marsh, approached by a single causeway. During the summer months the besiegers suffered severely from malaria. The siege was entrusted to Serrurier's division, but hitherto all assaults on the fortress had failed. Bonaparte planned to storm the place finally on 30 July.

By the end of June the Austrians were beginning to recover from the shock they had sustained by Bonaparte's lightning conquest of Piedmont and Lombardy. Field-Marshal Count Wurmser, a still older veteran than Beaulieu, was transferred with 20,000 men from the Rhine to the Italian front. Wurmser had collected in the Trentino a force of 47,000 men, rather more than Bonaparte's 44,000; his orders were to relieve Mantua and drive the French out of Italy.

Owing to the mountainous nature of the country Wurmser's advance was confined to the narrow valleys leading south from the Tyrol. He decided to move in three parallel columns, east and west of Lake Garda and by the Val Lagarina (upper Ádige valley), while a fourth column would cross the Venetian plain from Vicenza to threaten Verona. All four columns would converge on the front Bréscia–Peschiera–Verona, and then advance on Mantua.

Apart from Serrurier's division besieging Mantua and Kilmaine's cavalry division in reserve at Valéggio, Bonaparte's army was extended on a front of 75 miles, from Legnago on the lower Ádige, along the right bank of that river through Verona to Monte Baldo (north of Rivoli) and then westwards to Lake Garda (p. 65). Beyond the lake the front extended farther west to the Lago d'Iseo. This was a dangerously extensive line to hold, but Bonaparte could not tell where the main blow would be struck.

Wurmser's offensive opened on 29 July, his main thrust being directed on

64

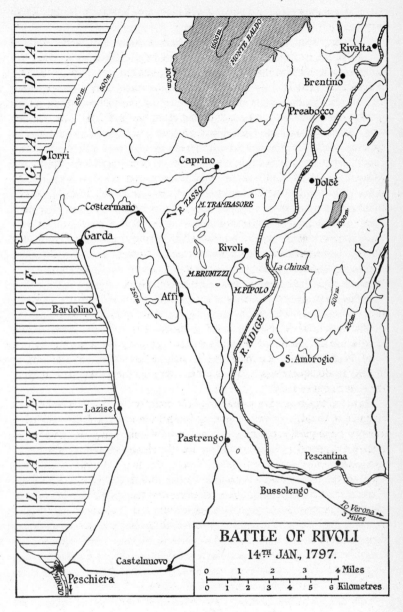

LAKE OF GARDA

Rivalta

Brentino

Preabocco

Torri

1500 m.
MONTE BALDO
1000 m.

Caprino

Dolcè

R. TASSO
M. TRAMBASORE

Costermano

Garda

Rivoli

La Chiusa

1000 m.

M. BRUNIZZI

M. PIPOLO

250 m.

Affi

R. ADIGE

Bardolino

500 m.

250 m.

Lazise

S. Ambrogio

Pastrengo

Pescantina

Bussolengo

To Verona
3 Miles

Castelnuovo

Peschiera

ADICE

BATTLE OF RIVOLI
14TH JAN., 1797.

0   1   2   3   4 Miles
0 1 2 3 4 5 6 Kilometres

the centre sector between the narrow Ádige gorge and Lake Garda, which was held by Massena's division (13,000). Wurmser's two centre columns (24,000) drove Joubert's brigade of Massena's division off the lower slopes of Monte Baldo and the Rivoli plateau. By nightfall Massena's division had fallen back 12 miles to the line Castelnuovo–Peschiera.

Bonaparte reacted swiftly to this blow, which threatened to split his front in two. He abandoned the siege of Mantua and pulled back all his troops holding the Ádige line and concentrated them south of Lake Garda in the area Lonato–Castiglione–Solferino. Wurmser's right-hand column under Quasdanovich had captured Bréscia, but it was retaken by a French counter-attack. Bonaparte succeeded in interposing four divisions (Sauret, Despinois, Massena and Augereau) between Quasdanovich and Wurmser's main body south-east of Lake Garda. Serrurier's division was moved from Mantua to Marcária 20 miles south of Castiglione. Wurmser played into Bonaparte's hand by moving on Mantua, thus increasing the gap between his main body and his right column under Quasdanovich. The latter captured Lonato on 2 August, but was fiercely counter-attacked by Massena and driven back to Peschiera. Too late, Wurmser turned westwards to join hands with Quasdanovich, but Bonaparte confronted him at Castiglione on 5 August with Massena's and Augereau's divisions. The village of Castiglione, on a rocky plateau which dominates the surrounding plain, was held by Wurmser. While Despinois and Massena held him frontally, Augereau and a cavalry brigade under Beaumont swept round his left flank, Bonaparte's A.D.C., Lieutenant-Colonel Marmont, leading the horse artillery at a gallop into action. Although the French troops were exhausted from their long marches, the threat to Wurmser's flanks caused him to fall back to the Mincio, and he retreated northwards through Peschiera, having lost 6000 killed and wounded. The French regained their old positions along the Ádige, including Verona and Rivoli. Mantua, however, still remained isolated with an Austrian garrison of 16,000, having been revictualled and reinforced by Wurmser.

Never had Bonaparte been nearer to defeat than on the day before the battle of Castiglione. His situation looked so alarming that at one moment he thought of retreating to the Adda. Wurmser had penetrated the French centre and driven a deep wedge down the Mincio valley; had he maintained touch with Quasdanovich, he might have crushed the French divisions before they could concentrate. Bonaparte saved his army by quick thinking and swift movement, drawing his dispersed formations together to strike alternate blows at his divided enemy.

Although his troops were very exhausted after a hard week's fighting and marching, Bonaparte was determined to give his enemy no rest. He still hoped to carry out before the onset of winter the pincer movement which would deal Austria a mortal blow, a drive by his own army through the Tyrol on Innsbruck, combined with an advance down the Danube valley by Moreau's Army of the Rhine and Moselle. This was his long-cherished dream, so he sent a cipher message to Moreau saying that he would attack Wurmser on 2 September and would reach Trento by the 5th.

When Massena was told to act as vanguard for this advance, he protested angrily that his division was incapable of offensive operations; the men were in rags and 'absolutely barefoot'. Bonaparte, however, would listen to no excuses and started off with three divisions on 2 September. Massena drove in Wurmser's outposts at Rovereto on 4 September and entered Trento on the 5th, as Bonaparte had promised Moreau, but the latter had only stirred sluggishly.

Wurmser now turned eastwards, hoping to outflank Bonaparte by advancing on Mantua by Bassano and Vicenza, leaving a division under Davidovich at Lavis to block the upper Ádige valley. Bonaparte pursued Wurmser down the Valsugana and the upper valley of the Brenta, catching up with the Austrians at Bassano on 8 September. He outflanked them with Massena's and Augereau's divisions, capturing 3000 prisoners and 35 guns. The remnant of Wurmser's army eluded the French pursuit and gained the shelter of Mantua on 15 September. The fortress now became for the second time a mouse-trap for the Austrian commander.

The campaign of 1796 was not yet over, for the Austrians made a further effort to relieve Mantua. During October an elderly Hungarian Field-Marshal, Baron Allvintzy de Berberek, was given a fresh army of 40,000 in the Piave valley, with orders to move on Mantua, seize Verona and effect a junction with Davidovich, who with a force of 18,000 would advance down the Ádige from the Tyrol.

Bonaparte again found himself in a weak position. Vaubois's division (8000) was holding the Ádige gorge near Rivoli, and Kilmaine (9000) was blockading Mantua, so that only Massena's and Augereau's divisions (11,000) were available to meet Allvintzy's attack. The French had 14,000 sick and 4000 wounded in hospital. Serrurier was down with malaria, and so were a number of commanding officers. Few reinforcements had been received and the morale of the troops was low. Even Bonaparte was depressed and wrote a pessimistic letter to Joséphine, now at Milan.

Early in November Allvintzy moved forward, pushing Massena's outpost line slowly back from Bassano to Vicenza. Bonaparte ordered Massena and Augereau to withdraw steadily to the line of the Ádige. He hoped to draw

Allvintzy southwards from Verona to prevent him effecting a junction with Davidovich. On 11 November Massena fought a stiff rearguard action on the Caldiero ridge, ten miles east of Verona, suffering heavy casualties. On the 14th Allvintzy turned south, intending to cross the Ádige by a pontoon bridge at Zévio, eight miles below Verona, in order to march on Mantua. On the night of the 14th/15th, therefore, Bonaparte quietly withdrew the divisions of Massena and Augereau through Verona and moved them 15 miles down the right bank to Ronco, where he had ordered Major Andréossy to construct a pontoon bridge. Having crossed the Ádige, they moved down the left bank, and then turned up the right bank of a small tributary, the Alpone, and halted opposite the little village of Árcole. Bonaparte had thus manoeuvred his striking force on to the left flank of Allvintzy's marching columns.

Árcole lies just east of the Alpone stream. The surrounding country was low-lying, marshy and partly cultivated with rice-fields. Off the roads, the countryside was impassable owing to recent heavy rains, and movement was restricted to the high embankments which enclosed the streams and paddy-fields. As it was impossible for troops to deploy, the few bridges and dykes formed important tactical points. Bonaparte had hoped that by marching north up the Alpone he could strike the Austrian columns in flank at San Bonifacio on the Vicenza–Verona road.

On the morning of 15 November Augereau's division on the right encountered the Austrian outposts at Árcole. There was a stern struggle for the wooden bridge there, which the Austrians held, but no progress could be made. Bonaparte himself came up and found Augereau's troops unable or unwilling to storm the bridge. Seizing a regimental colour he led the troops forward to attack the bridge, accompanied by his brother Louis and by two other A.D.C.s, Marmont and Muiron, both gunners. Another officer dragged the Commander-in-Chief back, telling him that it meant certain death to go on. A confused struggle ensued, during which Bonaparte slipped over the embankment and fell into the canal, Lieutenant-Colonel Muiron being shot dead. Two soldiers dragged the Commander-in-Chief out of the marsh.

During the night Bonaparte withdrew Augereau's and Massena's divisions to the right bank of the Ádige, and constructed another pontoon bridge below the junction of the Ádige and Alpone. On the 16th further unsuccessful attacks were launched against the bridgehead at Árcole. On the 17th Massena and Augereau attacked Árcole once more; this time Massena's attack succeeded, and a turning movement by the new bridge on the right flank caused Allvintzy to retire to Vicenza. On the 18th the French re-occupied their old positions. As soon as Davidovich heard of Allvintzy's withdrawal, he retired northwards to Trento.

It is hard to understand why Allvintzy retired so abruptly after the struggle at Árcole, for the French were in a weak position. The Austrians had lost over 6000 men in the three days' fighting, the French some 4500, but the latter had fewer reserves to fall back on. Bonaparte had to some extent repeated his Castiglione manœuvre, warding off one hostile column while he concentrated his striking force to deal with the enemy's main thrust. One can, however, make no tactical comparison between the Castiglione and Árcole battles, for they were fought over terrain so entirely dissimilar. Both battles show that Bonaparte was as brilliant in fighting a defensive action as an offensive one.

The 1796 campaign closed with the French army holding the line of the Ádige up to Lake Garda, with a foothold in Venetia. There still remained, however, an Austrian corps locked up in Mantua, behind their front line.

VI

Rivoli and the
Conquest of Venetia
1797

The opening of the year 1797 saw the Austrians still determined to rid northern Italy of the extraordinary young commander who had successively defeated Colli, Beaulieu, Wurmser and Allvintzy, all in one year. Allvintzy was now ordered to make a fresh attempt to relieve Mantua, which was at its last gasp from sickness and famine. Allvintzy had 43,000 men at his disposal. To oppose him, Bonaparte had 34,000 mobile troops and 78 guns, with another 10,000 blockading Mantua.

The French were holding the same line that they had held when attacked by Wurmser at the end of July. Augereau (9000) held the lower Ádige at Legnago; Massena (9000) held the important centre sector at Verona, while Joubert, newly appointed to command a division (10,000), had the difficult mountain sector between the Ádige gorge and Lake Garda, with his command post at the little village of Rivoli (Veronese) (p. 65). Another new divisional commander, Rey (4000), covered the left flank west of Lake Garda, while Victor had a brigade of 1800 in immediate reserve at Castelnuovo.

Bonaparte knew that the Austrians were preparing to attack him in mid-January, but he was still ignorant as to where the main thrust would come. The Austrians were concentrated in three strong groups: Bajalich (6200) was advancing on Verona; Provera (9000) was marching with a pontoon train from Padua towards Legnago and Mantua; while Allvintzy (20,000) was moving down the upper Ádige on Rivoli. Although the last column was the strongest, it seemed unlikely that the main operation would be carried out in mid-winter in the snow-bound mountainous sector.

Bajalich was the first to strike; he reached the Caldiero ridge, ten miles east of Verona, on 10 January and attacked Massena at dawn in a fog on the 12th. The Austrian attack was repulsed, and Brune's brigade counter-attacked, taking 600 prisoners and three guns. Provera's column halted in front of Augereau at Legnago and remained there inactive.

On the same day Allvintzy launched his main stroke against Joubert's division between the Ádige and Lake Garda. Joubert knew this sector thoroughly, as he had commanded a brigade on Monte Baldo at the time of Wurmser's attack in July. The mountain was now deeply covered with snow; Joubert's troops, greatly outnumbered, were gradually driven back to the village of Rivoli, where their left flank was being turned by an Austrian column under Lusignan, which had moved along the shore of Lake Garda. On the afternoon of the 13th Joubert reported that he could no longer hold out unless reinforced. Bonaparte reacted swiftly. He now knew that All-vintzy's main thrust was directed on the northern sector; he ordered Massena to take seven battalions, a cavalry regiment and five guns from the Verona sector and march through the night to Rivoli, where they were to launch a counter-attack the following morning. Victor's brigade was ordered from Castelnuovo to Rivoli, and Rey's division from the left flank was also directed there.

Bonaparte left Verona at 8 p.m. and rode 15 miles to Rivoli, reaching Joubert's command post there at 2 a.m. on the 14th. He at once ordered Joubert to mount a counter-attack, and as dawn broke Massena's column arrived. Sweeping along the ridge west of Rivoli, it drove back the head of Lusignan's division which was turning Joubert's left flank. The other Austrian columns, pinned in the narrow defile of the Ádige gorge, found themselves hemmed in and were unable to deploy. The whole French line counter-attacked and the Austrian columns broke and fled, Allvintzy himself narrowly escaping capture. On 15 January Joubert took up the pursuit north-wards and 5000 Austrians were made prisoners.

On the afternoon of the 14th, however, the battle flared up in another quarter. On the previous night Provera, unnoticed by Augereau at Legnago, had thrown a pontoon bridge across the Ádige at Angiari, two miles farther up stream. After slipping past Augereau, Provera headed straight for Mantua, and reached the outskirts of the fortress, but was held up by Serrurier near La Favorita, the country residence of the Dukes of Mantua, 1½ miles north of the town. The news of this alarming threat to his right flank reached Bona-parte at Rivoli on the evening of the 14th, just as the battle there was won.

There was no time to be lost. Bonaparte ordered Victor's brigade and four of Massena's battalions, which had been marching and fighting for 24 hours, to prepare to move; after half an hour's rest at Rivoli, they were ordered to start on a 30-mile march southwards to Mantua through Villafranca and Roverbella. Reaching the latter place at 8 p.m. on 15 April, very exhausted, they were given two hours' rest, and reached La Favorita at dawn on the 16th. It was an incredible feat of endurance.

Provera, having arrived in front of Mantua on the 15th, signalled to the garrison to make a sortie to join him. Wurmser, however, decided to wait until the following day, a delay which proved fatal. At dawn on 16 April Wurmser's sortie broke out to the north against the besieging troops at La Favorita. The French, however, had just been reinforced by Victor's brigade and two of Massena's battalions from Rivoli. Simultaneously the head of Augereau's column, which had been pursuing Provera, appeared in his rear on the Legnago road. Provera was now trapped between three French columns, as the sortie by the garrison failed to make progress. By noon Provera realized that his position was hopeless, and capitulated to Serrurier. His force of 7000 men with 22 guns was made prisoner.

Provera's surrender at La Favorita was a crowning touch to the victory of Rivoli. It finally extinguished Austrian hopes of relieving Mantua. As Bonaparte claimed in his despatch to the Directory, in four days his army had fought two pitched battles and six engagements, in which it had taken nearly 25,000 prisoners, 20 colours and 60 guns, and killed or wounded 6000 Austrians.

The battle of Rivoli shows us Bonaparte at his best as a fighting commander. With a long line to defend and with the enemy-held fortress of Mantua at his back, he was unable to retain any real tactical reserve; in fact, his only reserve was Victor's brigade of 1800 men. He was liable to attack by superior forces either from the north or from the east, and up to the last moment was in the dark as to where the enemy's main thrust would come. The coolness and quick decision with which he switched Massena's troops from Verona to Rivoli and then back to Mantua was a masterpiece of manœuvre on the battlefield. Of course Bonaparte was greatly indebted to the superb marching and fighting powers of Massena's units, and to the latter's bold and vigorous conduct of his counter-stroke, as well as to the tough resistance put up by Joubert's division. On the other hand he was badly let down by Augereau's negligence in guarding the crossings of the Ádige. One may wonder what the result of the battle would have been had Allvintzy's and Provera's attacks been driven home simultaneously with equal vigour, for

7 *The Battle of Castiglione, 5 August 1796. After a painting by Carle Vernet (1758–1836)*

8 *(overleaf) The Battle of Lodi, 10 May 1796. From a contemporary print*

9 *The Battle of Rivoli, 14 January 1797*
After a painting by Louis Bacler d'Albe (1761–1824). Monte Baldo on left;
Adige gorge on right; Rivoli plateau in foreground

Bonaparte had not sufficient reserves in hand to meet both attacks at the same moment.

On 2 February the garrison of Mantua, on the point of starvation and decimated by fever, surrendered to Serrurier. Bonaparte generously permitted Field-Marshal Wurmser, with 500 infantry, 200 cavalry and a token field battery, to march out with their arms and return to Austria on parole. The remainder of the garrison of 16,000 were made prisoners of war.

The victory of Rivoli and the capitulation of Mantua opened up the whole territory of Venetia to Bonaparte, and he was quick to take advantage of it. Joubert with three divisions was sent in pursuit of Allvintzy into the Tyrol. Massena was ordered to advance from Vicenza and Bassano up the Brenta valley to support Joubert. Meanwhile Bonaparte himself made another excursion southwards to deal with Pope Pius VI, who seemed dilatory in carrying out the terms of the convention signed at Bologna the previous June. Victor, now promoted to be a Divisional Commander, was sent with a punitive expedition to Imola and Faenza. After looting a quantity of Papal treasures and again threatening to march on Rome, Bonaparte signed a treaty with the Pope's delegates at Tolentino, south of Ancona, on 19 February. The Pope ceded to France the Papal States of Bologna, Ferrara, Romagna and Ancona, thus giving Bonaparte a foothold on the Adriatic. After these easy victories, Bonaparte returned to Mantua on 2 March.

In order to pursue the Austrians into their own country, Bonaparte had asked for further reinforcements, and the Directory had given him General Jean-Baptiste Bernadotte* with a fresh division from Kléber's Army of the Sambre-et-Meuse. Like Massena and Augereau, Bernadotte was a ranker from the old army, but junior to both of them. Bonaparte now reorganized his Army for the advance into Austria. On the left, Joubert with three divisions (14,000) was to drive Allvintzy northwards into the Tyrol. Massena's division (10,000) was to advance up the Piave valley as a separate flank guard, while Bonaparte's main body, consisting of Guieu (10,000), Serrurier (6000) and Bernadotte (7000), would make a wide sweep through Venezia and cross the Carnic Alps. Victor's division (6000) was left to secure the rearward communications. The total force amounted to 53,000.

The Austrians also had reorganized their forces. To command their troops in Italy they had brought from the Rhine front the Archduke Charles,†

* Jean-Baptiste Bernadotte (1763–1844) married (1798) the sister-in-law of Joseph Bonaparte. Created a Marshal (1804) and Prince of Ponte-Corvo (1806). He founded the present royal house of Sweden, having been elected Crown Prince (1810) and succeeded to the throne in 1818.

† Carl Ludwig, Erzherzog von Österreich (1771–1847), third son of the Emperor Leopold II.

younger brother of the Emperor. He was the youngest and ablest of the Austrian commanders, but they were slow in sending him the reinforcements he badly needed.

Bonaparte's forward move commenced on 10 March. Six days later he crossed the Tagliamento, a broad, shallow river; his advance had been so rapid that he encountered only slight resistance; the Austrians retired with the loss of 500 men and six guns. On the 19th Bernadotte's division captured Gradisca after a sharp fight and crossed the Isonzo. The main body then swung northwards up the Isonzo valley to Caporetto (Kobarid), and occupied Cividale and Údine.

Meanwhile Massena on the left flank encountered much stiffer opposition, but pushed his way north-eastwards by Feltre and Belluno. Brushing aside all resistance, Massena turned northwards up the upper Tagliamento by Spilimbergo and Gemona. He advanced through difficult mountain country in spite of increasing opposition, and on 23 March forced the Tarvisio Pass on the crest of the Carnic Alps. Massena's division now formed the advanced guard to the whole French army. The Archduke could only bring up brigades piecemeal, and Massena swept aside all opposition, entering Villach on 27 March and Klagenfurt on the 28th. The French had now penetrated into Austria proper, and moved almost unopposed along the mountain valleys of Carinthia.

On 2 April Massena's advanced guard forced the narrow Dürnstein gorge and entered the province of Styria. He pushed on down the valley of the Mur through Scheifling and Judenburg, where Austrian resistance finally ceased on 4 April. Massena continued on through Leoben, reaching Bruck on the 9th, when he was 92 miles from Vienna. On 7 April plenipotentiaries from the Archduke met Bonaparte at Judenburg, and an armistice was agreed to. On the 18th a preliminary peace treaty was signed at Schloss Eggenwald, near Leoben, between Bonaparte on behalf of the French Directory and the representatives of the Austrian Emperor. The young military commander had now assumed the role of a statesman. A year earlier he had dictated an armistice to a King; now he was dictating peace terms to an Emperor.

In 30 days Bonaparte's army had marched 400 miles from Mantua to Bruck, an average of 13 miles a day, mostly through mountainous and easily defensible country, and sometimes in the face of tough opposition. It was a fine military achievement. He had now gained the complete confidence of his officers and men, who were ready to follow him anywhere. The young commander had indeed impressed his own personality on his troops in a remarkable way. Madame de Staël, a keen critic and no friend of Bonaparte's, expressed it well when she wrote: 'The Army of the Rhine belonged to the

French Republic; the Army of Italy belonged to Bonaparte.' He took particular pains to foster an *esprit de corps* among his units; he had inscribed on their regimental colours the names of the battles in which they had taken part, and also slogans commemorating some special achievement.* General Desaix, who came to the Army of Italy that summer from the Army of the Rhine and Moselle, was greatly impressed by his methods of encouraging *esprit de corps*:

He has never seen a regiment which he has not persuaded that he considered it the best in the army; he often talks to them, and always says something impressive.

Desaix, however, was less flattering when he gave his own personal impression of Bonaparte:

He is proud, dissimulating, vindictive and never forgives. He follows his enemy to the end of the world, and is a great intriguer. He has plenty of money, naturally, since he receives the revenue of a whole country. He never presents any accounts.

Although so popular with his men, Bonaparte failed to win the personal affection of the senior officers, such as Massena and Augereau. In Massena's case, no doubt, there was a certain mutual jealousy; in the first place Massena was disappointed at being passed over for command of the Army of Italy, and Bonaparte always regarded him as a potential rival to his own military pre-eminence; indeed the two men detested each other; although Bonaparte was fully alive to Massena's great military qualities, he frequently exasperated Massena by belittling his achievements in official despatches.

Another habit of Bonaparte's which did not endear him to his Divisional Commanders was his trick of sending forward his own favourite staff officers or A.D.C.s at the climax of a battle, and then giving them the credit which was really due to the troops who had borne the brunt of the fighting. This tendency to favouritism marked Bonaparte's handling of his subordinates throughout his career; although it certainly gained him much devoted service, it frequently proved disadvantageous.

One cannot say that Bonaparte was always a good judge of military qualities in others; it is difficult, for instance, to understand why he took such a liking to Brune, who can hardly be called either an outstanding soldier or a likeable character. Others whom he thought highly of, such as Junot, Kilmaine, Lannes and Reynier, were only mediocre commanders. It may indeed have been that his favourites were chosen for their mediocrity, against which the star of his own genius shone the more brightly.

Looking back on the campaigns of 1796 and 1797, it is difficult to detect a

* For instance: 'The terrible 57th, which nothing can stop.'

single flaw in Bonaparte's strategy and tactics. He was from the start thoroughly grounded in the basic principles of warfare, so that his quick mind always reacted correctly to every fresh situation, however unexpected, and he was never thrown off balance. Indeed the only criticism that one can make, and this is more to do with administration, is that he failed to impose a strict code of discipline on his army. This was always a difficult matter with any French troops of the Revolutionary period, especially in the case of the Army of Italy which was in such a bad state when he took it over. Bonaparte himself fully realized the necessity for a high standard of discipline in the ranks; as he once said himself: 'Without discipline victory is impossible.' Throughout 1796 and the early part of 1797 his Army Orders are full of complaints about the disorderly conduct of the troops (just as Wellington's were later during the Peninsular War), but no improvement seems to have taken place. When the army settled down in its billeting areas after the fighting was over, an orgy of looting and drunkenness broke out, possibly because some of the senior commanders, such as Massena and Augereau, were bad disciplinarians, and many of the good regimental officers had become casualties.

The spring campaign of 1797 had put Bonaparte in possession of the mainland territories of the Venetian Republic, which also possessed part of the Dalmatian coast and the Ionian Islands. Although the Republic was nominally neutral, Bonaparte seized on the excuse that it had assisted the Austrians in the war, and so he treated it as an enemy country. By trickery and bullying he extracted enormous sums from the Venetian treasury, and also robbed Venice of all the art treasures he could lay hands on. At the end of June he sent a French naval expedition to seize Corfu and the Ionian Islands, which he thought would form a useful naval base against the British fleet.

Bonaparte then settled down in the Palazzo Mombello, near Milan, to administer his newly won territories and to reorganize his army, which of course could not be demobilized until the conclusion of a final peace treaty with Austria. Joséphine was installed at Mombello, together with *Madame Mère* and several other members of the Bonaparte family, and a Court was established on sumptuous and almost regal lines.

Meanwhile Bonaparte kept a close eye on the political situation in Paris, where he sensed that a crisis was developing. Of the five Directors, three were strong Republicans, while two (Carnot and Barthélemy) were liberal in their views and suspected of Monarchist leanings. In April Bonaparte had sent Massena to Paris, but he had got involved in the political world, and Barras had even put his name forward to fill a vacancy among the Directors.

So to keep himself informed about the situation, on 11 July Bonaparte sent his trusted A.D.C., Lavalette, to Paris, where he kept in touch with Barras, the craftiest of the Directors, who was scheming to get rid of his moderate-minded colleagues, Carnot and Barthélemy. Bonaparte, though opposed to mob rule, had always been a Jacobin, for he had felt all along that the extreme Republican party was bound to win, especially if backed by military force. The last thing he wanted to see was a Bourbon restoration, for that would extinguish his own chance of grasping political power, an ambition which was already germinating in his mind. Barras needed a strong military arm to support him in the *coup* which he was plotting, and applied to Bonaparte for assistance. Accordingly, at the end of July, Bonaparte sent Augereau to Paris, ostensibly to convey captured colours to the Directory. Augereau was a good choice; he was far too stupid and vulgar to become a dangerous rival, but he was a vain and arrogant swashbuckler who could intimidate politicians and use force unscrupulously.

On 8 August Barras persuaded his fellow Directors to appoint Augereau to command the Military District of Paris. On the night of the 3/4 September Barras struck his blow. Augereau's troops took control of the legislative bodies. Barthélemy was arrested, together with General Pichegru, who was known to be in traitorous correspondence with the Bourbons, and both were deported to Cayenne. Carnot managed to escape to Switzerland. It was the *coup d'état* of 18 Fructidor.

There now remained the task of settling the final peace terms with Austria, which had been provisionally outlined at the preliminary convention signed by Bonaparte at Leoben in April. The Directors were not too well pleased with the way in which Bonaparte had rushed through this negotiation, which had contributed so powerfully to his personal prestige. They felt that if he had waited until the French armies on the Rhine developed their spring offensive, Austria could have been more decisively crushed and better terms might have been obtained. In December 1796 they had sent General Clarke, a War Ministry official, to Bonaparte's headquarters to negotiate with the Austrians on their behalf; but Bonaparte had overridden this arrangement and insisted on retaining all the political transactions in his own hands. This the Directors eventually agreed to.

After protracted and acrimonious negotiations with the Austrian plenipotentiaries, a final peace treaty was signed at Campo-Formio, near Udine, on 17 October. By this treaty France acquired the Austrian Netherlands (Belgium) and all the German territories on the left bank of the Rhine, together with the whole of northern Italy up to the frontier of the Venetian Republic. As compensation for Austria, the Republic of Venice lost its independence and was handed over to the Emperor Francis as an Austrian province. It was a cynical and unscrupulous arrangement, but it consolidated Bonaparte's conquests, and it established French hegemony in northern Italy as far east as the river Ádige. The Corsican soldier-statesman had shown that he could drive a hard bargain.

VII

The Egyptian Adventure
1798-1799

The final Treaty of Campo-Formio reduced the activities of the *Armée d'Italie* to those of an army of occupation, with an outpost line on the new frontier with Austria along the river Ádige. The King of Sardinia went into exile, Piedmont was made into a Department of France, while Lombardy with the adjoining Duchies was formed into a new State, under French sovereignty, known as the Cisalpine Republic. A smouldering feud still existed between the Directory and the Pope, and Bonaparte's brother Joseph was sent as Ambassador to Rome in order to stir up republican feelings there and to undermine the Pope's temporal power. As a result of Bonaparte's victories France had now expanded beyond her 'natural frontiers'.

Meanwhile the Directors had to find fresh occupation for the victorious young General who had defeated their most active enemy, Austria. There only remained Britain to be dealt with. On 27 October 1797, ten days after the Treaty of Campo-Formio was signed, Bonaparte was appointed to command a new *Armée d'Angleterre*, with General Desaix from the Rhine as his Second-in-Command. The cream of the French troops on the Rhine and in Italy were allotted to this new army. At the beginning of December Bonaparte was recalled to Paris by the Directors, and on the 9th, much to Massena's disappointment, Berthier assumed command of the *Armée d'Italie*. Bonaparte received a triumphal welcome when he arrived in Paris on 5 December. On the 10th the Directors accorded him an official reception at the Palais du Luxembourg, and Talleyrand* gave a dinner in his honour at

---

* Charles-Maurice de Talleyrand-Périgord (1754-1838) became Bishop of Autun (1788), President of the National Assembly (1790) and Minister of Foreign Affairs (July 1797); he was created Prince of Benevento (1806) by Napoleon.

the Ministry of Foreign Affairs. He was elected a member of the Institute of France.

Bonaparte lost no time in drawing up plans for his new task, which was none other than the invasion of England, a combined naval and military operation which had not been successfully attempted since the year 1066, although General Hoche had made an abortive effort in December 1796 to land in Bantry Bay, south-west Ireland. Another ill-planned attempt to land at Fishguard, Pembrokeshire, in February 1797 had been an ignominious failure. This time an operation on a grander scale was envisaged. One of the first things that Bonaparte did was to order the ordnance factories to cast cannon of British calibres, so that 'once we are in that country we can use English cannon-balls'. This was a sensible precaution for a gunner officer to take. However, when he made further enquiries about the number of transports which the Navy could provide, the invasion project began to look less feasible. In mid-February 1798 he made a tour of inspection of the Channel ports in order to study the embarkation facilities. On his return he decided that the project was not possible as the French Navy had not sufficient command of the sea. On 23 February he reported in this sense to the Directory.

Talleyrand now put forward to the Directors an alternative project of sending an expeditionary force to conquer Malta and Egypt, and thus cut the communications between Britain and her Indian possessions. This scheme appealed strongly to Bonaparte, who had discussed it previously with Talleyrand. On 5 March Bonaparte wrote a report for the Directors on his estimate of the forces required for the operation: 25,000 infantry, 3000 cavalry, 60 field-guns and 40 siege-guns. Consequently, a decree establishing an *Armée d'Orient* under Bonaparte's command was issued on 12 April.

The idea of conquering Egypt had appealed strongly to the rulers of France ever since the days of the Crusades. Louis XIV had toyed with it, and it had been the dream of Louis XV's Foreign Minister, Choiseul, in the year when Bonaparte was born. The project, however, was beset with the embarrassing diplomatic drawback that, since 1536, France had been the ally of the Sultan of Turkey, the titular sovereign of Egypt. On 16 August 1797 Bonaparte had written to the Directory: 'The day is not far off when we shall appreciate the necessity, in order effectively to destroy England, to seize Egypt' (*Corr.* 2103). His idea was that the subtle Talleyrand should go on a special mission to Constantinople to persuade the Sultan to let the French recover Egypt on behalf of Turkey from its *de facto* rulers, the Mameluke Beys.

In the year 1517 Sultan Selim I had conquered Egypt from the Mameluke Sultans. The word 'Mameluke' (Arabic *mamluk*, meaning 'slave') is slightly

10 *Bonaparte in Egypt, 1798* (aged 2
Engraved by Lacauchie from a contemporary sket

misleading. The Mamelukes were originally Moslemized slaves imported from the Caucasus in the thirteenth century by the Arab Sultans of Egypt to form the core of their army. The Mamelukes soon became so powerful that they usurped the government of Egypt, until they were conquered by the Turks in the sixteenth century. Even then they continued to form the ruling caste, paying an annual tribute to the Ottoman Sultan and Caliph as their titular sovereign. The Sultan maintained in Cairo a Turkish viceroy, the Pasha of Egypt, who nominally presided over the *Diwan* or Mameluke governing council, but in fact exercised no real authority. The Mamelukes thus enjoyed undisputed sway over the cultivated Nile valley and its Delta, while the surrounding deserts were left to the sheikhs of the nomad Bedouin tribes.

In aiming at the conquest of Egypt Bonaparte had an ulterior objective in mind, namely to destroy the growing power of England in India. Using Egypt as a stepping-stone, he intended to march eastwards in alliance, as he hoped, with Turkey, and then join forces with Tipu Sultan of Mysore to drive the British from India. By a curious chance an expedition was then being organized in India to deal with Tipu Sultan by a British officer named Lieutenant-Colonel Arthur Wellesley. The idea of advancing to India was not so fantastic as it might seem, for the Island of Mauritius in the Indian Ocean, a French possession, would form another stepping-stone eastwards. It is significant that, when he embarked for Egypt, Bonaparte's portfolio of maps included James Rennell's *Bengal Atlas containing maps of the Theatre of War and Commerce on that side of Hindoostan*, published in 1781.

Malta, on the way to Egypt, was also a tempting prize to be had for the picking. That strategically important island, commanding the Sicilian Channel, was owned by the inert successors of the Knights Hospitaller of St. John of Jerusalem, a relic of the medieval orders of chivalry and of the Crusades. An Austrian Grand Master of the Order had recently been appointed, and the eccentric new Tsar Paul of Russia was throwing covetous eyes on its possession. It was an important French interest that Malta should not fall into Austrian or Russian hands, and Valletta harbour would form an excellent base for operations against the British fleet. The Directors, in hastily approving the design of seizing Malta and Egypt, may have also been glad to find some useful task which would keep their ambitious young General far from Paris for as long as possible.

The organization of the *Armée d'Orient* was pushed on rapidly, and Bonaparte was given a free hand in choosing his officers and units. Berthier, of course, was to be his Chief of Staff, and his personal staff consisted of his brother Louis, his stepson Eugène Beauharnais, Colonels Marmont, Murat

Battle of Abu Qir, 25 July 1799
After a painting by Louis-François Lejeune (1775–1848)
Murat's cavalry drove the Turks into the sea

and Junot, Lieutenant-Colonel Duroc and Captain Lavalette. Colonel Bessières commanded the personal escort of *Guides-à-cheval*. Bonaparte reached Toulon from Paris on 9 May and supervised the final preparations for the embarkation of his army of 37,000 men. On the eve of embarkation he issued a stirring address to the troops, promising each man six acres of land when he returned home.

Perhaps the most remarkable feature of the expedition was the inclusion of a team of 167 civilian experts, scientific, technical and cultural, who were to investigate and report on the natural resources and antiquities of Egypt. This team was made up of naturalists, physicists, chemists, cartographers, engineers, archaeologists and artists. In assembling it Bonaparte had been assisted by his scientific friend and adviser, Gaspard Monge (1746–1818), whose relations with his chief may be compared with those between Lord Cherwell and Mr. Churchill in the Second World War. Bonaparte had a wide range of scientific and literary interests, and he was a good mathematician. As it turned out, the archaeological and scientific results of the expedition were far greater than its military value.

The great armada sailed from Toulon on 19 May. It consisted of some 300 transports, carrying 25,000 infantry, 3000 cavalry, and 3000 gunners and sappers. The convoy was escorted by 13 ships-of-the-line and six frigates, under command of Vice-Admiral Brueys (1753–1798). Bonaparte sailed in Brueys's flagship *l'Orient*. On passage, the main body was joined by additional convoys from Corsica, Genoa and Civita Vecchia.

The secret of the expedition's destination had been well kept; only a few of the senior officers knew that they were going to Egypt. It was up to the last moment officially known as the left wing of the *Armée d'Angleterre*. No word of its sailing reached England till a fortnight later, and even then Pitt thought that it was intended to land in Ireland. Fortunately the Royal Navy was wide awake. Lord St. Vincent with the Mediterranean Fleet was then blockading Cadiz, where a Spanish squadron was anchored; on 2 May he despatched Vice-Admiral Sir Horatio Nelson into the Mediterranean with orders to seek out the French convoy and destroy it. Nelson's fleet was eventually made up to 14 battleships, two frigates and a sloop, which could easily have played havoc with the French expedition, had it been able to intercept it. Owing to storms and contrary winds, Nelson did not arrive off Toulon until after the expedition had sailed. He then unfortunately got separated from his frigates, which handicapped him in searching the width of the Mediterranean for his elusive enemy. The launching of Bonaparte's slow convoy on the high seas when the whereabouts of the British fleet was unknown was an incredibly rash venture. The gamble succeeded, but only by a narrow chance.

Bonaparte reached Malta without incident on 9 June. Landing parties were put ashore at several points of the island and converged on the fortified harbour of Valletta. The Knights put up only a token resistance and surrendered their impregnable fortress at 3 a.m. on 12 June. For the next six days Bonaparte was extremely busy reorganizing the administration and economy of the island as a French dependency. Leaving a garrison of 4000 under General Vaubois to hold Malta, he sailed on 19 June, reaching Egyptian waters on the 30th.

The whole journey from Toulon to Alexandria took six weeks. Several storms were encountered, and the troops, who were uncomfortably crowded, suffered badly from seasickness. The food deteriorated rapidly, as few provisions had been found at Malta. On the eve of their arrival at Alexandria Bonaparte issued a proclamation to the troops to prepare them for the hardships which they would encounter, and calling on them to respect the Moslem religion and to refrain from looting.

As his armada approached the Egyptian coast, Bonaparte sent ahead a frigate to reconnoitre the port of Alexandria. The frigate reached harbour on 29 June, picked up the French Consul Magallon and took him back to the flagship the following day. From the Consul Bonaparte learnt that one of Nelson's vessels had called at Alexandria two days earlier; the Consul also told him that the town would resist attack and that the Egyptian authorities would not allow any of his ships to enter the port. Bonaparte was most uneasy at Nelson being in the vicinity, and decided to land immediately on the open beach west of the harbour. Admiral Brueys advised him strongly not to do so; owing to the offshore shoals the transports would have to anchor three miles out, and a northerly gale was springing up. He pointed out that there was a sheltered anchorage and beach at Abu Qir Bay, 14 miles east of Alexandria, which would be a far more suitable place to disembark (p. 84). Bonaparte, however, fearing that the British fleet might turn up at any moment, rejected his Admiral's advice, and insisted on landing straight away at the little fishing village of Marabut, eight miles west of Alexandria, near the modern airport of El Dikheila.

In 1798 Alexandria was a very different place from the rich commercial emporium, with nearly a million inhabitants, into which it developed more than a century later under the British occupation. In those days Alexandria was a dilapidated native town of 16,000 people, with a small and undeveloped harbour. The main port for Cairo was Damietta, at the eastern mouth of the Nile, 120 miles further east.

In spite of the northerly gale, the troops began to disembark at Marabut at noon on 1 July. The operation was long and arduous, but by dawn the next

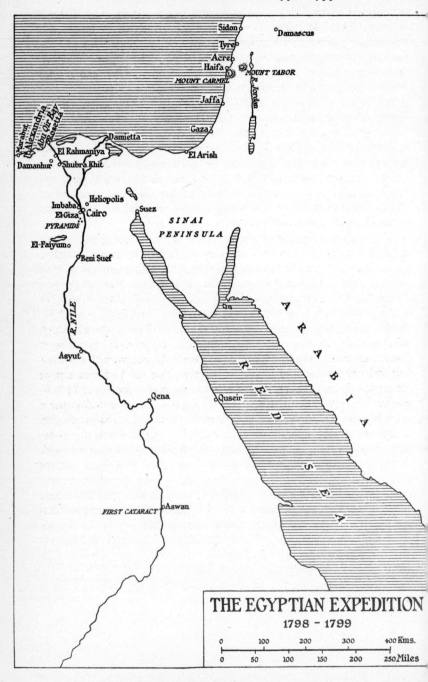

THE EGYPTIAN EXPEDITION
1798 – 1799

morning part of three divisions, commanded by Bon, Menou and Kléber,* had been landed, but without guns, horses, stores or rations. Everybody was seasick and a number were drowned. Bonaparte decided to march at once on Alexandria, although he had only 4000 men ashore, and no artillery. They had a painful march along the sand dunes without food or water, and at once assaulted the town. The resistance was feeble and sporadic, and by noon the French were in possession of Alexandria at the cost of some 300 casualties. Two of the divisional commanders, Kléber and Menou, were wounded.

Bonaparte issued to the inhabitants a remarkable proclamation in Arabic, assuring them that the French had not come to fight the Egyptians, but only the Mameluke Beys who oppressed them. He also announced that the French were true Moslems and had deposed the Pope, 'who always incited the Christians to make war on the Moslems'. He therefore called on all true Egyptians to assist the French in driving out the Mamelukes. He then decorated the local sheikhs and imams with tricolour scarves and badges.

Six days later, having disembarked all the troops and stores, and sorted out the army into its five divisions, Bonaparte started his march to Cairo. Kléber was left behind as Governor of Alexandria with a garrison of 2000 men, and Menou was sent to occupy Rosetta as Governor. Menou's division was taken over by Vial, and Kléber's by Dugua. Dugua's division was sent east to Rosetta, from where it was to march up the western arm of the Nile, escorting the heavy baggage, ammunition and civilian personnel, which would be transported up stream in a flotilla of boats, protected by gunboats under command of *Capitaine de vaisseau* Perrée. Bonaparte with the other four divisions, commanded by Desaix, Reynier, Bon and Vial, took a short cut across the desert via Damanhur to reach the Nile higher up at El Rahmaniya. This involved a march of 52 miles across an almost waterless desert at the hottest season of the year, with swarms of mounted Arabs hovering on their flanks, ready to pounce on any straggler. It seems incredible that Bonaparte had neglected to provide his troops with tropical clothing, or even with water-bottles. The troops suffered terribly from thirst, and their only rations were dry ship's biscuit. Any stragglers that could not keep up with the column were physically violated and mutilated by the desert Bedouin. The troops obtained no relief until they reached the Nile bank, where they gorged themselves on water-melons and then suffered from violent diarrhoea. The morale of the troops was low, and the Divisional Commanders complained bitterly

* General Jean-Baptiste Kléber (1753–1800) distinguished himself in the Army of the Rhine between 1789 and 1796. In August 1799, when Bonaparte left Egypt, he handed over command of the *Armée d'Orient* to Kléber, who was assassinated by an Egyptian fanatic on 14 June 1800.

to the Commander-in-Chief about the conditions to which they were subjected.

At El Rahmaniya the desert column was joined by Dugua's division, which had had a much easier march up the Nile from Rosetta. Bonaparte decided that, in spite of the hardships suffered by his four divisions, he could waste no time in giving them a rest, but must push on at once to Cairo, more than 100 miles up river, before the Mamelukes recovered from the first surprise of his landing, ten days previously. That afternoon, 11 July, he held a review of his army, and told them that they would possibly meet the enemy on the following day. He had learnt that the Mameluke advanced guard under Murad Bey was at Shubra Khit, eight miles farther south, supported by a flotilla of gunboats. The French continued their advance on the night of the 12th/13th, reaching Shubra Khit before dawn. Here Bonaparte made each division form a square, six ranks deep, with the guns at the corners of the squares. The five divisional squares were in echelon formation to the rear from Dugua's division on the left, nearest the river, in touch with the boat flotilla. As the sun rose, the regimental bands inside the squares played the *Marseillaise*, and the French saw the Mameluke horsemen drawn up for battle. They appeared to number 10,000 or 12,000.

Murad Bey's warriors advanced to reconnoitre the French squares, but found themselves faced everywhere with a thick hedge of bayonets. Eventually they started to charge, but were met with a hail of musketry and grapeshot. They attacked repeatedly, but failed to break any square. On the left flank Perrée's flotilla had a more difficult time, for it was engaged by a Mameluke flotilla of seven gunboats manned by Greek sailors. Perrée had only three gunboats and two sailing barges with all the scientists and other civilians aboard. The French boats suffered about 30 casualties, but Perrée's gunboat scored a direct hit on the ammunition magazine of the Mameluke flagship, which blew up with all hands. This caused a general panic, and the Mameluke force melted away.

The formation of his divisions in squares to confront the Mameluke horsemen was a remarkable tactical procedure improvised by Bonaparte in the engagement at Shubra Khit, for there is no evidence that this formation had ever been adopted previously by French troops. It was standard practice in the British army during the Peninsular War to form battalion squares whenever infantry were exposed to cavalry attack, but never on so large a scale as a whole division in square formation. Bonaparte may have evolved it from his historical studies of Alexander's Macedonian phalanx; it certainly supplied the answer to the Mameluke tactics.

Immediately after the engagement Bonaparte pushed on in pursuit of the

retreating Mamelukes. The French advanced steadily in spite of the difficult
stony terrain and the intense heat. On the evening of 20 July they reached the
point where the Nile divides into its Damietta and Rosetta branches, within
12 miles of Cairo. There Bonaparte learnt that the whole Mameluke army
was awaiting him just north of Cairo on both banks of the Nile, Murad Bey
on the left bank at Imbaba, and Ibrahim Bey on the right bank at Bulaq.
Between them the river was guarded by a Mameluke flotilla of armed vessels.

The French marched at 2 a.m. on the 21st and about 2 p.m. were confronted
by the Mamelukes entrenched at Imbaba, consisting of some 12,000 infantry
with 5000 mounted warriors on the flank. The five French divisions numbered 25,000 fighting troops. In the distance loomed the Pyramids of Giza.
As at Shubra Khit, Bonaparte formed his five divisions into squares, Desaix
on the right and Dugua on the left, next the Nile bank. The French squares
had barely time to form before Murad charged with the whole of his cavalry.
The result was the same as at Shubra Khit, but on a larger scale. The Mameluke horsemen charged repeatedly with incredible bravery, but were decimated by the French grape and musketry volleys. After two hours' fighting,
in which they lost 700 or 800, the Mamelukes abandoned the field, Murad
Bey retreating up the Nile past Cairo, while Ibrahim Bey with the right bank
contingent fled north-eastwards towards the Sinai Desert. The French casualties amounted to 300 or 400.

Ten days later Bonaparte's good fortune deserted him. He had left his
fleet at Alexandria under Admiral Brueys with rather vague instructions as
to his future course of action. He was either to take shelter in the Old Port
there, or to anchor in the fairly sheltered bay of Abu Qir, 14 miles to the east;
alternatively, if neither of these were suitable, he could sail to Corfu, 800
miles away. Brueys took soundings at the Old Port and decided that it could
not hold all his ships, which in any case would be trapped there if Nelson's
fleet were to appear, so he anchored his 13 battleships and four frigates in line
in Abu Qir Bay, parallel to the shore and about $1\frac{1}{2}$ miles from it.

On the afternoon of 1 August Nelson's fleet of 14 battleships, carrying over
1000 guns, bore down on Abu Qir Point with a following wind. Brueys was
caught out; half his crews were ashore, collecting water and provisions.
Nelson's ships sailed in on them, some venturing into the narrow navigable
channel between the French fleet and the beach. The French ships, not
expecting attack from the land side, had not manned their landward batteries.
They were now raked by devastating broadsides at close range from both port
and starboard; they put up a gallant fight, but were defeated by better seamanship and gunnery. Admiral Brueys was killed, and during the night his
flagship *l'Orient* was on fire and blew up. By dawn the next morning all the

French ships were out of action, except for Admiral Villeneuve's squadron in the rear, which had not been seriously engaged. Villeneuve, with two battle-ships and two frigates, made his escape, Nelson's vessels being too badly damaged to pursue.

Bonaparte threw all the blame for the disaster on the unfortunate Admiral, although his own instructions had been so vague. His army was now cut off from France, except for two frigates and a few despatch boats at Alexandria, which would have to run the gauntlet of the squadron under Commodore Samuel Hood, left by Nelson to blockade the Egyptian coast.

The resulting situation of the conqueror of Egypt was not an easy one. Although he had defeated the Mamelukes in two battles, he had not destroyed them. Ibrahim Bey had withdrawn across the Sinai Peninsula to Palestine, while Murad Bey had retreated southward to Upper Egypt. On 2 September, a month after the disaster at Abu Qir Bay, Turkey declared war on France. It was some time before Bonaparte became aware of this, and even then he affected to ignore it, although it seriously prejudiced his position. Firstly, it stiffened the resistance movement against the French, not only by the Mame-lukes, but also by the peasantry and the Bedouin tribes, for the Sultan and Caliph had declared a holy war against the infidels; secondly, it made non-sense of Bonaparte's propaganda theme that he was liberating Egypt from Mameluke oppression on behalf of his friend and ally, the Sultan; thirdly, it meant that the French troops isolated in Egypt would eventually be attacked by a Turkish army allied with a British fleet. Bonaparte, however, turned a blind eye to this future danger and proceeded to consolidate his power throughout the country. Having driven Ibrahim Bey northwards into Palestine, at the end of August he despatched Desaix with a weak division and some gunboats up the Nile in pursuit of Murad Bey. This task Desaix carried out with great energy and determination, but without achieving decisive success. In the face of tremendous difficulties, he chased Murad up river as far as Aswan, where he was held up by the First Cataract. He even sent a column mounted on camels to occupy Quseir on the Red Sea, to pre-vent Murad being reinforced by Arab forces from Mecca. Although the Mamelukes and their Arab allies were defeated in several engagements, they usually managed to evade a pitched battle.

Meanwhile Bonaparte in Cairo had his own troubles to contend with. He had learnt that Joséphine was being unfaithful to him, which rendered him morose and short-tempered. He consoled himself by seducing the wife of a cavalry subaltern, who had smuggled herself on board with her husband at Toulon. On 21 October a revolt against the French occupation broke out unexpectedly in Cairo, but it was stifled in two days by ruthless reprisals and executions. The El Azhar Mosque, believed to be the focus of the rebellion, was subjected to a destructive bombardment. As Bonaparte wrote to Menou at Rosetta, 'Here in Cairo I have heads cut off at the rate of five or six a day.'

Towards the end of December Bonaparte led a small reconnaissance party to Suez, which had been occupied earlier by General Bon. His main object was to gain the friendship of the Arab tribes of the Sinai Peninsula in order to realize the great dream of a march to India, which was floating in his mind like a desert mirage. He had indeed planned this project before he sailed for Egypt, but he had then intended to carry it out in alliance with Turkey. Now that by his own action he had antagonized the Turks, he hoped to rouse the Arab world against them, thus anticipating the dream of T. E. Lawrence. He had recently learnt that a Turkish army for the invasion of Egypt was being assembled near Acre by the Turkish Governor of Syria, Ahmed Pasha Jezzar ('the butcher').

Bonaparte decided to anticipate Jezzar's plans. He would march on Acre and defeat Jezzar's forces; then, with a freshly recruited army of 50,000 French, Arabs and Nubians, he would force the Sultan to make peace and assist him in his march to India (*Corr.* XXX. 14). On 19 November he sent an ultimatum to Jezzar: 'If you continue to give asylum on the borders of Egypt to Ibrahim Bey, I shall regard this as an act of war and shall march on Acre' (*Corr.* 3644). Receiving no reply, Bonaparte went ahead with his plans. He assembled an expeditionary force for the invasion of Palestine, consisting of four divisions under Kléber, Bon, Lannes and Reynier. Dugua was left to garrison Cairo, and Menou at Rosetta. Desaix's division was still campaigning against Murad Bey in Upper Egypt. On 25 January 1799 Bonaparte wrote to Tipu Sultan at Seringapatam, telling him that 'an innumerable and invincible army' was setting out to liberate him 'from the iron yoke of England' (*Corr.* 3901). Little did he suspect that four months later Tipu Sultan would be lying dead under the shattered ruins of his fortress, with Lieutenant-Colonel Arthur Wellesley officiating as Governor.

Bonaparte left Cairo on 10 February. Reynier's division, forming the advanced guard, had started a fortnight earlier, but was held up by the Turkish frontier fort at El Arish on 8 February. The French troops were now more acclimatized and better equipped for desert warfare; most of them had water-bottles and they had also been given cotton tropical uniforms. This was unfortunate, for Bonaparte had not realized how cold and wet the Palestine coast can be in February. On this occasion the weather was very severe and the troops had a miserable time.

When Bonaparte reached El Arish on 17 February, he was annoyed to find that both Reynier's and Kléber's divisions were still held up, besieging the

Turkish fort. With unfortunate optimism he had embarked all his siege artillery at Damietta and despatched it by sea to meet him at Acre, where in due course it was intercepted by the Royal Navy. Concentrating every available field-gun, he subjected the fort to a heavy bombardment; on 20 February the garrison of 900 Turks and Mamelukes surrendered and the French resumed their advance. Gaza was entered without resistance on the 24th, but on 3 March they were confronted by the walled town of Jaffa, strongly garrisoned by Jezzar's troops. On 7 March a breach was blown in the wall by the French sappers, and the town was stormed and sacked; an orgy of rape and pillage ensued, which was perhaps paralleled by the behaviour of British troops at Badajoz 13 years later. Worse, however was to come; 2500 Turkish troops were still holding out in the citadel, and these surrendered on the following day on the understanding that their lives would be spared. Bonaparte's order to massacre these prisoners of war was one of the worst blots on his character and career. On the pretext that he could spare neither sufficient troops to escort them back to Egypt, nor enough rations to feed them, he had them driven into the sea and there shot down or bayoneted. In the town the French had found 400,000 biscuit rations and 100 tons of rice; they also found bubonic plague, and from now onward 30 men were dying from it daily.

There were many curious and contradictory facets to Bonaparte's nature; he was firmly convinced that the plague could only be contracted by those who were afraid of it; in order to prove this, and to raise the morale of his troops, he visited the plague hospital in the Jaffa mosque on 11 March and helped to carry the corpse of a plague-stricken victim without suffering any ill result. The incident has been commemorated in Gros's famous picture in the Louvre. It was a brave thing to do, and had a reassuring effect on his troops.

On 17 March Bonaparte reached Haifa and established his headquarters on Mount Carmel, whence he could see to the north, across the bay, the frowning fortress of Acre, Jezzar's stronghold. Acre, an old Crusader fortress of the Knights Hospitaller, was crumbling to ruins. Its real strength lay in its geographical position, for it was perched on a rocky peninsula surrounded on three sides by the sea. It had an armament of 250 cannon, and was defended by an elderly but very determined Turk, who was supported by a British squadron of two battleships and several gunboats, commanded by a remarkable officer, Commodore William Sidney Smith (1764-1840), who had relieved Commodore Hood in the blockade of the Egyptian coast. He had with him in his flagship, H.M.S. *Tigre*, an equally remarkable French artillery officer, holding the rank of a British Colonel, named Louis-Edmond Le

Picard de Phélipeaux, who had emigrated from France in 1791; among other daring feats, he had in the previous year rescued Sidney Smith from a French prison. Phélipeaux had been Bonaparte's class-mate at the École Militaire, and they had both been commissioned on 1 September 1785. The two cadets had cordially detested each other.

On the day after Bonaparte reached Carmel the convoy of vessels transporting his siege train arrived off Acre. Their arrival was well timed, but it was a foggy day and they ran straight into the arms of the British squadron and were captured. Not only did Bonaparte have to begin the siege without his heavy guns, but these were now used by the Turks against their besiegers. Undeterred by this handicap, Bonaparte invested the land wall of the fortress, and launched a first unsuccessful assault on 28 March. After springing a mine, a further assault was made on 1 April, but also without success. The French lost heavily, and they were also falling victims to the plague at the rate of 140 cases a week. Sidney Smith had reinforced the Turkish garrison with 800 marines, and Phélipeaux's skill in directing the artillery fire was invaluable.*

Another danger now threatened the French. The Pasha of Damascus sent a large Turkish force to attack the besiegers from the rear. On 16 April Kléber, with a detachment of 2000 men, was attacked at Mount Tabor in the Plain of Esdraelon, south-east of Acre; the French resisted stoutly for ten hours, but were running out of ammunition when, at the critical moment, Bonaparte arrived with Bon's division and drove the Turks off. Bonaparte slept that night in a Christian monastery at Nazareth. During the next three weeks Bonaparte launched repeated attacks on the fortress, regardless of loss, but they all failed. His Chief Engineer, General Caffarelli, was killed. The walls had now been breached by mining, and on 10 May a final assault was organized, but was repulsed with heavy casualties. Bonaparte at last decided to abandon the siege.

On 16 May Bonaparte suggested to Dr. Desgenettes, his principal medical officer, that he should give an overdose of opium to all his plague patients; Desgenettes refused, saying that his duty was to preserve life, not to destroy it. On the following day Bonaparte issued a peculiarly mendacious proclamation to his troops, telling them that, having accomplished their mission, they would now return to Egypt. The retreat began on 20 May, and four days later the Army reached Jaffa. On 27 May the Commander-in-Chief described in a despatch to the Directory 'the glorious events accomplished during the past three months in Syria'; he explained that he had not allowed his troops to enter Acre owing to the plague that was raging there (*Corr.* 4156). He then

* Phélipeaux died, either of exhaustion or plague, in the last week of the siege of Acre.

cleared the military hospital of all the men fit to walk and ordered the chief pharmacist to poison the 50 who remained. On the following day the French blew up the fortifications of Jaffa, and continued their painful retreat across the Sinai Desert. Demoralized and on the verge of mutiny, they reached Cairo on 14 June. A week later Bonaparte ordered Admiral Ganteaume to keep two frigates in readiness at Alexandria for a possible sortie.

On 14 July news reached Cairo that a Turkish fleet had arrived off Alexandria and was preparing to land troops. Bonaparte immediately led a column 100 miles down the Nile to El Rahmaniya, where he learnt that a fleet of Turkish transports, escorted by Sidney Smith's squadron, had landed about 8000 men at Abu Qir Bay and had captured the French garrison holding the fort at the point. Instead of advancing, the Turks entrenched a beachhead south of the fort. Bonaparte had now collected a force of 10,000 and attacked the Turkish lines at dawn on 25 July. Brigadier-General Murat, at the head of a cavalry brigade, charged and broke through the Turkish lines, personally wounding and capturing the Turkish Commander-in-Chief. The Turks were driven into the sea, several thousands being killed or drowned, though a few survivors held out in the fort until 2 August. The French casualties did not exceed 1000.

During an exchange of prisoners which took place after the battle of Abu Qir, Bonaparte learnt from newspapers sent to him by Sidney Smith that affairs in France were going badly. The French armies on the Rhine and in Italy had been defeated by the Austrians and Russians, and there was alarm and confusion throughout the country. This was a good excuse for Bonaparte —*la patrie en danger!* He decided to return to France at once. On 11 August he went to Cairo for a week. On 18 August, with only a few picked companions, he left Cairo stealthily by night, and went down the Nile by boat, saying that he was going to visit Upper Egypt. Abandoning his troops, and also his mistress, Madame Pauline Fourès, he reached Alexandria on the 22nd and after dusk embarked with Admiral Ganteaume on board the frigate *la Muiron*. On the following morning he sailed with the dawn breeze, leaving behind a letter for Kléber, ordering him to assume command of the *Armée d'Orient*. After an uneventful voyage of 47 days, having successfully eluded Nelson's frigates, Bonaparte landed at St. Raphaël on 9 October.

The story of the Egyptian expedition has here been told at some length and in considerable detail, as it marked the transitional stage between Bonaparte the soldier and Bonaparte the soldier-statesman. As a soldier, he had added the experience of desert warfare to his campaigning skills acquired amid the mountains and plains of Europe. In Italy he had tried his prentice hand at political science and administration; he had levied tribute on subject princes and peoples; he had dictated treaties to King, Pope and Emperor. But in Egypt his achievement had been more constructive: he had acted as an independent ruler and lawgiver in a disparate country; by grafting the throbbing growths of Western technology onto the decaying trunk of Oriental tradition, he had created a new hybrid civilization; in fact he had laid the foundations of modern Egypt. The scientific and cultural achievements of his team of civilian experts, headed by Monge and Berthollet, were immense; far greater indeed than the military fruits of his expedition, which was costly and barren. This cultural endeavour was due solely to Bonaparte's vision and energy.

Above all, the Egyptian expedition throws into relief the chiaroscuro of Bonaparte's character. On the one hand, the soaring ambition, the supreme self-confidence, the dynamic magnetism, the determined courage, the matchless military skill. On the other, the callous brutality and cynical disregard for human life and feelings, the innate selfishness, the Machiavellian trickery and the meanness of the final evasion. From this amazing compound of incongruent elements was shortly to emerge the First Consul of the French Republic.

VIII

The Consulate and Marengo
1800

When Bonaparte returned to France from Egypt in October 1799 he found the country in political confusion and administrative chaos. The rule of the five Directors had proved to be corrupt and inefficient. Rewbell, the ablest of them, had been replaced in May by the ex-Abbé Sieyès (1748–1836), a crafty, but unstable political intriguer. The military situation was appalling; although Massena in Switzerland had saved France from invasion, the *Armée d'Italie*, which Bonaparte had led from victory to victory three years earlier, had during the summer suffered a succession of defeats at the hands of the Austrians and Russians, and was now reduced to a starving rabble. Almost all the Italian territories conquered by Bonaparte had been lost. The country was in fact ripe for a revolutionary change which could bring about administrative and financial stability coupled with military security.

Three clever politicians, Sieyès, Talleyrand and Fouché, all with a clerical background, were the central figures in plotting a *coup d'état*, which required a strong military leader to ensure success; Bonaparte was their obvious ally. Exactly a month after his return to France, an alleged terrorist conspiracy was made the excuse for transferring the legislative councils to St. Cloud. The fact that Bonaparte's younger brother Lucien was Speaker of the Lower Chamber facilitated the plot. The resignation of three of the Directors, Sieyès, Ducos and Barras, deprived the remaining two of any legal authority, so the Upper Chamber appointed Bonaparte, Sieyès and Ducos to act as temporary Consuls in order to carry on the government. This measure met with strong opposition in the Lower Chamber, whereupon Bonaparte burst into the Council and harangued them in a tactless and provocative manner. The members demanded that Bonaparte be outlawed and arrested, but Lucien saved the situation by calling in the troops from outside to protect his brother from 'assassination'. The troops cleared the Chamber in Cromwellian manner, and the *coup d'état* of Brumaire was effected.

Having been raised to Consular status, Bonaparte's first step was to enlist the support of the army. He at once issued a proclamation to the troops:

Soldiers, the extraordinary decree of the Upper Chamber is in conformity with Articles 102 and 103 of the Constitutional Act. It has placed me in command of the city and army.

The Republic has been badly governed for two years. You hoped that my return would put an end to so many evils. . . . Liberty, victory and peace will regain for the French Republic the position which it formerly occupied in Europe, and which it has only lost through ineptitude and treachery. *Vive la République!* (*Corr.* 4387)

On the following day he had Berthier appointed as Minister for War, thus gathering the reigns of power into his own hand. A month later a new 'Constitution of the Year VIII' was enacted; Sieyès and Ducos were quietly eliminated from the Consulate, and Bonaparte was nominated as 'First Consul', the second and third being Cambacérès and Lebrun. This effectively, though not in name, gave Bonaparte dictatorial powers, and he quickly set about putting France's house in order. He worked incessantly to introduce administrative reforms, but his real preoccupation was with the external dangers which threatened the country, confronted as it was by the Coalition of Austria, Britain, Russia, Sicily and Turkey.

The first step was to reorganize the armies on the eastern frontier with a view to resuming the offensive against Austria. Orders to this effect were issued on 24 November; Massena was transferred from Switzerland to command the *Armée d'Italie*, and the Armies of the Rhine and Danube were merged in a new *Armée du Rhin* under Moreau.

Bonaparte then stepped into the arena of foreign policy. Disregarding all conventions of diplomatic protocol, on Christmas Day he addressed personal letters to King George III and to the Emperor Francis of Austria, suggesting that the time was now ripe for the peaceful settlement of all outstanding questions on the basis of the *status quo*. In the case of Austria, he hinted that this would mean the withdrawal of Austrian troops to the Ádige line, as settled by the Treaty of Campo-Formio. The hypocrisy of these pacific gestures was illustrated by his issue on the same day of a proclamation to the French army:

Soldiers! It is no longer your frontiers that you are called upon to defend; we must invade the countries of our enemies. (*Corr.* 4449)

On the same day he had his brother Lucien appointed Minister of the Interior, so that he could keep his hand on police, internal security and censorship. On the following day he decreed the establishment of the Consular Guard, 2100 strong, consisting of two battalions of foot grenadiers with a light infantry company, two cavalry squadrons and a battery of artillery. This was to develop later into the Imperial Guard. Its earlier prototype was the personal bodyguard which he had organized after his narrow escape at Valéggio in 1796 (see p. 62).

In order to rebuild the armed forces it was necessary to restore the country's finances, for the corrupt and extravagant rule of the Directory had emptied the treasury and France's credit was at a low ebb. On 13 January 1800 he instructed Talleyrand, the Minister of Foreign Affairs, to negotiate a loan from the Portuguese Government:

It would be extremely useful if we could obtain a loan of eight or nine million francs. . . . At the present moment we cannot provide eight to ten thousand draught horses needed for the siege trains. (Corr. 4521)

And again: 'Perhaps we could get four millions from Hamburg.' In March he sent Marmont on a mission to Amsterdam to negotiate a loan of 12 million francs from the Dutch merchants, on the security of the timber sales for the current year, at the rate of 12 per cent per annum interest.

By dint of these expedients Bonaparte scraped together sufficient funds to reorganize and equip his army. For now a grand design was germinating in his mind to throw the Austrians back from the forward positions which they had regained in Lombardy and Piedmont during his absence in Egypt. Four years earlier he had made his lightning thrust through the Cadibona Pass and split the enemy's forces by striking at their centre. They were now strongly established along the Ligurian Apennines and they would expect him to repeat the same strategic plan. This time he would carry out a quite different and far more audacious project. He would rivet the attention of the Austrian forces in Piedmont by the manœuvres of the Army of Italy, while he himself with a newly raised Reserve Army would advance through Switzerland, cross the Alpine barrier and take the Austrians in rear. Meanwhile the Rhine Army would advance through the Black Forest, swing southwards through the eastern Swiss Cantons and cut the enemy's last line of communication with Austria. It was grand strategy on the most audacious scale, and involved the solution of complex administrative problems, as well as demanding the boldest leadership on the part of commanders and troops. It was similar in conception to Suvórov's attempt to encircle Massena the previous year, an operation which had ended in ignominious failure. To carry it out an entirely new army was required.

12 *Passage of the Grand Saint-Bernard, 14 May 1800*
From a painting by Charles Thévenin (1764–1838). Bourg Saint-Pierre in the middle
distance; the French gunners mounting their 4-pounders on locally made sledges

13 *The invasion flotilla assembled at Boulogne, August 1803*
After a painting by Bougeau

14 *John Bull's reaction to the threatened invasion, August 1803*
From a cartoon by James Gillray (1757–1815)

On 25 January Bonaparte wrote a minute to Berthier, his War Minister:

My intention, Citizen Minister, is to organize a Reserve Army which will be commanded by the First Consul in person. It will be divided into three corps, each of two divisions. (*Corr.* 4552)

This was the first occasion on which a French army was definitely organized in corps of two or more divisions. Six weeks later Bonaparte followed this up with a further decree:

A Reserve Army will be created, 60,000 strong. It will be commanded directly by the First Consul. It will concentrate at Dijon and be billeted within a radius of 20 leagues of that town. (*Corr.* 4651)

Early in February the formation of the Reserve Army was begun with the greatest secrecy. Units were withdrawn quietly from the different sectors and from the garrisons and depots in the interior, and were assembled in the Saône valley between Dijon and Chalon, as if they were intended as reinforcements for the Rhine Army.

The whole strategic plan of operations depended on General Melas,* the Austrian Commander-in-Chief, being pinned to his position in Piedmont sufficiently long for the Reserve Army to outflank him from behind the screen of the Alps. This vital task was assigned to André Massena, with his poorly equipped and awkwardly placed Army of Italy. On 5 March the First Consul wrote to Massena:

I am collecting a Reserve Army at Dijon which I shall command in person. In eight or ten days I shall send you one of my A.D.C.s with the plan of operations for the coming campaign, when you will see that your role will be important and within the means at your disposal. During March and April, if I were you, I should have four-fifths of my force, say 40,000, in Genoa. Then I should have no fear of the enemy capturing Genoa. (*Corr.* 4642)

This contained a considerable mis-statement; Massena's whole army only comprised 36,000 fighting troops, who were holding a front of 180 miles, and less than 30,000 of these were available for the defence of the Genoa sector. He was faced by an Austrian army of 95,000. Massena in fact was to be the tethered goat put out to attract the tiger, which would then fall an easy prey to the hunter, Bonaparte.

During March someone must have drawn the First Consul's attention to the fact that the ex-Abbé Sieyès had craftily inserted a clause in the new

* General Baron Michael Friedrich Benedikt von Melas (1729–1806).

Constitution which made it illegal for any Consul to command an army in the field. So on 2 April a fresh Consular Decree was issued:

General Berthier, Minister of War, is appointed Commander-in-Chief of the Reserve Army. Citizen Carnot* is appointed Minister of War.

Bonaparte thus evaded the constitutional brake on his military activities and outwitted his political rivals by putting his own yes-man in nominal command; this devolution of command proved to be a complete farce.

According to Bonaparte's original plan, communicated to Berthier on 22 March (*Corr.* 4694), the Reserve Army would ascend the upper Rhône valley from the Lake of Geneva, cross the St. Gotthard Pass, and descend into the plain of Lombardy by Lake Maggiore (Suvórov's 1799 operation in reverse). Within the next week, however, he modified this plan and allotted the St. Gotthard to the Rhine Army.

On 6 April Berthier, the new Commander-in-Chief of the Reserve Army, ordered his Chief of Staff, General Dupont,† to set up the Army Headquarters at Dijon, while he himself went to Bâle for a conference with Moreau, Commander-in-Chief of the Rhine Army, in order to coordinate their respective movements during the coming offensive. Moncey, commanding the right wing of the Rhine Army, was to cross the St. Gotthard with a division, and join forces with the Reserve Army near Milan. Meanwhile the rest of the Rhine Army would invade the Black Forest and engage Kray's Austrian Army there.

On 18 April Berthier returned from Bâle and took over command of the Reserve Army at Dijon. Bonaparte had already concentrated there 32,000 men, organized in four divisions under Boudet, Chabran, Loison and Watrin, with the nucleus of a cavalry division under Murat. The units were all very short of arms, equipment and transport, and were being brought up to strength with batches of conscript recruits. It was intended to bring the Reserve Army up to a strength of 50,000, but there were not enough horses or equipment available for a force of that size. The First Consul, being precluded by law from commanding in person, acted as a sort of supernumerary Quartermaster-General and issued a stream of orders to Berthier through Carnot in order to rectify the defects in the organization.

A key point in the plan of operations was the selection of the route by

* Lazare Nicolas Carnot (1753–1823), a very competent engineer officer, had been one of the Directors proscribed after the *coup d'état* of 18 Fructidor (4 Sep. 1797). He was allowed to return to France in December 1799.

† Pierre Dupont (1765–1840) was a competent officer, but while commanding a corps in Spain in July 1808, had the misfortune to be surrounded by the Spaniards and forced to capitulate (see pp. 185 and 186).

which the Reserve Army would cross the Alps. Bonaparte was anxious to move as soon as possible, in order to gain the benefit of surprise, but it was still early in the season and the Alpine passes were all blocked by snow. Hannibal, on whom Bonaparte consciously modelled himself, had crossed the lower Cottian Alps in September or October in 218 B.C., when the snows had mostly melted.* But to cross the Cottian Alps would merely threaten Melas's right flank, whereas Bonaparte's plan was to attack his rear. He must therefore cross the main Alpine chain somewhere east of Mont Blanc, which left him with the choice of only two passes possible for the passage of artillery, for the St. Gotthard (6935 feet) was already allotted to the right wing of the Rhine Army. That left only the Great St. Bernard (8110 feet) and the Simplon (6,590 feet). During March the First Consul had sent a staff officer to reconnoitre these two passes; he reported that, although the Simplon was lower, the Great St. Bernard was easier, as the difficult sector was only about six miles long, whereas the Simplon route presented difficulties over a much longer stretch. Bonaparte decided on the Great St. Bernard, which led directly to Turin, and which involved a shorter march from the base at Dijon. The same officer had suggested that it would be possible to transport guns across the pass if they were mounted on special sledges. Bonaparte ordered ten gun-sledges on rollers (affûts-traîneaux) to be constructed in Paris, and another batch at the artillery workshops at Auxonne.

The first stage in the operation was to move the whole army 120 miles further south to a new concentration area round Geneva. Thence the army would march 56 miles round the northern shore of the lake by Lausanne to Villeneuve at the far end, the heavy baggage and stores being moved by boat from Geneva to Villeneuve. The independent Republic of Geneva had been forcibly annexed by France two years earlier and converted into the Département du Léman. At the same time the 13 neutral Swiss Cantons had been occupied and federated into a French satellite State called the République Helvétique, so that the First Consul was able to do what he liked with Swiss territory.

While the Reserve Army was still concentrating in the Dijon area the First Consul's plans were forestalled by an unexpected initiative on the part of the Austrians. On 5 April Melas launched 60,000 men in a sudden attack on Massena's Army of Italy, which held the crest of the Ligurian Apennines north of Genoa. Massena, under assault by double his own numbers, put up a spirited resistance, but his army was split in two, the right wing (17,000)

---

* The pass by which Hannibal crossed the Alps has been the subject of much controversy between historians and geographers. Sir Gavin de Beer (*Alps and Elephants*, 1955) favours the Col de la Traversette (9825 feet).

under Soult being driven into the Genoa perimeter, while the left wing (11,000) under Suchet was pushed westwards towards Nice. Massena made a series of determined counter-attacks, but was unable to break out of the Genoa perimeter, where he remained closely blockaded, on the land side by Ott's Austrian corps and from the sea by a British squadron under Admiral Lord Keith. At the beginning of May another Austrian corps under Elsnitz drove Suchet back behind the river Var and captured Nice, Massena's base. Melas still held in reserve in Piedmont Keim's corps of 35,000.

This unwelcome news from the Genoa front caused the First Consul considerable anxiety. On 24 April he issued the following urgent directive to Carnot, the War Minister:

The Army of Italy is at grips with the Austrians. Whether it wins or loses, the Reserve Army must move at once. If it wins, the Austrian army will be considerably weakened and unable to resist the Reserve Army. If it is beaten, it is still essential that the Reserve Army should attack Piedmont or Lombardy in order to create a diversion. . . . I ask you therefore to order General Berthier:

(1) To move the Reserve Army forward to Geneva as quickly as possible.
(2) To transport all the ammunition and supplies collected at Geneva by the lake to Villeneuve.
(3) To invade Piedmont and Lombardy as rapidly as possible, either by the Great St. Bernard or the Simplon.

Repeat the order to General Moreau to attack the enemy. Impress on him that his delays are compromising the safety of the Republic. (*Corr.* 4728)

On the same day he wrote direct to Berthier:

The Reserve Army must invade Italy immediately, without waiting for the Rhine Army. To do that you have two passes, the St. Bernard and the Simplon. . . . Nothing in Italy will be able to resist the 40,000 men that you have. (*Corr.* 4729)

To which Berthier, somewhat plaintively, replied:

I intend to operate by the St. Bernard or the Simplon. I must sacrifice everything for Massena; I should be in the mountains already if I had enough ammunition and sledges. . . . I shall be meeting the enemy without a single round of ammunition. . . . My sledges are away in rear. I shall therefore have my army on the Lake of Geneva and in the Valais, confronting the enemy, but with nothing to fight him with. . . . I have done everything possible which the situation demands. There is no credit in doing easy things; we shall do the impossible. . . . Instead of the 40,000 men which you think my army consists of, I have at the most 25,000. . . . The Simplon is not passable for artillery.

On 27 April Dupont reported to Carnot that three divisions were moving by forced marches to Geneva and Lausanne. He added: 'What we are most worried about is our weakness in artillery and the almost complete lack of ammunition. Our means of transport are almost nil.' Three days later Berthier, still at Dijon, wrote a complaint about Carnot to Bonaparte:

In spite of my repeated orders, no provision has been made for either rations or forage. . . . Why has the Minister not taken the necessary steps? Why has he counter-ordered the arrangements which I had already signed? No; others are not inspired as I am with the will to foresee everything and to organize all the services.

Bonaparte, meanwhile, was doing his best to provide the Reserve Army with commanders on whom he could rely. He appointed his former A.D.C., Colonel Marmont, with the rank of Brigadier, to command the artillery of the army, and General Joachim Murat, who four months earlier had married his sister Caroline, to command the cavalry. The latter arm was in poor condition; on 1 May Murat reported to his brother-in-law:

Yesterday I inspected the 7th Regiment of *Chasseurs à Cheval*; I found it in a pitiful condition. It has no weapons and no horses; its regimental store is empty. . . . It consists only of conscripts, and can only put 140 men into the field; they will be without clothing and badly armed.

On 3 May Berthier moved his headquarters from Dijon to Geneva. Four of his divisions were already on the march, and he had now raised a fifth division, commanded by Chambarlhac. On 4 May Bonaparte sent Berthier the following rather depressing message:

If Massena is forced to surrender Genoa, General Melas only requires eight days to move from Genoa to Aosta [250 kilometres]. If he gets there before you arrive with only 20,000 men, that will put him in a most advantageous position to prevent you invading Italy. (*Corr.* 4751)

To which Berthier replied four days later:

I am beset by difficulties, but shall do my best to overcome them. If the sledges arrive, I shall try to cross the St. Bernard on the nights of 10 and 11 May. There is a lot of snow and the avalanches are dangerous; one can only cross at night and up to midday without too much danger. . . . The medical officers have not arrived; we have not got a single set of surgical instruments; everything is behindhand.

On 5 May Bonaparte ordered Moreau to send from the Rhine Army a column, 25,000 strong, to cross the St. Gotthard and Simplon Passes and reinforce the Reserve Army. On the following day the First Consul left Paris and reached Geneva on the 9th.

Meanwhile Massena's situation in Genoa was daily growing more serious. On 24 April he sent a despatch to Bonaparte by the hand of Major Franceschi, who slipped through the British naval blockade and handed the despatch to the First Consul in Paris on 5 May. Bonaparte sent Franceschi back with the message:

The Reserve Army is marching rapidly. I leave myself tonight. I count on your holding out as long as possible, at least until 30 May.

When Bonaparte reached Geneva on 9 May, the leading division (Watrin) had reached St. Maurice in the upper Rhône valley; the divisions of Boudet, Loison and Chambarlhac were strung out along the north side of the lake; a fifth division (Chabran) was ordered to move south from Geneva by Annecy and Chambéry and cross the Alps south of Mont Blanc by the Little St. Bernard Pass (7175 feet). Bonaparte now instructed Berthier to put Lannes in command of the advanced guard, while the other four divisions were to be formed into two corps under Duhesme and Victor.

On 12 May Bonaparte moved on from Geneva to Lausanne, where he received a final message from Massena, written on 29 April, which had been smuggled through the enemy lines:

For heaven's sake relieve me! The town is blockaded by land and sea. . . . I have rations for 30 days.

Bonaparte replied on the 14th:

I have been at Lausanne for two days, Citizen General. The army is on the way. . . . You are in a tight corner; but what reassures me is that it is *you* who are in Genoa: it is at times like these that one man can be worth 20,000. (*Corr.* 4795)

This was the last message which Massena received; it reached him on 27 May. A week later, when his rations were completely exhausted, he was forced to capitulate.

On 14 May Lannes's advanced guard, with Watrin's division in the van, reached Bourg St. Pierre, 5360 feet above sea level, the last inhabited village at the foot of the pass. Wheeled vehicles could proceed no further, but a rough mule-track, 18 inches wide, led up for a distance of eight miles to the monks' Hospice at the col (8110 feet). Infantry and cavalry could follow this track in single file, the ammunition being carried on pack mules, but the guns could get no further, as the *affûts-traîneaux* proved to be quite useless. The local peasants, however, came to the rescue, and showed the French gunners how to get their guns across. Pine-trunks were sawn longitudinally into two halves; these were cut into five-foot lengths and hollowed out into trough-like sledges in which the gun-barrels were packed, muzzle to the rear. Sixty men hauled on a rope attached to the breech-ring, while a gunner with a handspike in the gun-muzzle steered the sledge from behind. By this means six of the ten guns of Watrin's division were hauled to the summit of the pass by nightfall. After a few hours' rest at the Hospice, where the monks regaled them hospitably with wine, the troops began the descent into Italy at 2 a.m. on the 15th. On reaching Étroubles in the valley below, the guns were re-mounted on their field-carriages, which had been transported by pack-mule.

By 17 May Berthier had succeeded in bringing over the pass 15,000 infantry and 1000 cavalry, and Chabran's division, which had crossed by the Little St. Bernard without difficulty, also reached Aosta. Bonaparte himself left Lausanne on 16 May and crossed the Great St. Bernard in the early hours of the 20th, not on a fiery charger as depicted by David, but riding a mule led by a local guide.

So far, practically no resistance had been encountered. Lannes with the advanced guard pushed on rapidly down the valley of the Dora Baltea from Aosta to Châtillon, where 300 Austrians and two 4-pounder guns were captured. On 18 May, however, the vanguard was held up by an obstacle which proved far more troublesome than the St. Bernard Pass.

Just north of the village of Donnaz, 30 miles down stream from Aosta, the Dora Baltea forces its way through a narrow, precipitous defile. On a rocky promontory on the left bank, surrounded on three sides by a loop of the rapid torrent, rose Fort Bard, which commanded the road at point-blank range. Berthier himself reconnoitred the fort on 19 May and sent Bonaparte the following report:

Today I reconnoitred Fort Bard, which presents a very real obstacle. It is perched on a rock difficult of access, and enclosed by two ramparts containing two tiers of batteries, 12 guns in the lower and five in the upper. The road passes through Bard village between precipitous rocks on one side and the unfordable river on the other. The road, which is covered by the guns of the fort, is cut by three drawbridges. We may be able to get some infantry past Bard, but we must capture the fort before any guns can pass.

Watrin's division managed to by-pass the fort by climbing a mule-track over the mountain, but no guns could pass. The division pushed on without its artillery, and on 22 May captured the important town of Ivrea, taking 300 prisoners and 14 guns. In spite of bombarding the fort day and night with the 11 guns which they had been able to bring up so far, the French did not succeed in breaching the rampart until 1 June, when the garrison of 400 men finally capitulated. The resistance of Fort Bard had blocked the passage of the artillery of the Reserve Army for a whole fortnight, except for six guns which had been smuggled past by night on muffled wheels.

The First Consul had hitherto followed in the wake of the Reserve Army, urging forward its supplies and ammunition. On reaching Aosta, he took over direct charge of the operations, in spite of the clause of the Constitution forbidding a Consul to command an army. Berthier, however, remained nominally the Commander-in-Chief and passed on to Dupont, his Chief of Staff, the orders received from Bonaparte. On 25 May Lannes with the advanced guard was ordered to push on southwards to Chivasso on the Po, 15 miles north-east of Turin, where Melas was believed to be concentrating. The remainder of the army, however, headed by Murat's cavalry and Duhesme's corps, was diverted south-eastwards to Vercelli.

On the evening of 26 May Bonaparte arrived at Ivrea. He was clear of the Alpine region and the plain of Piedmont stretched in front of him. Had he really wanted to relieve Massena at Genoa, he now had the opportunity to make the attempt. Genoa lay 120 miles to the south, only eight days' march, if the enemy did not interfere; he could have reached it by the 30th, the date to which he had told Massena to hold out. The Reserve Army was now 40,000 strong, stronger than any one of Melas's widely scattered groups. But a more tempting morsel was within easier reach. Milan, the capital of Lombardy and the advanced base of Melas's army, lay only 70 miles to the east of Ivrea, and was practically undefended. Massena was expendable. Disregarding Melas at Turin, the First Consul with the bulk of his army marched eastwards by Novara to Milan. Murat's cavalry and Duhesme's corps forced the crossing of the Ticino on 1 June, driving Vukássovich's Austrian division eastwards to Bergamo. On 2 June Lannes, forming the right flank guard, marched unopposed through Mortara to Pavia, from where he sent the following message to the First Consul:

The enemy is still blockading Genoa, which he bombards continuously. There is not a moment to lose if you want to march on it. The place cannot hold out much longer, according to my information.

This information was precisely accurate, but the First Consul ignored it. That night he reached Milan, where he remained for the next seven days.

Napoleon in later years at St. Helena explained at considerable length his reasons for turning eastwards to Milan, instead of pushing southwards to relieve Genoa. In his Memoirs (*Corr.* XXX. 375-377) he described the three courses open to him as follows:

(a) Should he march on Turin and attack Melas, thus effecting a junction with Turreau's division which had crossed the Mont Cenis Pass to Susa? This would enable the Reserve Army to open a new line of communication with France by Grenoble and Briançon.
(b) Should he cross the Po at Chivasso and march to the relief of Genoa?

(c) Should he leave Melas behind him, cross the Ticino and make for Milan, thus effecting a junction with Moncey's corps of 15,000 from the Rhine Army which had crossed the St. Gotthard?

Napoleon answered these three questions thus:

(a) This would have been contrary to the true principles of war, for Melas was in considerable strength. The French army would have run the risk of fighting a battle with its line of retreat unsecured, as Fort Bard had not been captured.
(b) This would have been too risky; the French army between the Po and Genoa would have its line of communication and line of retreat exposed to a powerful Austrian army.
(c) The third alternative offered every advantage. Once in possession of Milan, the French army would capture all the base depots and hospitals of the Austrian army. By effecting its junction with Moncey, it would ensure a safe retreat by the Simplon and St. Gotthard.

It is perhaps rash to criticize the strategic decisions of such a master of the art of war as Napoleon, but it may be argued that when Bonaparte reached Ivrea on 26 May, Melas's forces were very widely separated; the Reserve Army could have crossed the Po, not at Chivasso which was too close to Turin, but at Casale or Valenza with comparative safety, and could have defeated Ott's corps besieging Genoa before Melas or Elsnitz could have come to the rescue. The capture of Milan, and eventually of Piacenza, could have been left to Moncey's corps, which was then crossing the St. Gotthard. However, Bonaparte chose the third alternative, sacrificed Massena and won the campaign, although only with the assistance of a certain amount of luck.

Melas had at first thought that the Reserve Army was merely a corps of 6000 or 7000 men. When he discovered that the threat to his rear was much more serious, he endeavoured to concentrate his scattered forces in the Alessándria area. On the 29th he moved to Asti and then to Alessándria, and sent an order to Ott to raise the siege of Genoa and march north to Voghera and secure the Po crossing at Piacenza.

Bonaparte, having established himself at Milan, intended to seize the Po crossings between Valenza and Piacenza, thus cutting all possible lines of retreat of the Austrian army. Lannes, at Pavia with Watrin's division, was on 4 June ordered to cross the Po and seize Stradella; Murat, at Piacenza with Boudet's division, was to cross the Po there and march westwards to support Lannes. A new division was now formed under Gardanne. Lannes and Murat both crossed the Po with only minor opposition on 7 June, and Lannes occupied the important road junction of Stradella. On the following day Lannes received orders from Bonaparte to advance south-westwards to Voghera on the road to Alessándria. Early on 9 June his advanced guard,

Watrin's division, encountered the advanced guard of Ott's corps, which had left Genoa on 5 June and had been ordered by Melas to seize the Po crossing at Piacenza. Victor, with Chambarlhac's division, came up to support Lannes, and a nine-hour battle ensued at Castéggio. Ott's corps was severely defeated and driven back to the little village of Montebello, leaving behind 5000 prisoners and six guns, and suffering a loss of 2000 killed and wounded. The French casualties were 500.

On 10 June Bonaparte and Berthier crossed the Po and established Army Headquarters at Stradella. On the following day Bonaparte reorganized his fighting formations with a view to the battle which he considered imminent in the Tortona area. General Desaix, the fine fighting commander who had carried out such an active campaign in the upper Nile valley in 1798, had now returned from Egypt and joined the Reserve Army; Bonaparte gave him command of a corps (8900) consisting of Boudet's and Monnier's divisions. Victor's corps (9000) had Chambarlhac's and Gardanne's divisions, and Lannes's corps (5100) had Watrin's. These three corps (23,000 infantry) and four cavalry brigades under Murat (3700) formed Bonaparte's striking force south of the Po; Duhesme's corps (11,600) and Moncey's corps (9900) were north of the Po guarding the lines of communication.

On 11 June Bonaparte had concentrated his striking force of 27,000 near Voghera, ten miles north-east of Tortona, a small fortress guarding the bridge by which the Voghera–Alessándria road crossed the Scrivia, now flooded by heavy rain. Bonaparte thought that this river would be held by the Austrians and that the decisive battle would be fought there. Orders were issued for the advance to be continued on the following day to the Scrivia on a five-mile front, Lannes's corps on the right directed on Castelnuovo di Scrivia, Victor's corps on the left to Tortona; Desaix's corps in reserve at Ponte-Curone. To each corps was attached a cavalry brigade from Murat's division. Lapoype's division (from Moncey's corps) was ordered to cross to the south bank of the Po from Pavia and join the reserve at Ponte-Curone. Army Headquarters moved forward from Stradella to Castéggio, and then to Voghera.

On 12 June the Army advanced to the Scrivia, but there was no opposition, and on the following day the forward movement was continued towards Alessándria. Bonaparte was extremely puzzled by the Austrian withdrawal, and concluded that Melas was trying to elude him, and would either cross the Po at Valenza or retreat southwards to Genoa. He thought that the latter alternative was more likely, so at midday he broke up the reserve corps at Ponte-Curone; Monnier's division was sent up to Torre di Garofoli in close reserve to Lannes's corps, while Desaix with Boudet's division was despatched to Serravalle, 12 miles south of Tortona, to block the Alessándria–Genoa road. Meanwhile the corps of Lannes and Victor continued their westward advance to the sinuous valley of the river Bórmida, which now barred the approach to Alessándria. At the little village of Marengo, 2½ miles south-east of Alessándria, Gardanne's division of Victor's advanced guard was held up by an Austrian rearguard. After a sharp engagement, the Austrians withdrew at 6 p.m. to Alessándria, leaving behind two guns and several hundred prisoners. Lannes's and Victor's corps halted for the night on a two-mile front between the villages of Castel-Ceriolo and Marengo (p. 108). Bonaparte rode up from Voghera to reconnoitre the front, and at dusk he sent a staff officer forward to report whether the bridge over the Bórmida was still intact. The officer reported (incorrectly) that the bridge had been demolished, which confirmed the First Consul in his conviction that Melas was evacuating Alessándria; he went back to spend the night at Torre di Garofoli, seven miles east of Marengo.

On the evening of 13 June, when he was expecting a decisive engagement, Bonaparte had concentrated in the Marengo plain between the Scrivia and Bórmida rivers the corps of Victor and Lannes (17,700 infantry) and Murat's cavalry (3700). In reserve at Ponte-Curone were Lapoype's division and the Consular Guard (in all 4300). His total strength was therefore 25,700, for earlier in the day he had sent off Desaix with Boudet's division (5300) to block the Genoa road. He was unaware of his opponent's strength or intentions. The Austrian Commander-in-Chief had in fact decided to force his way eastwards to cross the Po at Piacenza. With this purpose he had previously ordered Ott's corps to move on Piacenza from Genoa, but that attempt had been frustrated by Lannes's victory at Castéggio-Montebello on 9 June. Now Melas meant to break through with his whole army concentrated. This consisted of 23,300 infantry and 5200 cavalry, for he had detached a cavalry brigade (2300) towards Acqui to ward off Massena and Suchet. As regards numbers available, therefore, the French and Austrians were fairly evenly matched.

The battle of Marengo has given rise to more legends than any other battle in history, except perhaps Waterloo. The French official bulletin, published on 15 June (*Corr.* 4910), and Napoleon's Memoirs (*Corr.* XXX. 386) are equally misleading, so that one has to reconstruct the sequence of events from other official documentary evidence.

The night having passed quietly, Bonaparte was still convinced that Melas had slipped away, either to the north or south. At an early hour on the 14th he ordered Lapoype's division, in reserve at Ponte-Curone, to cross over to the north bank of the Po and reconnoitre westwards towards Valenza.

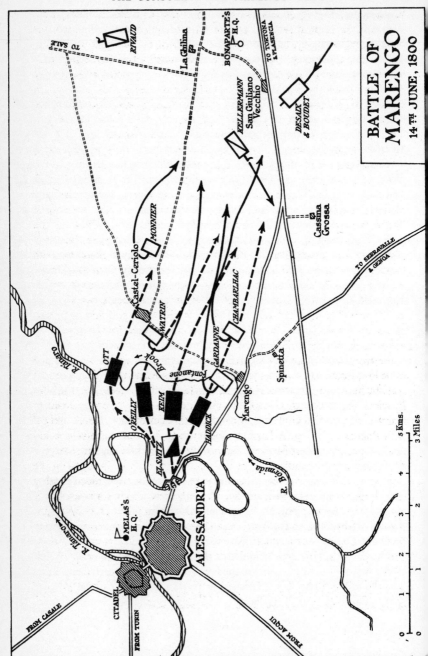

BATTLE OF
MARENGO
14TH JUNE, 1800

Rivaud's cavalry brigade was also sent out to the right flank at Salé. At the same time he sent an order to Desaix, who had been despatched towards Novi the previous day, to send a patrol westwards to Pozzolo-Formigaro to try to locate the enemy. No sooner had these orders been despatched, than the battle suddenly opened about 9 a.m. with an unexpected attack by the Austrians across the Bórmida bridge. Far from the bridge being broken, as reported to Bonaparte, there were two boat bridges leading to an entrenched bridgehead, from which three strong Austrian columns attacked the outpost line held by Lannes and Victor. A desperate battle ensued, and after two hours' fighting Gardanne's division was driven out of Marengo. Victor sent up Chambarlhac's division to reinforce, but the French could not regain the ground lost. On the right flank Watrin's division was driven out of Castel-Ceriolo; at 11 a.m. Bonaparte supported it with Monnier's division, his only available reserve, as he had sent Lapoype's division to the other side of the Po; he despatched an A.D.C. to recall Lapoype, but the order did not reach him till the evening. Monnier's division re-took Castel-Ceriolo, but were eventually driven out. The situation was now extremely serious, for both Lannes's and Victor's corps had suffered heavily and were running out of ammunition. The French were hopelessly out-gunned, for they had only been able to bring 15 guns into action, while the Austrians could deploy nearly 100. The two French corps were forced to retreat and withdrew 4½ miles to the village of San Giuliano Vecchio, covered to some extent by the counter-charges of their three cavalry brigades.

Bonaparte and his staff rode up to San Giuliano, but the battle now seemed to be lost, for he had no more troops in reserve. Earlier in the day, when he realized he was being attacked by the whole of Melas's force, he had sent Bruyères, one of his A.D.C.s, to Serravalle, 12 miles away, to order Desaix to march at once to San Giuliano. At 5 p.m., in the nick of time, Desaix arrived with Boudet's division. A hurried conference took place on horseback between Bonaparte, Berthier and Desaix. The latter said he must have a strong artillery preparation before he counter-attacked; he brought up the eight guns of Boudet's divisional artillery, to which Marmont added another ten, all that remained on the battlefield. With these 18 guns a rapid fire of canister was opened on the victorious Austrian columns at close range. Boudet deployed his two infantry brigades on either side of the Alessándria road, and Desaix led the counter-attack, but fell, mortally wounded. Bonaparte ordered Kellermann * to support the attack; his brigade had only 400

* François-Étienne Kellermann (1770–1835) commanded one of Murat's cavalry brigades. He was the son of General François-Christophe Kellermann (1735–1820) the hero of Valmy (1792). The son fought at Vimeiro (1808) and Waterloo (1815).

men left, but, collecting two squadrons of the Consular Guard, he charged the left flank of the shaken Austrian column and cut his way through to Cassina Grossa. This combined counter-attack by all three arms seemed to break the Austrian morale. A panic arose and they withdrew in disorder to the bridgehead, where a confused mass of men and horses struggled to cross the river. The French bivouacked for the night on the line Castel-Ceriolo–Marengo which they had held the previous evening.

The losses were heavy on both sides; the French casualties were 5835, while those of the Austrians amounted to 9400, a third of Melas's force. On the following morning he sent an officer with a flag of truce asking for an armistice. On the evening of the 15th the Convention of Alessándria was signed by Berthier and Melas; under its terms hostilities on the Italian front would be suspended until the conclusion of a final peace treaty; meanwhile by the 26 June the Austrian army would retire to the territory north of the Po and east of the Mincio, and a demilitarized zone between the rivers Chiese and Mincio would separate the French and Austrian forces.

Exactly a month had elapsed since the vanguard of the Reserve Army had crossed the Great St. Bernard Pass. Hostilities in Italy being now ended, the First Consul had more important matters to attend to on the home front. He merged the Reserve Army with the Army of Italy, handed the whole over to Massena, and on 25 June left for Paris to rejoin his fellow Consuls.

One is bound to admire the boldness of Bonaparte's strategic conception of crossing the Alpine watershed in order to attack from the rear the Austrian forces in North Italy. The execution of this audacious manœuvre, however, was marred by numerous faults, administrative, strategic and tactical, which might have ended in disaster, as did Suvórov's similar attempt in the previous year; defeat, indeed, was only averted by a stroke of luck on the climactic battlefield of Marengo.

In November 1799, when Bonaparte became First Consul after the *coup d'état* of Brumaire, he not only assumed command of all French land and sea forces, but he also took over the administration of a country of 30 million people in a state of chaotic confusion. The treasury was empty; the stocks of arms, ammunition and equipment in the military depots had been run down to nothing; the army was dispirited by the succession of military disasters in Italy. Despite this state of penury and disorder Bonaparte was able, besides maintaining an army of 100,000 on the Rhine and another of 50,000 in the Maritime Alps, to create within four months an entirely new Reserve Army of 40,000 for his bold enterprise. It was not surprising that, when this force crossed the Alps, it was short of arms and ammunition and lacked its proper complement of artillery and cavalry. Bonaparte, aided by Berthier, had made tremendous efforts and had, as Berthier claimed, 'achieved the impossible.'

The actual crossing of the Alps, however, was not very cleverly planned, and the physical difficulties were underestimated. Bonaparte's first intention had been to take his army by a long détour over the Splügen and St. Gotthard Passes. When Melas attacked Massena's army in the Ligurian Apennines in early April, it became urgent to move at once by a shorter route, so Berthier was ordered to cross by the Simplon and Great St. Bernard; in the end, the St. Gotthard and Simplon were allotted to the Rhine Army contingent. The preliminary reconnaissance of the Alpine passes was assigned to a *sous-lieutenant*, who actually did his job very well, but the problem of artillery transport across the Alps had been insufficiently studied, and Bonaparte's *affûts-traîneaux* proved useless. Had it not been for the lumber-men of Bourg St. Pierre, the French guns would never have got across.

A second bottle-neck in the advance was caused by the unexpected resistance of Fort Bard, which delayed the army's progress for a fortnight owing to the lack of medium artillery to reduce it.

When Bonaparte eventually reached Ivrea on 26 May, he completely abandoned his original plan of marching on Genoa to relieve Massena, whose army was then at the point of starvation. Instead, he turned eastward and established himself for a week at Milan. He might, however, have left the occupation of Milan to Moncey's corps, which at that moment was crossing the St. Gotthard. Bonaparte himself could have marched on Turin and defeated Melas, who was there with only two divisions, Keim's and Haddick's, in all 8600 men, for the other Austrian divisions were either engaged with Suchet at Nice, 130 miles away, or investing Massena at Genoa, 115 miles away. Alternatively, he could have safely ignored Melas at Turin and marched south to relieve Genoa. With a callous disregard for the fate of Massena's army, Bonaparte remained at Milan for a week, devoting his attention to occupying the Po crossings between Pavia and Cremona, in order to stop all the escape routes by which Melas could bolt back to Mantua. This in itself was a wise precaution, but it could have been effected equally well by the divisions of Moncey's corps (7700), then in the Milan area, instead of employing Duhesme's corps for the purpose. The result was that Bonaparte was left without any tactical reserve in the final encounter at Marengo. Had he relieved Duhesme's corps of its secondary role, he would have had the divisions of Chabran (3400) and Loison (5300) available as a reserve on the day of battle.

On the day before the battle Bonaparte was rash enough to send away his ablest corps commander, Desaix, and one of his strongest divisions (5300) on a wild-goose chase to the south, based on a wrong guess as to Melas's intentions; on the very day of the battle he despatched Lapoype's division (3500) on a reconnaissance in the opposite direction. Consequently, at noon on the day of the crucial battle he had left himself with no army reserve, and would have been defeated if Desaix had not turned up in the nick of time.

The lack of infantry reserves at Marengo was paralleled by the inadequacy of the French artillery support. Before the arrival of Boudet's division at 5 p.m. Marmont had only been able to get 15 guns into action in support of four infantry divisions, which were being attacked by an overwhelming weight of artillery. This deficiency seems quite inexcusable, considering the number of guns which the French had captured in the arsenals at Milan, Pavia and Piacenza.*

The French cavalry, consisting of four brigades and a reserve brigade in Murat's hands, was also used on the whole ineffectively. Murat attached a cavalry brigade to each infantry corps, but these got engaged in the infantry battle and produced little result until the end of the day, when Kellermann made his gallant charge near Cassina Grossa to add the *coup de grâce* to Desaix's counter-attack. The French official account states that on 13 June:

All the light cavalry of the French army received the order to scour the plain. The army followed, but only with the purpose of discovering the enemy's intentions, and without thinking of fighting a serious battle in the Marengo plain.

The results of these reconnaissances were completely negative. Bonaparte would have done better to have sent a cavalry brigade instead of Boudet's division to Serravalle, and another north of the Po instead of Lapoype's division.

One can hardly study the events of the Marengo campaign without being struck by the inefficiency of Bonaparte's intelligence service. He never seemed able to estimate correctly either the location, strength or intentions of the Austrian commander, in spite of the fact that he was operating in a country which had been occupied by French troops four years earlier. An Austrian source† alleges that Bonaparte was deceived by a double agent planted on him by Zach, the Austrian Chief of Staff, who led him to believe that Melas was preparing to cross the Po at Valenza and Casale in order to outflank the

---

* Bonaparte's gunner A.D.C., Colonel Lauriston, had on 4 June discovered 30 field-guns and 35 limbers at Pavia; 39 field-guns on their carriages were found at Milan.
† *Österreichische Militärische Zeitschrift*, XXIX. 137–139.

French at Pavia. This would account for Bonaparte's sending Lapoype's division across the Po on 14 June and diverting Rivaud's cavalry brigade to Salé. When Massena finally capitulated at Genoa on 4 June, Bonaparte at Milan did not hear the news until the 8th, and then only from a despatch sent by Melas to Vienna, intercepted by Murat at Piacenza.

One may deduce that Bonaparte learnt many useful lessons from the Marengo campaign, for never again do we find him engaging the enemy without adequate reserves of infantry and artillery. In future campaigns he used his light cavalry extensively for reconnaissance, keeping his heavy cavalry massed for shock tactics. He also took care to organize an efficient intelligence service.

The First Consul was fortunate in having as his opponent the lethargic, 71-year-old Baron Melas. A tougher and quicker witted enemy might have punished his mistakes more severely.

IX

Consulate to Empire
1800–1805

The battle of Marengo had been converted by a hair's breadth from a defeat into a victory, but it proved decisive so far as the war on the Italian front was concerned; the Austrian forces were withdrawn to the east of the Ádige in accordance with the terms of the Convention of Alessándria. But this armistice did not apply to the German theatre of war, where Moreau's Army of the Rhine faced the Austrians under the Archduke Charles and Kray in the Black Forest. On 19 June Moreau crossed the Danube at Höchstädt and inflicted a severe defeat on Kray, after which he occupied Augsburg and Munich. In the following month hostilities in that theatre were temporarily brought to an end by the Convention of Parsdorf.

But, as Britain still remained undefeated, and as Austria was pledged not to sign a separate peace before February 1801, the political situation was complicated and the peace negotiations dragged on. The French position was rendered difficult by the fact that the Army of Egypt, which Bonaparte had abandoned in that country, was still isolated there, although in no immediate danger, for on 20 March Kléber had decisively defeated the Grand Vizir's army at Heliopolis. On the day of Marengo, however, Kléber had been assassinated in Cairo, and the command of the army had devolved on Menou, a less forceful leader. Communication with Egypt was further hampered by Lord Keith's capture of Malta in September. Exasperated by these set-backs and delays, on 5 November Bonaparte ordered his Army Commanders to break the armistices on both fronts and resume hostilities (*Corr.* 5161).

Bonaparte had now four armies in the field: one in Italy of 70,000, Moreau's on the Danube (100,000), a new reserve army in Switzerland under Macdonald (14,000) and a Gallo-Batavian army (14,000) under Augereau on the lower Rhine at Mainz. In August he had removed Massena from command of the Army of Italy for alleged maladministration of his army funds, and had replaced him by the less competent Brune. When hostilities were renewed at the end of November, Moreau took the initiative on 3 December and inflicted a crushing defeat on the inept Archduke John at Hohenlinden. This resulted in the armistice of Steyr three weeks later, when hostilities ceased on the Danube front.

On the Italian front Brune displayed his usual lack of energy and made little progress, but Bonaparte ordered Macdonald to cross the Splügen Pass in midwinter, a feat which he accomplished successfully, and pushed on through the Trentino to Bolzano. This resulted in the armistice of Treviso, and eventually, on 9 February 1801, a definitive peace treaty between France and Austria was signed at Lunéville.

The Peace of Lunéville brought to an end the Second Coalition against France. The territorial settlements were much the same as those enacted by the Treaty of Campo-Formio in 1797: France retained Belgium and the left bank of the Rhine; in Italy, Austria as compensation was given the territory of Venetia as far west as the Ádige. Lombardy became the Italian Republic, to which were added the Duchies of Parma, Módena and Tuscany. The Batavian, Helvetian, Italian and Ligurian Republics were recognized as nominally independent States, but were in reality subject to French domination.

Austria being out of the war, Bonaparte had now only Britain to contend with, but here he was baffled by British supremacy at sea. Abercromby's victory at Alexandria in March 1801 resulted in the final evacuation of Egypt by the French in the autumn, thus finally shattering Bonaparte's dreams of oriental expansion. The assassination of Tsar Paul on 23 March and Nelson's destruction of the Danish fleet at Copenhagen on 2 April combined to frustrate the league of northern States which Bonaparte was trying to organize to injure British commerce. He therefore turned to the consolidation of his own position in France and to reorganize the financial and economic resources of the country.

Bonaparte's seat in the saddle was indeed none too secure. The arbitrary manner in which he had usurped power after the *coup d'état* of Brumaire had antagonized a great number of Frenchmen. There were two distinct currents of popular opinion opposed to him: firstly, the Royalists, who looked for the return of the legitimate Bourbon dynasty in the person of the exiled Comte de Provence, brother of the late King. The Royalist movement was particularly strong in the south of France and in the north-west. In the latter region (La Vendée) the *chouans* were in open rebellion and were being ruthlessly repressed. In September 1800 Bonaparte had written to the Comte de Provence: 'You need not think of returning to France; you would have to walk over 100,000 corpses' (*Corr.* 5090).

In order to conciliate the more conservative elements in the country, Bonaparte decided to come to terms with the Roman Catholic Church, which had been disestablished and despoiled by the Revolution. He was not himself religious-minded, indeed he was an agnostic, but he had great psychological perception, and he realized that the Church could still sway popular sentiment. There were still 40,000 parish priests in France, and these exerted a powerful influence on the minds of the people. A new Pope, Pius VII, had been elected in March 1800 in succession to Pius VI, who had been so roughly treated by the Directory in 1798 and ejected from Rome. In July 1801 Bonaparte concluded with the new Pope a Concordat, by which the Catholic Church was officially re-established in France as a Department of State under government control.

Bonaparte's arbitrary seizure of power had also offended the extreme Republicans, or Jacobins, who regarded his autocratic rule as a negation of all the principles for which the Revolutionary armies had fought. The Jacobins were roused to indignation by the Concordat, which in their eyes was a reaction against the precepts of the Revolution, and foreshadowed a return to the *ancien régime*. On Christmas Eve, 1800, an attempt had been made to assassinate Bonaparte by means of a time-bomb as he was going to the theatre. The plot was found to have been hatched by Royalist agents, but Bonaparte made it an excuse to seize and deport some of his most violent Jacobin opponents as well.

Bonaparte's firm rule quickly re-established law and order. He effected many administrative reforms and restored the financial and economic stability of the country, so that his autocratic régime was generally accepted. After hard and protracted negotiations with the British Government, peace terms were finally agreed and the Treaty of Amiens was signed on 25 March 1802.

By a Consular Decree of 19 May Bonaparte instituted the Legion of Honour for outstanding services to the nation, in replacement of the orders of chivalry formerly awarded by the French monarchs, and abolished by the Revolution. This innovation provoked criticism, as it seemed at variance with the spirit of *égalité* which had been one of the Revolutionary slogans. There is, however, no doubt that the creation of the Legion increased the First

Consul's popularity with the army and civil service, particularly the former. The first list of *Légionnaires*, which was not issued until 18 months later, contained 2238 names, of which only 104 were civilians.

The conclusion of peace with Austria and Britain, which left France with such a dominating position in Europe, greatly enhanced Bonaparte's prestige, and at the beginning of August 1802 he was nominated as Consul for life, though not without a certain amount of opposition. Many dyed-in-the-wool Republican Generals, such as Carnot, Massena and Moreau, voted against the measure.

The Peace of Amiens was not to be of long duration. It soon became obvious that the French ruler was employing every means to tighten his stranglehold on the whole European Continent. In September 1802 he incorporated Piedmont into France without compensating the King of Sardinia, as he had promised, and he also annexed the island of Elba; in particular, he irritated the British Government by refusing to evacuate Holland. In December 1802 he clearly exposed his attitude towards Swiss neutrality in an address which he made to a Swiss deputation in Paris:

So far as France is concerned, Switzerland must be French, like all other countries contiguous to France. (*Corr.* 6483)

The Swiss were forced to accept this position under threat of an invasion by General Ney with a force of 14 battalions. Bonaparte followed this up by intervening in the constitution of Switzerland, and in February 1803, on the pretext of terminating internal Swiss political feuds, he established effective control of that country by an 'Act of Mediation'.

Under the terms of the Treaty of Amiens the British were obliged to evacuate Malta, which was to be handed back to the Knights of St. John, protected by a Neapolitan garrison. Pitt, very prudently, refused to evacuate Malta so long as France's expansion beyond her natural frontiers continued, although, in fact, nothing had been said about this in the Treaty of Amiens. On 11 March Bonaparte wrote to the Tsar of Russia and to the King of Prussia, denouncing the British failure to evacuate Malta and seeking their support. On the same day he ordered the formation of two 'national flotillas', consisting of 520 landing craft, at Dunkirk and Cherbourg (*Corr.* 6628). On the 13th he wrote to his Minister of Marine, Vice-Admiral Decrès:

I want a memorandum on how we can inflict the greatest damage on British commerce in the event of a naval war now. (*Corr.* 6632)

On the same day he had a violent altercation with Lord Whitworth, the British Ambassador; it was quite obvious that he was bent on provoking hostilities, and his frame of mind was well described by the French historian Thiers:

> Now all of a sudden he was mastered by a patriotic and at the same time personal wrath, and from now on to conquer, humiliate, trample down and annihilate England became the passion of his life. (*Thiers*, I. 460b)

On 12 May Lord Whitworth left Paris, and on the 16th Britain declared war. Bonaparte now saw himself in the guise of a Roman ruler, with Britain as Carthage.

Already on 15 March Bonaparte had mobilized the French Navy, and on 12 April he ordered Berthier to have the whole Channel coast, from the Somme estuary to the mouth of the Scheldt, put in a state of instant readiness. On 29 May, after Britain's declaration of war, he ordered the Minister of Marine to design a flat-bottomed barge capable of transporting 100 men; on 3 June he ordered the keels of 21 new ships-of-the-line (64 or 74 guns) to be laid down, and on the 14th he ordered the formation along the Channel and Atlantic coasts of six camps, each to train an army corps in embarkation manœuvres.

From June onwards the pace of these preparations was accelerated. Bonaparte spent the first week of July in reconnoitring on horseback the Channel coast from the mouth of the Somme to Dunkirk, and then spent three weeks in Belgium. As a result of this study tour he evolved his invasion plan. The operation would be launched from two main harbours, Boulogne and Étaples; two subsidiary harbours were to be constructed at Ambleteuse and Wimereux, north of Boulogne. Four invasion camps were to be formed, each to take an army corps, at Utrecht (Marmont), Bruges (Davout), St. Omer (Soult), and Montreuil (Ney); a fifth camp (Augereau) was to be formed at Brest for a subsidiary landing in Ireland. A flotilla of 2000 landing craft was to be constructed in all the North Sea and Channel ports and assembled in the four invasion harbours under the command of Vice-Admiral Bruix at Boulogne. These landing craft were to be of three types:

> *chaloupe canonnière*, carrying 30 crew and 90 soldiers.
> *bateau canonnier*, carrying 25 crew and 55 soldiers.
> *péniche* carrying 10 crew and 66 soldiers.

They were to be organized in divisions, each of 27 boats, and each boat was to be armed with one or more 24-pounder guns. The troops were constantly practised in embarking and disembarking, and all soldiers were taught to row.

In November Bonaparte spent another fortnight at Boulogne to push forward the preparations and to supervise the training of the troops. On the 16th he wrote to his fellow Consul, Cambacérès:

> From the cliffs of Ambleteuse I could clearly see the English coast. . . . It is a ditch which one can jump whenever one is bold enough to try it. (*Corr.* 7279)

On returning to Paris, he wrote to his senior Flag Officer at Toulon, Admiral Ganteaume:

> I hope to have at Boulogne in the first week of January 300 gun-sloops, 500 gun-boats, and 500 pinnaces; each sloop carries three 24-pounders, each boat one 24-pounder, and each pinnace a 36-pounder howitzer. Give me your opinion about this flotilla. Do you think it will carry us to the shores of Albion? It can transport 100,000 men. Eight hours of darkness with suitable weather would decide the fate of the universe. (*Corr.* 7309)

The satellite Dutch Government was also forced, against its will, to contribute an additional invasion flotilla at Flushing and the Texel, comprising 400 boats capable of transporting a force of 60,000 men.

The invasion operation depended on the Channel being kept clear of the British Navy for at least 12 hours, preferably during darkness. Bonaparte's original plan was that on 11 January 1804 one naval squadron would break out from Toulon heading for Egypt, and another from Rochefort heading for Ireland; these would lead the British blockading squadrons under Nelson and Cornwallis on a false scent in opposite directions, while a third squadron would sail up the Channel from Brest to escort the invasion force. Bonaparte hoped to launch the operation on 20 February while the nights were still long. On 7 December he consulted Admiral Ganteaume about the feasibility of this plan, adding:

> On 20 February I shall be at Boulogne with 130,000 men in 2,000 boats. . . . Our only four ports will be Étaples, Boulogne, Wimereux and Ambleteuse, all close together; if the wind is favourable we shall only want the squadron for 12 hours. (*Corr.* 7359)

On 1 January 1804 Bonaparte visited Boulogne, where he made a thorough inspection of the flotilla and reviewed the troops. On 1 February he wrote to Davout, commanding the Bruges camp: 'The time approaches when operations will start.' But a week later the whole invasion plan was interrupted by the discovery of an amazing conspiracy, organized by the Royalists in exile, to kidnap the First Consul on his way from Paris to St. Cloud or Malmaison. Three parties, of about 40 in all, had landed by night from England between Le Tréport and Dieppe. They were led by General Pichegru, who had been deported to Cayenne after the *coup d'état* of 18 Fructidor in September 1797, and had escaped to join the Royalists. Fourteen of the conspirators were rounded up by Bonaparte's secret police on 13 February, Pichegru was arrested in Paris on 28 February, and another ringleader, Georges Cadoudal, was captured on 9 March. To avenge this attempt on his person, on 10 March Bonaparte ordered a squadron of 300 dragoons to cross the Rhine by night, invade the neutral territory of Baden and kidnap the young Duc d'Enghien, grandson of the Prince de Condé, the former Commander-in-Chief of the *émigré* Royalist forces. The unfortunate young officer was imprisoned in the Château de Vincennes, tried by a summary military court, and sentenced to death for bearing arms against his country. He was executed on 21 March. Pichegru died mysteriously in prison; Cadoudal and the other conspirators were executed. General Moreau, the hero of Höchstädt and Hohenlinden, who was suspected of having been in touch with Pichegru, was arrested on 19 February but, as no proof of his guilt could be found, he was banished; he later joined the Allies.* Bonaparte and Moreau had always disliked each other.

Thoroughly alarmed by this extensive plot, the First Consul decided that he must consolidate his personal authority in a more definite way by establishing a hereditary monarchy. After carefully preparing the ground, on 18 May he had himself proclaimed Emperor of the French, with the title of Napoléon Ier. Seven months later his coronation took place in the Cathedral of Notre Dame de Paris in the presence of the Pope.

On the day following his proclamation as Emperor in May, Napoleon awarded to 18 of his leading Generals the honorific title of *Maréchal de l'Empire*, a revival of the *Maréchaux de France* of the *ancien régime*. Of these, 14 were on the active list, while four others, between the ages of 50 and 69, were considered unsuitable for active employment.† The oldest of the active Marshals, Berthier, was 51, while the youngest, Davout, was 34. The title of Marshal carried an additional annual allowance of £1600.

After the distractions caused by the February plot and by his elevation to imperial status, Napoleon resumed active preparations for his grand design of invading England. Success, of course, depended on the Channel being kept clear of the British Navy for several days of suitable weather. The French, however, were handicapped by the superiority of the Royal Navy in numbers and seamanship, and their squadrons were closely blockaded in their home ports at Toulon, Rochefort and Brest. By an alliance with Spain on 9 October 1803 Napoleon had added 32 Spanish ships-of-the-line to his

* General Jean-Victor-Marie Moreau (1763–1813) was an able commander. He had commanded the Army of the Rhine and Moselle in 1795, the Army of Italy in 1799, and the Army of the Rhine in 1800. He joined the Allies in 1813, but was killed at the battle of Dresden.

† See Appendix for a nominal roll of all Marshals created by Napoleon.

own fleet, and this imposed a further strain on the Royal Navy, which had also to watch the harbours of Cartagena, Cadiz and Ferrol.

Napoleon now conceived a new plan for luring the British fleet away from the Channel to leave it clear for the invasion operation. Admiral Latouche-Tréville with the Mediterranean squadron (10 ships) was to evade Nelson's blockade in foggy weather, slip past Gibraltar, pick up six more ships at Rochefort and cross the Atlantic to the West Indies, whither Nelson would doubtless pursue him. After reinforcing the French islands of Martinique and Guadeloupe with fresh troops and stores, the Mediterranean squadron would sail back to Ferrol and Brest, combine with the French and Spanish squadrons there and proceed up the Channel to cover the invasion. This final phase of the operation was timed to take place in September. On 2 July Napoleon wrote to Latouche-Tréville:

Think over the great enterprise which you are to carry out. Tell me your plan before I sign your orders. Rochefort has five ships-of-the-line and four frigates ready to sail. At Étaples, Boulogne, Wimereux and Ambleteuse we have 1,800 landing craft, 120,000 men and 10,000 horses. If we are masters of the Channel for six hours, we shall be masters of the world. If you hoodwink Nelson, he will sail to Sicily, Egypt or Ferrol. You should leave by 29 July, sail round the north of Ireland and arrive off Boulogne in September. (*Corr.* 7832)

On the following day he sent detailed instructions to Vice-Admiral Bruix, commanding the invasion flotilla at Boulogne; the landing craft were to be distributed as follows:

		boats	battalions
Right wing:	Ambleteuse	300	(Dutch): 32
Reserve wing:	Wimereux:	180	12
Centre wing:	Boulogne	540	52
Left wing:	Étaples	180	16
		1200	112

In addition, there would be 625 transports carrying horses and guns, of which 75 would sail from Calais (*Corr.* 7840).

On 19 July the Emperor went himself to Boulogne and spent the next six weeks on the Channel coast, supervising the training of the troops, distributing awards of the Legion of Honour and rehearsing embarkation exercises. On 26 July he reviewed the whole flotilla, and on the following day wrote to Marshal Brune, his envoy at Constantinople:

I have with me here nearly 120,000 men and 3,000 landing craft, which only await a favourable wind to carry the Imperial Eagle to the Tower of London. (*Corr.* 7874)

The landing craft were waiting, however, not only for a favourable wind, but for the dispersal of the British squadrons blockading Brest, Rochefort and Toulon. Of these the most important was that of Admiral Sir William Cornwallis at the western approaches to the Channel, which maintained a close blockade of Brest. In the Mediterranean Nelson kept a looser control of Toulon, as his policy was to tempt the French squadron out and then destroy it on the open sea. Napoleon became increasingly impatient at the inactivity of his Admirals. At the end of May he had written to his Minister of Marine:

Admiral Truguet at Brest has been inactive and has made no attempt to force the English blockade. He must be replaced at once by a more active officer. (*Corr.* 7800)

But Truguet had already resigned his command, as he was a staunch Republican and did not approve of emperors. He was replaced by Ganteaume, three years younger, who was promoted to Vice-Admiral. It was Ganteaume who, five years earlier, had brought Bonaparte back from Egypt in the frigate *la Muiron*. Another change took place at Toulon, for the 59-year-old Latouche-Tréville died on 19 August and was replaced by the 41-year-old Villeneuve, who had escaped from Nelson's clutches at the Battle of the Nile in 1798.

The weeks wore on, but the French squadrons remained blockaded, and all hope of a September invasion vanished. On 6 September the Emperor evolved a new plan and wrote to Ganteaume at Brest:

If you and your squadron could make a sortie from Brest in Brumaire [23 Oct.–21 Nov.] and land 16,000 men and 500 horses in Ireland, it would deal a deadly stroke to our enemies. Discuss the landing places with the Irish General O'Connor. (*Corr.* 7996)

On 27 September he wrote to Berthier:

The Irish expedition is decided on. You will discuss it with Marshal Augereau. There is sufficient shipping at Brest for 18,000 men. Marmont, on his side, is ready with 25,000. He will try to land in Ireland and will be under Marshal Augereau's orders. The *Grande Armée* of Boulogne will embark simultaneously and will try to invade Kent. Tell Augereau that he must act according to circumstances. If the reports received from Irish refugees and from the agents I have sent to Ireland are confirmed, a large number of Irishmen will join him when he lands; he must then march on Dublin. The navy hopes to be ready by 22 October. (*Corr.* 8048)

Two days later Napoleon's fertile brain produced a still more complicated naval enterprise for his blockaded squadrons. On 29 September he wrote to his harassed Minister of Marine, Vice-Admiral Decrès:

> We must send off three expeditions: from Rochefort, to secure Martinique and Guadeloupe against enemy action and seize Dominica and St. Lucia; from Toulon, to capture Surinam and the other Dutch colonies; from Brest, to capture St. Helena. The Toulon squadron might sail on 10 October, the Rochefort one on 1 November and the Brest one on 22 November. (*Corr.* 8057)

But the Emperor still had the Irish expedition in mind, for on the same day he wrote another letter to Decrès:

> I agree to the place you suggest for the landing; I think the north and Lough Swilly Bay is the best place. . . . The landing in Ireland is only the first act. The squadron must then enter the English Channel and sail to Cherbourg to get news of the Boulogne army. If, on arriving off Boulogne, it meets with several days of contrary winds, it must go on to the Texel, where it will find seven Dutch ships with 25,000 men embarked. It will convoy them to Ireland. One of the two operations must succeed; whether I have 30,000 or 40,000 men in Ireland, whether I am in England or in Ireland, we shall have won the war. (*Corr.* 8063)

But, with all this confused thinking and planning, the French squadrons remained harbour-bound throughout the autumn. On 23 December the Emperor wrote impatiently to Decrès: 'The season is already well advanced and every hour lost is irreparable' (*Corr.* 8231).

He had indeed already made his final plan for the naval operations which were to enable the invasion of England to be launched in the spring or summer of 1805. Villeneuve was to break out from Toulon, eluding Nelson, and sail for the West Indies; at the same time Rear-Admiral Missiessy was to break out from Rochefort and join Villeneuve at Martinique. This would disperse the British squadrons, which would pursue them across the Atlantic. The two French squadrons would then give their pursuers the slip and double back to Brest, where they would release Ganteaume's squadron. The combined French fleet would then sail up the Channel and clear the Straits for the Boulogne invasion flotilla.

In accordance with this plan, Missiessy broke out from Rochefort on 4 January 1805 and reached Martinique successfully. Villeneuve broke out from Toulon on 18 January, but encountered a bad storm and had to put back to port three days later to repair his battered ships. This infuriated the Emperor, who then played his last naval card. On 2 March he ordered Ganteaume to break out from Brest with 21 ships-of-the-line and six frigates; he was to proceed to Ferrol, where he would pick up four more ships and two frigates, as well as a Spanish squadron. Ganteaume was then to sail to Martinique and take under his flag the Toulon and Rochefort squadrons, in all 40 ships-of-the-line, with which he would sail back to Ushant, defeat Cornwallis's squadron and arrive off Boulogne between 10 June and 10 July, where Napoleon would be waiting for him. On 24 March Ganteaume reported that he was ready to sail, but that there were 15 British ships waiting for him outside the anchorage.

At last, spurred on by the Emperor's repeated orders, Villeneuve broke out from Toulon on 30 March with 11 ships-of-the-line and eight frigates. He was lucky enough to elude Nelson's squadron, and passed Gibraltar on 8 April. On the following day at Cadiz he picked up another French ship and six Spanish ships, and succeeded in reaching Martinique on 14 May with 18 ships. Meanwhile Missiessy, instead of waiting for him, had returned to Rochefort on 20 May. Nelson, delayed by contrary winds, eventually tracked Villeneuve across the Atlantic and back again, but without catching up with him. Villeneuve's subsequent manœuvres ended with his disastrous defeat at Trafalgar five months later.

While the Emperor impatiently awaited the outcome of his naval plans, other events were developing on the Continent. On 11 April the Tsar of Russia signed a treaty of alliance with Britain. This was kept so secret that when Fouché, the Minister of Police, reported it to Napoleon on 29 May, the latter refused to believe it. He proceeded, however, to strengthen his grip on the Continent. On 26 May he crowned himself King of Italy with the iron crown of Lombardy, once worn by Charlemagne. A fortnight later he delegated the government of Italy to his 23-year-old stepson, Eugène Beauharnais, as Viceroy. On 4 June Napoleon annexed the Republic of Genoa, incorporating it in his Kingdom of Italy. This continuous expansion of the French Empire in Europe thoroughly alarmed the Austrians, who began to prepare for a war of revenge and entered into secret negotiations with Russia.

Napoleon spent the whole month of June in Italy, consolidating his hold on that country, but all the time waiting anxiously for news of his naval expeditions. On 14 June he wrote to his Minister of Marine:

I have no idea where Nelson is, I think he must have returned either to England or to the Mediterranean. His ships are not capable of making a long voyage. (*Corr.* 8892)

Nelson at that time was off Trinidad, looking for Villeneuve. On 27 June Napoleon wrote to Decrès from Parma:

My intention is that after 9 July the Dutch squadron at the Texel will make a sortie and return, and that on 20 July the whole army will embark and remain on board. Certainly 30,000 men embarked, which has never been done before. (*Corr.* 8955)

On the following day he wrote to Berthier from Piacenza:

Keep an eye on everything—rations, brandy, boots, and all embarkation details. Embark plenty of artillery accessories, you know one is always short of them in war. I shall have to besiege Dover Castle, Chatham and perhaps Portsmouth. . . . Order my Guard Artillery to move from La Fère to Wimereux; it will do if they are there by 14 July. (*Corr.* 8957)

On 12 July Napoleon returned from Italy to Fontainebleau, but there was still no word of his fleet movements. On 18 July he wrote to Decrès:

Why has Ganteaume not made a dash from Brest? He should sail up the Channel to his objective. (*Corr.* 8991)

Two days later he wrote to Berthier:

No British warships have been seen off Brest for five days. Embark at once all the artillery powder and ammunition so that the expedition can start at 24 hours' notice. My intention is to land at four places close together. Ney, Soult, Davout and the Reserve Corps must each detail a Brigadier and some officers to embark in pinnaces to make the first landing. Tell the four Marshals that there is not a minute to lose. (*Corr.* 8996)

On 26 July Napoleon despatched the following order to Villeneuve:

Pick up the Spanish warships at Cadiz and Ferrol and arrive off Brest; from there proceed to Boulogne, where you must gain mastery of the Straits for three days only, when, with God's help, I shall terminate England's existence.

150,000 men are embarked at Boulogne, Étaples, Wimereux and Ambleteuse in 2000 landing craft, anchored in a continuous line from Étaples to Cap Grisnez. Your voyage alone, with luck, will make us masters of England. (*Corr.* 9022)

On 2 August the Emperor left Paris for Boulogne, where he remained for a whole month. On the 9th he at last heard the result of Villeneuve's trans-atlantic excursion. It was not good news. On 9 June Villeneuve had left the West Indies with 20 ships-of-the-line and headed for Ferrol to fulfil his mission. On 22 July he ran into Admiral Sir Robert Calder's weaker squadron of 15 ships off Cape Finisterre. It was a misty day and an indecisive action took place, in which Villeneuve lost two Spanish ships and eventually sought refuge in Ferrol. That finally extinguished all chance that remained of the invasion of England being launched. On 22 August the Emperor wrote to Decrès:

I consider that Villeneuve has not the character to command even a frigate. He is a man without resolution or moral courage. (*Corr.* 9112)

However, the Emperor refused to acknowledge failure; on the same day he sent a final instruction to Villeneuve:

Sail; do not lose a moment; enter the Channel with my assembled squadrons; England is ours. We are all ready, everything is embarked. Show yourself for 24 hours and all is over. (*Corr.* 9115)

He wrote this under the impression that Villeneuve had reached Brest, whereas he had sought safety at Ferrol. On the following day Napoleon decided to cancel the invasion plan, as he knew that he was now threatened by a coalition of the Austrian and Russian Empires, and that he must strike quickly before they joined forces. On 23 August he wrote to Berthier:

Tell General Marmont that my Ferrol squadron sailed on 14 August. If it arrives, I shall carry on with the expedition. If contrary winds or the lack of boldness of my Admirals detain it at Cadiz, I shall postpone the operation till another year. My intention is that, within 24 hours of receiving his new orders, he will disembark and return to his camps. He must then march for Mainz as secretly and rapidly as possible. I want to be in the heart of Germany with 300,000 men before anybody knows about it. (*Corr.* 9120)

Thus finally collapsed the great invasion plan, to which for two and a half years Napoleon had devoted so much effort, time and expense. He ascribed its failure to the incompetence and timidity of his Admirals. They were not a very brilliant lot, but they were neither incompetent nor cowardly. Masterly as he was at handling troops in the field, Napoleon never grasped the technique of naval warfare, nor did he sufficiently appreciate the factors of wind, tide and weather, by which naval operations are limited. Sir Julian Corbett has well summed up the Emperor's attempt to manœuvre his scattered squadrons in the face of British sea-power:

Englishmen with judgment unoppressed by the Napoleonic legend will see in it the work of a self-confident amateur in naval warfare, the blindness of a great soldier to the essential differences between land and sea strategy, and something perhaps of the exasperated despot who refused to own himself beaten (*The Campaign of Trafalgar*, 1910, pp. 41–42).

X

Ulm and Austerlitz
1805

The summer of 1805 saw Napoleon approaching the zenith of his military career, a career which was to end so disastrously ten years later. This may therefore be an appropriate place to analyse briefly his military achievements so far.

The first Italian campaign of 1796, opening with Bonaparte's swift defeat of the combined Piedmontese and Austrian forces, was a masterpiece of offensive strategy. Acting on interior lines, he drove a wedge between his allied opponents, whose combined strength was greater than his own; he then crushed each of their divided groups by rapid alternate blows. Following up this initial success with a ruthless pursuit, he won the spectacular, though perhaps unnecessary victory of Lodi. Later, when thrown on the defensive by the weight of superior numbers, he rapidly returned to the offensive, having seized the opportunity afforded by a temporary separation of Wurmser's forces; this gave him the victory of Castiglione in early August. Another ruthless pursuit of a beaten enemy brought about the victory of Bassano in the following month. The defensive struggle at Árcole was turned into a victory by the skilful switching of his reserve divisions.

The successes of 1797 were no less dramatic. The campaign opened in mid-winter with a hard-fought defensive battle, which was crowned with victory by the brilliant tactical counterstroke at Rivoli, followed by the swift strategic switch to Mantua. A relentless pursuit for 400 miles brought the victorious Army of Italy to within 100 miles of the enemy's capital.

The Egyptian expedition of 1798 was carried out under very different conditions. The tactical training and equipment of the enemy was of medieval standard, but the physical hardships of desert warfare in an arid climate called for improvisations in organization, training and tactics which Bonaparte effected with marked success. No less remarkable was the moral ascendancy which he exerted over his officers and men, and the supreme confidence with which he inspired them in the face of appalling physical privations. The disembarkation of the troops at Alexandria, it is true, was badly organized and would have led to disaster had it been opposed by an efficient European enemy. The subsequent administration of a conquered Oriental country undoubtedly developed Bonaparte's organizational capacity and prepared him for the larger task ahead of governing the French nation. His rash advance to Acre, however, was a strategic error which was punished with failure.

The Marengo campaign of 1800, though brilliantly conceived as a strategic manœuvre, nearly failed owing to the neglect of reconnaissance and to faulty tactical planning. The decisive battle revealed uncertain leadership on the part of the First Consul; he deserved to lose it, for he had retained no tactical reserve with which to influence the combat, and his front-line infantry were given most inadequate artillery support; nor had he retained any cavalry reserve with which to follow up his victory. Marengo was a lucky win, gained mainly through the ineptitude of his opponent. Bonaparte's conduct of the battle of Marengo compares unfavourably with the swift decision and tactical skill which he displayed in his earlier Italian campaigns.

We can now turn to the events of 1805. On 9 August Austria joined Britain and Russia in the Third Coalition to prevent French domination of the Continent. Napoleon was then at Boulogne with his huge invasion flotilla and the *Grande Armée* was ready to embark, awaiting the arrival of the combined squadrons of Villeneuve and Ganteaume to clear the Straits of Dover for the crossing. He was, however, already aware of the trouble brewing in his rear; on 31 July he had written to his Foreign Minister, Talleyrand:

> The information I get from Italy points to war, and indeed Austria barely conceals it. Prepare a note for Monsieur de Cobenzl [the Austrian Ambassador], to be handed to him at the right moment; this note should be sweet and reasonable. (*Corr.* 9032)

Napoleon was still anxious to strike a mortal blow at England before tackling his Continental enemies, but on 9 August he learnt that Villeneuve's squadron, on returning from the West Indies, had on 22 July been intercepted by Calder off Ferrol, and that Ganteaume had not yet left Brest. His hopes of

launching the invasion began to fade. On 12 August he wrote to Talleyrand:

> Tell Monsieur Cobenzl that I await his reply. If I don't get it, I shall invade
> Switzerland and strike my Ocean camps; that I won't be put off with words; that
> I won't allow any army in the Tyrol, and that the Austrian troops must return to
> their garrisons; otherwise I shall go to war. (*Corr.* 9069)

This in itself was a crafty bit of deception, as it led the Austrians to believe
that the main French attack would come through Italy. On the following
day he wrote to Cambacérès:

> Austria is arming; I wish it to disarm; if it does not do so, with 200,000 men I
> shall pay a visit which it will remember a long time. Austria would be mad to go to war
> with me. There is no better army in Europe than the one I have today. (*Corr.* 9069)

However, he remained at Boulogne in the hope that, at the eleventh hour,
his fleet might still turn up. Finally, on 23 August, he abandoned the invasion plan and decided to attack Austria before the Russian reinforcements
could arrive. On that day he wrote to Talleyrand:

> The more I reflect on the European situation, the more I feel it urgent to take
> decisive action. By April, I shall find 100,000 Russians in Poland, paid by England,
> 15 or 20 thousand English in Malta, and 15,000 Russians in Corfu. I should then
> be in a critical situation. (*Corr.* 9120)

In order to crush Austria once and for all Napoleon was now determined
to occupy Vienna. There were two strategic corridors leading to the Austrian
capital, the valleys of the Danube and the Po. In his campaigns of 1796 and
1797 he had successfully advanced towards Vienna by the Po valley, and it
was again in that valley that he had defeated Melas at Marengo in 1800. In
order to prevent another victorious advance on this strategic axis, the
Austrian High Command had assembled an army of 95,000 men to hold the
Ádige frontier under the command of their best fighting commander, the
Archduke Charles, aged 34. Politically too, the Po valley was the more
important region for the Austrians, as they wished to regain possession of
Lombardy. To bar the Danube valley approach, the Austrians had concentrated another army of 60,000 on the line of the Inn, their frontier with
Bavaria, under the young and inexperienced Archduke Ferdinand, aged 24,
who had as his Chief of Staff the veteran General Mack, aged 53. As the result
of the Austro-Russian alliance, this army would be reinforced in October by
100,000 Russians who were advancing westwards through Poland and Moravia.

The Austrian plan of campaign was that the Archduke Charles would deal
with the French *Armée d'Italie*, which held the line of the Ádige from
Verona to its junction with the Po; simultaneously the Archduke Ferdinand

would advance by the upper Danube valley to the line of its tributary the Iller, in the hope of enlisting the support of the Elector of Bavaria with his useful army of 25,000. There the Austrians would be able to check any French advance until the arrival of the Russian army, which would give them a considerable superiority in numbers with which to invade France.

This was a sound enough plan, which Napoleon could only defeat by rapidity of movement and action. His main objective was to attack the Archduke Ferdinand in the Danube valley before the arrival of the Russians; at the same time he must pin down the Archduke Charles in the Po valley to prevent him from reinforcing the Danube front. On 23 August he decided to switch the whole *Grande Armée* of 176,000 men from the Channel coast by forced marches to the Danube, a distance of 500 miles, while the veteran Marshal Massena (47) was dug out of retirement and given command of the Army of Italy (65,000) to engage the Archduke Charles in front of Verona.

Napoleon was quick on the draw, and he lost not a moment in putting his plan into execution. The first measures to be taken were not only military but also political. On 24 August he despatched to Berlin General Duroc, his Grand Marshal of the Palace, to negotiate a secret treaty with the King of Prussia, in order to ensure Prussian neutrality in the coming campaign; in exchange he offered Hanover, which he had recently annexed. He then wrote personal letters to the Electors of Bavaria, Baden and Württemberg and to the Landgrave of Hesse-Darmstadt, inviting them with a combination of threats and bribes to become his allies, an offer which they somewhat reluctantly accepted. He thus obtained the right to use their territories as a battle ground, and gained a reinforcement of 40,000 men to his own army; of these, only the Bavarian contingent of 25,000 was of any considerable fighting value.

Having cleared the diplomatic terrain, Napoleon on the same day told Berthier to issue orders for the five independent cavalry divisions (21,000 sabres) to march by parallel roads to the Rhine, and hold the crossings of that river from Neuf Brisach to Strasbourg. These divisions would form the advanced guard of the *Grande Armée*. On the following day he sent off his brother-in-law Prince Murat, disguised as 'Colonel Beaumont', to make a rapid reconnaisance of the Palatinate, Bavaria and the Black Forest, and to report on the state of the roads and width of the rivers. Murat was to return to Strasbourg by 11 September, when he was to assume command of the *Grande Armée* until the Emperor's arrival; he would then take over command of the Cavalry Corps.

General Bertrand, Napoleon's senior Engineer Officer, was sent off to the same area to make a more detailed reconnaissance of all bridges, ferries and fords, taking special note of the nature of the banks of the Danube, Inn, Lech and Isar. General Savary, another trusted member of the Emperor's staff, was sent to make a similar reconnaissance of Württemberg territory. Berthier was then instructed to prepare a card-index showing every unit of the Austrian army, with its latest identified location, so that the Emperor could check the Austrian order of battle from day to day. Berthier had been a trained staff officer before Napoleon went to school, but this order is typical of the Emperor's attention to every minute detail of staff work.

On 26 August Napoleon instructed Berthier to issue march orders for the *Grande Armée*. The most northerly corps (I), Bernadotte's, which was occupying Hanover, was to start on 2 September and reach Göttingen on the 9th; Marmont's II Corps from Bruges was to reach Mainz on the 15th; both corps would then advance to Würzburg in the Palatinate, where they would join hands with the Bavarian contingent under General von Wrede. The III, IV, V and VI Corps were to march on 27 August, and by 26 September were to reach the Rhine crossings on a front of 80 miles between Strasbourg and Mannheim. The VII Corps (Augereau) at Brest, which had the longest distance to march, was to cross the Rhine at Neuf Brisach and occupy the Freiburg area in order to block the exits from the Black Forest.

The march of the *Grande Armée* from the Channel coast to the Rhine, a distance of 375 miles, is one of the great strategic moves in history; it recalls Marlborough's march from the Low Countries to the Danube a century earlier, but Napoleon's army was nine times more numerous than Marlborough's. The final march orders were issued from the Imperial Headquarters on 29 August. The *Grande Armée* was then organized as follows:

I Corps (Bernadotte)	2 divisions (each 9 battalions) 1 light cavalry division	15,000
II Corps (Marmont)	3 divisions 1 light cavalry division	20,000
III Corps (Davout)	3 divisions 1 light cavalry division	25,000
IV Corps (Soult)	3 divisions 1 light cavalry division	28,000
V Corps (Lannes)	3 divisions 1 light cavalry division	26,000
VI Corps (Ney)	3 divisions 1 light cavalry division	21,000
VII Corps (Augereau)	2 divisions	14,000
Imperial Guard (Bessières)	1 division, 2 cavalry regiments	6,000
Cavalry Corps (Murat)	5 cavalry divisions	21,000
Total: 20 divisions and 11 cavalry divisions with 286 field-guns		176,000

131

The landing craft assembled in the various invasion harbours were concentrated at Boulogne, and a bogus invasion army under Marshal Brune, consisting of the 3rd battalions of the line regiments, was left in the camps there in order to deter the British from attempting a landing. On 4 September the Emperor left Boulogne for Malmaison. The *Grande Armée* was already on the march; every corps, except Augereau's, reached the Rhine by 26 September.

The feeding and supply of this vast army presented a considerable administrative problem. Every man started with a bread or biscuit ration for four days; after that, units requisitioned supplies and forage from the countries they marched through; fortunately they were fertile ones, and the harvest had been gathered.

On 13 September Napoleon, while still in Paris, learnt that the Austrian army had crossed the Inn on the 10th and had invaded Bavaria. The Elector, Prince Maximilian Joseph, now Napoleon's ally, had withdrawn from Munich to Würzburg, where he and his army were in touch with Bernadotte's corps. A week later Murat reported that the Austrian army was approaching Ulm and was digging in on the line of the Iller, which joins the Danube at that fortress. This news was almost too good to be true, for by crossing the Danube below Ulm Napoleon would be able to interpose himself between the Austrians and their Russian allies; he would also cut their easiest line of communication with Vienna. His two right-hand corps (Lannes and Ney) had originally been ordered to march on Ulm; they were now directed to march by Stuttgart and Ludwigsburg to Heidenheim and Gundelfingen (north and north-east of Ulm) in order to locate the enemy's north flank. The I, II, III and IV Corps were to continue their advance south-eastwards, cross the Danube between Ingolstadt and Donauwörth, and march on Munich and Augsburg; they would thus be astride the main line of communication of the Austrian army and separate it from the approaching Russians.

The *Grande Armée* was now marching towards the Rhine frontier at the rate of 15 miles a day, and the Emperor had time to deal with other matters, such as naval strategy. On 13 September he wrote a long and unconvincing memorandum entitled 'My object in creating the Boulogne flotilla' (*Corr.* 9209). Having finally abandoned the invasion plan, on the 14th he sent fresh instructions to Villeneuve, commanding his main fleet of 32 French and Spanish ships-of-the-line, blockaded at Cadiz by the Royal Navy. Villeneuve was to break out and sail into the Mediterranean; after picking up another Spanish squadron at Cartagena, he was to sail to Naples and land French reinforcements there, after which he was to proceed to Toulon to refit (*Corr.*

9210). This disastrous order resulted, a month later, in the total destruction of Villeneuve's fleet by Nelson at Trafalgar. On the next day, however, having lost confidence in Villeneuve, he ordered him to hand over his command to Admiral Rosily. The latter only reached Madrid in time to hear that Villeneuve's fleet had been destroyed.*

In order to keep the rest of his navy usefully employed, on 17 September Napoleon ordered his Minister of Marine to send out half-a-dozen small naval expeditions to visit St. Helena, Martinique, Barbados, San Domingo, Jamaica, Cayenne, Senegal and Mauritius, in order to show the French flag, raid British commerce and 'ravage the shores of Ireland'. As all the French Atlantic harbours were effectively blockaded by the British Navy, these excursions never took place.

The campaign against Austria was now calling for the Emperor's undivided attention, and he ceased issuing wild directives to his harbour-bound navy. On 24 September he left Paris for Strasbourg to pursue the war on land, an element with which he was better acquainted.

Before leaving Paris Napoleon had already on 17 September issued orders for the heads of his columns to cross the Rhine on the 25th and advance south-eastwards to the upper Danube. His six northerly corps, preceded by Murat's Cavalry Corps, extended themselves across southern Germany on a front of 70 miles like the tentacles of a giant octopus, to seek out and enfold their prey (p. 128). Only near Ulm, where the Austrian commander, Mack, had established himself, was any resistance encountered.

The march from the Channel coast to the Rhine had been favoured with fine summer weather but, in the first week of October, as the French columns penetrated the Odenwald and the Suabian Jura, the rains came and the country became a sea of mud. On the extreme left flank, Bernadotte's I Corps and Wrede's Bavarians, who had assembled at Würzburg, advanced through Ansbach and Weissenburg, crossed the Danube at Ingolstadt and continued southward to Munich. In this march Bernadotte had somewhat brusquely violated the neutral Principality of Ansbach, which was Prussian territory. The Prussians were extremely annoyed, and Napoleon had to apologize profusely, and narrowly avoided throwing the King of Prussia into the arms of the Austrians.

Marmont's II Corps, which had crossed the Rhine at Mainz and also assembled at Würzburg, followed a parallel course to that of I Corps by Rothenburg and crossed the Danube at Neuburg; that bridge was also

---

* The unfortunate Admiral Villeneuve, after being taken prisoner at Trafalgar, was exchanged and returned to France in 1806. He received such a chilly reception that he committed suicide.

used by Davout's III Corps, which had crossed the Rhine near Mannheim. In the centre, Soult's IV Corps was directed to march through Heilbronn, parallel to III Corps, and after crossing the Danube at Donauwörth to continue southward to Augsburg. Ney's VI Corps and Lannes's V Corps, which had crossed the Rhine near Karlsruhe and Strasbourg respectively, had originally been directed on Ulm; as that fortress was now known to be held by the bulk of Mack's army, Ney and Lannes were diverted to a more northerly route through Stuttgart and Ludwigsburg, and ordered to cross the Danube at Dillingen, 25 miles down stream from Ulm.

The Emperor himself, having left Paris in the early morning of 24 September, reached Strasbourg two days later, where he found the Imperial Guard. He then moved his headquarters successively to Ludwigsburg, Gmünd, Aalen and Nördlingen, crossing the Danube at Donauwörth on 8 October, by which date the whole of the *Grande Armée* was on or across that river. The French being now firmly established astride the Austrian line of communications, the campaign had been virtually won before the fighting began.

In reality Mack was in command of the Austrian army, for the young Archduke Ferdinand was a mere figure-head. Mack was now in a hopeless position; he had never imagined that the French could envelop his right flank so swiftly, so he was still facing westwards on the river Iller, from which direction he expected the French to appear. On his right flank Kienmaier's corps was watching the Danube bridges between Ulm and Donauwörth. On 8 October Murat, supported by the corps of Marmont and Soult, drove Kienmaier southwards towards Munich. Murat then turned westward and at Wertingen (15 miles south-west of Donauwörth) encountered a strong division of 12 battalions under Auffenberg which Mack had sent up in support of Kienmaier. Murat at once attacked and drove back this force, taking 3800 prisoners. Bernadotte (I) then took up the pursuit of Kienmaier, entered Munich on 12 October and drove Kienmaier beyond the Inn at Wasserburg, causing him considerable loss.

Mack with some 50,000 men was now being constricted into the immediate neighbourhood of Ulm; the tentacles of the octopus were steadily throttling him (p. 135). Napoleon ordered Marmont (II) to move south to Augsburg and then west to the ridge overlooking the Iller south of Ulm. Davout (III) was moved south-east to Dachau (14 miles north-west of Munich) to act as a reserve and support Bernadotte (I) in case the Russians should arrive. Soult (IV) was to move south through Augsburg and ascend the Lech valley as far as Landsberg; he was then to swing west to Memmingen, cross the Iller and cut the communications of Ulm with the south. Lannes (V) and

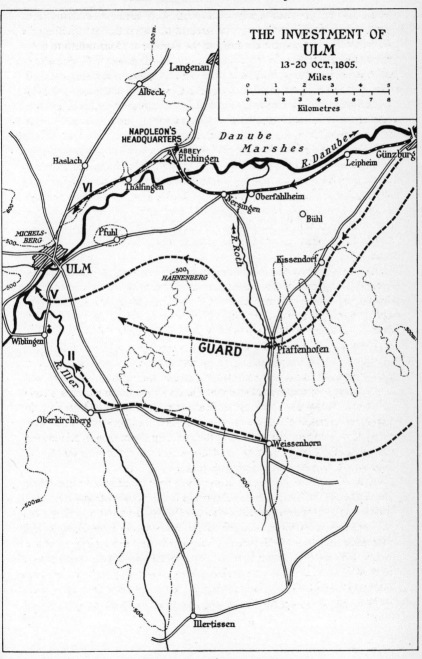

THE INVESTMENT OF
ULM
13-20 OCT., 1805.

Miles

0   1   2   3   4   5

0 1 2 3 4 5 6 7 8

Kilometres

Langenau

Albeck

NAPOLEON'S
HEADQUARTERS

Haslach

VI

Thalfingen

*Danube
Marshes*

ABBEY
Elchingen

R. Danube

Günzburg

Leipheim

Oberfahlheim

Nersingen

R. Roth

Bühl

MICHELS-
BERG

500

Pfuhl

Kissendorf

ULM

500
HAHNENBERG

V

500 m.

Wiblingen

II

R. Iller

GUARD

Pfaffenhofen

500 m.

Oberkirchberg

Weissenhorn

500 m.

500

Illertissen

Ney (VI) were to advance westwards on Ulm, following both banks of the Danube. The encirclement of Ulm would then be complete.

Napoleon knew that he had only to draw the noose tight to crush Mack, but he was also aware that the Russian army was marching through Moravia, and might reach Munich within a week or two. In order to be free to deal with any such fresh situation, on 12 October he placed his brother-in-law Murat in command of a task force to complete the destruction of Mack's army at Ulm. Murat, in addition to his own Cavalry Corps, was given the two corps of Lannes and Ney. Lannes was to advance up the right bank of the Danube and Ney up the left bank, so as to close the ring round the doomed fortress. His final directive to Murat, written on the 12th from Augsburg, shows the meticulous care with which Napoleon had thought out every detail of the operation:

My Cousin, Marshal Soult has advanced to Landsberg, which he reached yesterday at midday. Today Soult is marching on Memmingen, but he cannot get there until very late tomorrow evening. My intention is that, if the enemy maintains his present positions and is prepared to give battle, it will not be fought tomorrow, but the day after, in order that Soult with his 30,000 men can take part; he will outflank and attack the enemy's right, a manœuvre which will ensure us certain and decisive success. Meanwhile, throw a bridge over the Danube, as close to your line as possible, opposite Albeck, so that the corps at Albeck [Ney's] is connected with the rest of the army. . . . Order your Generals to inspect the arms and ammunition, and to recall all their men on baggage escort; all baggage and vehicles are to be sent back beyond Burgau and parked in the fields, so as to clear the main roads. Fix the positions for the artillery ammunition refilling points for the Cavalry Corps, and for the corps of Lannes and Ney. See that all the parks have enough ammunition and that it has not been spoilt by the rain. Also fix the positions of the main dressing stations for each corps. I am not referring to the field ambulances, which must follow the front-line troops at not less than half a mile. This is not going to be a skirmish or an encounter action; it will be a full-scale attack on an army which may be more numerous than you think, on the success of which will depend the most vital results. I shall be there myself. Establish my command post where you consider most suitable. I shall be there tomorrow. (*Corr.* 9372)

To this clear directive the Emperor added a postscript reprimanding his brother-in-law for having in his last report omitted any indication of place, date or hour of despatch—'*c'est un oubli très-capital*' he added; Murat was no Berthier.

On the same day Napoleon sent the following message to Soult, who had now reached Landsberg:

The decisive moment has come. Push forward your cavalry and horse artillery to Memmingen, which you must reach with your leading division before 0900 hours.

15 *Guard Cavalry*

16 *Guard Infantry*

17 *Line Cavalry and Infantry*

18 *Light Infantry and Cavalry*

UNIFORMS OF THE GRANDE ARMÉE, 1804–1815
from contemporary water-colours and prints

19 *The Battle of Austerlitz, 2 December 1805*
Engraved from a painting by Carle Vernet (1758–1836). Napoleon's command
post in the foreground; the Pratzen plateau in the distance to the right

Attack the place immediately and get astride the Iller during tomorrow. . . . Try to seize the bridge at Kellmünz. . . . Get in touch with Prince Murat at Weissenhorn. . . . The enemy's morale is at rock bottom. I am sending Marmont with his corps to Krumbach; he will be on the Iller tomorrow. . . . There is no question of just beating the enemy; not a man must escape. (*Corr.* 9374–75)

Not a man would have escaped, had the Emperor's orders been intelligently carried out. Unfortunately the Marshal to whom Napoleon had entrusted the final *coup de grâce* was not equal to his task. Murat, though a dashing cavalry leader, was no strategist. Contrary to the Emperor's instructions, he ordered Ney's corps, which was on the left bank of the Danube near Günzburg, to cross over to the right (south) bank, thus leaving a gap to the northeast of the fortress. Fortunately Ney only transferred part of his corps to the south bank, but this partial withdrawal created an escape route for the Austrians. Mack took advantage of this gap to push Werneck's corps of 20,000 men, accompanied by the Archduke Ferdinand, north-eastwards. Heavy fighting with one of Ney's divisions took place at Albeck, in which the French captured 3000 prisoners. Werneck, however, broke away through Langenau, Heidenheim and Neresheim, in fact, right across the French lines of communication. Napoleon sent Murat's cavalry in pursuit, and Werneck was eventually rounded up on the 18th near Nördlingen, where he surrendered with 8000 men. The Archduke, with a few hundred cavalry, having deserted his command at Ulm, made good his escape by Nürnberg to Bohemia. Another of Mack's divisions under Spangen tried to break out to the south, but was intercepted at Memmingen by Soult, who captured 5000 prisoners and ten guns. The corps of Jellachich, 6000 strong, had already escaped southwards to the Vorarlberg before the ring closed.

Napoleon was burning to redeem his failure to invade England. On 13 October he issued a long and bombastic proclamation to his army, as he expected the final battle to take place on the following day:

Soldiers, a month ago we were camped on the Ocean coast, facing England, but an impious Coalition has forced us to fly to the Rhine. . . . But for this army in front of you, we should today have been in London; we should have avenged the outrages of six centuries and restored the freedom of the seas.

Soldiers, tomorrow will be a hundred times more famous than the day of Marengo; I have put the enemy in the same position. The most remote posterity will recall your deeds on this memorable occasion. (*Corr.* 9381)

Murat's stupidity had left the Austrians in possession of the Danube bridge at Elchingen (6 miles north-east of Ulm). The village, crowned by an imposing abbey, occupies a dominant site commanding the wide valley. This position was held by 15,000 Austrians with 40 guns. On the morning of

General Mack surrenders to the Emperor Napoleon at Ulm, 20 October 1805
From a painting by Charles Thévenin (1764–1838)

14 October Ney, with great gallantry, attacked this formidable centre of resistance and stormed it after hard fighting, capturing 3000 prisoners and 20 guns. The remainder retired to Ulm, which was now closely invested.

On 16 October Napoleon bombarded Ulm and summoned Mack to surrender, threatening him with the fate of the Turkish garrison of Jaffa, if he refused; Napoleon was indeed most anxious to conclude matters, for by this time he had completely outrun his supplies. On the 19th Mack finally capitulated, and on the morning of the 20th the whole garrison, consisting of 16 Generals and 33,000 officers and men with 60 guns, filed past the Emperor and laid down their arms. The French losses in the campaign amounted to 500 killed and 1000 wounded, mostly in Ney's corps at Albeck and Elchingen.

On the following day Villeneuve's fleet, in attempting to carry out Napoleon's orders, was destroyed at Trafalgar.

Napoleon's triumph at Ulm had been achieved at insignificant cost; as he himself said, he had won his victory with his soldiers' legs, not with their bayonets. They were now to engage in more serious fighting, and in the ensuing campaign we see Napoleon at his best as a commander in the field.

The Emperor had destroyed the bulk of Mack's army, but he was still faced with many uncertainties in attaining his next objective, the occupation of Vienna. In the first place his way to the Austrian capital was barred by Kienmaier's corps of 20,000, which had now been reinforced by Kutúzov's* army of 30,000 Russians, and these were now holding the line of the lower Inn and its tributary, the Salzach. Behind the river Inn a succession of right-bank tributaries of the Danube, such as the Traun, the Enns and the Ybbs, offered the enemy good defensive positions which it was difficult to turn. Jellachich's division of 6000, which had escaped southwards from Ulm, had now joined the Austrian forces in the Tyrol. As the French advanced eastwards, their communications would lengthen and would be exposed to attack from the south. The powerful Austrian army in Venetia under the Archduke Charles was for the time being pinned down by Massena's Army of Italy, which attacked the Archduke on the Caldiero ridge east of Verona on 28 October; a stern struggle ensued, in which each side suffered 6000 casualties. On hearing of Mack's disaster at Ulm, the Archduke withdrew northwards towards Vienna, but not in time to interfere with Napoleon's advance.

A second Russian army under General Buxhövden was advancing through Moravia, and Napoleon rightly decided that, if he was to reach Vienna

---

* Mikhail Ilariónovich Kutúzov (1745–1813) had achieved a great reputation in the Russo-Turkish wars, and was a disciple of Suvórov.

before the arrival of the Russians and the Archduke Charles, he must strike at once. Still another danger threatened, for the attitude of Prussia was becoming daily more hostile. A week after the capitulation of Ulm, the *Grande Armée* began its eastward march on 26 October. On the following day Murat's Cavalry Corps crossed the Inn with only slight opposition, and the fortress of Braunau, with a large stock of supplies and ammunition, fell intact into the hands of the French. Murat was followed by Davout (III), Soult (IV) and Lannes (V). On the right flank Bernadotte (I) entered Salzburg on the 30th. On 31 October the Traun was crossed after a rearguard action at Lambach. It now turned very cold and the ground was covered with snow. On 2 November the Russians fought a sharp rearguard action on the Enns, but on the following day Kutúzov continued his retreat. On the 6th Napoleon formed a new VIII Corps under Marshal Mortier, consisting of one cavalry and two infantry divisions. This was ordered to cross to the left bank of the Danube at Linz to form a left flank guard; Ney (VI) and Marmont (II) had already been detached to Innsbruck and Leoben to act as right flank guard, and Augereau (VII) formed a rearguard on the line of communication. Napoleon was thus prepared for all eventualities.

Kutúzov, seeing that Vienna was now doomed, decided on 9 November to cross the Danube at Mautern and retreat north-eastwards into Moravia to join the second Russian army which had now reached Olmütz (Olomouc). Having destroyed the Danube bridge at Mautern, Kutúzov on 11 November ambushed one of Mortier's divisions in the Dürnstein gorge* and nearly annihilated it. He then retired through Krems to Znaim (Znojmo) across the Moravian border, after fighting a stiff rearguard action near Hollabrunn.

Meanwhile the French advance on the right bank of the Danube progressed with little opposition, and on 13 November Murat's advanced guard reached the outskirts of Vienna. This was contrary to Napoleon's orders, for he had already told Murat to cross the Danube and follow Kutúzov; he sent to his brother-in-law a sharply worded reprimand:

I cannot approve your march orders; you are rushing ahead like a madman and you do not follow the orders I give you. The Russians, instead of covering Vienna, have crossed the Danube at Krems. Without knowing the enemy's plans or considering my intentions, you are going to get my army boxed up in Vienna. But you received my order, sent to you by Marshal Berthier, to pursue the Russians closely. It is a curious way to pursue them to make forced marches in the opposite direction. I find it impossible to explain your conduct. . . . The Russians will now be able to play havoc with Mortier's Corps, which would not have been left exposed if you had obeyed my orders. . . . You have lost me two days in order to acquire glory

* It was in the Castle of Dürnstein that King Richard Cœur de Lion was imprisoned by the Emperor in 1193.

for yourself by being the first to enter Vienna. Glory can only be won where there is danger; there is none in entering an undefended capital. (*Corr.* 9470)

On 14 November Napoleon entered Vienna and established his head-quarters in the magnificent Palace of Schönbrunn, built by the Empress Maria-Theresa. The Austrian Emperor and his Court fled to Brünn (Brno), the capital of Moravia, where he was joined a week later by the Tsar Alexander. In Vienna, with its population of 250,000, the French were able to re-equip themselves on a lavish scale after their arduous marches; Napoleon ordered that no more guns or ammunition need be forwarded from France, as he had found all he required in the Austrian arsenals.

Napoleon decided to pursue the enemy into Moravia without delay, before the winter was too advanced and before the Archduke Charles could arrive from the Italian front. He therefore ordered an energetic pursuit by the corps of Murat, Lannes and Soult; Davout was detached to Pressburg (Bratislava) to ward off danger from the east; Bernadotte was sent westward to Budweis (Budovice) to watch the corps of the Archduke Ferdinand, and Mortier was left to garrison Vienna. After making all these detachments, the *Grande Armée* was considerably reduced in strength.

Napoleon became impatient at the lack of energy shown by his Marshals; on 15 November Bernadotte was reprimanded:

The Emperor is displeased that, while Marshals Lannes and Soult are fighting two days' march beyond Vienna, you have not got a single man across the Danube. The Emperor expects that, by the hand of my staff officer on his return, you will inform him that your whole corps has crossed, and that you are pursuing the Russians and prodding their backsides with your bayonets. (*Corr.* 9491)

On the same day he was roused to fury by a gross piece of stupidity on the part of Murat. The latter's vanguard had been checked by Prince Bagratión's * division, which was holding a rearguard position near Hollabrunn, 15 miles south of the Moravian border. Murat thought he would be clever in offering to conclude an armistice with the Russian commander, allowing him to withdraw unmolested to Moravia, while he himself awaited the arrival of the French infantry. The Russian was only too pleased to agree, and withdrew to Znaim. This incident produced the following fulmination from Napoleon:

It is impossible for me to find terms in which to express my displeasure with you. You are only my advanced guard commander and have no right to arrange armistices without my orders; you rob me of the fruits of victory. Break the armistice at once and march against the enemy. Tell the General who signed this agreement that he had no right to do so; only the Tsar had the right. (*Corr.* 9497)

* Prince Peter Bagratión (1765–1812) had served under Suvórov in 1799. He later distinguished himself at Eylau and Friedland and was mortally wounded at Borodinó, 1812.

After that things moved more quickly and Kutúzov retired to Brünn. On 17 November Napoleon set up his headquarters at Znaim; on the following day he received the news of Trafalgar, and wrote to his Minister of Marine:

I have received your letter about the battle off Cadiz. I await your further details before forming a definite opinion about this affair. Meanwhile, I assure you that this makes no change in the naval raids which I ordered; I am annoyed that these were not ready before this. They must start without further delay. (*Corr.* 9507)

The Russian rearguards evacuated Brünn on 19 November and Murat entered it, finding 60 guns and a large stock of ammunition. Napoleon made it his headquarters the following day, and the Austrian Emperor retired to Olmütz. Murat was held up by some 4000 Austrian cavalry on rising ground in front of a village called Austerlitz (Slavkov in Moravian),* 13 miles east of Brünn (see map facing p. 144).

The Austrian Emperor, now driven to the furthest limits of his domains, sent two plenipotentiaries to Napoleon to discuss peace terms; the latter sent them back to Talleyrand at Vienna, saying that his principal condition would be the incorporation of Venice with the Kingdom of Italy. The sending of these envoys back to Vienna was merely a subterfuge on Napoleon's part to delay matters, for he was determined, before making peace with Austria, to make mincemeat of the Russian army.

On 25 November Napoleon sent his principal A.D.C., General Savary, under a flag of truce to Olmütz, bearing a hypocritical message of good will to the young Tsar Alexander. The real object of this mission was to discover the location of the various enemy corps. As a result of this intelligence Napoleon obtained considerable insight into the Austro-Russian intentions.

Hitherto, Napoleon had never been in the habit of issuing orders to his troops about tactical procedure, for the standard French battle-drill had proved adequate when engaging Austrian troops. Now, however, they were to meet the Russians, who relied less on firepower and more on the bayonet, wielded by dense columns in shock action. This was the traditional Russian practice, inherited from the doctrine of Suvórov. In order to destroy the Russian mass formations before it came to hand-to-hand fighting, Napoleon insisted that the French infantry should develop their maximum firepower, while still retaining sufficient cohesion to deal with shock assaults. On 26

* The French and Austrian authorities use the Germanized version of Moravian place-names. The latter are given here in brackets, to facilitate reference to modern Czechoslovak maps.

November Berthier issued the following instruction to the Corps Commanders:

> The Emperor desires me to communicate to you, Marshal, his ideas on the order of battle to be adopted against the Russians, whenever possible.
>
> Each brigade will have its leading regiment deployed in line, the second regiment in close company column (*en colonne serrée, par division*).
> 1st battalion, to the right and in rear of the 1st battalion of the leading regiment. 2nd battalion, to the left and in rear of the 2nd battalion. The artillery, in the interval between the two front battalions in line, with some guns on each flank. If the division has a fifth regiment, it should be held in reserve, 100 yards in rear; there should be a squadron, or at least a troop of cavalry, behind each brigade, in order to pass through the intervals to pursue the enemy if he is broken, and to deal with the Cossacks.
>
> In this order of battle you will be able to engage the enemy with the fire of the line and with close columns ready formed to meet his. (*Corr.* 9527)

Napoleon now made his final concentration for the decisive battle. Bernadotte (I) was called in from Bohemia, where he was facing the 18,000 men under the Archduke Ferdinand, and was replaced by Wrede's Bavarian corps; Davout (III) was brought up from Pressburg; Mortier (VIII) remained behind, holding Vienna. By 30 November a French army of 65,000 was concentrated at Brünn, facing an Allied army of 52,000 Russians and 30,000 Austrians under the command of their respective Emperors, Alexander and Francis.

On 1 December Napoleon deployed his army facing east, on a six-mile front, along the right bank of a marshy stream known as the Goldbach (Zlatyp). The position was six miles east of Brünn, and midway between that town and the village of Austerlitz. The left flank of the French line rested on a prominent knoll, just north of the Brünn–Austerlitz highway, known to the French as the Santon; the French right flank was protected by a chain of frozen lakes and marshland into which the Goldbach flowed, just south of the village of Telnitz (Telnice). The centre of the line was overlooked by an undulating plateau, held by the Austro-Russians, centred on the village of Pratzen (Prace).

The left sector of the French position, between the Santon and Puntowitz (Ponětovice), was held by Lannes (V) and Bernadotte (I), with Murat's cavalry, Oudinot's grenadier division and the Imperial Guard under Bessières behind them in reserve. Napoleon had his command post here, just south of the highway and a mile behind the front line, but on rising ground from which he had a view down the Goldbach valley and across it to the Pratzen plateau. The right sector, extending from Puntowitz along the

Goldbach to Sokolnitz (Sokolnice) and Telnitz, was held more thinly by Soult (IV), holding a front of three miles. Four miles west of Telnitz, at Raigern abbey (Rajhrad), Davout (III) was held in reserve, well out of sight of the enemy.

The 60-year-old Kutúzov was nominally in command of the Allied army, but by protocol he was obliged to adopt the plan laid down by the Austrian and Russian Emperors, who had met a few days earlier at Wischau (Vyškov) and agreed to accept a plan put forward by General Weyrother, Kutúzov's Austrian Chief of Staff. This plan was based on the belief that the French were at the end of their tether, and that Napoleon was on the point of retreating to Vienna. Weyrother's plan was to pin down the French left (northern) sector, while the main Austro-Russian army would move south-westwards down the Litava valley and turn Napoleon's right flank, thus cutting his communications with Vienna. Actually, Napoleon had no intention of retreating to Vienna; had he been defeated, he would have withdrawn westwards into Bohemia, which would have afforded him an easier line of retreat to the Rhine. Kutúzov and the other Russian Generals strongly disapproved of Weyrother's plan, as they would have preferred to await the arrival of further Russian reinforcements, but they were overruled.

On 1 December Napoleon issued a proclamation to his army:

Soldiers, the Russian army is facing you to avenge the Austrian army of Ulm. These are the same battalions that you beat at Hollabrunn and have pursued to here.

The position we occupy is a formidable one; while the enemy marches to turn my right, he will expose his flank to me. . . . .

This victory will end our campaign, and we can go into winter quarters where we shall be reinforced by the new armies forming in France. Then the peace that I shall make will be worthy of my people, of you and of me. (*Corr.* 9533)

This proclamation, which was published in the *Moniteur* a fortnight later, and is dated 1 December from Napoleon's bivouac, is suspiciously prophetic and resembles the spurious one which he claimed to have addressed to his troops on assuming command of the Army of Italy in March 1796. If it was genuinely issued at the time, it shows his supreme confidence in himself and his troops, and reveals an uncanny insight into his enemy's intentions.

After dark on 1 December the Emperor rode along the whole front, inspecting the troops in their bivouacs. He noted the concentration of the enemy's camp-fires behind the Pratzen plateau and in the Litava valley between Křenovice and Aujest (Ujezd), which confirmed his forecast that the enemy would try to turn his right flank. As he passed through the lines, the troops illuminated the scene with blazing torches made from their bedding-straw, and cheered him with their battle-cry of '*Vive l'Empereur!*', which had now replaced the '*Vive la République!*' of Marengo days. Strange to say, this demonstration was considered by the enemy as a feint to cover a French withdrawal.

Before dawn on 2 December the Austro-Russian columns began their advance; there were six of these: the two northerly ones, commanded by Prince Bagratión and Prince Liechtenstein, astride the Brünn–Austerlitz highroad, attacked the northern sector of the French front, held by Lannes (V) and Bernadotte (I). Behind them, in reserve, was the Russian Imperial Guard under the Grand Duke Constantine. In the centre, Kolowrat's corps of 25,000 Austrians attacked Soult's corps at Kobelnitz (Kobylnice), while the main assault was launched south of the Pratzen plateau by three columns numbering 33,000 men, under the Russian General Buxhövden, against the southern sector of Soult's corps on the Goldbach, held by Legrand's division. This attack, by sheer weight of numbers, at first made progress; the villages of Telnitz and Sokolnitz were taken, and the French were driven back to Maxdorf (Dvorska) and Turas (Tuřany). Napoleon at once brought up Davout's corps from reserve at Raigern; the Russian left flank was counter-attacked and after stiff fighting, was driven back with heavy loss to the Gold-bach. The Allied Commander-in-Chief, Kutúzov, instead of remaining on the Pratzen plateau, where he could have controlled the battle, had followed Kolowrat's corps in its attack on the French centre between Puntowitz and Kobelnitz.

About 7.30 a.m. the thick mist which had covered the valleys lifted, and the sun shone out brightly. Napoleon from his command-post observed that the Pratzen plateau was now entirely unoccupied. He ordered Soult to advance with the divisions of Vandamme and Saint Hilaire and seize this key-point. This they accomplished almost without opposition, and Napoleon had thus driven a wedge between the two wings of the Allied army. Kolowrat's column was attacked in flank while still in column of route, and driven back in disorder.* As this column was accompanied, not only by Kutúzov and his staff, but also by the Tsar Alexander, all centralized control of the Allied army now broke down, and their centre column was driven back to Kreseno-witz. Meanwhile, on the northern sector, Lannes's infantry had held the important Santon hill against Bagratión's repeated attacks.

As soon as Soult had established himself on the Pratzen plateau, Napoleon ordered a general advance by the whole of his left wing, namely the corps of Lannes and Bernadotte, supported by the Imperial Guard and Murat's

---

* A vivid picture of the confusion that occurred here is given in Tolstoy's great historical novel *War and Peace*.

cavalry. After heavy fighting this resulted in the rout of Bagratión and Liech-tenstein. In the southern sector the Allies fared still worse. Buxhövden's columns were caught between Soult, advancing south from Pratzen to Hosteradek and Aujest (Ujezd), and Davout striking east from Telnitz. The Russians tried to escape across the frozen lakes and marshes between Tel-nitz and Žatčany,* but the ice was broken up by the French artillery, and many perished by drowning. The rout of the Allies was now complete.

With 65,000 men engaged, the French casualties amounted to 8800. Of 82,000 Austrians and Russians, 12,200 were killed or wounded, while 15,000 prisoners and 133 guns were taken. Early on the following morning the Austrian Emperor asked Napoleon for an armistice, which was granted on condition that all Russian troops were withdrawn to Poland. Peace negotiations were then continued at Pressburg, and a final peace treaty be-tween France and Austria was signed there on 27 December. It was the end of the Third Coalition, and Austria ceded to France the Venetian territories, which were added to the Kingdom of Italy.

The battle of Austerlitz was Napoleon's military masterpiece.† His handling of the action was impeccable, both strategically and tactically, and his timing of the counter-stroke was brilliant. None of the mistakes made at Marengo were repeated. With a marked inferiority of numbers, he induced his opponents to attack him in a strong defensive position; then, when the enemy committed the cardinal error of abandoning the high ground in the centre, Napoleon seized the opportunity like lightning and separated their two wings. He had thoroughly reconnoitred the ground beforehand, knew where his opponents' forces were located, and had accurately predicted their plans. Above all, despite his numerical inferiority, he retained adequate troops in reserve to influence the battle and carry out the pursuit.

The victory of Austerlitz was won on the first anniversary of Napoleon's coronation as Emperor of the French; it crowned his laurels as the foremost military leader in Europe. Throughout Germany the battle became known as the *Dreikaiserschlacht*; the French Emperor certainly surpassed his Austrian and Russian rivals in both military and political stature.

* These lakes were drained many years ago, but are shown on contemporary maps (see Plate 21).

† On returning to St. Petersburg, General Kutúzov submitted to the Tsar a despatch on the battle of Austerlitz, which was published in the *Moniteur* of 30 April 1806, together with Napoleon's comments on it (*Corr.* 10032). Both versions made equally mendacious claims.

XI

The Jena Campaign
1806

After the defeat of the Austro-Russian army at Austerlitz the European Continent settled down to an uneasy peace. During the previous campaign Napoleon had been anxious to ensure Prussian neutrality, for the addition of a Prussian army of 150,000 to the ranks of his enemies would have faced him with a serious situation. Bernadotte's trespass on the Prussian Principality of Ansbach during the march to the Danube had aroused the indignation of Prussia and nearly provoked her into war, which was only averted by Napoleon offering the bribe of Hanover. That country was of course not legally in Napoleon's power to give away, but its cession to Prussia was confirmed in a convention signed by Napoleon and Count Haugwitz at Schönbrunn a fortnight after Austerlitz, though this convention was modified in France's favour two months later. The weak and vacillating King Frederick William III was dominated by the war party in Berlin, which was ardently supported by Queen Louise. Anti-French feeling in Berlin was further exacerbated by Napoleon's demand that Ansbach should be handed over to Bavaria in compensation for the cession of Hanover.

The tension between France and Britain had relaxed slightly since Pitt's death on 23 January 1806, and with the advent of a Whig administration in the following month, but the peace negotiations came to nothing, for the questions of Holland, Sicily and the overseas colonies proved intractable. Matters were not improved by Napoleon's brother Louis being elevated to the throne of Holland in June.

The Treaty of Pressburg had forged a chain of French satellites in south

146

Germany: the Electoral Princes of Bavaria and Württemberg had been created kings and their territories increased at the expense of Austria; the Margraves of Baden and Hesse-Darmstadt had been made Grand Dukes. Napoleon had acquired a daughter of the Bavarian ruler as a bride for his stepson, Prince Eugène*; in July the heterogeneous German territories in the Rhineland and Palatinate had, without consulting Prussia, been welded into a satellite Confederation of the Rhine; Napoleon's brother-in-law, Marshal Murat, had been appointed Grand Duke of Berg and Cleve, thus acquiring the important Rhine bridgehead at Wesel. These political barriers to *Deutschtum* were reinforced by the continued presence of overwhelming military power. The *Grande Armée*, 192,000 strong, far from having been demobilized, was still billeted at war strength throughout south-west Germany at the expense of the local territories, which did not increase the popularity of the French presence. Bernadotte (I) occupied Ansbach; Davout (III) and Lannes (V) were in Suabia; Soult (IV) and Ney (VI) were in Bavaria, and Augereau (VII) at Frankfurt. Marmont (II) had been sent to subdue Dalmatia, and Massena, under Napoleon's elder brother Joseph, was overrunning the Kingdom of Naples.

Napoleon being fully occupied in Paris with his political and dynastic designs, the command of the *Grande Armée* was delegated to Berthier at Munich. The latter, however, was given clearly to understand that he was a mere *locum tenens*; on 14 February he received the following curt directive:

Adhere strictly to the orders I give you; carry out your instructions to the letter; everyone must be ready and at his post; I alone know what is to be done. (*Corr.* 9810)

Since the battle of Austerlitz the Emperor had acquired supreme confidence in his own infallibility.

Throughout the summer of 1806 Napoleon's military precautions, and the maintenance of the *Grande Armée* on a war footing, were aimed solely at preventing the resurgence of Austria and at overawing the Court of Vienna while he was discussing peace terms with the British delegates, Lord Lauderdale and Lord Yarmouth. He had no intention whatever of arousing the hostility of Prussia. In July Prince Murat had tactlessly expelled the Prussian garrison of Werden, in his newly acquired Grand Duchy; on 2 August the Emperor addressed a severe rebuke to his brother-in-law:

Your decision to eject the Prussians by force from the territory they occupy is downright folly; by this you are insulting Prussia, which is quite contrary to my

---

* Napoleon also married off a niece of the King of Bavaria to Berthier, whom he created Prince of Neuchâtel, a principality in the Swiss Jura which he had obtained from Prussia.

intentions. I have good relations with this Power, and I am breaking off negotiations with England in order to keep Hanover for Prussia. I do not want to antagonize her by such follies; I want to remain on good terms with her. Your role is to be very conciliatory towards the Prussians. (*Corr.* 10587)

And on the same day he instructed Talleyrand to smooth over the incident with the Prussian Government.

But, in his negotiations with the Whig Government in London, Napoleon had surpassed all his previous acts of political duplicity by offering to restore Hanover to Britain, after having already ceded it to Prussia. This piece of treachery came to the ears of the Prussian Government at the end of July, and war now was inevitable.

Napoleon seems to have been strangely unconscious of the growing enmity which his expansionist policy had evoked in Prussia. This hostility sprang from two sources: firstly, the bellicosity of the Prussian officer corps, steeped in the military tradition of Frederick the Great; secondly, the sudden upsurge of *Vaterlandsliebe* which had begun to nucleate in Berlin since the dissolution of the old German Empire based on Vienna. The Prussian army, proud of its victories over Austrians and French in the Seven Years' War, had learnt nothing from the mobility and tactical elasticity developed by the French Revolutionary armies. Immersed in the Frederician doctrine of rigid formations, slow manœuvre and ordered volley-firing, which had proved effective half a century earlier, the Prussian officers held in contempt the loose skirmishing lines and laxer fire-discipline of the French troops. The mobility of Prussian units was further impaired by their magazine system of supply and the cumbrous baggage columns, without which they were unable to move.

Anti-French feeling in Berlin rose to such a pitch that King Frederick William III was compelled to declare general mobilization on 9 August, though he made no immediate effort to concentrate his troops. At a council of war on 25 August it was decided to form two armies, under the Duke of Brunswick and Prince Friedrich Hohenlohe–Ingelfingen, with a separate corps under General Rüchel, the whole being under the supreme command of the 71-year-old Duke of Brunswick.*

During the following month the Prussian troops, together with those of their Saxon allies, moved south in leisurely fashion; by the end of September

---

* Karl Wilhelm Ferdinand, Duke of Brunswick (1735–1806), had distinguished himself in the Seven Years' War and was a Prussian Field-Marshal; he was a nephew of Frederick the Great, but was a cautious soldier. He was mortally wounded at the battle of Auerstedt. His son and successor, Duke Friedrich Wilhelm, was killed at Quatre-Bras, 1815.

they were assembled on a 70-mile front, close to the southern frontier of Prussian territory, in three groups as follows:

Right:	Rüchel's corps (3 divisions)	25,000	Eisenach.
Centre:	Brunswick's army (6 divisions)	58,000	Gotha – Erfurt.
Left:	Hohenlohe's army (5 divisions)	47,000	Jena – Saalfeld.
		130,000	

Hohenlohe, whose command included the Saxon contingent, 20,000 strong, had pushed Tauentzien's corps forward to Schleiz and Hof to protect the left flank. The whole concentration was screened by the wooded ridge of the Thüringer Wald and Franken-Wald, a range of hills 80 miles long and rising to a height of nearly 1000 metres, which forms the watershed between the Elbe basin to the north and the right-hand tributaries of the Main to the south. The Thüringer Wald is the western extension of the Erzgebirge, which separates Saxony from Bohemia.

Far from anticipating any hostile move on the part of Prussia, Napoleon was thinking in the middle of August of withdrawing the bulk of the *Grande Armée* from Germany. On 20 July the Russian delegates in Paris had signed a peace treaty with France. On 6 August he wrote to Soult, who was at Braunau, keeping an eye on the Austrians:

The peace with Russia and the negotiations that I am conducting with England lead me to think that everything is going to calm down, and that a profound peace will follow all these warlike movements. (*Corr.* 10606)

On the 17th he wrote to Berthier:

We must think seriously about the return of the *Grande Armée*, for it seems to me that all doubts about Germany are cleared up. You may announce that the army will march, but actually I do not intend to hand back Braunau [to the Austrians] until I know that the treaty with Russia has been ratified. Meanwhile, stop all warlike preparations and don't let any more troops cross the Rhine; everyone must be ready to return to France. (*Corr.* 10660)

But on 3 September Napoleon learnt that on 24 August the Tsar had refused to ratify the treaty of 20 July, so he cancelled his preparations for the return of the army to France. On the following day, however, he granted compassionate leave to two of his corps commanders, Ney and Davout, for three weeks, as their wives were expecting confinement. Berthier also was told he could return to Paris on leave.

On 5 September intelligence was received that the Prussian army was moving south to the frontier, and Napoleon called up 50,000 conscripts of the 1806 class and also 30,000 reservists. On that day he wrote to Berthier:

The new turn of events in Europe makes me think seriously about the situation of my armies. (*Corr.* 10743)

and he instructed Berthier to send engineer officers, '*à tout hasard*', to reconnoitre the roads leading from Bamberg towards Berlin; all the corps of the *Grande Armée* were to be ready to concentrate within eight days in the area Bamberg–Bayreuth.

My intention is that in eight days all my corps should be assembled beyond Kronach. From that place on the frontier of Bamberg I reckon it to be ten days' march to Berlin. . . . I want to know what the rivers Saale and Elster are like at Gera. . . . What about the Elbe crossing at Wittenberg? How are the towns of Dresden, Torgau and Magdeburg fortified? Collect the best maps that can be found in Munich and Dresden. Send intelligent officers to Dresden and Berlin to ascertain, for your information, the meaning of these moves and concentrations of Prussian troops. You must be very discreet in obtaining this information, for I have no intentions against Berlin; I want these details solely as a measure of precaution. I imagine that Magdeburg is the only fortress between Bamberg and Berlin. (*Corr.* 10744)

Within a week he realized that the Prussians intended to fight, for on 10 September he wrote to Berthier:

Prussia's movements continue to be very strange. They need a lesson. Tomorrow I am sending off my horses, and in a few days my Guard. If information confirms that Prussia has gone mad, I shall go straight to Würzburg or Bamberg. (*Corr.* 10757)

and he ordered Caulaincourt, his Master of the Horse, to send on eight of his horses and all his field-glasses, but to give out that he was only going to hunt at Compiègne.

On 19 September Napoleon ordered the initial concentration of the *Grande Armée*, to be completed by the first week of October, as follows:

I (Bernadotte)	25,000	Bamberg
III (Davout)	33,000	Bamberg
IV (Soult)	35,000	Amberg
V (Lannes)	23,000	Königshofen
VI (Ney)	21,000	Ansbach
VII (Augereau)	16,000	Frankfurt
VIII (Mortier)	15,000	Mainz
Cavalry (Murat)	20,000	Würzburg
Guard (Lefebvre) (Bessières)	12,000	Mainz
Bavarians (Wrede)	8,000	Nürnberg
	208,000	

It was the most formidable concentration of force that the Emperor had yet achieved. In addition, his brother Louis, King of Holland, had a corps of 15,000 Dutch auxiliaries holding the crossing of the Rhine at Wesel. General Headquarters were set up at Bamberg. The line of communications was to be Strasbourg–Mannheim–Mainz–Würzburg–Bamberg, and advanced supply and ammunition depots were to be formed at Forchheim and Würzburg. The whole strategic concentration was to be covered by the deployment of Murat's six cavalry divisions on the line Kronach–Coburg–Königshofen, facing the exits of the Thüringer Wald. In order to intimidate the Austrians on his right rear behind the Inn, Napoleon left a French garrison in the fortress of Braunau, supported by a corps of 15,000 Bavarian troops in south Germany.

Although completely ignorant of the enemy's intended plan of operations, Napoleon had, by his initial concentration of the *Grande Armée*, prepared for all eventualities. If the Prussians were to advance south-westwards to threaten his line of communications with the Rhine valley, he could strike at their left flank with superior forces; if, on the other hand, they were to invade Bavaria so as to join forces with the Austrians, he could equally attack their right flank and drive them into Bohemia. To guard his communications with the Rhine, and to act as a general reserve, Napoleon formed an VIII Corps of two divisions under Marshal Mortier, which he stationed at Frankfurt. At the back of his mind, however, irrespective of the enemy's plans, was germinating his great strategic project of enveloping the left flank of the Prussian and Saxon forces by a lightning thrust down the valleys of the Saale and the Elster, thus cutting their communications with Berlin and Dresden. As soon as the *Grande Armée* was assembled in the area south of the Thüringer Wald in the first week of October, this strategic plan was put into operation (p. 154).

Napoleon's last week in Paris before leaving for the front was an exceptionally busy one. He was indeed his own Chief of Staff, and drew up personally all the movement and concentration orders for the *Grande Armée*, Berthier being merely used as a post-office to ensure that these reached the correct destinations. On the morning of 19 September, for instance, he spent two hours in dictating to General Clarke the operation orders, but a host of other matters, financial, administrative and political, also called for his attention: he wrote directives to his brothers, Joseph in Naples and Louis in Holland, and to his stepson Eugène in Italy; he reproached Admiral Decrès for giving wrong orders to the Navy; Davout and Ney were recalled from leave and ordered to rejoin their corps by 28 September; detailed instructions were issued for improving the coast defences at Boulogne, Quiberon Bay and Antwerp. The Emperor even found time to write to the King of Württemberg, asking for the hand of his daughter Catherine as a bride for his youngest brother Jérôme, who was already married to an American lady, and had a son by her. On 20 September, on studying the strength returns of the *Grande Armée*, he was annoyed to find that Berthier had omitted to organize any bridging train; 'How shall I cross the Elbe without any bridging equipment?' he demanded angrily. On the following day he received in audience an old soldier aged 102, to whom he granted a gratuity of 2400 francs.

On 20 September Napoleon summoned from the headquarters of VI Corps a young staff officer of Swiss origin, Major Antoine-Henri Jomini, who had acquired a reputation as a writer on military history and tactics; the 27-year-old Jomini was now attached to the Emperor's personal staff, but unfortunately did not find favour with Berthier.

All these preoccupations, great and small, having been dealt with, the Emperor left Paris on 25 September, and reached Mainz three days later; on 2 October he moved forward to Würzburg, and on the 6th assumed personal command of the *Grande Armée* at Bamberg.

Napoleon was not yet very clear as to the enemy's movements, strength or intentions; all he did know was that Saxony and Prussia were now allies, so he would have to meet their combined forces. He had already instructed Berthier to send engineer officers to reconnoitre the roads leading into Prussia and Saxony through the Thüringer Wald, and he had given his corps commanders fairly large sums to spend on secret intelligence, though their reports had hitherto been somewhat conflicting. On 29 September he had written from Mainz to Berthier:

Order Marshal Bernadotte to advance to Kronach and occupy the exits from the Saxon hill-country, remaining on the frontier, but taking up a good position to cover the crossings into Saxony and reconnoitring the roads to Leipzig and Dresden. . . . Marshal Bernadotte must make his reconnaissances and movements secretly, so as to intercept the road from Erfurt to Hof. . . . War is not yet declared; our language must be peaceful; no hostile act must be committed. (*Corr.* 10893)

On the same day he wrote to Murat:

You will send spies towards Fulda. You may cross the frontier at certain points, if necessary, to occupy a good position to cover our crossing into Saxony. Send engineer officers to Königshofen and Fulda to reconnoitre the roads carefully. (*Corr.* 10895)

On the following day he wrote to Berthier:

We must have cavalry detachments on the hills between Meiningen and Neustadt, as far as the Bavarian frontier, in order to mask our movements when the moment comes. My intention is to reach Saalfeld before the enemy gets there in force. Send an engineer officer to reconnoitre the Bavarian frontier as far as Heldburg and up to the watershed, which I think is beyond Coburg. Send another to reconnoitre the watershed between Meiningen and Mellrichstadt beyond Neustadt. . . . I await the result of these reconnaissances which are most important. (*Corr.* 10911)

The new theatre of war was quite unfamiliar to the French army, and Napoleon rightly insisted on collecting every scrap of topographical intelligence he could before embarking on operations; on 1 October he wrote to Berthier:

I want you to keep at Würzburg the engineer officers who have carried out the road reconnaissances, as I want to interrogate them about the nature of the terrain. . . . It is essential to establish at Bamberg a bakery to make bread for 80,000 men for four days. Bamberg is the central point for all the major moves of the army. I want to be able to start operations before the 10th if we are forced to. (*Corr.* 10929)

On reaching Würzburg on 3 October, Napoleon interviewed these officers, who had obtained most interesting and accurate information. One of them, Colonel Blein, had been bold enough to ride openly in uniform through the Prussian lines on the pretext of going to the Leipzig Fair to buy maps! The Prussian outposts, taking him for a Saxon officer, let him pass, and he proceeded by Coburg, Jena and Saalfeld to Naumburg, where he found the G.H.Q. of the King of Prussia and the Duke of Brunswick. Having successfully located the main body of the Prussian army, he returned safely to the French lines.

Bernadotte had also been able to collect valuable intelligence. He reported on 3 October that the Prussian main body, 80,000 strong, was still at Naumburg; Prince Hohenlohe had been expected at Plauen on 1 October; he had an advanced detachment of 2000 men under General Tauentzien at Hof. On the same day the V Corps on the left flank reported that there were no Prussian troops between Cassel and Fulda, but that their forces were assembling at Eisenach, Erfurt and Gotha.

As a result of all this intelligence work, the Emperor had a pretty clear idea of the enemy's dispositions, and he now made ready to strike. The enemy forces were evidently deploying on the line Eisenach–Jena, with only a weak detachment covering their eastern flank in the Franken-Wald. This flank could thus be turned by a swift advance down the valleys of the Saale and the Elster, directed on Plauen, Gera and Naumburg. Preceded by Murat's six cavalry divisions, the six corps which formed the striking force of the *Grande Armée* were now organized in three columns as follows:

Right :   Soult (IV), Ney (VI) and Bavarians: Bayreuth–Münchberg–Hof.
Centre :   Bernadotte (I), Davout (III), Guard: Bamberg–Kronach–Lobenstein.
Left :   Lannes (V), Augereau (VIII): Schweinfurt–Coburg–Neustadt.

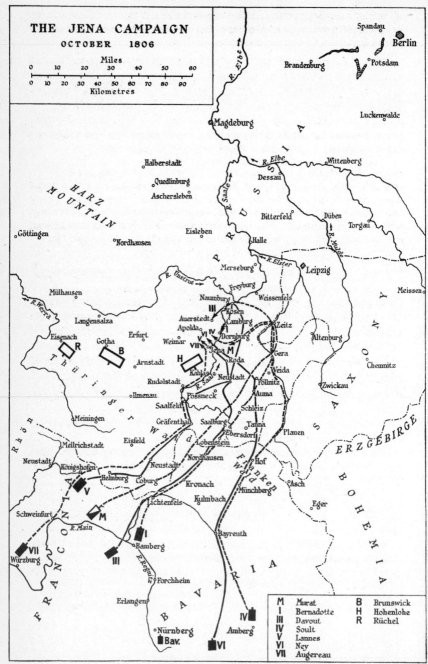

THE JENA CAMPAIGN
OCTOBER 1806

Miles
0   10   20   30   40   50   60

0   10   20   30   40   50   60   70   80   90
Kilometres

M	Murat	B	Brunswick
I	Bernadotte	H	Hohenlohe
III	Davout	R	Rüchel
IV	Soult		
V	Lannes		
VI	Ney		
VII	Augereau		

This made a striking force of 180,000 men moving forward in three parallel columns on a front of 30 miles, so that all corps were within mutually supporting distance.

The outer flank of the great 'left wheel' movement to envelop the Prussian army would be led by Soult (IV), whose bold tactical leadership had contributed so greatly to the victory of Austerlitz. Napoleon intended that this time there should be no misunderstanding of his strategic plan by his subordinates, as had happened the year before when Murat's stupidity had nearly botched his arrangements for the investment of Ulm. On 5 October, therefore, he dictated the following directive to Soult:

The country between Bayreuth and Hof is unsuitable for cavalry. I want you to know my plans, in order to guide you in important eventualities. My advanced depots are at Würzburg, Forchheim and Kronach; I shall invade Saxony by three routes. You are at the head of my right column, with Marshal Ney's (VI) Corps half a day's march behind you; 10,000 Bavarians will be half a day behind him, making in all more than 50,000. Marshal Bernadotte (I) is leading my centre; behind him is Marshal Davout (III) with the reserve cavalry and my Guard, in all 70,000. He will march by Kronach, Lobenstein and Schleiz. My left column is headed by V Corps, followed by Augereau (VII), and will march by Coburg, Gräfenthal and Saalfeld, in all 40,000. On the day you reach Hof the other columns will be abreast with you. I shall generally be at the head of the centre column. With this immense superiority of force concentrated on so narrow a front, you will realize that I am taking no chances and shall attack the enemy, wherever he may stand, with double his strength.

I believe that the cavalry is the most formidable part of the Prussian army; but with the infantry that you have, and if you can manage to form squares, you will have nothing to fear. But no precaution of warfare must be neglected; see that 3 to 5000 entrenching tools are always carried well forward with your divisions, in order to throw up a redoubt when necessary, or even a simple trench.

If you encounter the enemy in less strength than 30,000, you may, in conjunction with Marshal Ney, concentrate and attack him; but if he is in a prepared and entrenched position, act with prudence. On arrival at Hof, your first task must be to establish communication with Lobenstein, Ebersdorf and Schleiz. I shall then be at Ebersdorf. The information which you get about the enemy when you leave Hof will either cause you to feel in toward my centre, or take up a more advanced position, your objective being Plauen. According to the reports I receive today, the enemy seems to be moving towards my left, for his main body appears to be at Erfurt.

I must insist that you send me frequent reports and keep me informed of everything that you discover on the road to Dresden. You may well think that it will be a fine achievement to envelop that place with a *bataillon carré* of 200,000 men. It will require some skill and many actions. (*Corr.* 10941)

Never has a Commander-in-Chief expounded his plan and methods more clearly or fully to a subordinate. This concept of the *bataillon carré*, three parallel columns of 50,000 men each, advancing on a front of 30 miles, was the acme of Napoleonic strategy. If the enemy were encountered in front, he could be held by one column and out-flanked by the other two; if he were on a flank, two corps could always deploy to the right or left and engage him, supported by the remainder of the army. This was the principle underlying the Jena campaign; owing, however, to an error of judgement on the battle-field on the part of Napoleon, it did not entirely work out in the way that he intended.

On 7 October the Emperor received an ultimatum from the King of Prussia, which had been despatched on the 1st, demanding that all French troops should evacuate German territory forthwith. Napoleon needed no further pretext, and hostilities began that day, though he claimed that the first shot was fired by the Prussians; the *Grande Armée* began its northward march through the sparsely inhabited woodlands of the Thüringer Wald. Each man carried four days' ration of *pain biscuité*, and biscuit rations for ten more days were held in the corps bakeries at Würzburg, Bamberg and Forchheim. Napoleon had neglected no administrative detail.

We can now turn to the situation in the Prussian camp. In the days of the Great Frederick the Prussian army, like Napoleon's, had been the instrument of one supreme and brilliant commander. His great-nephew, King Frederick William III, had not inherited the same qualities of leadership; the higher direction of the army was now vested in the *Ober Kriegs-Kollegium*, an Army Council of elderly officers, though the King was nominally in supreme command. The command in the field had been delegated to the elderly Duke of Brunswick, who had under his orders the main Prussian army, an independent corps under General von Rüchel, and a mixed Prussian-Saxon army under the 60-year-old Prince Friedrich Ludwig von Hohenlohe-Ingelfingen. The latter army consisted of five divisions; one was Prussian and one Saxon, while the other three were composed half-and-half of Prussian and Saxon units, a mixture which did not conduce to smooth cooperation. Added to this, Brunswick and Hohenlohe held widely divergent views on strategy and tactics, while their respective chiefs of staff, von Scharnhorst and von Massenbach, were hardly on speaking terms with each other.

Although the Prussian army had mobilized as early as 9 August, and had then moved in leisurely fashion towards the frontier, it was not until 25 September that Brunswick submitted his plan of operations to the King; his intention was to advance south-west from Eisenach towards Fulda and Würzburg in order to threaten the French line of communications. This plan was opposed by Hohenlohe, who wished to operate on the right (east) bank of the Saale, close to the Saxon border. On 5 October the question was referred to a Council of War at Weimar, and Brunswick's plan was eventually adopted with some modifications; Brunswick's army, which was concentrating on the line Eisenach–Gotha–Erfurt, was to advance south-west, its left flank being covered by Hohenlohe's army, which would block the exits from the Thüringer Wald. Accordingly, Hohenlohe's advanced guard, commanded by Prince Louis Ferdinand of Prussia, advanced southwards from Jena to Saalfeld, while Tauentzien's Saxon division was pushed out to Hof, 45 miles south-south-east of Jena. It took some time, however, for these moves to take place; the Prussians had not yet adopted the formation of army corps, so the Commander-in-Chief's orders had to be transmitted to 14 divisions separately whereas Napoleon's operation orders were despatched only to six corps commanders.

Into this welter of indecision and lethargy Napoleon's *bataillon carré* of six army corps advanced like a steam-roller, though it was not altogether an easy walk-over. Augereau's VII Corps had to march for nine consecutive days at an average pace of 24 miles a day, and all the columns had an arduous march through the narrow defiles of the Thüringer Wald, from which they pushed back the enemy outposts. The first clash came at Hof, where Soult's vanguard encountered Tauentzien's Saxons on 8 October and drove them 20 miles northward to Schleiz, where they ran into Bernadotte's advanced guard and were severely handled.

Prince Louis Ferdinand, commanding Hohenlohe's advanced guard, had reached Rudolstadt when he heard of the French advance. He moved south to Saalfeld, where on 10 October he ran into the French left column, headed by Lannes's advanced guard. His division of 10 battalions and 10 squadrons, half Prussian and half Saxon, was completely defeated and the young Prince Louis was killed.

The news of these early reverses caused consternation at Brunswick's headquarters. He realized his mistake in advancing on Würzburg and exposing his left flank and rear to Napoleon's superior force, and decided on an immediate retreat to Magdeburg and the Elbe valley in order to cover his communications with Berlin. Rüchel's corps on the right flank was ordered back to Weimar, where the bulk of the army was concentrated on the 11th, while Hohenlohe was ordered to assemble his divisions on the plateau west of Jena in order to protect the left flank. This again was a bad mistake, for Hohenlohe ought to have been told at all cost to hold the crossings over the river Saale.

North of the Thüringer Wald an undulating plateau descends gradually to the Elbe valley. This Thuringian plain is intersected by a left-bank tributary of the Elbe, the Saale, which has cut a deep trench in the limestone plateau, especially between Jena and Naumburg, where the river flows through a gorge several hundred feet below the level of the plateau. The defeat and dispersal of Prince Louis's and Tauentzien's divisions had left the whole region east of the Saale open to the advance of Napoleon's *bataillon carré*.

On 11 October the French right column, headed by Soult (IV), had reached Plauen; the centre, with Bernadotte (I) in the van, was north of Auma, while on the left Lannes (V) was at Saalfeld. Misled by a report sent by Soult late on the 9th that the enemy were retiring from Plauen to Gera, Napoleon now thought that the main Prussian army was concentrating there, and prepared to give battle. But later in the day Murat reported that his cavalry had passed through Gera and found it unoccupied; the Saxons appeared to have withdrawn westward through Roda towards Jena. Bernadotte (I) also reached Gera and Lannes (V) moved up from Saalfeld to Neustadt, followed by Augereau (VII). Napoleon now had all his corps well concentrated, but he was still in the dark about the enemy's dispositions.

After midnight on 11/12 October Napoleon at Auma received a report from Murat which at last gave him a clue to the enemy's whereabouts. Saxons captured north of Gera had stated that 'the King of Prussia was at Erfurt with 200,000 men'. This vague exaggeration was partly confirmed by intercepted correspondence. At 4 a.m. on the 12th the Emperor made the following communications to two of his corps commanders; to Lannes (V), after congratulating him on the result of his victory at Saalfeld, he wrote:

All the intercepted letters show that the enemy has lost his head. They hold consultations day and night, not knowing what to decide. You will see that my army is concentrated and that I block their road to Dresden and Berlin. The thing now is to attack everything we meet in order to defeat the enemy in detail, while he is trying to concentrate. (*Corr.* 10982)

At the same time he wrote to Murat:

Before noon today I shall be at Gera. From the situation of the army you will see that I am completely enveloping the enemy. But I must have information about his intentions. The post-office at Zeitz may afford you some intelligence. Attack boldly anything on the march. Marshal Davout is sending all his cavalry straight to Naumburg. With your cavalry you must sweep the whole Leipzig plain. (*Corr.* 10983)

Napoleon was now so full of confidence that he wrote to Talleyrand:

Things here are working out exactly as I had calculated, two months ago, in Paris, step by step, event by event; I have not been wrong once. Everything tends to confirm my conviction that the Prussians have not got a chance. Their Generals are complete idiots. (*Corr.* 10989)

At 2 a.m. on 13 October, after snatching a few hours' sleep at Gera, the Emperor wrote to Joséphine:

My affairs are going well, and exactly as I had hoped. . . . I am in splendid health; I have already put on weight since I left notwithstanding that every day I cover 45 to 60 miles, either on horseback or in my carriage. I go to bed at eight o'clock and rise at midnight. (*Corr.* 10992)

Napoleon's intention was to close in on Jena with IV, V, VI and VII Corps, cross the Saale and on the 16th attack the main Prussian army, which he believed to be concentrated between Weimar and Erfurt. Meanwhile Murat, Bernadotte (I) and Davout (III) were to seize the Saale crossings at Dornburg and Kösen (west of Naumburg) in order to cut the enemy's line of retreat to Leipzig or the Elbe valley. At 7 a.m. he wrote to Lannes (V), whose vanguard was now approaching Jena:

Today at 1 p.m. I shall be at Jena. I shall pass through the little town of Roda. See that you let me have there news of your own movements and of those of the enemy. I have not issued any movement orders today to the army, as I want it to get some rest and to close up. Only Marshal Ney will move up to Roda today, so he will be within less than seven miles of you. If the enemy attacks you, don't fail to let me know at once. (*Corr.* 10998)

The Emperor then received an important situation report from Davout (III), dated the previous evening, saying that he had occupied Naumburg; from the statements of prisoners and deserters it was certain that the King of Prussia had reached Weimar on the 11th and that his army was between Erfurt and Weimar; there were no enemy troops between Naumburg and Leipzig. This report confirmed Napoleon's conviction that he had got the whole Prussian army in the net; he decided to carry out at once the enveloping movement with his right wing which would cut off their retreat to the Elbe. At 9 a.m. he dictated a message to Murat:

At last the veil is torn aside; the enemy is beginning his retreat to Magdeburg. Move as soon as possible with Bernadotte's corps to Dornburg, a big village between Jena and Naumburg. Take specially your dragoons and cavalry. . . . I think that the enemy will either attempt to attack Marshal Lannes at Jena or else he will retreat. If he attacks Lannes, you will be able to support him from Dornburg. (*Corr.* 11000)

He thus made his intentions admirably clear to Murat, but unfortunately did not make them equally clear to Bernadotte (I), who had a vital role to play in the enveloping movement (p. 162).

At 3 p.m. on the 13th, when Napoleon was within four miles of Jena, he received a report from Lannes to say that he had occupied the town and had driven an enemy force of about 12,000 in the direction of Weimar; a force of 30,000 men was encamped three miles west of Jena on the Weimar road. An hour later Napoleon himself reached Jena and joined Lannes on the Landgrafenberg hill, 1½ miles north-west of the town, and from here he reconnoitred the position held by the enemy outposts, a long ridge known as the Dornberg* a mile to the north, between the villages of Closewitz and Lützeroda. This position was in fact only held by Hohenlohe's advanced guard, consisting of Tauentzien's Saxon division which had been badly mauled at Hof and Schleiz during the French advance. Napoleon, however, thought that the enemy might attack him the next day, and the other corps had not yet reached Jena, and would have to cross the bridge there during the night, so he at once pushed up the Imperial Guard to support Lannes.

After snatching a few hours' sleep in his bivouac on the Landgrafenberg, the Emperor dictated the following operation order in the early hours of 14 October:

Marshal Augereau (VII) will command the left wing; he will place his leading division in column on the Weimar road, as far forward as General Gazan has got his guns into position on the plateau; he will maintain sufficient forces on the left sector of the plateau, on a level with the head of his column. He will have skirmishers along the whole enemy line at the various approaches from the high ground. As soon as General Gazan advances, he will deploy his whole army corps on the plateau, and will march as circumstances direct so as to form the left wing of the army.

Marshal Lannes (V) will at daybreak have all his artillery in the intervals and in the firing line where he has passed the night.

The artillery of the Imperial Guard will be placed on the ridge and the Guard [infantry] will be behind the plateau, drawn up in five lines, the front line, composed of light infantry, holding the crest.

The village on our right [Closewitz] will be bombarded by the whole of General Suchet's divisional artillery, and will then immediately be attacked and captured.

The Emperor will give the signal, everyone must be ready at dawn.

Marshal Ney (VI) will at daybreak be stationed at the edge of the plateau, so as to be ready to ascend and advance on the right of Marshal Lannes the moment the village is captured, and from there the troops will deploy.

Marshal Soult (IV) will deploy from the track which has been reconnoitred on the right, and will remain in touch there to form the right wing.

The Marshals will form their order of battle in two lines, not counting the line of light infantry; the distance between the lines is not to exceed 200 yards.

* Not to be confused with the village of Dornburg, on the Saale, five miles further north-east.

21 Plan of the Battle of Austerlitz from a contemporary French map in the collection of the Royal Geographical Society. The lakes have now been drained

The light cavalry of each army corps will be placed as most suitable, so that each corps commander can employ it according to circumstances.

The heavy cavalry, as soon as it arrives, will take up position on the plateau and will be in reserve behind the Guard, to be employed as circumstances dictate.

The important thing today is to deploy on the level ground; later on we can make further dispositions in accordance with the movements and strength of the enemy, so as to drive him out of the positions which he occupies and which are necessary for our own deployment. (*Corr.* 11004)

This order is of great interest; Napoleon dictated it in the middle of the night by the light of his bivouac fire on the Landgrafenberg. It gave no map references and no place-names, for the *Grande Armée* had marched so fast and so far that no large-scale maps of the country were available; the topographical features mentioned—'the plateau', 'the village on our right'—had been hastily noted by Napoleon while he surveyed the enemy position in the fading daylight; there had been no time for detailed reconnaissance or for locating the enemy's flanks. This was not an operation order for a full-scale attack at dawn; it was intended merely to set in motion a preliminary advance of the *bataillon carré* in order to drive back the enemy outposts, so as to gain elbow-room on the level plain in front of Weimar, where the Emperor hoped to encircle the whole Prussian army. Napoleon's position was indeed a somewhat precarious one; during the night of the 13th/14th he was assembling on the narrow plateau-scarp above Jena four corps, the cavalry corps and the Guard, in all more than 80,000 men.

Another interesting point is that Napoleon had now changed his mind about the employment of Murat's cavalry corps. He had originally intended to put Murat in charge of the envelopment of the enemy by his right wing, and Murat would have coordinated the movements of Bernadotte (I) and Davout (III) as well as of his own cavalry. It may be that Napoleon remembered Murat having bungled a similar task which had been assigned to him in the investment of Ulm; anyway he now brought Murat's corps over to the left bank of the Saale in order to follow up the expected rout of the Prussian army, which left Bernadotte and Davout to act independently, and resulted, as we shall see later, in the failure of Bernadotte's corps to participate in the coming battle.

During the night of 13/14 October the Saale valley and the plateau west of it were covered in mist. This was fortunate for the French, for the corps of Ney, Soult and Augereau were struggling throughout the night along the narrow, winding tracks leading up from Jena to the plateau above. Much difficulty was experienced in hauling the guns up, and Napoleon himself in person supervised the operation at midnight.

2 *Napoleon entering Berlin by the Brandenburger Tor after the Jena campaign, 27 October 1806 After a painting by Ulrich Ludwig Wolf (1772–1832)*

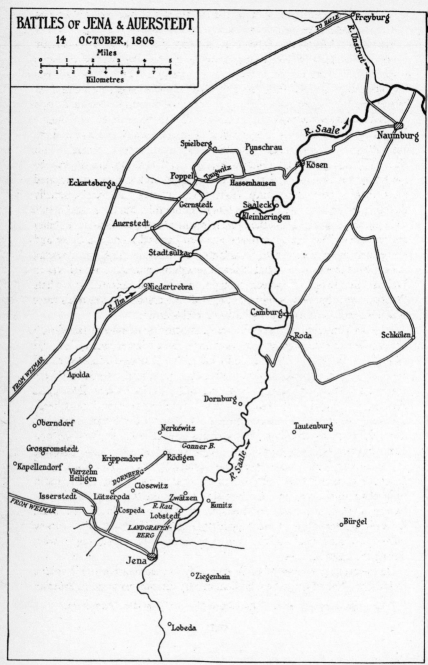

BATTLES OF JENA & AUERSTEDT
14 OCTOBER, 1806

Miles

Kilometres

TO HALLE

Freyburg

R. Unstrut

R. Saale

Naumburg

Spielberg
Punschrau
Kösen

Poppel
Taugewitz
Hassenhausen

Eckartsberga

Gernstedt
Saaleck
Kleinheringen

Auerstedt

Stadtsulza

Niedertrebra

R. Ilm

Camburg

Roda

Schkölen

FROM WEIMAR

Apolda

Dornburg

Oberndorf

Nerkéwitz

Tautenburg

Grossromstedt

Gonner B.

Krippendorf
Rödigen

R. Saale

Kapellendorf

Vierzehn
Heiligen

DORNBERG

Closewitz

Isserstedt

Lützeroda

Zwätzen

Kunitz

FROM WEIMAR

Cospeda

R. Rau
Lobstedt

Bürgel

LANDGRAFEN-
BERG

Jena

Ziegenhain

Lobeda

At dawn Lannes (V), followed by the Guard, at that time the only French troops in position on the plateau, advanced and cleared the Saxons out of Closewitz and Lützeroda. Hohenlohe then brought up the rest of his army from Kapellendorf, and also Rüchel's corps, until he assembled some 47,000 troops on the plateau. With these he occupied the next ridge between Isserstedt and Vierzehn-Heiligen, and hard fighting ensued. At 9 a.m. Ney arrived with VI Corps; the early mist had now dispersed; Ney had been ordered to form up on the right of Lannes (V) but, seeing a gap on Lannes's left, he dashed in there with his usual reckless impetuosity and captured the key village of Vierzehn-Heiligen. The battle now became general. With Soult (IV) deployed on the right and Augereau (VII) on the left, the French outflanked the Prussian line at both ends. Napoleon had now concentrated more than 75,000 men against Hohenlohe's 47,000, and was personally directing the action. The Prussians fought stubbornly, but their movements were too slow and rigid, and the French infantry outclassed them in mobility and initiative. The French artillery was also handled more effectively and cooperated more closely with its infantry. By mid-afternoon the Prussian defeat had become a rout, and Murat's squadrons pursued the fugitives to Weimar and Erfurt. Napoleon thought that he had defeated the whole Prussian army, but he was mistaken; he had only crushed Hohenlohe's force which was acting as flank-guard to Brunswick's army.

After the Prussian reverses at Saalfeld and Schleiz, and now menaced with envelopment by the advance of the French right wing towards Gera and Naumburg, the King of Prussia and the Duke of Brunswick decided to fall back on their line of communication through Merseburg and Halle. By the night of 13 October their main body, marching north-east from Erfurt and Weimar, reached Eckartsberga, 14 miles north of Jena. From Eckartsberga the main road to the north-east crosses the Saale at the Kösen defile and continues through Naumburg. In the early morning of 14 October the Prussian army resumed its retreat through Eckartsberga and Auerstedt * heading for Naumburg. The advanced guard was formed by Schmettau's division and Blücher's cavalry division. As the early morning mist lifted, the Prussian vanguard ran into the head of a French column near the village of Hassenhausen, four miles north-east of Auerstedt, and heavy firing broke out. It had in fact encountered the advanced guard of Davout's III Corps. We must now turn to the movements of the two corps forming Napoleon's right wing during the past two days.

On the evening of 12 October Davout (III), in accordance with his orders, had reached Naumburg, where his light cavalry division captured 12 Prussian

* Also spelt Auerstädt. I have adopted the spelling used in modern German maps.

pontoons with their transport. On the following day Davout was joined at Naumburg by Bernadotte (I). Napoleon's intention was that these two corps should cross the Saale (III Corps by the bridge at Kösen, and I Corps at Dornburg) and then march to Apolda, where they would cut off the retreat of the Prussian army. Unfortunately, this intention was not made absolutely clear to both corps commanders in the orders issued by Berthier.

At 3 a.m. on 14 October Davout (III) at Naumburg received from Berthier an order despatched the previous evening at 10 p.m. from Napoleon's bivouac on the Landgrafenberg. This order informed Davout that the Emperor had located the Prussian army on the plateau between Jena and Weimar, and would attack it on the 14th. The III Corps was to move from Naumburg to Apolda and envelop the enemy's left flank; the order continued:

If Marshal Bernadotte is with you, you can both march together; but the Emperor hopes that he will have reached the position assigned to him, at Dornburg.

Berthier had omitted to despatch a separate order to Bernadotte. On receipt of Berthier's order, Davout at once took it to Bernadotte's billet and showed it to him, suggesting that they should march together to Apolda, and offering to place III Corps under Bernadotte's orders. The latter rejected this suggestion, saying that his previous orders had been to march to Dornburg, which he proceeded to do, thereby blocking the road for three of Murat's cavalry divisions.

In accordance with Berthier's order, Davout moved off from Naumburg before dawn on 14 October. At 6 a.m. his leading division (Gudin) crossed the Saale unopposed at the narrow Kösen defile and reached Hassenhausen two hours later. Here in the fog an encounter battle took place between Gudin's advanced guard and that of Graf von Schmettau's division, which was leading the retreat of Brunswick's army northwards. Schmettau was supported by Blücher's cavalry division, which charged the French column. The latter saved themselves by forming square, giving Davout time to bring up in succession Friant's and Morand's divisions, which deployed between Hassenhausen and Auerstedt, and the battle became general. At this juncture the Duke of Brunswick came up and reinforced Schmettau and Blücher with the divisions of Wartensleben and the Prince of Orange, so that the bulk of the Prussian army was now engaged against Davout's corps. The Duke, however, fell, mortally wounded by a bullet in the head, and Schmettau also was killed. The King of Prussia arrived and took charge, but confusion was already spreading in the Prussian ranks. Davout brought his guns into action on the Sonnenberg ridge which enfiladed the Auerstedt ravine, and the Prussian reinforcing columns were mown down. The Prussian King then ordered a retreat to Weimar, but this only added to the confusion, for his retreating troops encountered the thousands of fugitives from the Jena battlefield, who were being cut down by Murat's cavalry. The French continued the pursuit until late in the day.

The double victory of Jena and Auerstedt resulted in the complete destruction of the Prussian army as a fighting body. But Napoleon's success had not been won by skilful tactical manœuvre, as at Austerlitz. He took an unjustifiable risk in squeezing four corps and his Guard through the narrow defile at Jena in close proximity to the enemy. Had that enemy been vigilant and enterprising, Lannes's corps might have been destroyed, and the other corps defeated in detail. Napoleon's manœuvre was all the more hazardous, for on the Landgrafenberg he imagined that he was dealing with the whole Prussian army; it is hardly surprising that, with 75,000 men at his disposal, he defeated the 47,000 which Hohenlohe brought up piecemeal. By comparison, Davout's achievement at Auerstedt was the more meritorious, for with only 26,000 French troops he routed 45,000 Prussians; it was a hard-fought battle, for the French had 7000 casualties, Gudin's division alone losing 3630, or over 40 per cent of its strength.

One may fairly say that Napoleon's success in the Jena campaign was mainly due to the ineptitude of the Prussian commanders; first of all, strategically, when they exposed their left flank and rearward communications to Napoleon's enveloping movement between the Saale valley and the Saxon border; secondly, tactically, when they neglected to hold the crossings of the Saale between Jena and Naumburg. Napoleon would have had great difficulty in getting his *bataillon carré* across the deep trench of the Saale in the face of determined opposition, and Davout could hardly have reached Auerstedt had the Prussians seized and held the defile at Kösen.

The spoils of the double victory were immense; 25,000 prisoners, 200 field-guns and 60 colours were taken. There was little more resistance on the part of the Prussian army, and Napoleon made his triumphal entry into Berlin on 27 October, three weeks after the start of the campaign. On the way he spent three days at Potsdam, and removed from the Palace of Sans-Souci Frederick the Great's sword and military decorations, which he sent as trophies to the Hôtel des Invalides in Paris.

The only French military leader who failed to achieve distinction on 14 October was the commander of I Corps, Marshal Jean-Baptiste Bernadotte, Prince of Ponte-Corvo. His conduct during the battle earned him a severe reprimand from his chief (*Corr.* 11060). After refusing to accompany Davout in the march from Naumburg to Apolda, which was evidently the Emperor's wish, he obstinately adhered to his previously assigned rendezvous,

Dornburg. There he remained inactive throughout the battle until 4 p.m., although he must have heard the gun-fire all day from both Jena and Auerstedt, for he was half-way between and seven miles distant from both battlefields. In later years, at St. Helena, the Emperor expressed his own feelings about this incident in the following words:

Bernadotte's conduct at Jena was such that the Emperor had signed the warrant ordering him to be court-martialled; he would certainly have been sentenced, so great was the indignation of the army. It was only out of consideration for the Princess of Ponte-Corvo that, when on the point of handing the warrant to Marshal Berthier, the Emperor tore it up.

Bernadotte's wife was Désirée Clary, who had been Bonaparte's fiancée before he met Joséphine; she was also the sister of Julie Clary, his brother Joseph's wife. This was neither the first nor the last time that Napoleon had occasion to reprimand his brother-in-law for his behaviour on the field of battle. The Emperor's continued lenience to Bernadotte was due less to considerateness for the Princess than to reluctance to tarnish the reputation of any member of the Imperial family.

XII

Poland and East Prussia
1806-1807

Napoleon lost no time in pursuing his defeated and demoralized enemy. The remnants of the Prussian field army retreated to the north-eastern corner of their territory in order to gain contact with their Russian allies, who were now approaching the frontier. The Prussian Government had indeed been extremely foolish to challenge Napoleon at the beginning of October, long before the Russians could come to their assistance. Had they waited another two months, Napoleon would have been faced with a winter campaign against greatly superior forces.

The *Grande Armée* was now loosed like a pack of hounds in pursuit of the scattered Prussian columns. Prince Hohenlohe, who had retreated through Magdeburg, was rounded up by Murat at Prenzlau on 28 October, when he surrendered with 16,000 men. Blücher, more elusive, was pursued by Bernadotte and Soult through Lübeck, and finally laid down his arms with 10,000 men near Travemünde on the Baltic coast on 7 November; Lübeck was stormed and sacked by the French troops. On the following day Kleist with 20,000 men surrendered the fortress of Magdeburg to Ney. The King of Prussia had already signed the terms of an armistice, but Napoleon repudiated this and invaded Prussian Poland in order to confront the Russians.

The Russians were thirsting to avenge their defeat at Austerlitz, which they ascribed, with some justice, to the inept strategy imposed on them by the Austrians. Two Russian armies were now approaching, one of 55,000 under Bennigsen* at Pultusk, 30 miles north of Warsaw, the other of

---

* General Levin August Bennigsen (1745-1826) was a Hanoverian who had entered the Russian service in 1773.

36,000 under Buxhövden, farther in rear. Both were under the over-all command of Field-Marshal Kamenski, an inefficient octogenarian. The King of Prussia and his Court had withdrawn to Königsberg (Kaliningrad) in East Prussia, but there was still in the field a Prussian corps of 15,000 under General L'Estocq near Thorn (Torun).

Being now in occupation of the whole German coastline as far east as the mouth of the Oder, Napoleon seized the opportunity to strike another blow at British commerce by declaring a complete blockade of the British Isles; all British persons or goods found in territory occupied by the French or their allies were to be seized, and any ship trading with Britain or a British colony was liable to confiscation. These decrees were promulgated from Berlin on 21 November, and meant ruin for the Hanseatic traders of Hamburg, Bremen, Lübeck and Danzig. On 7 January 1807 the British Government retaliated with an Order in Council declaring any neutral vessel liable to seizure which carried goods to or from any French port.

Napoleon now formed a IX Corps, composed of the Bavarian and Württemberg contingents, which he placed under the command of his youngest brother, the incompetent and inexperienced 22-year-old Jérôme, and sent it to reduce the Prussian fortresses in Silesia, which were still holding out.

In order to safeguard his communications in the coming campaign against Russia, it was important for Napoleon to gain the friendship and cooperation of the Poles. As a result of the Seven Years' War their country had been partitioned between Austria, Prussia and Russia, with capitals respectively at Krakow, Posen (Poznan) and Warsaw. With his usual astute statecraft Napoleon considered the claims of various candidates as future head of State for a resurrected Poland, which could act as a buffer against Russian aggression. He at once discarded the patriot Kosciuszko, the acknowledged champion of Polish liberty, as being too much of a Paoli; he also rejected Prince Czartoryski, as being too friendly with Tsar Alexander; his final choice settled on Prince Joseph Poniatowski, a prominent nobleman who had been hostile to Russian rule.

After making these political preparations for detaching Poland from Russia, the Emperor set his army in motion once more to meet the Russian threat. Winter was now approaching, but he could not afford to await the spring, for by then the Russians would have assembled a vast army, and Austria might be tempted to join them for a renewal of the struggle. In the first week of November Davout (III) was sent to occupy Posen, and Berthier was ordered to send four surveyors to map the surrounding country, 'for it is there that I mean to deliver battle to the Russians if they intend to advance' (*Corr.* 11195). But the Russians were slow movers. After attending to the fortification of Spandau, Stettin and Küstrin in order to guard his line of communications, and calling up 80,000 conscripts of the 1807 class to replenish the ranks of the *Grande Armée*, Napoleon transferred Imperial Headquarters from Berlin to Posen on 27 November. On the following day Murat's cavalry entered Warsaw, driving the Russian advanced guard out of the citadel of Praga on the right bank of the Vistula (back endpaper).

To engage a Russian army of unknown strength and potential at the onset of winter was a formidable enough military venture, but the strategic problems involved were dwarfed by the administrative ones. The *Grande Armée* of 140,000 men, which had marched a thousand miles and fought a strenuous campaign, had not only to be fed, but had also to be entirely re-equipped and provided with winter clothing, and that in an inhospitable land of forests, marshes and lakes. Napoleon's genius on the battlefield was only equalled by his brilliance as an organizer. A study of his correspondence during the two months from 27 October, when he reached Berlin, and 26 December when he first encountered the main Russian army, reveals the vast range of problems with which he had to wrestle. He was certainly gifted with an infinite capacity for taking pains, and no cog in the machine of government escaped his alert attention.

On the day after the battle of Jena the Emperor had issued a decree fixing the war contributions to be levied on the city of Berlin and on each of the Prussian feudatory States, such as Hesse-Cassel and Brunswick. State-Councillor Daru,* the Intendant-General of the *Grande Armée*, was told to have 280,000 greatcoats and 250,000 pairs of boots manufactured in the principal Prussian towns. Six general hospitals were to be organized, including special ones for cases of scabies and venereal disease; 6000 hospital mattresses were to be made up in Berlin, and 12,000 Prussian tents were to be cut up to make 9000 hospital sheets.

Military administration was not the only subject which engrossed the Emperor's attention; he dictated orders to Admiral Decrès about the launching of new warships, and about winter cruises to keep his naval squadrons at Toulon, Rochefort and Lorient occupied. Foreign affairs, too, were woven into his far-reaching designs. Talleyrand was instructed to press the King of Spain to send a contingent of 14,000 men to occupy Hanover. The Sultan of Turkey and the Shah of Persia were urged to invade Russian territory on the lower Danube and on the Caucasus front in order to divert the Russian

---

* Pierre-Antoine-Noël Daru (1767–1829), after serving in the artillery, became a *commissaire des guerres* under the Revolution. In 1799 he displayed conspicuous administrative ability as Massena's Chief Commissary in Switzerland. He performed similar services for Napoleon in the Marengo and Austerlitz campaigns.

military effort. A Polish division was organized under Generals Dombrowski and Zaionczek, and armed with rifles surrendered by the Prussian army. Finally, Saxony was induced to break away from Prussia and join the Rhine Confederation, her Elector, Frederick Augustus, being given the title of King.

These various matters having been dealt with, the Emperor turned to his military campaign. On 24 November Murat was given a task force of 66,000 men, comprising the corps of Davout (III), Lannes (V) and Augereau (VII), besides his own cavalry, and ordered to occupy the line of the Vistula between Warsaw and Plock. He was also told to secure bridgeheads over the rivers Bug, Narew and Wkra, which all unite and join the Vistula within a radius of 20 miles north of Warsaw, that city being the key-point which gives access to the whole plain of northern Poland. On the left wing Ney (VI) was ordered to cross the Vistula and occupy Thorn, thus opening a corridor to the East Prussian region of the Masurian Lakes.

On being confronted with Murat's army, Bennigsen, commanding the Russian advanced guard, abandoned Warsaw and withdrew 30 miles northward to Pultusk on the Narew. Napoleon at once ordered Murat to advance on Pultusk, and on 13 December issued a general directive for a forward move by the rest of the army, namely Soult (IV), Ney (VI), Bernadotte (I) and the Imperial Guard, beyond the Vistula to the line of the Wkra, the next river obstacle (*Corr.* 11458). The Emperor himself left Posen on 15 December and established his headquarters at Warsaw on the 19th. The weather was unusually mild for the time of year, but it now started to rain heavily.

The Emperor took over personal command of the operations and the French advance began on 23 December. On the left flank, Ney (VI), followed by Bernadotte (I), advanced eastwards from Thorn for 60 miles and crossed the Wkra at Biezun, where they engaged and drove back L'Estocq's Prussian corps. In the centre, Soult (IV) crossed the Vistula near Plock and advanced 25 miles to Plonsk. On the right wing, Lannes (V), Davout (IV) and Augereau (VII), after crossing the Bug, pressed forward to the line Serock–Nasielsk. This concentric advance caused the Russians to withdraw 12 miles to the line Golymin–Pultusk. The elderly Kamenski, feeling that his communications with the north were threatened, ordered a general retreat up the Narew valley to Ostrolenka, but his subordinates, Bennigsen and Buxhövden, decided to stand firm.

The real fighting took place on 26 December. Lannes (V) on the French right made a gallant attack on Bennigsen's position at Pultusk, but was repulsed with considerable loss, mainly due to the Russian artillery fire. Napoleon then made a concentrated attack further north at Golymin, against the sector held by Buxhövden's troops, with the corps of Soult (IV), Davout (III) and Augereau (VII). This eventually forced the Russians to retire to Makow, and under cover of the night they continued their retreat for 25 miles north-eastwards to Ostrolenka. Rain had fallen continuously; there was no frost and the marshy Narew valley had become a sea of mud. The French had lost more than 3000 killed and wounded, and were quite incapable of pursuing the Russians. The mud was so deep that the latter had to abandon nearly all their guns. On 29 December the Emperor wrote to Joséphine:

I can only write you a word, my dear; I am living in a wretched barn. I have beaten the Russians, and taken 30 guns and their baggage, and made 6000 prisoners. But the weather is awful; it goes on raining, and the mud is up to our knees. (*Corr.* 11517)

That was a fairly concise account of the battle of Pultusk. Napoleon remained there until the end of the month and then returned to Warsaw, where he established himself for the winter.

The battle of Pultusk, though a French victory, was not a brilliant one. Napoleon had attacked the Russians frontally, making his main effort on the right wing, in the marshy valleys of the Narew and Wkra, where tactical manœuvre was impossible. Had he made his main attack with his left wing on the higher ground, from Thorn towards Mlawa and Ostrolenka, he might have inflicted a more decisive defeat on the enemy and cut off his retreat.

The morale of the *Grande Armée* was now very depressed; the state of the roads was appalling, and the troops were completely exhausted after their long marches. There were no more shouts of '*Vive l'Empereur!*', as at Austerlitz, but only scowls and growls when he rode past his men. The mud had rendered any further operations impossible until the frost came to harden the roads, and both sides went into winter quarters, the Russians between Lomza and the Masurian Lakes, the French to the east of the Vistula between Warsaw and Elbing (Elblag). Marshal Kamenski was now removed from command of the Russian field army and replaced by Bennigsen. Prussian garrisons were still holding out in the fortresses of Danzig (Gdansk) and Graudenz (Grudziadz) on the lower Vistula; to reduce these Napoleon formed a X Corps under Marshal Lefebvre, consisting largely of Polish troops.

The left wing of the *Grande Armée* was formed by Bernadotte (I) at Elbing and Ney (VI) at Gilgenburg (Dabrowno), south of Osterode. Ney found it difficult to feed his troops in the sparsely inhabited frontier district, so in his usual impulsive way he conceived the idea of making a raid into the more fertile territory farther north. He started off in the first week of January 1807 and penetrated 60 miles into East Prussia. Near Bartenstein (Bartszyce) on the river Alle (Lyna) he encountered L'Estocq's Prussian corps and was forced to retrace his steps. Ney's rash raid, however, led Bennigsen to think that this was the commencement of a French offensive; he advanced westwards with his army of 63,000 men in order to drive Ney and Bernadotte back across the lower Vistula. The Russian counter-offensive reached Mohrungen (Morag) on 25 January, when it was halted by Bernadotte's corps.

Napoleon was very angry with Ney for stirring up trouble, for he had intended to settle down in winter quarters and give his troops a rest, but Bennigsen's advance made him anxious about the safety of his advanced base at Thorn, on which depended the supplies of the I and VI Corps. He also saw that the Russian advance westwards had exposed their left flank to attack from the south. On 27 January, therefore, Napoleon decided to take the offensive himself; Bernadotte (I) was to retire and lure the Russians on towards the Vistula, while the rest of the *Grande Armée* would advance northwards through Allenstein (Olsztyn) and cut off their retreat. Orders were at once issued for the III, IV, VI, VII and Cavalry Corps to break up from their winter quarters on 1 February and march northward to a concentration area between Mlawa and Ortelsburg (Szczytno).

This sudden change of plan disrupted the French transport and supply organization, which had hitherto been based on Warsaw. The Emperor immediately transferred his main advanced base to Thorn, which afforded an easier line of communications with Berlin; he also returned to the magazine system of supply. On 2 February he wrote from Willenberg to his Intendant-General in Berlin:

Monsieur Daru, urgent circumstances have obliged me to revert to the magazine system. The greatcoats and boots despatched from Berlin are worthless. The greatcoats from Leipzig are ridiculously short; I have seen some which barely reached the knee. . . . The boots, especially those supplied from Berlin, are of the worst quality. (*Corr.* 11767)

Although it had snowed heavily, there had also been a very hard frost and movement was now easy. The Emperor himself moved his headquarters with amazing rapidity; he left Warsaw at 6 a.m. on 30 January and reached Willenberg (Wielbark) at midday on the 31st, having travelled 80 miles. By 3 February Napoleon had reached Allenstein and the *Grande Armée* was concentrated in the forward area ready to strike. But at this moment one of those mishaps which so frequently occur in war deprived him of the chance of attacking the Russian left flank with overwhelming force. An A.D.C.

despatched by Berthier to Bernadotte with the operation order was captured by a Cossack patrol, so that not only did Bernadotte fail to cooperate in the intended concentric attack, but the Emperor's entire plan was revealed to the Russian commander. Bennigsen at once realized his danger and hurriedly retreated northwards towards Königsberg.

As Napoleon travelled north from Warsaw, he found that Lannes had fallen sick, so he replaced him in command of V Corps by his own senior A.D.C., General Savary, and detached the corps to act as right flank guard in the Narew valley to watch a Russian corps under General Essen which was assembling farther east. The remaining corps of the *Grande Armée* marched northward in pursuit of Bennigsen, with the exception of Bernadotte (I), who was left inactive owing to his orders having miscarried.

After crossing the river Alle at Heilsberg (Lidzbark), the advanced guard, consisting of Murat's cavalry and Soult (IV), came up with the Russians on 7 February at the little town of Preussisch-Eylau,* now renamed Bagrationovsk, 24 miles south of Königsberg (Kaliningrad). The town was held by the Russian rearguard under Prince Bagratión, who had checked Murat's pursuit at Hollabrunn before the battle of Austerlitz. A sharp encounter took place; Soult's corps deployed and enveloped the Russian flanks, and the latter retired after dark to a strong position held by their main body, four miles long, on a ridge east of Eylau. Napoleon came up during the night and took charge. Soult (IV) and Augereau (VII) were to attack frontally from Eylau at daybreak, supported by the Imperial Guard, while Davout (III) was to turn the Russian left flank and Ney (VI) was to engage L'Estocq's Prussian corps on the Russian right flank.

On the following morning the battle opened with an artillery duel, the Russians having a greater weight of metal. Augereau's corps then advanced from Eylau to attack the Russian position, but a blinding snow-storm came on; Augereau's men lost their direction in the blizzard and were enfiladed at close range by the massed Russian batteries. Augereau himself was suffering from acute rheumatism and was slightly wounded; one of his divisional commanders was killed. The corps suffered such heavy casualties that it had to be withdrawn. The Russians then counter-attacked and recaptured Eylau, but Napoleon brought up a battalion of his Guard and drove them out again. A desperate struggle then took place, both sides suffering heavily. Eventually Davout's outflanking movement turned the scale and, as night fell, Bennigsen withdrew his army towards Königsberg.

* Preussisch-Eylau should not be confused with Deutsch-Eylau (Ilawa), between Graudenz and Osterode. It is now in the territory annexed by the Russians after the Second World War.

The French were far too exhausted to pursue the enemy. Out of 80,000 engaged they had lost 15,000,* while the Russians had suffered still more heavily, losing 18,000 out of 73,000. It was the most sanguinary battle that Napoleon had yet conducted and, though his troops remained in possession of the battlefield, it can hardly be regarded as a French victory; the *Grande Armée* was, for the time, incapable of further fighting. The IV and VII Corps had suffered exceptionally heavy losses and some units were so reduced in numbers that they had to be broken up. Napoleon ascribed the tactical blunders of his infantry to the blinding snow which prevailed, but this did not prevent the Russian gunners from doing murderous execution.

Murat, some of whose squadrons had not been engaged, on the next day slowly followed the Russians to within five miles of Königsberg, but found them in a strong position on the right bank of the Pregel (Pregola). Napoleon then withdrew his shattered troops 50 miles to the south-west, where they went into winter quarters west of the rivers Passarge (Pasleka), Alle and Omulew. A fortnight later the Imperial Headquarters were established at Osterode, and were on 1 April transferred to Schloss Finckenstein, 20 miles east of Marienwerder (Kwidzyn). The army was then refitted and brought up to strength. As Lannes was still on the sick list, Massena was brought back from southern Italy and given command of V Corps at Pultusk.

Napoleon took advantage of this cessation of active hostilities to reorganize his exhausted army and to consolidate his position in the northern part of occupied Germany. Augereau's VII Corps, which had suffered so heavily at Eylau, was broken up; throughout France the 1808 class was called up prematurely, 25,000 of the 80,000 conscripts being assigned to replenish the ranks of the *Grande Armée*. Mortier's VIII Corps was sent to occupy Pomerania and Stralsund, then under Swedish sovereignty, and was later reinforced by a Spanish contingent of 30,000 under General La Romana. Three Prussian fortresses still held out: Danzig and Graudenz on the lower Vistula and Kolberg on the Baltic coast. Danzig was the hardest nut to crack, being held by 12,000 Prussians and three Russian battalions under General Kalckreuth. The siege was entrusted to the 51-year-old Marshal Lefebvre with his mixed X Corps of French, Germans and Poles. Lefebvre did not display the energy expected by his chief and received frequent admonitions. After a vain attempt by the Russians to relieve it from the sea, Danzig finally capitulated on 24 May and X Corps was then broken up. On 5 May Lannes

---

* No comprehensive casualty lists for the Napoleonic battles are to be found in the French military historical archives. One can only obtain totals by adding up the losses of every unit engaged. The figures computed by different historians vary considerably; those given in Napoleon's bulletins are completely mendacious.

returned from sick leave and was given command of a new Reserve Corps, 15,000 strong.

When the *Grande Armée* retreated to the south-west corner of East Prussia after the battle of Eylau the Russians had followed up slowly, and the two armies now faced each other on the river Passarge.

After the capture of Danzig Napoleon changed his line of communications once more. Thorn being now too far to the south, he transferred his advanced base to Danzig, with his communications running forward through Marienburg, Marienwerder and Elbing.

On 4 June Bennigsen, whose army had been reinforced to 100,000 men, took the offensive and attacked Ney's Corps, which held an exposed salient between Guttstadt (Dobre Miasto) and Allenstein. Ney was forced to retire behind the Passarge, but Napoleon promptly counter-attacked with I, III, IV, VIII and Lannes's Corps and restored the situation. In this fighting Bernadotte was wounded, and the Emperor replaced him in command of I Corps by General Victor,* one of his own favourites. Napoleon now decided to take the offensive himself in order to drive the Russians out of East Prussia. With Murat and Soult (IV) acting as a general advanced guard, the whole army advanced on 8 June, but the Russians had constructed a strongly entrenched camp at Heilsberg, where fighting took place on 10 June and the French suffered heavy casualties. Napoleon, however, pressed forward with his left wing in order to turn Bennigsen's right flank and cut him off from his base at Königsberg. The Russians were forced out of Heilsberg and retreated to Bartenstein (Bartozyce). Napoleon occupied Heilsberg on the 12th and the next day reached Eylau, where the indecisive but costly battle had been fought four months earlier. Bennigsen continued his retreat to Friedland, the last place where he could cross the river Alle before its junction with the Pregel at Wehlau (Snamensk).

Friedland, now renamed by the Russians Pravdinsk, is a small town 27 miles south-east of Königsberg and 15 miles east of Eylau. Napoleon quickly decided to seize this strategic key-point to frustrate the Russian retreat. He now had the choice of two routes by which to intercept the Russians, either to the west of the Alle or to the east of that river. The western route was the shortest and easiest, leading directly to Königsberg, the Russian advanced base, where they had collected vast quantities of supplies and equipment. But, from the strategic point of view, this approach would merely drive

---

* Claude-Victor Perrin (1764–1841), who took the surname of Victor, distinguished himself as an artillery sergeant at the siege of Toulon (1793) and gained Bonaparte's friendship. Napoleon made him a Marshal after Friedland (1807) and Duke of Belluno (1808).

Bennigsen back on his line of communications through Riga and Kovno, and Napoleon could not afford to pursue him into the depths of Russia. The more easterly approach, by-passing Friedland, would cut the Russian line of communications between Königsberg and Tilsit (Sovetsk), and would drive Bennigsen's army into the Königsberg peninsula, 17 miles wide, where they would be hemmed in against the Baltic coast. Jomini, a competent military critic, who at the time was serving on Napoleon's staff, considers that the Emperor should have advanced by the eastern route but, in fact, Napoleon chose to keep to the left bank of the Alle. The wider turning movement to the east would have involved far longer marches, and his right flank would have been exposed to attack; the difficulties of supply would also have been greatly increased.

In either case, Friedland was the main point to aim at, and the Emperor now directed the bulk of his army there from Bartenstein, while detaching his left wing, consisting of Murat's cavalry, Davout (III) and Soult (IV) to pursue L'Estocq's corps northward to Königsberg. The Emperor himself, with the main body of the army, moved eastward toward Friedland, where Bennigsen's main army was now holding the crossing over the Alle. Mortier (VIII) formed the left wing, Lannes the centre, and Ney (VI) the right wing. The Imperial Guard and Victor (I) formed the general reserve behind the centre.

The following day, 14 June, was the seventh anniversary of the battle of Marengo. Napoleon, somewhat credulous of omens, determined to give Bennigsen the *coup de grâce* that day. At 3 a.m. he dictated the following operational directive to his corps commanders for the attack on Bennigsen's bridgehead at Friedland:

Marshal Ney will form the right wing, from Posthenen towards Sortlack, ... Marshal Lannes will form the centre, extending from Marshal Ney's left, at Heinrichsdorf, as far as almost opposite the village of Posthenen. Oudinot's grenadiers, who at present form Marshal Lannes's right, will gradually feel to their left so as to attract the enemy's attention. Marshal Lannes will disengage his divisions as much as he can, in order to organize them in two lines. The left will be formed by Marshal Mortier, holding Heinrichsdorf and the Königsberg road, and from there extending to face the Russian right wing. Marshal Mortier will not advance at all, as the turning movement must be made by our right wing, pivoting on the left.

General Espagne's cavalry and General Grouchy's dragoons, in conjunction with the cavalry on the left wing, will move so as to inflict the greatest possible damage on the enemy when he is forced to retreat by the vigorous attack by our right.

General Victor and the Imperial Guard, horse and foot, will form the reserve at Grünhof, Bothkeim and behind Posthenen.

176

23 *Battle of Eylau, 8 February 180*
After a painting by Jacques-François Swebach (1769–1823). The Frenc
right wing is attacking the Russian position east of the villag

24 Battle of Eylau. The French advanced guard stormed the churchyard the evening before the main battle; French guns crossing the frozen lake

25 Battle of Landshut, 21 April 1809. Massena's corps driving Hiller's Austrian corps across the Isar the day before the battle of Eckmühl

26 The Grande Armée deploying on 5 July 1809 from the wooded island of Lobau (near left) to attack the Archduke's position at Deutsch-Wagram (far centre)

These sketches were made on the battlefield by Captain Giuseppe Pietro Bagetti, a surveyor-cartographer on Berthier's staff. They are now reproduced for the first time by courtesy of the Musée de l'Armée, Invalides, Paris

Lahoussaye's dragoon division will be under General Victor's orders; Latour-Maubourg's will be under Marshal Ney's orders; General Nansouty's heavy cavalry division will be at Marshal Lannes's disposal and will act with the cavalry of the Reserve Corps in the centre.

I shall be with the reserve.

The advance must be made from the right, and the progress of the attack will be left to the initiative of Marshal Ney, who will await my orders to move off.

From the moment when the right attacks the enemy, every gun in action will double its rate of fire on its correct line, so as to cover the attack on that wing. (*Corr.* 12756)

This directive was admirably clear and concise; every corps commander was made aware of the Emperor's plan, while being given full discretion for the detailed moves to ensure its execution; the villages mentioned were already occupied by the French, so that their names were familiar to all units. An adequate reserve was kept under Napoleon's hand, while the fullest cooperation between all arms was ensured.

The Emperor had at once appreciated the tactical weakness of Bennigsen's position. His bridgehead had no depth, and he had crowded 50,000 men into a narrow river valley with one bridge in their rear. Nor was this river line a suitable one for defence, as the winding loops of the Alle formed several salient spurs which enabled the French artillery to enfilade every sector of the Russian position.

Napoleon at noon moved his command post up to the centre of the reserve line, while the corps of Ney, Lannes and Mortier deployed for the attack. At 5.30 p.m. he gave the signal for the advance to commence. Ney gave his assault columns the church spire of Friedland as their direction, but on reaching the Russian position they were met with a destructive fire and wavered. They could make no progress, in spite of a gallant charge by Latour-Maubourg's dragoons on the Russian flank. General Senarmont, commanding Victor's corps artillery in reserve, then pushed forward his 36 guns and brought them into action on a spur enfilading the bridge at Friedland. The concentrated fire of these massed batteries produced a devastating effect on the Russian columns in the valley below. Ney with great gallantry led his corps forward on the right flank, supported by Lannes's advance in the centre. By 8 p.m. Ney had gained possession of Friedland, and the remnants of Bennigsen's army retreated northwards during the night, pursued by the French cavalry, to Wehlau on the Pregel.

The victory of Friedland was one of Napoleon's most brilliant achievements. He had no opportunity of reconnoitring the battlefield beforehand, nor had he any fore-knowledge of the enemy's intentions, as at Austerlitz. But from the reports of his cavalry he had located the enemy's position and had obtained sufficient knowledge of the ground to enable him to dictate his battle orders with unerring skill. Although strategically he had merely driven the Russians back on their line of communications, his tactical victory at Friedland in fact proved decisive. On the following day Bennigsen crossed the Pregel at Wehlau and retreated to Tilsit on the Niemen. The casualties on both sides had been very heavy; the Russians lost 10,000 out of 46,000 engaged; the French lost 12,000 out of 86,000, but neither the Imperial Guard nor the bulk of Victor's corps, apart from his artillery, had been called upon to take part in the battle. The Russians left 80 guns in the hands of the French.

Meanwhile, on the same day, Murat, with Soult and Davout, drove L'Estocq's Prussian corps northward from Eylau to Königsberg, and established themselves on the left bank of the Pregel. The Prussians continued their retreat, and Murat pursued them to Tilsit.

The results of the battle of Friedland were far-reaching. On 19 June Bennigsen asked for an armistice, which the Emperor accepted. He had neither the intention nor the means to penetrate farther into Russian territory, with his lines of communication ever lengthening and becoming more vulnerable. He was now in occupation of all Prussian territory, excepting the Memel district north of the Niemen (Néman). He was also anxious to come to terms with Tsar Alexander in order to anticipate any movement on the part of Austria. On 25 June Napoleon and Alexander met on a raft anchored in midstream on the Niemen, where a pavilion had been erected. A conference took place between the two Emperors, and Talleyrand, who had already reached Danzig, was summoned to negotiate the terms of peace. After a further fortnight Napoleon signed a final peace treaty with the Russians on 7 July, and two days later with Prussia. By the end of the month Napoleon had returned to Paris. By the Treaties of Tilsit he had reorganized central and eastern Europe. A Grand Duchy of Warsaw was created as a buffer State between Prussia and Russia, ruled by Frederick Augustus, the puppet King of Saxony; all Prussian territory west of the Elbe was converted into a Kingdom of Westphalia, to provide a crown for Napoleon's incompetent young brother Jérôme; most important of all, Russia was enlisted as an ally in the war against British commerce.

XIII

Apogee of an Empire
1807-1808

The conclusion of the Treaties of Tilsit raised Napoleon to an unparalleled position as Dictator of the European Continent; not since the time of Charlemagne had such a hegemony existed. The French Empire now extended from the Pyrenees to the Elbe, a distance of 900 miles as the crow flies; in the south it continued to the toe of Italy, and in the east to the Dalmatian coast. The problems of administering such a vast area, peopled by so many different nations, were becoming too great a burden to be carried by one ruler, especially one who had such a meticulous mind for detail and who was averse from delegating authority.

The military problems which confronted the Emperor were alone stupendous. He had indeed in three successive years crushed his three principal rivals on land: Austria, Prussia and Russia; but the maintenance of military force was still required to keep them in subjection. His remaining enemy, Britain, was beyond his reach, thanks to her insular position, since his battle-fleet had been destroyed at Trafalgar; he could only hope to subdue Britain by completely strangling her overseas commerce through his 'Continental System'. This commercial blockade, however, could not be rigidly enforced until the long Atlantic seaboard of Spain and Portugal could be brought effectively under his own control. Spain, it is true, was his ally, but a very half-hearted one, especially since Trafalgar, while Portugal, except for a few francophiles, was definitely in the British camp. Within three weeks of signing the Treaties of Tilsit, Napoleon made up his mind to subjugate the whole Iberian Peninsula; on 29 July, as a first step, he ordered his War Ministry to organize at Bayonne, on the Spanish frontier, an army of 20,000 men and 40 field-guns.

Quem deus vult perdere prius dementat. Napoleon's insanely ambitious decision to extend his sway over all Spain and Portugal was the beginning of his downfall. Largely owing to the ineptitude of his enemies, his victories in central Europe had been too easy. He was now hypnotized by his own success and believed himself to be infallible, both in strategy and statecraft. He had proved himself to be the greatest soldier in Europe, and the *Grande Armée* to be invincible; he had outwitted the most astute diplomats and forced the crowned heads of ancient monarchies to bend the knee to him. It had all gone to his head; from now on a *folie de grandeur* increasingly clouded both his military judgment and his political perspicacity.

The Roman Empire had been based on the fighting strength of the legions; the Napoleonic Empire could only be maintained by the *Grande Armée*. But that was a tool which he himself had forged, and which only he could wield in person. This had been deliberate policy on his part, for he had studied ancient history, and knew how many Roman Emperors had been deposed by the legions under refractory commanders. On the day following his proclamation as Emperor of the French he had created 18 Marshals of the Empire, and after Tilsit he had added his friend General Victor to the list. They were mostly good tacticians and troop leaders, anyway under his own personal direction; none of them, with the exception of Massena, Davout and Soult, were capable of commanding an independent army. In fact, with the above exceptions, the Marshals were military mediocrities, and were never encouraged to think for themselves or attempt strategic manœuvre. All he required of them was blind obedience to his own personal leadership. By open-handed distribution of honours, gratuities and decorations he had also ensured that the loyalty of the rank and file was focused solely on himself. The imperial edifice which Napoleon had so far successfully erected was, in fact, an inverted pyramid; the whole structure rested on his own person, and would have crumbled to pieces had he fallen a victim to a stray round-shot at Austerlitz, Jena or Friedland.

By extending the theatre of war to the Iberian Peninsula the Emperor was incurring the risk of that bugbear of all strategists, a war on two fronts. Russia, it is true, was now his ally, and Prussia had been knocked out for some time to come. But there were already signs that Austria was dreaming of revenge for her defeat two years previously and was making stealthy preparations for a renewal of the struggle. Napoleon was alive to this danger; on 12 August 1807 he instructed his new Foreign Minister, Jean-Baptiste Nompère de Champagny, who had just replaced Talleyrand, to write a carefully worded warning to Metternich about Austria's warlike preparations (*Corr.* 13023). But the *Grande Armée*, 200,000 strong, had not been disbanded and was still occupying Prussia and Poland, distributed in six military *commandements* as follows:

1. Davout: H.Q. at Warsaw
2. Soult: H.Q. at Stettin
3. Mortier: H.Q. at Breslau
4. Victor: H.Q. at Berlin
5. Bernadotte: H.Q. at Hamburg
6. Brune: H.Q. at Hanover

The *Grand Quartier Général* under Berthier was established at Berlin. Davout, who at Warsaw was nearest to the Austrian frontier, warned the Emperor of what he heard from Vienna; Napoleon, however, preferred to discount the danger, and on 13 October wrote to Davout:

> The rumours of war with Austria are absurd. Your language must always be as pacific as possible; you must never mention the word 'war'. You must treat the Austrian officers as friends. (*Corr.* 13249)

This was rather an ostrich-like policy, but Napoleon thought that by forceful diplomacy he could absorb the whole Iberian Peninsula without having to fight for it, while the *Grande Armée* remained in eastern Europe to cow Austria. This decision led Napoleon to make the first great politico-strategic blunder of his career. By his brutal and cynical treatment of the Spanish monarch and the Crown Prince Ferdinand,* acting in concert with the treacherous Prime Minister, Godoy,† he outraged the patriotic instincts of the Spanish people. It is strange that Napoleon, who in his youth had shared in the militant nationalism of the Corsicans against French domination, should have so underestimated the fervent patriotism of the Spanish people. Spain was for him a mere stepping-stone, which he could gain by bribery and corruption, for the subjugation of Portugal.

In secret negotiations with Godoy, Napoleon arranged for the free passage of French troops across Spain into Portugal, which country would then be partitioned among his nominees; Godoy himself was to receive all Portuguese

---

* Charles IV (1748–1819) was a slothful and nearly imbecile ruler, who left everything in the hands of his Prime Minister, Godoy. His son, the Prince of the Asturias, who succeeded him as Ferdinand VII, was even more incompetent and vicious.

† Manuel de Godoy (1767–1851), the Prime Minister, was Queen Maria Luisa's lover, but also enjoyed the King's favour. He practically ruled Spain between 1792 and 1808, and his intrigues with Napoleon caused the Peninsular War. After his negotiation of the peace treaty between Spain and France in 1795 he had been created 'Prince of the Peace'.

territory south of the Tagus as his personal reward. On 8 September the Emperor wrote to his ally, the Spanish King:

> Above all, we must snatch Portugal from the influence of England, and force that country to seek and sue for peace. (*Corr.* 13131)

On the same day he wrote a threatening letter to the Infante Dom João, Prince Regent of Portugal, warning him of the consequences if he remained in alliance with Britain.

Meanwhile a British Expeditionary Force under Lord Cathcart had landed in Denmark and destroyed the Danish fleet, which Napoleon was about to seize in concert with Tsar Alexander. This roused Napoleon to fury and he decided to act at once. On 12 October he wrote to the King of Spain:

> For the last 16 years Portugal has behaved scandalously as a vassal of England. The port of Lisbon has been for them an inexhaustible treasure-house. . . . It is high time to close the harbours of Oporto and Lisbon to them. I expect the army commanded by General Junot to be at Burgos by 1 November, united with that of Your Majesty, and we shall then be able to occupy by force Lisbon and all Portugal. I shall arrange with Your Majesty what to do with that country, but in any case suzerainty over it will be yours. (*Corr.* 13243)

On the same day he wrote to Champagny:

> I consider myself at war with Portugal; by 1 November my troops will be at Burgos. If Spain wants more troops, she has only to ask and I shall send them. As regards Portugal, winter is the best time to act; General Junot's corps will be nearly 20,000 strong. (*Corr.* 13235)

On 22 October Napoleon declared war on Portugal, and on the 27th he signed the iniquitous secret Treaty of Fontainebleau between himself and the King of Spain, by which Portugal was to be partitioned at his own discretion under nominal Spanish suzerainty. The Portuguese colonies were to be divided between France and Spain.

On 31 October the Emperor issued detailed instructions to Junot with his army of 22,000 for his march through Spain and the occupation of Portugal. He reckoned the distance from Bayonne to Lisbon at 500 miles (it is actually over 560), and calculated that, at the normal French marching rate of 14 miles a day, Junot would reach Lisbon on 1 December if the Portuguese offered no resistance, and by 10 December if the Prince Regent, with his army of 15,000, put up a fight. On no account were any Portuguese fortresses to be handed over to the Spaniards. Actually there was little resistance, and Junot's army arrived in Lisbon on 30 November, but in half-starved and ragged condition. The French proceeded to take possession of the country, which was ordered to make a war contribution of one hundred million francs. Three days earlier the Prince Regent had sailed for Brazil.

But the rape of Portugal was not Napoleon's only objective. He had obtained permission to infiltrate an unspecified number of troops into Spain; he now decided to take advantage of the chaotic condition of that country, ruled by a slothful and incompetent monarch, to incorporate it into his own Empire, and to place one of his own family on the throne. Thirteen years previously, when he was a staff officer in the plans division of the War Ministry, the young Brigadier-General Buonaparte had written a strategic memorandum for the Committee of Public Safety: 'Nobody in their senses', he wrote, 'would ever dream of taking Madrid.' The mature Emperor's aims had now become more ambitious and less balanced; he did not realize what his inordinate thirst for military expansion was going to cost him.

In the first week of November Napoleon ordered a 'Corps of observation of the Gironde', 30,000 strong, to be formed at Bayonne under command of General Dupont.* This corps then crossed the Pyrenees, ostensibly to support Junot's 'Army of Portugal', with orders to march across Spain on Cadiz, in order to take possession of that important Atlantic naval base. Dupont's corps was the spearhead of what was shortly to be called the 'Army of Spain'. It was soon followed by a second corps under Marshal Moncey, previously in command of the troops watching the Channel and the Atlantic coast. By the end of January 1808 Dupont had reached Valladolid and Moncey was approaching Burgos. In February a further corps of two divisions under General Duhesme entered Spain at the Mediterranean end of the Pyrenees and occupied Catalonia, while Merle's division seized the important fortress and road junction of Pamplona. On 20 February Murat was appointed to command all the French troops in Spain as the Emperor's deputy—'Lieutenant de l'Empereur en Espagne'—and ordered to set up his headquarters at Vitoria. On 5 March Napoleon could write to his brother Joseph at Naples with the boast:

I have 80,000 troops within 75 miles of Madrid and Junot has 30,000 in Portugal. . . . Nevertheless I have not recalled a single man from the Grande Armée, where I have 300,000 in Poland and on the Oder. (Corr. 13622)

On 9 March Napoleon informed Champagny, his Foreign Minister, that a French army of 50,000 would enter Madrid on the 24th, and instructed him to explain to the Spanish Government that it was merely on its way to Cadiz

---

* General Pierre-Antoine Dupont de l'Étang (1765–1840) was a capable divisional commander who had distinguished himself in Ney's corps at Ulm (1805) and at Friedland (1807). He was to suffer an unfortunate reverse five months later (see p. 186).

to besiege Gibraltar. This barefaced effrontery so incensed the Spaniards that a popular insurrection broke out on 18 March at Aranjuez, 25 miles south of Madrid; Godoy was arrested as a traitor and Charles IV was forced to abdicate in favour of his eldest son, the Prince of the Asturias, who was proclaimed as Ferdinand VII. This of course did not suit Napoleon's book, so he now threw off the mask. On 24 March Murat entered Madrid at the head of Moncey's and Dupont's corps; Bessières with the Imperial Guard was sent up to Burgos in support; on 5 April the Emperor arrived at Bordeaux, and on the 14th moved on to Bayonne, whence he proceeded to direct the occupation of Spain.

Napoleon now had 110,000 French troops in Spain, distributed in three groups: Bessières on the right wing had 30,000 at Burgos; in the centre Murat had 50,000 in and around Madrid, while the left wing consisted of Duhesme's 30,000 in Catalonia. The Emperor still believed that this overwhelming show of force would obviate any serious resistance. He was rather proud of his psychological intuition; only recently he had written to his younger brother, Louis: 'I am an old hand in my knowledge of mankind'; but he made a grave mistake in underrating the tenacity and strength of character of the proud and independent Spanish people. On 15 April from Bayonne he sent Murat the following directive:

If there are any operations in Spain, they will be like those we had in Egypt. So you must keep your troops concentrated and have your supply columns well protected. (*Corr.* 13746)

And on the following day he instructed Bessières: 'There must be no isolated post, that is the main thing.' This was sound advice, but difficult to follow in a country like Spain, where Murat's army was extended on a front of 400 miles, with a line of communications already 250 miles long and ever lengthening.

Although Ferdinand had been proclaimed as King of Spain, Napoleon had no intention of allowing this stupid and intractable young man to succeed his more pliable father. He refused to recognize Ferdinand's title and summoned the whole royal family to Bayonne; there he forced Ferdinand to hand the crown back to his father, and then bullied Charles IV into abdicating once more, this time in favour of the Emperor's nominee, namely his own brother Joseph, who was at once summoned from Naples to Madrid. This was too much for the people of that city, who broke into open revolt—the famous *dos de Mayo*—on 2 May. A crowd of 30,000 collected in the streets, and shots were fired from windows at French soldiers. The crowd was dispersed by two French battalions and a cavalry regiment of the Imperial Guard, 2000

Spanish civilians being killed. The Emperor congratulated Murat on the 'vigour' he had shown. On 6 June Joseph was proclaimed King of Spain, and entered his new capital on 21 July.

When Charles IV abandoned his country to Napoleon Spain was left without centralized leadership, either political or military, but it is a land of strong and traditional local loyalties, and the revolt against French domination spread rapidly to all the provinces, from Galicia in the north-west to Andalusia in the far south. In each region resistance crystallized round the Provincial Council, or *Junta*, and as early as May some of these bodies had appealed to Britain for assistance, although Spain and Britain were still technically at war. Meanwhile the scattered and badly organized Spanish forces had to fend for themselves. Local leaders arose in the various provinces: the elderly General Gregório de la Cuesta in Extremadura, Joaquin Blake in León and the Asturias, Francesco Xavier Castaños in the Tagus valley and José Palafox in the Ebro valley. Napoleon had not expected this stubborn resistance; on 6 May he wrote to Talleyrand:

I think the worst part of the job is over. There may be a little agitation, but the good lesson which has just been given to Madrid will settle things. (*Corr.* 13815)

The first sporadic risings were in fact put down without much difficulty; on 16 June Duhesme marched on Tarragona, killed 1500 peasants and burnt six villages. On 25 June some British marines were landed at Santander to support the insurgents, but were driven off.

Napoleon was now trying to control the operations from Bayonne, 300 miles away, with his columns widely scattered; on the left wing 14,000 French troops were held up by General Palafox, who was stoutly holding Zaragoza; on the right wing Bessières had advanced westwards into León to deal with Blake's Army of Galicia; in the south Dupont's corps, on its way to Cadiz, had crossed the Sierra Morena and sacked Córdoba. On 13 July the Emperor dictated to Savary an appreciation of the strategic situation for his brother Joseph, who was then on his way to Madrid with his not very able Chief of Staff, Marshal Jourdan:

Bessières has now 15,000 men at Medina de Rioseco [25 miles north-west of Valladolid]. He ought to have at least 8000 more. . . . The second point is Dupont's position; he has got more strength than is necessary there; if he suffers a reverse, that would be of little consequence. He would only have to recross the mountains. The real way to reinforce General Dupont is not to send him more troops, but to send them to Marshal Bessières. (*Corr.* 14191/14192)

Napoleon's strategic judgment was here completely at fault. On the very next day Bessières attacked the Army of Galicia, which was holding a strong position with 35,000 men and 40 guns; the Spaniards were routed, losing several thousand men and all their artillery, while the French casualties were 300.

The victory of Medina de Rioseco altered the whole position, and a week later, on 21 July, the Emperor issued a fresh directive:

Today the only important point is General Dupont. If the enemy were ever to seize the passes of the Sierra Morena, it would be difficult to dislodge them; we must therefore reinforce General Dupont so that he has 25,000 men. (*Corr.* 14223)

But Napoleon was too late in thinking this way; the Spanish General Castaños, with an army of 25,000 men, had indeed seized the passes of the Sierra Morena, thus cutting Dupont's line of communications with Madrid. Without food, water or ammunition, the unfortunate Dupont* had on the previous day been forced to surrender at Bailén, 160 miles south of Madrid, with his corps of 19,000 men. This was the worst reverse that French arms had suffered, and was a bad blot on Napoleonic strategy. To have pushed forward this corps through a barren country so far from Madrid, without taking any measures to protect its line of supply, was the height of folly. But of course the Emperor took no responsibility for the disaster. On 3 August he wrote to his War Minister in Paris:

I send you these papers for your eyes only; read them with a map in your hand, and you will realize that, since the world was created, there has been nothing so stupid, so inept or so cowardly. Everything that has happened is the result of the most inconceivable ineptitude. (*Corr.* 14242)

King Joseph, who had reluctantly quitted the comforts of Naples for the melting-pot of Madrid, reached his new capital on the day after the disaster. As soon as he heard the news he repacked his baggage and fled to the north. On 5 August the Emperor, who was then on his way back to Paris from Bayonne, wrote to his War Minister:

Yesterday I told you of General Dupont's horrible catastrophe. The King has seen fit to evacuate Madrid to be nearer his army; he must have left on 2 August. ... I have ordered the I and VI Corps of the *Grande Armée* and two dragoon divisions to return to Mainz; arrange for their march from Mainz to Bayonne. (*Corr.* 14244)

Napoleon realized at last that he was faced with the possibility of a war on two fronts.

* On his return to France, Dupont was convicted by the High Court of cowardice and treachery. He was publicly disgraced, deprived of his rank and sentenced to two years' imprisonment.

As a result of the Bailén disaster, Napoleon decided to adopt a more cautious defensive strategy in the Peninsula until he could withdraw some more highly trained formations from the *Grande Armée*. He laid down this policy in a memorandum dated 5 August. The Army of Spain was still to be divided into three corps; the main body in the centre (30,000) was to be under immediate command of King Joseph with headquarters at Aranda de Duero, 90 miles north of Madrid. The right wing under Bessières was to occupy Valladolid, 55 miles west of Aranda, while the left wing would hold the upper Ebro valley between Logroño and Tudela, covering Pamplona:

The first objective is to recapture Madrid, if possible; the second is to keep open the line of communication with Portugal; the third is to hold the line of the Ebro, and the fourth is to maintain our lines of communication through Pamplona and San Sebastian, so that when the *Grande Armée* arrives we shall soon defeat and annihilate all the insurgents. (*Corr.* 14245)

On 15 August the Emperor had returned to Paris, and two days later he ordered the I, V and VI Corps and three cavalry divisions to be transferred by forced marches from Germany to Spain; a siege train was to be assembled at Bayonne, comprising 12 24-pounders, 12 6-inch howitzers and six 8-inch mortars.

Meanwhile a new factor had contributed to upset Napoleon's expectations of an easy conquest of Spain and Portugal. In June the British Government had decided to arrest the Emperor's march to the Atlantic by sending an expeditionary force to the Peninsula. On 1 August Lieutenant-General Sir Arthur Wellesley landed with a corps of 10,000 men at the mouth of the river Mondego in Portugal and advanced on Lisbon. After defeating Junot's Army of Portugal at Roliça (17 August) and Vimeiro (21 August), he was reinforced, and under the 'Convention of Cintra' (30 August) Junot's whole army was evacuated from Portugal and conveyed by sea to La Rochelle. The British troops in Portugal, 35,000 strong, were then taken over by Sir John Moore, who was ordered to cooperate with the Spanish armies in expelling the French from the Peninsula. Having command of the sea, the British Navy was able to land at the Biscay and Atlantic ports ample supplies of arms and ammunition to maintain the Spanish and Portuguese resistance movement.

On returning to Paris, Napoleon wrote to his stepson, Prince Eugène, at Milan:

Spanish affairs are getting serious; the British have landed more than 40,000 men. . . . My troops in Spain have been victorious everywhere, except in one unfortunate place, where Dupont has made gross blunders and wrecked all my plans. (*Corr.* 14257)

Meanwhile he could only mark time and wait for his more seasoned troops to arrive from Germany, after which he intended to clear up the Spanish mess once and for all. On 16 September Joseph suddenly declared his intention of leaving garrisons in Pamplona, San Sebastian and Burgos, and advancing with 50,000 men to capture Madrid; he asked for the Emperor's approval. This produced a blast of Napoleon's most cutting sarcasm; on 22 September he replied to his brother:

> You proposed to march on Madrid with a mass of 50,000 men, abandoning your communications with France. The art of war has certain principles which one must never violate. To change one's line of communication is an operation which requires genius; to lose one's line of communication is such a serious error that a General who commits it is a criminal. . . . But now, if you were to shut yourself up in the middle of Spain without any organized base or proper depot, and with enemy armies on your flanks and rear, you would be committing an act of folly without parallel in the world's history. (*Corr.* 14343)

Napoleon was now handicapped by his own deliberate policy of having no competent second-in-command to whom he could depute the leadership when he himself was not present on the battlefield. The combination of Joseph and Jourdan was proving disastrous; Murat had gone sick and was undergoing a cure at a Pyrenean spa; Massena had just lost an eye (by the Emperor's hand) at a shooting party at Fontainebleau; Davout, the most capable Marshal on the eastern front, must be left to command the *Grande Armée*. So nothing could be done in Spain until Napoleon himself could return to take command. But he was continuously receiving reports that Austria was secretly rearming, so he summoned his recently acquired ally, Tsar Alexander, to a conference at Erfurt, to ensure that he would not be attacked from that quarter.

In a secret convention signed on 8 October the alliance between France and Russia, established at Tilsit, was confirmed, and the two countries agreed to make common cause against Britain, but the Tsar carefully avoided any obligation to enter the war, should hostilities break out between France and Austria. Partially reassured by the Erfurt Convention, Napoleon ordered the disbandment of the *Grande Armée* as from 15 October, the 75,000 troops remaining in Germany being designated the Army of the Rhine, under command of Marshal Davout. Bernadotte's corps was left at Hamburg to garrison the Hanseatic towns, but Soult and Lannes were ordered to the Spanish front. Having thus reduced his establishments on the eastern front, the Emperor returned to the west. On 5 November, followed by the Imperial Guard, he arrived at Vitoria and assumed command of his Army of Spain.

This army was now reorganized as follows:

Victor (I)	29,000
Soult (II)	20,000
Moncey (III)	24,000
Lefebvre (IV)	23,000
Ney (VI)	30,000
Saint-Cyr (VII)	30,000
Bessières (Guard and Reserve Cavalry)	35,000
	191,000

In addition, Mortier (V) and Junot (VIII) were assembling in France, making an additional 43,000. It was a formidable array, and appeared more than adequate to crush the 115,000 regular and militia troops which were scattered in a wide arc across central Spain. The Spanish troops too were poorly armed and equipped, and their discipline left much to be desired. Their forces were split up into five or six independent armies, without any centralized command or staff. The local commanders were jealous of each other and did not cooperate well.

Napoleon decided that his first objective must be the recapture of Madrid, while at the same time making sure of his line of communication with France by Vitoria and San Sebastian. He therefore started with a wide sweep to the west with his right wing, consisting of Victor (I), Soult (II) and Lefebvre (IV), which drove Blake's army back to León. Ney (VI) in the centre advanced south through Burgos and Aranda, the whole movement pivoting on the left wing at Logroño in the upper Ebro valley, where two corps were grouped under Lannes. This wing encountered two Spanish armies under Palafox and Castaños, the victor of Bailén. The Spaniards were enveloped by a converging movement of the corps of Ney and Lannes, and were severely defeated on 23 November at Tudela on the Ebro, losing 3000 prisoners and 26 guns. The main French army then swung southward from Burgos unopposed until it was confronted by the granite range of the Sierra de Guadarrama, 6000 feet high, which rose from the plain like a wall, shielding Madrid from the north. Although the Sierra was held by 12,000 Spaniards, Victor (I) forced the steep Somosierra Pass (4690 feet) on 30 November, capturing 16 guns and a number of prisoners. Napoleon then advanced on Madrid, which under the threat of bombardment surrendered to him on 4 December.

Soult (II) in the north at Burgos was now ordered to advance westward by Carrión de los Condes to León, in order to drive Blake's army, reinforced by the corps of the Marqués de la Romana, into Galicia. In the south Victor (I) was sent to hold the valley of the Tagus, from Toledo down to Talavera de la Reina, and Napoleon himself intended to follow in the same direction with an army of 42,000 to invade and subdue Portugal, where he knew that a British army had assembled.

In fact, Lieutenant-General Sir John Moore * had already, on the British Government's instructions, invaded Spain with an expeditionary force of 30,000 men, based on Lisbon. Leaving Lisbon on 27 October, Moore had marched eastward in several columns, the bulk of which had concentrated at Salamanca by 13 November, while the right column under Sir John Hope, consisting mainly of cavalry and artillery, had made a more southerly détour south of the Tagus as far as Talavera, where it turned north to join Moore near Salamanca. Moore could obtain no help from the local Spanish forces, either in the way of supplies and transport or in active military cooperation, but on 10 December, after Hope's column had joined him, he decided to move north in order to strike a blow at Soult's isolated corps at Carrión, 50 miles north of Valladolid. Soult had only 18,000 men, while Moore now had 28,000 and 66 guns, so the latter's chances were good. Moore's army marched north in bitter weather, and on 15 December crossed the Duero (Douro) between Zamora and Tordesillas, picking up on the way a number of prisoners from Franceschi's cavalry division of Soult's corps. On 21 December the British cavalry reached Sahagún, 50 miles north of Valladolid, where they defeated the French cavalry in a sharp encounter. But on the 23rd Moore learnt that Napoleon's army was marching north to cut him off from Portugal. There was no time to lose; on the following day he ordered his army to turn west; the retreat to Corunna had begun.

Meanwhile in Madrid Napoleon was busy reorganizing the government of Spain and preparing for his move down the Tagus valley to drive the British out of Portugal. On 12 December he heard that his advanced guard cavalry commander, Lasalle, had captured at Talavera a Hanoverian cavalry patrol belonging to Moore's army, actually from Hope's southern column. A week later he was still more amazed to learn from the interrogation of three deserters (of French birth) from Moore's army that Salamanca was occupied by 16,000 British troops. Later in the day he received a report from Soult in the north that on 13 December his cavalry had encountered a strong British force at Rueda, eight miles south of Tordesillas on the Duero. These reports upset all the Emperor's calculations and plans; he at once decided to march northwest to Valladolid in order to drive 'the leopard' into the ocean. Leaving

* Sir John Moore (1761–1809) was a distinguished soldier and an able tactician, who had raised the British light infantry regiments to a high pitch of efficiency. He was mortally wounded at Corunna (1809).

King Joseph with Victor (I) and Lefebvre (IV) to guard the Tagus valley, on 22 December, with Ney (VI) as advanced guard, Napoleon marched north-west with an army of 42,000 to support Soult in León.

Napoleon's army crossed the mountain range with considerable difficulty in a blinding snow-storm by the Puerto de Guadarrama pass (5000 feet). On the following day he reached Villacastin, 52 miles north-west of Madrid; he pushed on by forced marches, and on the evening of 25 December established Imperial Headquarters at Tordesillas on the Duero, 115 miles north-west of Madrid; this was a rapid move in four days. He now learnt from the interrogation of a few British stragglers that Moore was retreating to Corunna (La Coruña), so he sent Ney forward to Medina de Rioseco to gain touch with Soult and endeavour to intercept the British retreat. On 27 December the Emperor wrote to King Joseph, telling him to announce in the Spanish newspapers that he had surrounded 36,000 British. But the latter proved too elusive. On 31 December Napoleon reached Benavente on the Esla, and halted there for a week to rest his exhausted troops. On 4 January he realized that Moore had escaped his clutches, so he handed over the pursuit to Soult, who was to be supported by Ney. Two days later he himself moved back to Valladolid.

On 1 January the Emperor, realizing that he had failed to finish the war, signed a decree calling up 80,000 conscripts of the 1810 class.* He was now seriously perturbed about the intentions of Austria. On 9 January he wrote to his Foreign Minister, Champagny:

Tell the Bavarians that if Austria continues to arm I shall concentrate Oudinot's corps at Augsburg and Ingolstadt. Tell them that I have 150,000 men in my Army of Germany. (*Corr.* 14668)

On the 15th he wrote to Davout, commanding the Army of the Rhine at Erfurt:

Send Oudinot's corps to Augsburg at once, to await further orders there. It will be composed of his infantry regiments and his three cavalry regiments and 18 guns. He is to pretend that he is moving to Italy. In the course of March his strength will amount to 36 battalions and seven cavalry regiments. (*Corr.* 14711)

Napoleon now felt the position in central Europe to be so threatening that he decided to return to Paris. He instructed Berthier to remain at Valladolid and issue orders until the British had embarked, after which King Joseph was to take over command of the Army of Spain. On the same day he wrote to Joseph:

The circumstances of Europe oblige me to spend three weeks in Paris. If nothing happens to prevent it, I shall return about the end of February. Berthier will

---

* He had already used up the 1809 class to fill the ranks of the Army of Spain.

instruct you about my plan for invading Portugal by Oporto and Galicia simultaneously. I expect to reach Paris by 21 January; I shall ride most of the way. Keep my absence secret for a fortnight and say I have gone to Zaragoza. (*Corr.* 14716)

On the following day he wrote to King Jérôme of Westphalia at Cassel:

The Spanish business is finished. . . . If the Emperor of Austria makes the slightest hostile movement, he will soon cease to reign. That is very clear. As for the Russians, we have never been on better terms with them. (*Corr.* 14731)

That day he left Valladolid and arrived in Paris a week later. He was mistaken about the Spanish business being finished. It was certainly the day on which the British began their embarkation at Corunna, after fighting a gallant rearguard action, but they had no intention of abandoning the struggle for the mastery of the Iberian Peninsula.

Second Campaign
in the Danube Valley
1809

After the embarkation of Moore's army at Corunna, Napoleon imagined that he had eliminated all chance of further British intervention in Spain. Portugal, certainly, still remained to be subjugated, but that country could be dealt with after Austria had been finally crushed. The Emperor now applied his boundless energy and resourcefulness to his immediate objective, the occupation of the enemy's capital; the shortest way to Vienna was down the Danube valley, the same road that he had followed after his victory at Ulm in 1805.

Napoleon reached Paris from Valladolid on 24 January and at once began to reorganize his forces for the new Danube campaign. He did not think that the Austrians would move before 15 April, so he felt that he had ample time to prepare, and on 15 February he ordered Bessières, who was now commanding the northern provinces of Spain at Valladolid, to send the Imperial Guard to Paris. In the course of the next week his intelligence staff gave him a statement of the latest distribution of the Austrian forces, which were now organized in nine corps under the supreme command of the Archduke Charles:

Right wing, in Bohemia: Count Bellegarde⎱
                            Count Kolowrat ⎬ 120,000
                            Prince Rosenberg⎰
                            Prince John of Liechtenstein 45,000

193

Left wing, in Styria and Carinthia: Baron von Hiller ⎫
General Chasteler ⎬ 95,000
General Gyulay ⎭
_____
260,000

Two other corps, amounting to 100,000, were held in reserve, one in Galicia under the Archduke Ferdinand, the other, under the Archduke Louis, covering Vienna.

The Archduke Charles's striking force considerably outnumbered the French troops available in Germany, under Davout, Oudinot and Bernadotte, which barely amounted to 90,000, so there was no question of Napoleon taking the initiative immediately, as he had done in 1805. He therefore wisely decided to adopt an offensive-defensive form of strategy, and to group his forces so as to strike only when the enemy had disclosed his intentions. Initially, therefore, he ordered his troops in Germany to concentrate about Regensburg (Ratisbonne) in the Danube valley and to await the Austrian move. The most important thing was to reinforce the Army of Germany, but the situation in Spain was still too uncertain to withdraw many troops from that theatre.

On 21 February the Emperor ordered Clarke, his War Minister, to send for Marshal Massena, who had now recovered from the loss of his eye in a shooting accident, and give him command of a new 'corps of observation of the Rhine', which was to assemble at Strasbourg by 12 March and was to consist of four infantry divisions and one light cavalry division. Napoleon then warned the rulers of the allied German States forming the Confederation of the Rhine, namely Bavaria, Württemberg, Saxony, Baden and Hesse-Darmstadt, that their freedom was being menaced by Austrian aggression, and that they must mobilize and place their armies at his disposal by 20 March. He thus obtained a reinforcement of some 70,000 men. The Bavarian corps was of good fighting value, but the other German troops were more suitable for employment on the lines of communication. The satellite rulers had perforce to comply with this call-up; King Maximilian Joseph asked that his son, the Crown Prince, should command the Bavarian contingent, but Napoleon refused to allow this and gave command of the Bavarian Corps to Marshal Lefebvre, Duke of Danzig, whom he had just removed for incompetence from the Army of Spain. Bernadotte, from Hamburg, was ordered to Dresden to take over command of the contingent supplied by the King of Saxony.

Reports of Austrian concentrations on the right bank of the Inn continued to reach the Emperor, and on 24 March he ordered the Guard to be conveyed in wagons from Spain to Paris, so that they could cover a three-days' march in one day. Bessières was transferred from commanding the northern provinces of Spain to command the Cavalry Corps of the Army of Germany, as Murat had been promoted to the throne of Naples. Bessières was relieved at Valladolid by General Kellermann, who had distinguished himself at Marengo and who had been with Junot in Portugal.

On 28 and 30 March Napoleon issued to Berthier very long and detailed instructions as to the composition and location of the *Armée d'Allemagne*, as he expected the Austrians to attack on 15 April; Metternich, the Austrian Ambassador, was still in Paris and had not yet asked for his passports. If the Austrians attacked before 10 April, the French army was to concentrate behind the river Lech, with its right on Augsburg and its left resting on the Danube between Ingolstadt and Donauwörth; Imperial Headquarters would be at the latter place. Strasbourg was to be the main supply base, with advanced supply depots at Augsburg and Ingolstadt, and river transport was to be organized on the Danube for supplies and ammunition; immense quantities of bread and biscuit were to be baked, and general hospitals were to be established at Ulm, Augsburg and Donauwörth. The *Armée d'Allemagne* would be organized as follows:

		Infantry	Cavalry	Guns
II Corps—Lannes *	3 divisions	40,000		57
	1½ cavalry divisions		6,000	
III Corps—Davout	4 divisions	45,000		66
	2 cavalry divisions		6,000	
IV Corps—Massena	4 divisions	30,000		68
	1 cavalry division		5,000	
VII Corps—Lefebvre	3 divisions	30,000		60
(Bavarian)	1 cavalry division		4,000	
Cavalry Corps—Bessières	4 cavalry divisions		6,000	6
Total	14 inf. 9½ cav. divs.	145,000	27,000	257

This army would shortly be reinforced by the Imperial Guard, consisting of 18,000 infantry, 4000 cavalry and 60 guns. To guard the lines of communication, an VIII Corps under Augereau, a IX (Saxon) Corps under Bernadotte and a X Corps under King Jérôme were in process of formation.

Napoleon, however, was now being forced to fight on two fronts, a situation which he had not reckoned with. On 21 March he had to reprimand his brother Joseph for the mess he was making of the war in Spain. The Emperor

---

* Marshal Lannes was on his way to Germany from Spain, where he had distinguished himself by the capture of Zaragoza.

was beginning to reap the ill effects of his policy of over-controlling his sub-ordinate commanders and centralizing his system of command. His Generals were not made Marshals because of their qualities as independent leaders, but for the zeal and activity with which they carried out his orders when under his very eyes. Of the 18 Marshals, only Massena and Davout were capable of commanding anything more than a corps. Massena had saved France in 1799 by his skilful handling of the Army of Helvetia; Davout had won the battle of Auerstedt entirely on his own. But Ney at Elchingen and Soult at Austerlitz had been fighting directly under the Emperor's personal direction; they were good tacticians, but had displayed no strategic genius. The result of the Napoleonic command system became apparent the moment that the Emperor turned his back on the Spanish theatre of operations.

The Marshals in Spain had the greatest contempt for both their nominal Army Commander, the indolent King Joseph, and for his Chief of Staff, the incompetent Marshal Jourdan, who was not even a Duke, as Lannes, Ney, Soult, Mortier and Victor were. Split up by the geography of the country into widely separated commands, they persistently ignored the orders received from Madrid; worse still, their jealous personal rivalry prevented all mutual cooperation. Since the Emperor never returned to exercise personal command in Spain, these unhappy conditions prevailed throughout the next four years and contributed largely to Napoleon's failure to subjugate the Peninsula.

Before the Emperor left Spain in January he instructed Soult, as soon as the British had embarked, to invade Portugal from Galicia and occupy Oporto and Lisbon. Soult's advance was to be supported by Victor's corps moving down the Guadiana valley through Badajoz, and then by the Tagus valley to Lisbon. The link between these two corps was to be provided by Lapisse's division advancing from Salamanca. Soult, unsupported either by Victor or Lapisse, eventually overcame the resistance of the Portuguese militia and captured Oporto on 29 March. Six weeks later, however, he was driven out of Portugal by Sir Arthur Wellesley. Ney's corps, meanwhile, was immobilized in Galicia by La Romana's Spanish army. On 2 April Napoleon wrote angrily to Joseph:

Spanish affairs are going badly. How is it possible that you have been for so long without news of the Duke of Elchingen, and that, in spite of La Romana's moves between Galicia and Castille, together with the revolt in the Asturias, you sent Lapisse's division to the south, instead of using it in the north? I cannot understand what you are about, and I can only foresee trouble ahead. . . . Your primary objective must be to re-establish communication with the Duke of Elchingen [Ney]. (*Corr.* 14995)

But Spanish affairs were not Napoleon's only worry. For some time he had been dissatisfied with the attitude of the Pope, who, he thought, had been instigating the Austrians to fight him. On 5 April he wrote to Murat at Naples:

I have given orders to finish the Rome business and to destroy this hotbed of insurrection. . . . On receipt of this letter, assemble troops on the frontier and make a lightning raid on Rome. . . . I want Saliceti to remain at Rome as adviser to General Miollis, who must organize a new government. You may assure everyone that the Pope will remain a bishop, but he will no longer meddle in temporal affairs. (*Corr.* 15018)

The Emperor continued to be exasperated by the conduct of his Generals in Spain. On 9 April he instructed his War Minister:

Write to Marshal Jourdan that I note with displeasure that the army is not being commanded, and that this lack of activity will lead to disastrous results; that it was absurd to order General Kellermann to march to Villafranca, since he only has cavalry; that he could quite well march on Astorga and Benavente, but he must not get tied up in the mountains; that to take away his artillery was a bad mistake; that this General will now be without the means to destroy a house; that you will repeat to him, as you have already done many times, that his first objective must be to gain contact with the Duke of Elchingen; that the worst may result from this apathy and this neglect of the first principles of war. (*Corr.* 15037)

But more important things were now happening on the eastern front. On 10 April Napoleon wrote to Berthier at Strasbourg:

I think that the Emperor of Austria will soon attack. Go at once to Augsburg and act according to my instructions; if the enemy attacks before the 15th, you must concentrate the troops on Augsburg and Donauwörth. Order my Guard and my horses to Stuttgart. (*Corr.* 15047)

A few hours later he sent a further urgent message by semaphore signal:

Intercepted messages sent to Metternich * from Vienna and the fact that he has demanded his passports make it certain that Austria is about to commence hostilities, if she has not already done so. The Duke of Rivoli should move to Augsburg with his corps and you should go there yourself. . . . The Duke of Auerstädt should have his headquarters at Nürnberg. If the Austrians attack before the 15th, everyone must fall back on the Lech.

While Napoleon was fretting about the mismanagement of the Spanish campaign, and at the same time was initiating aggression against the Pope,

---

* Clement Wenceslaus Lothar Metternich (1773–1859) was a reactionary pillar of Austrian diplomacy. After serving as Ambassador in Berlin (1803) and Paris (1807), he succeeded Thugut as Foreign Minister in 1809 and was created Prince in 1813. He played a leading role at the Congress of Vienna (1814–1815).

the Austrians had, in fact, stolen a march on him. On 9 April, without pre-vious declaration of war, the Archduke Charles crossed the Inn frontier between Passau and Braunau with four corps numbering 140,000 men; a fifth corps under General Count Kolowrat formed the right wing and ad-vanced on Regensburg from north of the Danube (p. 128). The main body under the Archduke moved westward up the valleys of the Danube and the Isar, the left wing being directed on Munich. The Austrian invasion caught the French army in complete disarray. The Emperor was still in Paris, and Berthier, who was deputizing for him in command of the army, was back at Strasbourg. Davout (III) was, in accordance with Napoleon's earlier orders, moving south from Nürnberg to Regensburg; Oudinot's corps, which was to be taken over by Lannes when he arrived from Spain, was 75 miles further south-west at Augsburg. Lefebvre with the Bavarian corps was north of Munich with outposts in the Isar valley near Landshut. Massena (IV) was on the march from Strasbourg through Ulm to Augsburg. Bessières's Cavalry Corps was also far behind. Thus the French corps were widely dispersed, and if the Archduke had advanced rapidly on Landshut and Munich, a matter of three days' march, he could have destroyed the *Armée d'Allemagne* piecemeal before the Emperor had left Paris. Fortunately for Napoleon, the Austrian army was a cumbrous and slow-moving organism.

Napoleon had instructed Berthier to concentrate the army behind the Lech and to set up headquarters at Donauwörth. Berthier did not leave Strasbourg until 11 April and then moved to Augsburg. In the absence of his chief he was not the man to take command in an emergency. On 6 April he had re-ceived from Davout a report dated the 3rd indicating that the Austrian troops in Bohemia had moved to the south bank of the Danube and were massing on the frontier; Berthier neglected to forward this report to the Emperor, so that the latter got no warning of the imminence of the Austrian offensive until the day after the Archduke crossed the frontier. The Emperor himself was not blameless in the matter; knowing, as he did, that the Austrians were meditat-ing war, he should have covered the frontier with a cavalry screen to give him early warning of the enemy's movements. Napoleon had also instructed Berthier to concentrate Davout's corps at Regensburg 'in all circumstances', which was a grave error, as it placed Davout in an exposed position on the left flank of the army, especially as he had ordered the remainder of the army to be withdrawn behind the Lech. Berthier added to Davout's confusion by writing him an extraordinary letter while on his way from Strasbourg:

In the actual circumstances the Emperor's plan of concentrating at Regensburg seems impossible of execution, since General St. Hilaire's cavalry division must have retired from there. I shall reach Donauwörth this evening [13 April] and shall hear news of the army's situation. I shall move with General Oudinot's corps to Neuburg [on the Danube, 10 miles west of Ingolstadt]. Now we must think of concentrating the army to give battle to the enemy if the Emperor does not arrive in time. If we have an action, it must be a decisive one. Could we not find a good position between Neumarkt and Beilngries?

Berthier must have been temporarily insane when he wrote this letter; Beilngries is 30 miles west of Regensburg and 20 miles north of the Danube; Neumarkt is still farther north, on the road to Nürnberg; had this plan been carried out, the army would have been completely cut off from its line of communication along the Danube valley.

Napoleon on a later occasion summed up Berthier's abilities:

He had no decision of character and was quite unfitted to be a Commander-in-Chief, but possessed all the qualities of a good Chief of Staff. (*Corr.* XXIX. 107)

By appointing Berthier as deputy Commander-in-Chief at such a critical juncture, even for a few days, the Emperor imperilled the safety of his army. Either Davout or Massena could have handled the situation adequately, but Napoleon was always averse from subordinating one Marshal to another unless the latter happened to be a member of his own family, like Murat.

Amid this welter of indecision and confusion the Emperor at last proceeded to the front. Leaving Paris on 13 April, he reached Strasbourg two days later and pushed on to Ludwigsburg, where he stayed with the King of Württemberg. There he received Berthier's situation report of the 13th, which infuriated him. In the early hours of the 16th he wrote to him:

I have just got your letter telling me that you have moved Oudinot's corps to Regensburg; you don't explain what induced you to take this extraordinary step, which weakens and disperses my troops. . . . As for the order [to the Bavarians] to occupy Landshut, I think it senseless. Marshal Lefebvre was quite right to concentrate his troops at Munich. I cannot understand the idea behind your letter written on the evening of the 13th; I should have preferred to hear that my army was concentrated between Ingolstadt and Augsburg, with the Bavarians in the front line, as the Duke of Danzig has placed himself, until we know what the enemy's intention is. You must stick to my instructions, which were to concentrate the army and have it well in hand. That is just the opposite to what you have done. (*Corr.* 15070)

The Emperor then quickly dictated orders to Massena to concentrate his own and Oudinot's corps at Augsburg; he himself pushed on to Donauwörth, which he reached at 4 a.m. on 17 April.

The Emperor had not arrived a minute too soon. On that very day the Bavarian outposts between Siegenburg and Abensberg (south-east of Neustadt) were attacked by the vanguard of the Archduke's main body, which had crossed the Isar and was advancing slowly north-west towards Regensburg, where Davout's corps was already facing the threat of the Austrian right wing under Kolowrat, north of the Danube. Davout was thus in imminent danger of being crushed between the jaws of this pincer movement. Never since Rivoli, 12 years earlier, had Napoleon found himself in such a perilous military situation. It was largely his own fault; he had allowed the entanglement in Spain to divert his main *force de frappe* from the vital theatre of war. His Guard was still being transported in wagons from the Pyrenees to the Rhine, and his Cavalry Corps was not yet assembled. On the Danube front Davout's corps and the Bavarians, 35 miles apart, were being attacked by an Austrian army double their combined strength. His only available reserves were Nansouty's heavy cavalry division at Ingolstadt and the two corps of Oudinot and Massena, together 64,000 strong, concentrating at Augsburg, but exhausted by long marches. Any ordinary commander would have ordered the whole army to retire behind the Lech, Napoleon's intended assembly area. The Emperor's dynamic genius, however, instantly devised a plan which transformed almost certain defeat into victory. Davout was to retire slowly from Regensburg and effect a junction with Lefebvre's Bavarians in the tangled hill country south of the Danube; the two corps, shoulder to shoulder, were to withstand and hold the Archduke's frontal attack; meanwhile Oudinot and Massena would advance eastward by forced marches from Augsburg on Freising and Landshut, thus striking the left flank of the Archduke's main army attacking Regensburg, and cutting its line of communications. This *manœuvre de Landshut* was one of Napoleon's most brilliant strategic conceptions; in later years he considered it his greatest. Unlike the plan for Austerlitz, it had to be hastily improvised at a moment of great danger, and it demanded tremendous physical exertions, both in marching and fighting, on the part of his troops.

When the Emperor arrived at Donauwörth on the morning of 17 April he found his available troops distributed as follows:

	Infantry	Cavalry	Total	Location
III Corps (Davout)	48,600	8,600	57,200	Regensburg
II Corps (Oudinot)	16,000	5,300	21,300	Augsburg
IV Corps (Massena)	34,800	2,800	37,600	approaching Augsburg
VII Corps (Lefebvre)	22,500	4,500	27,000	Geisenfeld–Neustadt
Cuirassier division } (Nansouty)	—	5,100	5,100	Neuburg
	121,900	26,300	148,200	

The first thing to be done was to effect a junction between the III and VII Corps, to avoid them being defeated in detail. At 10 a.m. he despatched his senior A.D.C., General Savary, with a cavalry escort to Regensburg, ordering Davout to withdraw along the right bank of the Danube to Neustadt (28 miles south-west of Regensburg) and gain touch with the Bavarians. Lefebvre was ordered to concentrate his divisions between Siegenburg and Abensberg to cover Davout's withdrawal. Massena was ordered to take Oudinot's corps with him and to move from Augsburg before dawn the following morning on Aichach and Pfaffenhofen. Massena's men were to carry four days' bread and four days' biscuit ration. Napoleon also sent out several A.D.C.s to gather intelligence about the enemy's movements and to locate his left flank. During the night he learnt that four Austrian corps had crossed the Isar between Landshut and Freising.

Unfortunately Davout did not receive the Emperor's order until the morning of the 18th, and his columns did not get on the move for another 24 hours. During their march through the wooded hills south of the Danube they became heavily engaged with the vanguards of the three Austrian corps of Hohenzollern, Rosenberg and Liechtenstein. Lefebvre, as ordered, moved north-east towards Abensberg, but the officer whom he sent to get in touch with Davout was captured by the Austrians.

Massena, with Oudinot's divisions in the lead, reached Aichach at midday on the 18th, when he received a further long directive from the Emperor; after giving Massena a complete summary of the situation it ran:

> During tomorrow the 19th all of your corps which has reached Pfaffenhofen will move so as to fall on either Prince Charles's rear or on the column between Freising and Moosburg. Everything leads one to think that between the 18th, 19th and 20th the German business will be finished. . . . I regard the enemy as lost if Oudinot and your three divisions start before daylight and if, at this critical moment, you impress on my troops what they have got to do. . . . The importance of your move is such that I may myself accompany your corps.

As a postscript Napoleon added: *Activité, activité, vitesse! Je me recommande à vous* (Corr. 15087).

On 19 April the Emperor moved his headquarters 37 miles forward to Ingolstadt. He thought that the main action would take place that day, but it developed more slowly than he had anticipated, owing partly to the delay in his orders reaching Davout, and partly to the ponderous movements of the clumsily organized Austrian formations. The Archduke had deployed four corps on the front held by Davout and Lefebvre between Regensburg and Siegenburg, while his fifth corps under Hiller formed the left wing in the Isar valley. Contact had now been established with the enemy all along the front, and Massena's vanguard, advancing from Pfaffenhofen on Freising, had taken 400 prisoners of Hiller's corps. At midday the Emperor sent Massena a further order:

Push Oudinot's corps on to Au and Freising. From Freising and Au, according to the information which I get today, I shall direct you on Landshut; then Prince Charles will find his communications cut, as they are covered by the Isar, and we shall attack his left. . . . All this must be cleared up today, and minutes are precious. (*Corr.* 15092)

On 20 April Napoleon moved his headquarters 12 miles forward to Vohburg on the Danube, within 10 miles of the battle front, where the action was now developing. Lannes and Bessières now arrived at the Emperor's headquarters from Spain. Lannes was given command of two of Davout's divisions in a temporary grouping, while Bessières was sent to lead the cavalry of Massena's advanced guard. At 6 a.m. Napoleon sent Massena another directive:

All reports this morning show that the enemy is in full flight. The battlefield is covered with his dead. Only two French and one Bavarian division have so far been engaged. I am just mounting my horse to reconnoitre the outpost position, and will attack the enemy if he is still holding out anywhere, or pursue him hotly if he is retreating. I want you on your side not to lose a minute, and to catch him at the Isar crossing – preferably at Landshut, but at least try to get to Moosburg. (*Corr.* 15098)

This was an unduly optimistic appreciation of the situation, for the battle proper was only just beginning. Napoleon had tremendous confidence in himself, and he liked to inspire his subordinates with the same blind faith.

So far only the Austrian vanguards had been encountered, but on the evening of the 20th the Austrian right wing captured Regensburg, where Davout had left a small rearguard. The Archduke's main force was now deployed on a front of 20 miles, running due south from Regensburg, but a gap had developed between the four northerly corps and Hiller's corps, which was 10 miles north-west of Landshut. By dint of strenuous marching, Massena had concentrated his four infantry and two cavalry divisions between Freising and Moosburg in accordance with Napoleon's orders.

During the whole of 21 April the Archduke launched a strong offensive against Davout and Lefebvre between Regensburg and Eggmühl, 16 miles further south in the valley of the Gross-Laaber. The Austrian attacks lost cohesion in the wooded valleys and were delivered piecemeal; the French and Bavarians, though greatly outnumbered, not only held their ground, but drove the enemy back by well-timed counter-attacks.

Napoleon still imagined that the Isar valley was the key to the problem, so he diverted Lannes's corps and part of Lefebvre's corps southward towards Landshut to strengthen his right wing. The force of this thrust, together with Massena's advance from Moosburg, drove Hiller's corps out of Landshut by the evening. Bessières with two cavalry divisions pursued the Austrians to the south-east as far as Geisenhausen.

After a ride of 25 miles, the Emperor himself reached Landshut at 7 p.m. on 21 April. He then realized that, in driving Hiller's corps southward across the Inn, he was missing his principal objective, namely the destruction of the Archduke's main body in the Regensburg area. At 2 a.m. the following morning he received a message from Davout, saying that he was being hard pressed by three Austrian corps and was short of ammunition. Napoleon at once decided to go to Davout's assistance; at 3 a.m. he dictated to Berthier:

Order General von Wrede to move his division to support Marshal Bessières's advance from Geisenhausen in order to throw the enemy across the Inn. The Bavarian division will start at 4 a.m.

Order the Duke of Rivoli [Massena] to assemble between Landshut and Ergolding [4 miles north-east of Landshut] three of his divisions with their guns and Espagne's cavalry division. The leading division must be in column of route on the left bank [of the Isar] ready to march at 6 a.m. The Duke of Rivoli will march on Eckmühl with his three divisions and surround the enemy; the Emperor will march with him. (*Corr.* 15105)

He also ordered Oudinot with two fresh divisions to move north to reinforce Davout. He then despatched General Lebrun, one of his A.D.C.s, to Davout with the following message:

It is 4 a.m. I intend to march immediately and I shall be at Eckmühl at midday, and in a position to attack the enemy vigorously at 3 p.m. I shall have 40,000 men with me. . . . I am determined to exterminate Prince Charles today or at latest tomorrow. This letter is also for the Duke of Danzig [Lefebvre]. Show it to him. (*Corr.* 15104)

The little village of Eggmühl, called Eckmühl by the French, lies on the left bank of the Gross-Laaber stream, 16 miles south of Regensburg, and 25 miles by road north of Landshut. Napoleon knew from Davout's reports that the Archduke's left flank rested on the village, and as he rode north with Massena and Lannes at the head of the column he could hear the cannonade of Davout's guns holding back the assault of 66,000 Austrians. At 2 p.m. the head of the Emperor's column debouched in the Gross-Laaber valley at Eggmühl and struck the Archduke's left flank. Simultaneously Davout and Lefebvre launched their counter-stroke eastwards. The whole Austrian line was rolled up, and as darkness fell the enemy were retreating in disorder to the Danube bridges at Regensburg. Lannes, at the head of two cavalry divisions, continued the pursuit by moonlight as far as the bridgehead.

The French infantry were too exhausted by their long marches to pursue vigorously, and by the following day the Archduke had withdrawn the bulk of his army to the left (north) bank of the Danube, while Hiller's corps of 30,000 which had been defeated at Landshut, retreated across the Inn and followed the Vienna road south of the Danube. Leaving a strong rearguard to hold the bridgehead at Regensburg, the Archduke retreated north-east into the mountainous Böhmerwald (Šumava).

On 23 April Lannes, at the head of a storming party, scaled the wall of Regensburg and occupied the town. Napoleon, while watching Lannes's exploit from an observing post, received a painful injury from a spent bullet which struck his boot, officially recorded as '*forte contusion au pied droit.*' It was his first wound in battle since the bayonet thrust in his thigh by a British marine at the siege of Toulon.

Napoleon had failed in his main object, which was 'to exterminate Prince Charles' and cut him off from Vienna. He had, however, achieved a substantial success after four days of hard fighting and marching, on 20, 21, 22 and 23 April, which are individually recorded on the Arc de Triomphe in Paris as the victories of '*Abensberg*', '*Landshut*', '*Eckmühl*' and '*Ratisbonne*'. He had split the Austrian army into two fractions, and the way to Vienna by the shortest road south of the Danube was now only covered by the lesser fraction under Hiller. With casualties of only 5200 he had inflicted a loss on the enemy of 6000 men and 16 guns. The 'battle of Eckmühl' was not a preconceived strategic manœuvre as Austerlitz had been; it was perforce hastily improvised on the spur of the moment, while his corps were scattered and unready owing to Berthier's inability to effect their concentration, though he himself was largely to blame for that state of unpreparedness. The rapidity and firmness with which the Emperor turned the tables on his opponent, and snatched victory from a most disadvantageous situation, is a striking example of his masterly genius for warfare.

Napoleon quickly regrouped his forces for the march on Vienna, which he was anxious to reach before the Archduke. The main road south of the Danube crossed the Inn at the Austrian frontier fortress of Passau; 60 miles further east it crossed the Traun at the more easily defensible bridge of Ebelsberg, south of Linz. Beyond Ebelsberg, Vienna was only 110 miles distant, with few physical obstacles to cross. Massena (IV) was given command of the advanced guard, with orders to pursue Hiller's corps vigorously. Lannes (II) was to follow Massena; Davout (IV) was to guard the line of communications at Passau, until relieved by Bernadotte, who was to bring the

Saxon corps south from Dresden; Lefebvre (VII) was sent southward through the Kufstein Pass to Innsbruck, in order to act as right flank guard and suppress any resistance in the Tyrol. Prince Eugène in Venetia was engaged with an Austrian corps under the Archduke John.

Massena forced the passage of the Inn at Passau without difficulty on 27 April, but on 2 May he found the crossing of the Traun at Ebelsberg (south of Linz) disputed obstinately by Hiller's rearguard. The river here runs through a narrow defile and was crossed by a wooden bridge 200 yards long, enfiladed by the massed Austrian batteries. The Emperor had instructed Massena to push on at all costs, and the Marshal obeyed this order almost too literally. The result was a sanguinary battle in which the French suffered 5000 casualties, and the Austrians over 6000, but the latter were forced to abandon their position. Napoleon arrived on the scene before the battle was over, but made no attempt to outflank the enemy with Lannes's corps. When he was in a hurry, he was always ruthless in incurring casualties, and he was now anxious to forestall the Archduke in reaching Vienna.

Hiller, having delayed Massena at Ebelsberg, crossed the Danube at Mauthausen and rejoined the Archduke's army north of Vienna. Massena then continued his advance with little opposition and reached Amstetten on 7 May. On the 11th he occupied the western suburbs of Vienna; the Austrian garrison, under the 26-year-old Archduke Maximilian, offered a token resistance in the inner, walled city. Napoleon established his headquarters in the Imperial Palace of Schönbrunn, three miles south-west of the city centre, and ordered a bombardment of the inner city on 12 May. After a cannonade of four hours the capital surrendered, and the French army took possession on the morning of the 13th, exactly a month after the Austrian army had invaded Bavaria. Napoleon, who was now in occupation of the Austrian capital for the second time in four years, issued the following proclamation to its 300,000 citizens:

I take the good inhabitants under my special protection. But I shall inflict exemplary punishment on the turbulent and wicked. (*Corr.* 15203)

The Emperor now found himself in complete ignorance of his enemy's whereabouts, and he was still more annoyed to find that his staff had provided him with no intelligence about the country in which he was operating. He voiced his indignation in a letter to General Clarke, his War Minister in Paris, in the following terms:

I must express my extreme displeasure that you have left me absolutely destitute of any maps or topographical reports of the Nikolsburg and Austerlitz areas or the neighbourhood of Vienna. I cannot find in my topographic section any of the information which I myself ordered to be collected. You only sent me the reconnaissance reports on the Inn after they had become useless to me. Under some ridiculous rule, you only send me office copies, and as the copies take so long to make, the maps never arrive in time, and I am left without vital intelligence. . . . What is the use of the War Office if it cannot supply commanders with the reconnaissance reports they need for their operations? Issue an order that I am sent within 24 hours the originals (I won't have copies) of all maps, plans, reconnaissance reports and notes concerning Moravia, Bohemia, Hungary and Austria. (*Corr.* 15196)

Napoleon always disliked anything in the shape of red tape.

The Austrian Emperor having fled to Bohemia, and the Archduke's army having disappeared somewhere north of the Danube, Napoleon's problem was now to bring about a second Austerlitz and crush Austria's military power once and for all. The first step was to transport his army across the Danube, in flood from the melting of the snows in the Black Forest and Bavarian Alps; the Austrians had destroyed all the bridges. On 11 May Berthier issued the following instruction to General Songis, the army artillery commander: *

The intention of the Emperor, General, is to bridge the Danube tomorrow or the next day; you must therefore warn the pontoon unit and make every effort to collect boats, ropes and anchors. The Emperor wishes the bridge to be constructed between Pressburg [Bratislava] and Vienna. It is believed that at Fischamend [18 miles below Vienna] the Danube runs in a single channel without islands. You must therefore send an officer to reconnoitre this site, or any other that may seem suitable. The officer you nominate will report to the Duke of Rivoli, whose headquarters is at Simmering on the road to Pressburg. He will ask for a strong cavalry escort to cover his reconnaissance. (*Corr.* 15189)

The Emperor gave Massena charge of the whole bridging operation.

In attempting to pass his army across the Danube in flood, in order to attack a hostile army 100,000 strong, of whose whereabouts he was ignorant, Napoleon was undertaking the most hazardous military operation conceivable. He had always been a gambler; hitherto, in playing for bold stakes, he had always won. He had bluffed his way to victory against a succession of Austrian commanders—Beaulieu, Colli, Wurmser, Allvintzy, Melas and Mack. He had now only to get 100,000 men across a river to crush the Archduke Charles.

---

* In the French army the artillery staff was responsible for all bridging operations. General Nicolas-Marie Songis (1761–1810) had obtained his commission in the artillery five years before Napoleon. He had served under Bonaparte in Italy and distinguished himself at the siege of Acre (1799). His health broke down in June 1809 and he died a year later.

In its 40-mile course between Vienna and Pressburg the Danube, especially when in spring flood, presents a very formidable military obstacle. During the last century it has been extensively embanked and canalized, but in 1809 its course was far more sinuous, and was divided by islands into numerous channels.* The number of these channels involved the necessity of constructing additional bridges, but in compensation the length of each bridge was reduced and the strength of the stream diminished. After reviewing the reconnaissance reports, Napoleon decided to site his bridge opposite Kaiser-Ebersdorf, a village on the right bank six miles down stream from Vienna. Here the river was divided into two arms by the large low-lying island of Lobau. The main (southern) arm was 720 yards wide, and the bridging operation was facilitated by the existence of a small sandy islet in mid-stream. The island of Lobau was three miles long and two miles wide, affording ample space to assemble a large force; beyond it lay the lesser arm of the Danube, only 140 yards wide, with a more sluggish current than the main stream.

Massena's gunners and sappers got rapidly to work on the bridging operation. Timber, rope and barges were collected from Vienna, and a floating bridge was constructed from the right bank to Lobau island. Owing to the lack of pontoon anchors and chains, crates of cannon-balls were sunk in the river attached to the mooring cables. The first bridge over the main arm was completed by 19 May. Napoleon arrived at Kaiser-Ebersdorf that afternoon, and at dawn on the 20th the first of Massena's four divisions crossed to the island. This was followed by two light cavalry divisions and another of Massena's divisions. The lesser arm of the river was then bridged with some captured Austrian pontoons, and Massena occupied the villages of Essling and Aspern, two miles inland from the left bank of the Danube.

So far, there had only been slight opposition from the Austrian outposts. This indeed was in accordance with the Archduke's plan. He had assembled his army in the level plain north of the Danube, with his right flank resting on the river at the village of Aspern. He intended to allow the French to cross over to the left bank and then, while they were engaged in crossing, to drive them into the river. His trap was well laid, and it succeeded.

By dawn on 21 May Massena's four divisions and Lasalle's two cavalry divisions had deployed on the far bank between Essling and Aspern, and Napoleon himself crossed over from Lobau. Shortly before 2 p.m. the Arch-

* The map on page 208 is reproduced from one in the collection of the Royal Geographical Society. It was drawn in 1810 by the topographic section of the Austrian General Staff, and shows the bridges constructed by Napoleon in June–July 1809, and the names given by the French to the various small islands.

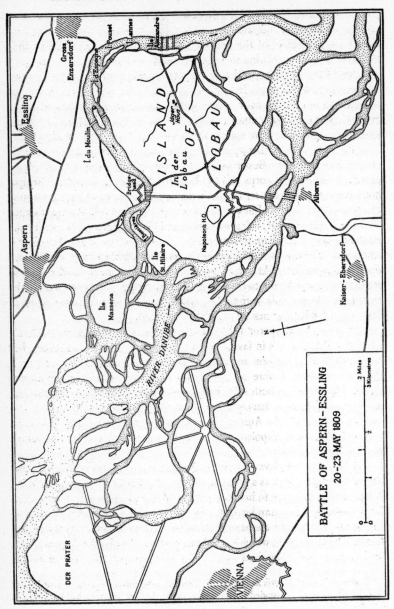

BATTLE OF ASPERN-ESSLING
20-23 MAY 1809

duke launched his attack and the French were driven out of Aspern. Lasalle's cavalry counter-attacked, and throughout the afternoon fierce fighting continued for possession of the two villages. Napoleon's operation was then struck with disaster. Owing to a sudden flood the river rose four feet and a number of the mooring cables of the main bridge snapped, the pontoon barges being carried away. It now became impossible to reinforce the 30,000 men isolated on the far bank, either with fresh troops or with ammunition. Meanwhile the Austrian attacks continued, led by the Archduke in person. Eventually, after desperate efforts, the bridge was repaired by midnight.

Undeterred by this calamity, the Emperor decided to continue the struggle on the following day. Bessières was sent up to take command of all the cavalry, and Lannes's corps and the Imperial Guard reinforced the bridgehead. Napoleon also sent for Davout's corps, which was watching the Danube crossings above Vienna. But before Davout could cross, disaster again struck the French. Fire-barges, laden with stone and blazing timber, released by the Austrians from farther up stream, crashed into the main bridge, breaking it once more. The troops on the left bank were now completely exhausted and short of ammunition. At 2 p.m. on the 22nd Napoleon ordered a general retreat from the left bank to the island, Massena being put in command of the rearguard. During this withdrawal, which was continued under cover of darkness, Marshal Lannes was mortally wounded.

At 7 p.m. the Emperor held a council of war on the island with his Marshals. Berthier was in favour of abandoning the attempt altogether, but Napoleon decided to form an entrenched camp on Lobau and to wait until the river subsided before making another attempt with fresh reinforcements. The losses on both sides had been shattering: the French, who had suffered more heavily, having had to abandon most of their wounded, lost over 44,000,* while the Austrian casualties amounted to 23,000. It was the first real defeat that Napoleon had suffered, and he had also lost one of his best fighting Marshals.

The Emperor still, however, retained possession of Lobau island, which he named 'Île Napoléon', as a jumping-off place for his second attempt. He left Massena with his corps to hold the island and to make adequate preparations for a crossing on a grander scale. He withdrew his own headquarters to Ebersdorf, but had an elevated observation post constructed on the island, screened by trees, from which he could inspect the river banks. Accompanied by Massena, both disguised as N.C.O.s in order to avoid attracting the

---

* Napoleon's 10th *Bulletin de l'Armée d'Allemagne* announced the French casualties as 1100 killed and 3000 wounded. The missing were not mentioned. See footnote to Chapter XII, p. 174.

attention of the Austrian outposts, he made a thorough reconnaissance of the river. He decided to mislead the enemy by making a feint crossing at the site of his previous pontoon bridge from the north end of the island towards Essling and Aspern. The real crossing was to be launched from a small island east of Lobau, which he named (after Berthier) 'Île Alexandre', three miles down stream from the original crossing. From this island pontoon bridges, ready-made further up stream, would be swung across the left arm on the night before the operation. Meanwhile a triple pile bridge of stout timbers was constructed across the right arm opposite Ebersdorf. The pile-driving involved considerable effort as the main stream was in places 25 feet deep. This triple bridge was protected up stream by a strong boom.

Having made these careful preparations for the crossing, the Emperor transferred his headquarters to Schönbrunn Palace and proceeded to re-organize his army. The corps which had suffered heavily were brought up to strength by reinforcements from France. Prince Eugène, with the Army of Italy, who had at last driven the Archduke John into Hungary, was recalled to Vienna, as was also Marmont's corps from Dalmatia. Oudinot was given command of II Corps, as Lannes had died of his wounds on 31 May. With these additional troops Napoleon succeeded in concentrating by 4 July, the date fixed for the crossing, a striking force of 25 infantry and 10 cavalry divisions, with 544 guns, organized as follows:

Imperial Guard (Walther)	11,000
Massena (IV)	30,000
Oudinot (II)	24,000
Davout (III)	35,000
Bernadotte (IX)	18,000
Prince Eugène's Corps	31,000
Marmont's Corps	10,000
Cavalry Corps (Bessières)	9,000
Bavarian Division (Wrede)	7,000
	175,000

Besides the above he had Lefebvre's VII and Vandamme's VIII Corps acting as flank guards, garrisoning Vienna and protecting the lines of communication.

Throughout the month of June Napoleon gave the closest attention to all the preparations for his great operation. On the 13th he wrote to General Bertrand, his Chief Engineer:

I sent for the officer in charge of works on the islands; I found him to be a miserable fellow who had no maps or plans of these islands. This is pitiful; every infantry officer has a map. The engineer services are not being carried out as they should be. The engineer Colonel in charge of the Vienna suburban defences should have plans of all the islands, keep them corrected by surveys, follow the enemy's movements, report these every day, and reconnoitre at dawn every important point. Instead of that, your engineer officer has seen nothing and done nothing. (*Corr.* 15345)

The Emperor's anger was also aroused by the leisurely way in which Marmont was marching his corps from Dalmatia through Ljubljana and Graz to join him at Vienna. On 28 June he wrote to Marmont:

You did not reach Graz by the 27th. You have committed the greatest military fault that a General can make. You should have been there by midnight on the 23rd. . . . You have the best corps in my army; I want you here for a battle, and you are several days late. Warfare demands more activity and mobility than you seem to have. (*Corr.* 15453)

On the evening of 30 June Napoleon made a feint crossing with a division of Massena's corps at the old pontoon site south of Aspern. To the Emperor's amazement, the enemy offered practically no resistance, and Massena was able to drive the Austrian outposts back to Aspern and construct a trestle bridge. In fact this was in accordance with the Archduke's plan of operations. He had drawn up his army of 130,000 men and 400 guns in a re-entrant semi-circular position, 12 miles in extent; his right flank rested on the Danube at Aspern, and the right wing, consisting of three corps, held the line Breitenlee–Süssenbrunn–Aderklaa–Deutsch-Wagram. The left sector, also consisting of three corps, continued from Deutsch-Wagram along the left bank of the Russbach stream to Markgraf-Neusiedl. Into this noose the Archduke intended to lure the whole of Napoleon's army. The Archduke John's corps of 14,000 at Pressburg, three days' march distant, was ordered to move west to close the gap south of Markgraf-Neusiedl, thus completing the encirclement of the French army. It was in fact an elaboration of the plan which had proved successful at Aspern-Essling.

Napoleon, ignorant both of the Archduke's plan and dispositions, felt that, as he had a bigger and better army, all he had to do was to transport it across the Danube to secure an easy victory. On 2 July he issued his operation orders for the crossing. Two battalions of light infantry were to be rafted across the left arm from the Île Alexandre at dusk on 4 July, covered by a bombardment to silence the Austrian guns on the left bank. A bridgehead was to be established on the low flats, known as the Hänsel-Grund, between Mühlleiten and Gross-Enzersdorf (p. 213). The pontoon bridges would then be swung across and made fast to the opposite bank, and the whole army would cross in three waves as follows:

First wave (from right to left): Davout, Oudinot, Massena.
Second wave (from right to left): Eugène, The Guard, Bernadotte, Marmont, Wrede (Bavarians).
Third wave: Bessières with the reserve cavalry.

General Reynier was left to garrison Lobau island with an infantry division and 113 guns, so as to cover the retreat in the event of failure. The whole army would deploy from the bridgehead in the above order of battle and would wheel to the north, pivoting on Massena's left flank at Aspern.

This carefully laid plan met with complete success. A violent thunderstorm, which broke on the evening of 4 July, distracted the attention of the Austrian outposts and the French army crossed without opposition, for the Archduke's main army was awaiting them seven miles to the north. The Austrian advanced troops were driven back and Napoleon's great left wheel was carried out according to plan. It was a triumph of staff work to have transported in a single night 150,000 men with their horses, guns and ammunition across one of the largest rivers in Europe. Napoleon, however, blamed Berthier for issuing inaccurate march tables, as a result of which Davout's corps crossed by the centre bridge instead of by the right one, causing a delay of some hours in the deployment.

North of the Danube between Vienna and Pressburg stretches a fertile plain known as the Marchfeld, 40 miles from west to east and 20 miles from south to north, where it is bounded by the uplands of Moravia. It is watered by the river March (Morava) and a number of smaller streams, left-bank tributaries of the Danube. One of the larger of these is the Russbach, along the left bank of which, between Deutsch-Wagram and Markgraf-Neusiedl, the Archduke had entrenched the left wing of his army, consisting of the corps of Rosenberg, Hohenzollern and Bellegarde; this sector was four miles in length. The Archduke's right wing hinged on the left at Deutsch-Wagram and extended for eight miles in a curve westwards and southwards through the villages of Aderklaa, Süssenbrunn, Breitenlee and Aspern, where its right wing rested on the Danube. This wing was held by the corps of Klenau, Kolowrat and Prince Liechtenstein. Klenau had taken over the command of Hiller's corps only on the previous day. (See Map on p. 213)

After the thunderstorm and torrential rain of the night before, the morning of 5 July dawned sunny and hot. By 3 p.m. the French army had completed its fan-like approach march and closed up to the concave arc presented by the enemy position. The Archduke was in no hurry to engage battle; his corps

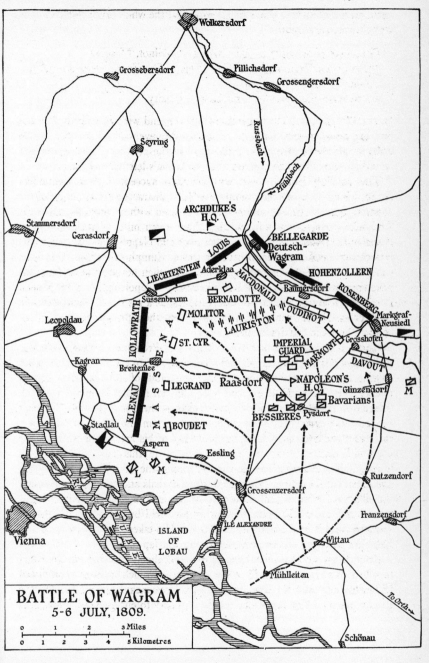

Wolkersdorf

Grossebersdorf

Pillichsdorf

Grossengersdorf

Russbach

Seyring

Mühlbach

Stammersdorf

Gerasdorf

ARCHDUKE'S H.Q.

BELLEGARDE

Deutsch-Wagram

LIECHTENSTEIN

LOUIS

Aderklaa

MACDONALD

HOHENZOLLERN

Süssenbrunn

BERNADOTTE

Baumersdorf

ROSENBERG

Leopoldau

KOLLOWRATH

MOLITOR

LAURISTON

OUDINOT

Markgraf-Neusiedl

ST. CYR

IMPERIAL GUARD

Grosshofen

MARMONT

DAVOUT

Kagran

Breitenlee

M A S S E N A

LEGRAND

Raasdorf

NAPOLEON'S H.Q.

Glinzendorf

M

KLENAU

BOUDET

Stadlau

BESSIÈRES

Pysdorf

Bavarians

Aspern

Essling

L   M

Grossenzersdorf

Rutzendorf

Franzensdorf

ILÉ ALEXANDRE

Wittau

Vienna

ISLAND
OF
LOBAU

D A N U B E

Mühlleiten

To Orth

BATTLE OF WAGRAM
5·6 JULY, 1809.

0   1   2   3 Miles

0   1   2   3   4   5 Kilometres

Schönau

were not yet fully deployed, and his brother John, whose arrival would have closed the ring, was still distant. Had he attacked the French at dawn before their crossing was completed, he might have annihilated them.

Massena's corps of four divisions formed the whole of the French left wing between Aspern and Aderklaa, and from the beginning its left wing was hotly engaged with Klenau's corps near Aspern. It was not until 6 p.m. that Napoleon had got his Guard and heavy cavalry reserve assembled behind his centre near Raasdorf, four miles south of Deutsch-Wagram. Having reconnoitred the enemy position, the Emperor decided to attack the Austrian left on the line of the Russbach, a deep and muddy stream. The attack was launched frontally by the corps of Davout and Oudinot, but was repulsed everywhere with heavy losses; some of the commanders received their orders too late, their attacks were delivered piecemeal, and the Austrians counterattacked fiercely. No ground was gained, and in the centre Bernadotte's Saxons were driven back from Aderklaa in disorder. As darkness fell the Emperor broke off the battle, intending to renew the attack next day.

Early on the morning of 6 July the Archduke surprised Napoleon by taking the offensive. Massena's four divisions, extended on a front of seven miles between Aderklaa and Aspern, had to withstand the main force of the assault by Klenau's and Kolowrat's corps. The Saxons on his right were again routed and his left division (Boudet) was forced out of Aspern with the loss of all its guns. The situation seemed desperate, for, if the Austrians advanced along the Danube bank, the French army would be cut off from its bridges and line of retreat. Faced with this crisis, Napoleon had the choice between moving his reserves across to support his threatened left, or of counterattacking the Austrian centre and left. The former course would have involved too lengthy and complicated a manœuvre; he decided to strike at Wagram, the central key-point at the hinge of the Austrian position; at the same time, with his right flank, he would roll up the whole line of the Russbach.

After telling Massena to hold the left wing at all costs, Napoleon ordered Lauriston and Drouot to bring the 60 guns of the Guard artillery into action opposite the Austrian centre between Wagram and Aderklaa. After a prolonged and massive bombardment, Bessières with his cuirassier divisions charged the shaken Austrian infantry. Then Macdonald with 20 battalions of Eugène's infantry, followed by Marmont and Wrede, broke through the Austrian centre. At the same time Davout on the right crossed the Russbach south of Markgraf-Neusiedl, rolled up the whole of the Austrian left and converged on Wagram. The fighting was fierce and the Austrians resisted stoutly, but at 4 p.m. the Archduke Charles learnt that his brother John was still 10 miles distant from the battlefield. He realized that his plan to encircle the French army had failed and felt it useless to continue the slaughter. He therefore ordered his troops to disengage and withdraw northward into the Moravian hill country.

The Austrians withdrew in good order, leaving behind only their severely wounded and some shattered guns. The French were too exhausted to pursue, Napoleon having used all his reserves. More than 400 guns had been in action at close range on each side, and the casualties were enormous, probably amounting to 30,000 for the French * and 26,000 for the Austrians. Wagram cannot be claimed as such a crushing victory for Napoleon as were Friedland or Austerlitz, but in the end it proved equally decisive. The Archduke's army retreated northward during the night in several columns. On the following day the French pursued slowly, and on 10 July Massena caught up with the rearguard at Znaim (Znojmo) and successfully engaged it. The Austrian Emperor then felt that his army had suffered sufficiently and on the 11th he sent Prince Liechtenstein to Napoleon requesting an armistice, to which the latter gladly assented; he was a long way from home and the news from Spain was not good. Hostilities came to an end, but it took three months of hard negotiation before a peace treaty was eventually signed at Schönbrunn on 14 October.

After the battle of Wagram the Emperor sent Bernadotte home in disgrace, not being satisfied with his handling of the Saxon Corps. Macdonald, Marmont and Oudinot were each awarded a Marshal's baton; Davout was created Prince of Eckmühl and Massena Prince of Essling.

* See footnote to p. 174.

XV

War on Two Fronts
1810–1812

While the *Armée d'Allemagne* was winning the Austrian war under Napoleon's personal leadership, his *Armée d'Espagne*, nominally commanded by his incompetent brother Joseph, was waging war in the Peninsula with less success. The Napoleonic system of command, with all authority concentrated in the Emperor's hands, broke down completely when he was not present in person. The distance from Vienna to Madrid via Paris is 1400 miles, and the Spanish war was too complicated to be waged by remote control. Not only was King Joseph useless as a soldier, but he was served by a mediocre Chief of Staff in Marshal Jourdan. The corps commanders, some of whom were competent leaders, such as Soult and Ney, were widely scattered over Spain and Portugal, trying to suppress local insurrections. Not only did they disregard the orders received from Madrid, but they were mutually jealous and refused to cooperate.

Three days after the victory of Eckmühl had opened up the Danube valley to Napoleon's march on Vienna, Sir Arthur Wellesley landed at Lisbon with a fresh British army; three weeks later he had thrown Soult out of Portugal, bag and baggage. When the Emperor at Schönbrunn heard of this disaster on 12 June he wrote to Clarke:

Send a staff officer to Spain with the order that the corps of Ney, Mortier and Soult are to be formed into an army which will be commanded by Soult. These three corps must march together against the British, pursue them relentlessly, beat them and throw them into the sea. Putting aside other considerations, I give the command to Soult, being the senior. These three corps should comprise in all

50 to 60,000 men. If this concentration takes place promptly, the British should be destroyed and the Spanish business finished, but they must march together and not in penny packets. (*Corr.* 15340)

But before this order became effective, Wellesley had defeated Victor and Sébastiani at Talavera. On hearing of this second disaster, Napoleon sacked Jourdan and replaced him by Soult.* Ney refused to take orders from Soult and returned to France. Gouvion Saint-Cyr also failed to fulfil the Emperor's expectations and was replaced by Augereau, who equally proved a failure. And so the war in Spain dragged on, with a quarter of a million men bogged down in an endless guerrilla struggle which involved a constant drain on France's military resources.

After the Peace of Schönbrunn had ended the war with Austria the Emperor returned to Paris and resumed the task of ruling his extensive, but not wholly consolidated empire. Austria being disposed of, he felt that he must now personally undertake the conquest of the Peninsula. There is no doubt that he could have achieved it, had he transferred to Spain the bulk of his Army of Germany, and had he assumed personal command of the operation. Wellington's 30,000 British troops, with a similar number of Portuguese, could not have withstood the attack of 200,000 French troops under Napoleon, advancing simultaneously by Ciudad Rodrigo and Badajoz. This indeed was the Emperor's intention: on 26 September, three weeks before the signing of the Treaty of Schönbrunn, he told Soult that he intended to march on Lisbon himself. On 23 November he confirmed this to Clarke, his War Minister, ordering him to bring the Imperial Guard up to a strength of 25,000, complete with medical officers, transport and field forges, ready to start for Spain about 15 January. On 1 December Berthier's post was altered to Chief of Staff of the Army of Spain, and he was told to arrange for 100,000 reinforcements to be sent to the Peninsula. On 3 December, in a speech to the Legislative Body, the Emperor pompously announced: 'When I show myself beyond the Pyrenees, the terrified "leopard" will seek safety in the Ocean to escape from shame, defeat and destruction.' (*Corr.* 16031).

But Napoleon's purpose was diverted from this enterprise by other ambitions. During his residence at Schönbrunn a young Saxon fanatic had made an attempt on his life, and he was disturbed by the thought that he had no legitimate successor, as he did not wish his heritage to be split up, as those of Alexander and Charlemagne had been. The Empress Joséphine was now barren, and had given him no heir to the throne. His brothers were all unsuitable to succeed him. He decided to divorce Joséphine and wed a younger

*Jourdan was later reinstated as Chief of Staff and Soult was given command of the Army of Andalusia.

bride who would give him a son. On 15 December 1809 Cambacérès, his Arch-Chancellor, issued a senatorial decree divorcing Joséphine, and giving her a state pension of 2,000,000 francs. The difficulty was to find a suitable bride, who must be of royal blood to maintain his imperial dignity. The choice lay between the Románov and Habsburg houses. He first sought the hand of one of the Tsar's sisters, either the Grand Duchess Catherine or her younger sister Anna, aged 14, but the Tsar discouraged the proposal. Napoleon then turned to Vienna, which he had recently conquered, and after negotiations with Prince Schwarzenberg and Metternich obtained the Austrian Emperor's consent to a marriage with his eldest daughter, the Archduchess Marie-Louise, aged 19. On 23 February 1810 Napoleon wrote to his mother:

> I hasten to let you know that the marriage contract between me and the Archduchess Marie-Louise, daughter of the Emperor of Austria, was ratified on the 16th at Vienna. (*Corr.* 16285)

The wedding was solemnized at the Louvre on 2 April. In the following March the new Empress gave birth to a son, who was given the title of 'King of Rome'.

The Spanish war now took a back seat among the Emperor's plans and he abandoned for ever his intention of assuming personal command of his armies in the Peninsula. A fortnight after his marriage he created a new Army of Portugal, consisting of only three corps: Reynier (II), Ney (VI) and Junot (VIII). André Massena, a sick man and ageing rapidly, was given the army command, which he only accepted with the greatest reluctance. His task ended in complete failure, for neither Napoleon nor Berthier took adequate steps to coordinate his operations with those of the other Marshals, Bessières, Soult and Mortier, who held adjacent commands. After sustaining a serious tactical reverse at Bussaco on 27 September 1810, Massena's march on Lisbon was frustrated by Wellington's* Lines of Torres Vedras. Owing to Napoleon's neglect to ensure the maintenance of Massena's line of communications, he was forced to evacuate Portugal in the following spring, and was finally defeated by Wellington at Fuentes de Oñoro, 3–5 May 1811. For the next two years the Peninsular War dragged on with a mounting record of French reverses and attrition of French manpower, for the Emperor was now bent on undertaking a still more ambitious operation.

Napoleon had indeed been caught up in the gears of the colossal empire which he had created. He had made too many conquests and had subjugated

---

* After the battle of Talavera (27–28 July 1809) Sir Arthur Wellesley had been created Viscount Wellington.

too many peoples with individual entities. He had abducted the Pope from the Holy See and been excommunicated. The subordination of so many national interests to his own despotic will had made him the most hated ruler in Europe. Above all, his ruthless enforcement of the Continental System, banning all commerce with Britain, had ruined the trading communities on the North Sea and Baltic coasts, including Russia. This was not the only source of friction with the Tsar: by the Treaty of Schönbrunn (14 October 1809) Austria had been forced to cede Galicia, which Napoleon at once incorporated into the Grand Duchy of Warsaw, thus upsetting the political equilibrium on Russia's western frontier; finally, in January 1811 Napoleon had, contrary to the Treaty of Tilsit, annexed the Grand Duchy of Oldenburg, allied to Russia by dynastic ties.

The causes which brought about the rupture between the Emperor and the Tsar were numerous and complex; Napoleon's main motive was that he could not tolerate on the boundary of his Empire the existence of a Power which was not entirely subservient to his own will. Napoleon had already beaten the Russians in battle and he had formed a poor opinion of their leadership. Once they were finally beaten, he could create a strong Poland as a buffer state and satellite of France. Unfortunately, Napoleon decided to conquer Russia before he had succeeded in conquering Spain.

Towards the close of 1811 Napoleon began to prepare for a campaign in Russia. On 4 December he discussed with his War Minister the artillery organization of '*la nouvelle Grande Armée*', which was to comprise 512 guns in artillery units and 176 attached to the infantry. On 16 December he ordered Bessières to bring home all the units of the Imperial Guard serving in Spain and to prepare them for active service. The Guard was to be reorganized in three infantry divisions with 128 field-guns and two cavalry divisions with 48 horse-artillery pieces. Three days later he issued confidential instructions for the purchase of 3000 horses in Poland, 1000 in Württemberg, 2000 in Hanover and Westphalia, and 4000 in Austria. On the same day his librarian was ordered to send him all the books available on the topography of Russia and Lithuania, as well as a history of Charles XII's campaign in Poland and Russia.

Napoleon's political advisers, such as Caulaincourt, who had been Ambassador at St. Petersburg, were strongly opposed to a war with Russia, and his military advisers pointed out the strategic difficulties, but they were all disregarded. On 26 February 1812 the Emperor made a treaty of alliance with Prussia and in March one with Austria. This new threat to his western frontier alarmed the Tsar, who demanded on 24 April that the French garrisons in Prussia and in the Silesian fortresses should be withdrawn. Napoleon rejected this demand and began to concentrate his troops. On 9 May he left Paris with the Empress and on the 16th set up Imperial Headquarters at Dresden, where a round of festivities took place for the next fortnight, while the *Grande Armée* advanced and deployed on the line of the Vistula.

Napoleon had now assembled the most powerful army that Europe had ever seen; it was organized as follows:

Old Guard (Lefebvre	
Young Guard (Mortier	40,000
I Corps (Davout)	70,000
II Corps (Oudinot)	42,000
III Corps (Ney)	40,000
IV Corps (Prince Eugène)	45,000
V Corps (Polish, Poniatowski)	35,000
VI Corps (Bavarian, Saint-Cyr)	22,000
VII Corps (Saxon, Reynier)	16,000
VIII Corps (Westphalian, Junot)	16,000
IX Corps (German, Victor)	32,000
X Corps (Prussian, Macdonald)	32,000
XI Corps (Reserve, Augereau)	50,000
Austrian Corps (Prince Schwarzenberg)	32,000
Reserve Cavalry (Murat, 4 corps)	38,000
	510,000

The whole comprised 40 infantry and 25 cavalry divisions. At least half the men were of non-French nationality, but most of the foreign corps were stiffened with a French division.

The Tsar's available forces were not so formidable, as Russia was still fighting the Turks in Bessarabia. The main army of 150,000, commanded by General Barclay de Tolly, a Latvian of Scottish ancestry, was concentrated behind the Niemen. The second army, under Prince Bagratión, covered the gap between the Niemen and the Bug and numbered 50,000; the Hetman Platov with 8000 Cossacks was in the Grodno area (back endpaper).

Napoleon left Dresden on 29 May and moved by stages via Posen, Thorn and Danzig to the East Prussian frontier. On 22 June he reached Wilkowyszki (Vilkaviškis) in Polish Lithuania, and on the 24th crossed the Niemen at Kóvno (Kaunas) into Russian territory. He did not underestimate the difficulty of supplying his huge army in the comparatively barren wastes of Lithuania and White Russia. On 26 May he wrote from Dresden to Davout:

As a result of all my movements 400,000 men will be concentrated in one spot; we can therefore expect to find nothing in the country itself, and we shall have to carry everything with us. (*Corr.* 18725)

But he never foresaw the possibility of a winter campaign. He expected to make early contact with the main Russian army under Barclay in the open country near Vilna (Vilnyus). He would there defeat it and dictate his own terms to the Tsar. He would then become the supreme Dictator of Europe. His plan was to pierce the extended Russian front by advancing directly on Vilna from Kóvno, while two subsidiary armies, each consisting of three corps, commanded by Prince Eugène and King Jérôme, would be echelonned behind his right flank to cover his lines of communication.

The crossing of the Niemen was unopposed and on 28 June Napoleon entered Vilna which the Tsar had evacuated only a few days previously. The Emperor had hoped to envelop Bagratión's army with his right wing while his main body would defeat Barclay in a decisive battle, but this plan was frustrated by Jérôme's indecision and ineptitude. The Russian armies eluded battle and retreated eastwards. This was not really a preconceived plan on their part, but resulted from the absence of any fixed policy and from the lack of cooperation between the various commanders, who were mutually jealous.

On reaching Vilna Napoleon halted for 18 days. There were several good reasons for this delay, but it had fatal consequences for the whole campaign. Matters now began to go seriously wrong. A heat-wave and heavy rains affected the health of the army from the Emperor downwards. The troops began to suffer from dysentery. There was a shortage of oats, and the horses, which were being fed on green rye, died by hundreds. For lack of gun-teams, 100 guns and 500 ammunition wagons had to be abandoned.

Meanwhile Davout (I) on the right flank had reached Minsk on 8 July, but Bagratión again eluded him. Displeased with Jérôme's slowness, Napoleon put Davout in command of the whole right flank guard over his brother's head; Jérôme took offence at being superseded and retired to his Kingdom at Cassel on 16 July. Davout then pushed on to Mogilev on the Dnepr.

Barclay had retired north-eastwards to the entrenched camp of Drissa on the Dvina, intending to cover the road to St. Petersburg. This left a gap between the two Russian armies; Napoleon took advantage of this gap to push on to Vítebsk which he reached on 28 July. The Tsar, realizing that Napoleon was aiming at Moscow, ordered Barclay to abandon Drissa and fall back on Smolénsk, where Bagratión was to join him and come under Barclay's orders, though Bagratión was the senior. Bagratión, hard pressed by Davout, made his way back to Smolénsk, where Barclay joined him on 3 August.

On reaching Vítebsk Napoleon found that his army had outrun its supply system and was in poor condition. It had indeed dwindled from its original strength to 230,000 men, and the enemy had not yet been brought to battle. On the following day he wrote to Davout, commanding his right wing:

The Emperor's principal intention, if the enemy does not oblige him to make other arrangements, is to give the army seven or eight days' rest in order to organize the supply service. (*Corr.* 19017)

But when he learnt that the two Russian armies had united at Smolénsk, he decided to push on and engage them. On 12 August he wrote to Davout:

Everything leads me to think that we shall have a big battle at Smolénsk. (*Corr.* 19095)

Ney, leading the advanced guard, reached the bank of the Dnepr facing Smolénsk on 16 August. The massive brick ramparts were strongly held by the Russians. The Emperor came up and ordered an immediate assault, which was repulsed with considerable loss. The French attack was resumed on the following day and heavy fighting took place. The town, constructed of wood, was set on fire by the French bombardment. The casualties on both sides were heavy. Covered by a strong rearguard holding the ramparts, the Russians retired on the night of the 17th/18th. The battle of Smolénsk, in which the French losses had not achieved a decisive result, faced Napoleon with the choice between abandoning the campaign altogether or continuing his pursuit of the elusive Russian armies. The latter course meant a dangerous extension of his tenuous line of communications. His army had already marched 480 miles from its advanced base at Königsberg (Kaliningrad), and a march on Moscow meant another 240 miles to go. The gambler in Napoleon prevailed, and he decided to go on.

After the battle of Smolénsk the Tsar, disappointed at the continued retreat of his armies, and alarmed by the growing discord between Bagratión and Barclay de Tolly, reluctantly decided to give the supreme command to the lazy but shrewd 67-year-old Kutúzov, who had been replaced after Austerlitz. Kutúzov continued the strategic withdrawal, but decided to make a stand on a good defensive position between Vyázma and Mozháysk. The position he selected was a ridge dominating the right bank of the Kolochá stream,* where it is crossed by the Smolénsk–Moscow road at the village of Borodinó. This ridge he fortified with several strong earthwork redoubts; the left flank, which was not protected by the stream, rested on a detached knoll, strongly entrenched, known as the Shevárdino redoubt.

On 5 September Murat's mounted advanced guard was held up by the

* A tributary of the river Moskvá; the latter covered the Russian right flank. The French know the battle of Borodinó as '*la Moskova*'.

Russian position at Borodinó. A determined attack by Davout on the French right flank captured the Shevárdino redoubt by nightfall, and the Russian left wing under Bagratión withdrew to the main position on the ridge between the villages of Borodinó and Semënovsk. During the following day the Emperor carefully reconnoitred the Russian position and then issued orders for a frontal attack by Davout and Ney on the main ridge the next morning, while Poniatowski on the right was to try to turn the enemy's left flank.

The Emperor rose early on 7 September and established his command post on the Shevárdino redoubt, but he was suffering from a feverish cold and was feeling very unwell; after ordering the initial moves he took little further part in directing the battle. The French attack was launched at 6 a.m. after a concentrated bombardment of the Russian redoubts by the French artillery. The Russians counter-attacked and very heavy fighting took place all along the line, particularly around the Semënovsk redoubt. Poniatowski's attempt to turn Bagratión's left flank failed, but Bagratión was mortally wounded. The battle developed into a succession of frontal assaults on the strongly held entrenchments in the centre of the position. About 6 p.m. the French, by sheer weight of numbers, succeeded in capturing the redoubts. The losses on both sides were very heavy: 28,000 for the French and 40,000 for the Russians. But the Russians hung on grimly and formed up again behind the captured redoubts. Napoleon's Marshals advised him to send in the Guard for a final assault to break their line, but the Emperor refused; he might have to fight another battle in front of Moscow, and he wanted to keep his Guard intact.

Leaving a rearguard on the battlefield, Kutúzov retired on the following day to Mozháysk. Napoleon was still feeling unwell and Murat's pursuit was not pushed vigorously. The Russians made no further stand; Murat's cavalry entered Moscow on 14 September and Napoleon occupied the Kremlin on the 15th; he found an almost deserted city; by that evening fires broke out in many places owing to the depredations of drunken looters both French and Russian. The houses being largely built of wood, the greater part of the city, outside the Kremlin walls, was gradually reduced to ashes.

After abandoning Moscow, instead of continuing to retreat eastwards, Kutúzov moved his army to Kalúga, 100 miles to the south-west. This was a clever move; not only did it protect the important town of Túla, one of the main Russian arsenals, but it was within 90 miles of Vyázma, a key-point on the French line of communication. Here he reorganized his army, bringing it up to a strength of over 100,000. Napoleon had already received the news of Marmont's defeat by Wellington at Salamanca and of Wellington's entry into Madrid. His own situation was now every day becoming more precarious. In order to protect his life-line he had been obliged to detach large covering forces to the north and south, and he had less than 100,000 men at hand in and around Moscow; Murat's cavalry formed a screen to the south watching Kutúzov. The convoys moving between Smolénsk and Moscow were under constant attack by Cossack raiders, and Napoleon had to give orders to Junot at Smolénsk that no convoy was to be allowed to leave without an armed escort of 1500 men.

On 20 September the Emperor sent an envoy to the Tsar with a peace feeler, but no response came. Another approach to Kutúzov was also fruitless. On 18 October Kutúzov launched a sudden attack on Murat at Tarútino, 50 miles south-west of Moscow; Murat was caught off guard and forced to retire with the loss of a number of men and guns. But Napoleon had at last realized that it was impossible to remain longer. After a mild autumn the first snow fell on 13 October; on the 19th the *Grande Armée* began its retreat from Moscow.

Murat's reverse at Tarútino made it essential for Napoleon to take that road to support him; the army's first direction was therefore to the south-west. On 24 October Kutúzov intercepted them at Málo-Yaroslávets, and a battle took place in which the French lost 5000 men, mostly Italians of Prince Eugène's corps. The French were in a very difficult position, but fortunately Kutúzov broke off the fight and withdrew, although as he marched west-wards he still threatened their line of retreat. Disturbed by the set-back at Málo-Yaroslávets, Napoleon turned north-west in order to continue his re-treat by the shortest road though Vyázma and Smolénsk.

The retreat of the *Grande Armée* now became a long nightmare. Its numbers had been reduced to 65,000 men, including 15,000 cavalry. The flank guards, and even the main columns, were harassed daily by swarms of mounted Cossacks, who killed every straggler. Many of the wounded had to be abandoned, as well as the booty-laden transport. At the beginning of November Ney, with his corps of 6000 men, was put in command of the rearguard; he was being pressed closely by Kutúzov's pursuit, and a stiff engagement took place at Vyázma on 3 November, the French casualties amounting to 5000. The first heavy snow-fall occurred on 5 November, which increased the miseries of the retreat. On the following day Napoleon heard the extraordinary news of the Malet conspiracy in Paris. A certain General Malet, who had been in prison for four years on a political charge, had escaped from hospital on 23 October, announced that Napoleon had died in Russia, and arrested General Savary, the Minister of Police. Malet was, however, soon apprehended, court-martialled and shot.

Several Russian armies were now closing in on the retreating French, and on the north flank Victor's corps had been driven out of Polótsk by Wittgenstein, who was covering the road to St. Petersburg. On 7 November Berthier was instructed to send the following order to Victor in clear:

His Majesty orders you to concentrate your six divisions and attack the enemy without delay, drive him beyond the Dvina, and recapture Polotsk.

The message continued in cipher:

This move is of the highest importance. Within a few days your rear may be flooded with Cossacks; tomorrow the army and the Emperor will be at Smolénsk, but very tired after a march of 300 miles without stopping. Take the offensive, the safety of the armies depends on it; every day's delay is a calamity. The army's cavalry is dismounted; all its horses have died of cold. March! It is the Emperor's order and that of necessity. (*Corr.* 19326)

It was not the cold which had killed the horses, but the fact that they had not been shod with frost-nails, as the Russian horses were. Whenever the French horses crossed a frozen river or lake, they fell and broke their legs.

On 9 November the Emperor reached Smolénsk, and the rest of the *Grande Armée* was collected there by the 13th. Only 50,000 now survived, and the cavalry had very few horses; 200 guns had already been abandoned. Smolénsk was a main depot on the line of communication, but Victor's corps which had been stationed there for two months to guard the base hospitals and depots had consumed all the reserve rations, so that the army found nothing to eat.

Napoleon left Smolénsk on 14 November, but on the 16th Eugène's advanced guard was held up at Krásnoye by Kutúzov's army which now barred their line of retreat. A sharp engagement took place, but Napoleon with considerable boldness brought up the Guard and Davout's corps, whereon Kutúzov withdrew once more. Ney with the rearguard was for a time cut off; after a gallant struggle he managed to break through and rejoin the column, but with only 800 survivors left out of his corps of 6000.

The *Grande Armée* was now faced with its most terrible ordeal. Napoleon intended to head for Minsk, his nearest supply depot, but on 22 November he learnt that Minsk had been captured by Admiral Chichágov, whose fresh army had been released from Moldavia by the conclusion of peace between Russia and Turkey. The Emperor was therefore forced to take a more northerly route and make for Vilna. Athwart his road lay the marshy valley of the Berezíná, a right-bank tributary of the Dnepr. The only bridge across the Berezíná was at Borísov, which was held by a Polish division, but on 21 November Chichágov's army descended on Borísov and burnt the bridge. Oudinot's corps recaptured Borísov, but it was impossible to rebuild the bridge with Chichágov's army on the opposite bank. A sudden thaw had melted the ice and the Berezíná was in flood with blocks of ice floating down, so that it was impossible to cross it on foot. Napoleon then sent one of his artillery Generals, Éblé, to build a bridge farther north. It was General Éblé who, as Massena's corps artillery commander, had successfully bridged the Danube before Wagram. Éblé found a suitable place at Studyanka, five miles north of Borísov, where the crossing was only watched by a weak Cossack patrol. Two trestle bridges, 160 yards long, one for infantry, the other for guns and transport, were constructed with great difficulty by 25 November, and the army crossed during the next two days.

The congestion at the two bridges was appalling. On 22 November the Emperor had issued the following laconic Army Order:

Baggage will be reduced. Every general officer or staff officer who has several carts will burn half of them and hand over the horses to the artillery park. (*Corr.* 19346)

But many disobeyed the order and the bridges were choked with a seething mass of men, women, horses and vehicles.* The Russian armies now closed in for the kill: Chichágov from the south, Wittgenstein from the north, and Milorádovich with Kutúzov's vanguard from the east. Russian guns came into action on the ridge overlooking the bridges to add to the confusion. Victor with the rearguard of 3000 men crossed the bridges on the morning of 29 November and then burnt them. The French losses were about 25,000.

The passage of the Berezíná was the swan song of the *Grande Armée*; it was no longer capable of fighting. At Molodéchno on 3 December Napoleon wrote his famous 29th Bulletin, which recounted, fairly factually, the operations since 6 November. Its final paragraph runs as follows:

Our cavalry was so dismounted that we had to collect together the officers who still had one horse, in order to form four companies of 150 each. Generals acted as Captains, and Colonels as N.C.O.s. This sacred squadron, commanded by General Grouchy, and under orders of the King of Naples, never let the Emperor out of its sight during all his moves. His Majesty's health has never been better. (*Corr.* 19365)

Two days later at Smorgón the Emperor handed over the command of his army to Murat and left for Paris in his travelling carriage with Caulaincourt. He reached the Tuileries on 18 December.

The Emperor was justified in leaving his army, which had ceased to be a fighting force, for his recent allies, but latent enemies, were turning against him; his Empire was now at bay. On reaching East Prussia, Yorck with the

* Among the vehicles burnt in accordance with this order was the one containing the Emperor's personal library.

Prussian corps signed an armistice convention with the Russians at Tauroggen on 30 December. Prince Schwarzenberg with the Austrian contingent also signed a separate armistice with Admiral Chichágov. Murat, on reaching Posen on 17 January, suddenly remembered that he was King of Naples and left for a warmer climate, after handing over the army to Prince Eugène.

Meanwhile the Army of Spain had been abandoned to the helpless hands of King Joseph. Wellington's victory over Marmont at Salamanca in July had caused Joseph to evacuate Madrid hastily; this had greatly stimulated the morale of the Spanish nation, which was still further encouraged by the news of Napoleon's disasters in Russia. The Army of Spain was also doomed to destruction, and the Emperor had fallen between two stools.

It is easy, with the advantage of hindsight, to put one's finger on the military mistakes which Napoleon made in the conduct of his Russian campaign. His first and greatest error was to embark on the enterprise before having ensured the conquest of Spain. He had gambled on defeating the Russian army during the summer months on the plains of Lithuania, without having to lead his cumbrous international array across the barren wastes of White Russia. When the Russian forces eluded him by slipping away to the north, east and south, the fate of the *Grande Armée* was already sealed. This evasion was no master-stroke of strategy on the part of the Russians; it was in fact due to the irresolution of their Generals and their lack of cooperation; but the result was the same. The appointment of the corpulent and lethargic Kutúzov to the supreme command at the end of August ensured that this evasive strategy was continued. Only once, and then reluctantly, did Kutúzov engage in a pitched battle. That battle found Napoleon ill and irresolute; it developed into a frontal assault against troops of imperturbable courage. The only decision made by Napoleon was to refuse to employ his Guard at the crisis of the struggle, when a crushing and decisive victory might have been gained.

The miseries of the retreat from Moscow might have been mitigated by better organization of the lines of communication, and more foresight in the provision of winter equipment for the men and frost-nails for the horses, when the decision was made to advance beyond Smolénsk. The normal Napoleonic system of living on the country broke down completely in the barren Russian wastes. It is a mistake to ascribe the disaster to an unusually severe winter; in fact the weather was milder than usual, at least until mid-November. Napoleon's worst bit of bad luck was the sudden thaw which melted the frozen Bereziná in the last week of November.

Napoleon's conduct of the Russian campaign shows that his military abilities were on the wane; they were, however, still far from fading out.

XVI

The Beginning of the End
1813

Although his invasion of Russia had ended so disastrously, Napoleon had no intention of throwing up the sponge. As soon as he reached Paris he set to work to organize a '*nouvelle Grande Armée*' to meet the counter-invasion which he knew would soon take place. It was vital to act swiftly before an overwhelming Russian army could concentrate on the Prussian frontier. The shield of Napoleonic invincibility had been sadly tarnished, and if time were allowed to slip by, his reluctant satellite allies, Austria, Prussia, Saxony and Bavaria, would escape from their orbits.

  After all, things were not so black as they seemed; half the casualties sustained in Russia were not French ones; the major losses were suffered by Bavarians, Württembergers, Saxons, Prussians, Poles and Italians who had been forcibly pressed into the *Grande Armée*. These allies were now summoned to furnish fresh contributions, both of men and horses. To replenish the cadres of his French troops he called up in advance the 1814 and 1815 classes of conscripts, which gave him 300,000 fresh recruits. He had previously reorganized the National Guard (Territorial Army) as an army reserve; its units were organized in *cohortes* to distinguish them from the battalions of the regular army and were constitutionally liable to serve only in France, but a large number of them were now induced to volunteer for transfer to regular units.

  There was a great dearth of junior officers; 200 cadets in the military schools were given immediate commissions, and 100 corporals with over ten years' service were promoted to *sous-lieutenant*. But the arm which had suffered most severely in the Russian campaign was the cavalry. On 26 February the Emperor ordered his War Minister to reorganize the whole cavalry arm for the 1813 campaign with the following establishment:

	Squadrons	Men
Army of Germany	255	58,600
Army of Spain	89	19,700
Home forces	116	26,700
	460	105,000

Of these, 27,000 would be recruits of the 1814 and 1815 classes. Gendarmerie officers were called in to assist in training recruits and breaking remounts.

Meanwhile on the eastern front Prince Eugène's depleted army of less than 20,000 men was being forced back by Wittgenstein's corps, which formed the advanced guard of Kutúzov's army. Napoleon sent his stepson urgent orders to hold the line of the Vistula, but by the time the order reached him, Eugène had already been driven back to the Oder; by the end of January he was behind the line of the Elbe and the Russians had entered Berlin. Napoleon had forgotten that in mid-winter the rivers of Poland and East Prussia are frozen hard, so that the Cossacks could cross them anywhere, outflanking the fortified bridgeheads held by the French. He was greatly annoyed at Eugène's retreat and kept sending him stern admonitions:

Stay in Berlin as long as you can. Make examples in order to maintain discipline. If there is any sign of revolt in any Prussian town or village, even Berlin, have it burnt down. If you are forced to retire to the Elbe, do not retreat any further. . . . The cavalry is being reorganized in France on a grand scale, but we still need the whole of April. By May I shall have assembled the three corps of the Army of the Main, with my Guard and plenty of artillery and cavalry; then I shall drive the Russians back to the Niemen. (Corr. 19664)

The Emperor was still more infuriated by the lack of information from the front. On 7 March he wrote to Eugène, who had now retreated to Wittenberg:

I cannot give you any orders or instructions, since you do not carry out any of your duties; you send me no details or strength returns; you tell me nothing, neither you nor your staff. I do not even know which Generals command your corps; or where they are; I do not know your situation, or what artillery you have. I get no information, I am completely in the dark. How do you expect me to give directions to my army? (Corr. 19687)

The trouble was that Berthier, who had been left to assist Eugène, had gone sick after the privations of Russia, and the Emperor himself was without a proper Chief of Staff; General Duroc, his Grand Master of the Palace, was functioning *ad interim*.

Napoleon's strategic plan for the 1813 campaign was to arrest the Russian advance on the Elbe with his left wing under Eugène, which he called the Army of the Elbe, while he reorganized in Franconia a striking force called the Army of the Main, which would advance through the Thüringer Wald and deploy on the line of the lower Saale. It would there join hands with the Army of the Elbe, sweep eastwards and drive the Russians out of Saxony and eastern Prussia. In writing to his ally, King Frederick of Württemberg, at the beginning of March, the Emperor asked him to concentrate his contingent at Würzburg and outlined his plan as follows:

> I have given orders that the Russians should be allowed to advance, and I have taken all measures necessary to open the campaign soon. But it is essential to cover the Thuringian mountains in order to protect the heart of the Confederation of the Rhine from being insulted by the raids of Cossack patrols. It is particularly important that Your Majesty should collect several thousand horses at Würzburg. (*Corr.* 19650)

The Cossack patrols were indeed spreading alarm throughout north-east Germany; on 12 March 200 of them actually raided Hamburg, and the local commanders, Lauriston and Gouvion Saint-Cyr, ordered its hasty evacuation by French troops, much to the Emperor's indignation. He wrote to Eugène:

> General Lauriston appears to have a very excitable temperament, and I much fear that he has no ability as a commander. (*Corr.* 19766)

He had just appointed both Lauriston and Saint-Cyr to be corps commanders; Lauriston, who had commanded his Guard artillery at Wagram, was allowed to retain his command, but Saint-Cyr was replaced by Macdonald.

On 12 March the Emperor issued a decree establishing the organization of the new *Grande Armée* as follows:

I Corps—Davout	VII Corps—Reynier
II Corps—Victor	VIII Corps—Poniatowski
III Corps—Ney *	IX Corps—Bavarians
IV Corps—Bertrand	X Corps—Rapp
V Corps—Lauriston	XI Corps—Macdonald
VI Corps—Marmont	

These corps were organized in 41 infantry and 11 cavalry divisions. In addition, the Imperial Guard, which had suffered least heavily in the retreat

---

* For his gallantry at Borodinó and during the retreat from Moscow, Marshal Ney had been created *Prince de la Moskova*.

from Moscow, was reorganized in two divisions under Mortier and Bessières, comprising 12,000 infantry, 3000 cavalry and 60 guns. The army cavalry consisted of 172 squadrons, organized in three cavalry corps.

After three months of ceaseless activity on the part of the Emperor, the new army began to take shape, though it was not completely up to establishment, particularly in cavalry, owing to the shortage of horses; this proved a great handicap in obtaining intelligence of the enemy's movements. Towards the end of March, when Berthier returned to duty, Napoleon had assembled in Franconia his striking force, the 'Army of the Main', consisting of III, IV, VI Corps, the Guard and a cavalry corps, comprising about 85,000 men. This exceeded the number of Russians and Prussians now assembling on the line of the Oder, as yet only some 50,000.

On hearing that the French garrison had evacuated Hamburg, the Emperor had ordered Eugène to send Davout there to restore the situation. On receiving this order, Davout, who was facing a Prussian corps at Dresden, blew up the Elbe bridge and evacuated the Saxon capital. This infuriated Napoleon, who wrote on 28 March to Eugène:

Everything that this Marshal [Davout] has done at Dresden and during the retreat proves that his notions of war are erroneous and stupid. (*Corr.* 19779)

In mid-April the striking force began its northward march through the Thüringer Wald, following the same roads that the *Grande Armée* had in October 1806 at the outset of the Jena campaign. In fact it traversed the battlefields of Saalfeld, Jena and Auerstedt. On 14 April the Emperor left Paris, reaching Mainz on the 17th after a 40-hour journey. Mainz was the main supply depot for the right wing of the army, and Napoleon spent a week there to inspect the administrative services. All was not to his liking. On the day of his arrival he wrote an angry note to Count Mollien, his Finance Minister in Paris:

The organization of our finances is in complete chaos. I have been obliged to waste several hours in unscrambling this mess and in working with junior clerks. I told you that the Army of the Main is quite separate from the Army of the Elbe and that each must have its own Paymaster. If you trouble to look at a map you will see that the Paymaster at Magdeburg is in the thick of operations and cannot look after affairs at Mainz. We are not short of money here, but we are short of good organization. (*Corr.* 19865)

And on the same day he found time to give a lesson in battle-drill to his VI Corps commander, who, being a gunner, he may have thought unversed in infantry tactics:

I must insist that the most important manœuvre is to form square by battalions. Battalion and company commanders must be able to execute this movement with the greatest rapidity; it is the only way to meet cavalry charges and save the whole regiment. As I expect that your officers are slow movers, explain the idea to them every day, to get it into their heads.

Your Spanish battalion must be given no opportunity to desert. It must never be sent on detachment, outpost or escort duty, but must always be kept concentrated and surrounded by French battalions. (*Corr.* 19868)

The Emperor moved up to Erfurt on 25 April and to Naumburg on the 29th. On the 30th Imperial Headquarters was established at Weissenfels. He now formed a new XII Corps, under Oudinot, by removing two divisions from the four in Bertrand's IV Corps. Oudinot was also given two Bavarian divisions, while Bertrand was made up with an Italian and a Württemberg division.

Meanwhile Napoleon had ordered Eugène to move the bulk of his Elbe Army southward and to concentrate on the left bank of the lower Saale between Halle and Merseburg. Thus by 30 April the Army of the Main (85,000) had effected its junction with the Army of the Elbe (60,000). The leading corps were then ordered to cross the Saale and move eastward on Leipzig.

Owing to his shortage of cavalry, Napoleon was uncertain of the enemy's strength and dispositions. They were in fact rather widely dispersed and in some disarray. Field-Marshal Kutúzov, who had been created Prince of Smolénsk after the recent campaign, had died of typhoid in Silesia on 25 March, and the Tsar, who had arrived in Dresden, appointed Count Wittgenstein to the supreme command of the Allied forces. Wittgenstein was concentrating the bulk of his army on the river Elster near Pegau, 15 miles south of Leipzig. He realized that Leipzig would be Napoleon's first objective, and he intended to strike at the French right flank as they crossed the Saale. His force immediately available was composed of 35,000 Russians and 33,000 Prussians under Blücher, with a detachment under Kleist holding Leipzig. Thus Napoleon had a superiority in numbers of more than two to one.

On the morning of 1 May the French army crossed the Saale and advanced eastwards on a front of ten miles between Weissenfels and Merseburg. Ney (III) and the Guard Cavalry under Bessières led the right column, followed by Marmont (VI). The left column, advancing from Merseburg, had Macdonald (XI) in the lead, followed by Lauriston (V). In rear marched Bertrand (IV) and Oudinot (XII). This order of march was a good example of Napoleon's strategic approach in a *bataillon carré*, ready for an encounter battle with an enemy either in front or on a flank.

Shortly after crossing the Saale the Guard Cavalry encountered enemy outposts on the Rippach stream. The first Russian salvo scored a bull's eye, for Bessières fell dead, struck by a round-shot; he was the second of Napoleon's Marshals to fall in battle. * By nightfall Napoleon, accompanying Ney's advanced guard, reached Lützen, the scene of the battle on 16 November 1632, where Gustavus Adolphus was killed. Lützen is a small town 12 miles south-west of Leipzig. Four miles farther north, Eugène's leading corps, Macdonald (XI), reached Markranstädt. Lauriston (V) on the extreme left was ordered to move on Leipzig.

Meanwhile Wittgenstein had concentrated the Allied army at Pegau, only eight miles south-east of Lützen, and on the morning of 2 May was on the march to meet Napoleon there. The Emperor seems to have had some warning of this approach, for at 4 a.m. he ordered Ney to send out strong reconnaissances in that direction. Ney cannot have carried out this order very effectively, for at 11 a.m. one of his leading divisions was caught, halted and cooking its dinners, by the Prussian advanced guard. The Allies were slow to take advantage of this opportunity and the battle became general south and east of Lützen, where the villages of Gross-Görschen and Kaja changed hands repeatedly. Napoleon at Lützen had expected the engagement to take place further north, near Leipzig, but as soon as he heard the roar of gun-fire to the south, he galloped three miles to Gross-Görschen and at once took charge. Ney (III) was to hold his ground at all costs and pin the enemy down; Marmont (VI) was to come up on Ney's right, and still farther south Bertrand (IV) was to attack the Allied left flank; the Guard was to march to the sound of the guns. The battle raged, backwards and forwards, all the afternoon. Ney's corps had suffered heavy casualties and showed signs of giving way, but Napoleon, exposing himself recklessly, rallied them again with his inspiring presence. He then ordered Drouot to bring into action a mass of 80 guns, with which he blasted a gap through the Allied centre, as he had done at Wagram, after which he launched an attack with 16 battalions of the Young Guard.

However, the Allied ranks still stood firm and Blücher's cavalry made several effective charges. When night fell, both sides were completely exhausted and bivouacked on the field of battle. The casualties were very heavy; Napoleon admitted to 10,000 killed and wounded on the French side, and the Allies must have lost as many. General Scharnhorst, Blücher's Chief of Staff, was mortally wounded and was replaced by Gneisenau.

Meanwhile on the northern flank Lauriston (V) had driven Kleist out of Leipzig, and consequently Wittgenstein withdrew his battered army eastward towards Dresden. The French, for lack of cavalry, did not pursue.

Napoleon was at his best at the battle of Lützen; he took personal

* Marshal Lannes had died of wounds in May 1809 after the battle of Aspern-Essling.

command in the thick of the fighting and displayed great courage. Considering that his army contained such a high proportion of raw recruits and inexperienced officers, there is no doubt that the result of the battle was due to the Emperor's dynamic leadership. On the day after the battle he issued a Proclamation to the Army in terms of more than usual extravagance:

Soldiers, I am pleased with you! You have fulfilled my expectations! You have achieved everything by your readiness to obey and by your courage. On the famous 2nd of May you defeated and routed the Russian and Prussian armies, commanded by the Emperor Alexander and the King of Prussia. You have added a new lustre to the glory of my eagles. The battle of Lützen will rank higher than the battles of Austerlitz, Jena, Friedland and the Moskova. . . . We shall hurl back these Tartars to their horrible climate, which they must never leave. Let them stay in their icy deserts, the abode of slavery, barbarity and corruption, where man is debased to the level of the brute. (*Corr.* 19952)

After the battle of Lützen the Allied forces retired eastwards on Dresden, but Napoleon's pursuit was not pushed vigorously for several reasons: he was still very short of cavalry, the discipline of many units broke down, and his supply arrangements were inadequate. The Allied retreat was ably covered by the fresh Russian corps of Milorádovich and also by Blücher's Prussian corps. The French pursuit was also frustrated by the inefficiency of the Emperor's stepson, Prince Eugène, who was still commanding the left wing of the army. On 4 May Napoleon ordered Berthier:

Write to the Viceroy that he marches far too slowly; that his columns take up too much space, which hinders the march of the army; that he has far too many vehicles in his corps, and that there is no discipline; that he must see that the regulations are carried out, and that no baggage accompanies the leading divisions on the march. (*Corr.* 19965)

The continued evidence of Eugène's ineptitude so annoyed the Emperor that, a week later, he dissolved the 'Army of the Elbe' and sent his stepson off to command the troops on the Italian front where peace still reigned.

Napoleon, as an expert gunner, was extremely indignant with the quality of the artillery ammunition supplied to the army. On 5 May he wrote to his War Minister:

During the last battle I was most annoyed to see that a good third of our shells failed to explode. This is a matter of the utmost importance. It results from keeping them too long in store; this must not happen; there are no 'buts' or 'ifs' which can excuse the corps of artillery for such negligence. I saw many of these shells lying on the battlefield; they had fuzes, but no priming. . . . A Director of Artillery who sends up unserviceable ammunition deserves to be shot in accordance with military law. (*Corr.* 19968)

Having got rid of Eugène, the Emperor now reorganized his army and formed a new left wing group under Ney, consisting of his own III Corps together with Victor (II), Lauriston (V), Reynier (VII) and a cavalry corps under Sebastiani, numbering nearly 100,000 men. His main body, comprising Bertrand (IV), Marmont (VI), Macdonald (XI), Oudinot (XII) and Mortier (Guard), with a cavalry corps under Latour-Maubourg, numbered rather more than 100,000.

The Allies abandoned Dresden, continuing their retreat to the east, and Napoleon entered the Saxon capital on 8 May and reinstated King Frederick Augustus. The French encountered considerable resistance from the Russian rearguard holding the right bank of the Elbe at Dresden. The country beyond the Elbe was broken and wooded, and Napoleon was very puzzled as to the enemy's intentions. On 13 May he wrote to Ney:

I am now beginning to collect some cavalry. In his four divisions, I have given General Latour-Maubourg some 12,000 men. The Guard Cavalry has 4000 horses and expects large reinforcements at any minute. I cannot yet see what the Prussians are up to; it is quite certain that the Russians are retiring on Breslau; but are the Prussians retiring to Breslau, as is claimed, or have they made a dash for Berlin, which seems natural, to cover their capital? These are the things I want to know. (*Corr.* 20006)

On the following day he received positive information that the Prussian corps under Blücher, Kleist and Yorck had retired by Königsbrück to Bautzen on the road to Breslau; they had therefore left Berlin uncovered.

After fighting several sharp rearguard actions, the Allies retired behind the upper Spree at Bautzen, 35 miles east of Dresden. Here they occupied a strongly entrenched position on the right bank, dominating the river line. The position extended northward from Bautzen for seven miles, and was reinforced by a second defensive line, three miles farther east, along a parallel ridge overlooking a small valley in which lay the villages of Kreckwitz, Preititz and Gleina. Covered by an outpost line along the Spree, this double defensive position was held by 85,000 Allied troops, with Barclay's fresh Russian corps on the right; Blücher, Kleist and Yorck formed the centre, while another Russian corps held the left (south) flank. The Allied position was tactically strong, but suffered from the strategic disadvantage that the Bohemian frontier lay 20 miles south of Bautzen; Austria being still neutral, the Prussians and Russians ran the risk of being interned if they were forced to retreat into Bohemia.

After reconnoitring the enemy's position on 19 May, Napoleon decided to pin down the Allied left near Bautzen by a frontal attack with Oudinot (XII), Macdonald (XI) and Marmont (VI), while Ney, with the four corps under his direct command, would cross the Spree at Klix, 7½ miles north of Bautzen, and would turn the Allied right flank by an attack directed on Preititz. Accordingly, on the morning of the 20th the French right wing advanced and drove back the outposts holding the river. Under cover of a heavy artillery bombardment, trestle bridges were constructed and the French obtained a footing on the right bank. The Emperor then halted his right wing to let Ney come up on the left, and sent Ney an order, hastily scribbled in pencil, to advance south-eastward from Preititz to cut off the enemy's retreat. This latter order was apparently not understood by Ney. Whether this was the fault of Berthier or of Colonel Jomini, Ney's Chief of Staff, or of Napoleon's handwriting,* is not clear, but after the battle Jomini, who could never get on with Berthier, deserted to the Allies.

After very heavy fighting, Ney reached Preititz at 10 a.m., but as his orders were to be there by 11 a.m., he sat down and waited, instead of pushing on. Seeing this threat to their right flank and line of retreat, the Allies quietly evacuated their position and withdrew eastward towards Görlitz. Their retreat was carried out in good order, covered by their cavalry and artillery; the French captured neither prisoners nor guns, and, owing to their weakness in cavalry, were unable to press the pursuit. The fighting had been very severe: the French lost 13,500, the Allies about 20,000. Napoleon's tactical victory at Bautzen was a barren one. His conduct of the battle was ineffective; vague orders were issued, and he left far too much to the initiative of Ney, who, though a gallant leader, had no real tactical vision and was incapable of commanding more than a single corps.

The reverse at Bautzen left the Allies in an unhappy position. They had sustained heavy losses, both at Lützen and Bautzen, and dissensions arose between the Prussians and the Russians. The Tsar replaced Wittgenstein by Barclay de Tolly; the latter, seeing that no military victory could be achieved for the moment, insisted on withdrawing the Russian troops from Silesia into Poland, and Napoleon occupied Breslau on 1 June. But the Emperor's strategic situation was equally unsatisfactory; he was in an inhospitable country and his lines of communication were becoming unduly extended; he was short of ammunition and had large numbers of sick and wounded. He was very near the Austrian border, and the Austrian attitude had recently become menacing; if they were to join the Allies, Napoleon's position would be perilous. Both sides were anxious for a breathing-space, and on 4 June an armistice was signed at Pleischwitz, to last until the end of June; it was later extended until 17 August.

* Napoleon's handwriting was extremely difficult to read. For another occasion when its illegibility may have caused confusion, see p. 272.

On 2 June the Emperor explained his own point of view to his War Minister:

> This armistice arrests the course of my victories. I decided on it for two reasons: my lack of cavalry, which prevents me from striking strong blows, and the hostile attitude of Austria. . . . The armistice will last, I think, all June and July. . . . If I can, I shall wait until September to make a decisive stroke. I hope then to be in a position to crush my enemies. (*Corr.* 20070)

Many authorities, including Jomini, consider that, in signing the armistice, Napoleon made the greatest mistake of his whole career; the respite afforded by it was probably more advantageous to the Allies than to the Emperor, but on the other hand his position was most precarious. On 10 June Napoleon established his headquarters at Dresden, which he converted into a strongly entrenched camp as a base for his future operations. He then set about reorganizing his army and bringing its units up to strength. He formed a XIII Corps under Davout at Hamburg, which he fortified strongly, to form a *point d'appui* for the defence of North Germany and of his left flank.

On 1 July Napoleon received the news of the crushing defeat of his Spanish armies by Wellington at Vitoria; he at once despatched Soult, who had been commanding his Guard, to take command of all the French troops in Spain, and to try to hold the line of the Ebro against Wellington.

By the end of July Napoleon had regrouped his forces to meet the danger involved by Austria joining the Allies, which every day became more certain. His main army, over 200,000 strong, was assembled in the area Dresden–Bautzen–Görlitz–Löwenberg, between the rivers Elbe and Bober, facing the Bohemian frontier. A separate group of IV, VII and XII Corps with 3rd Cavalry Corps, numbering 72,000 men, under Oudinot, was concentrated between the Elbe and the Spree, between Wittenberg and Luckau, ready to make a dash for Berlin.

On 12 August Austria declared war on France and joined the Allies, who thus acquired a distinct superiority in numbers over the French; however, they suffered the disadvantage of divided counsels in strategy. The Tsar, the Austrian Emperor and the King of Prussia had a joint headquarters where strategic policy was concerted, and the supreme command in the field was given to Prince Schwarzenberg, as it was assumed that Napoleon would try to carry the war into Bohemia. Schwarzenberg was 42 years old; he possessed little military talent, but had a pleasing personality and was easy to deal with; he had an able Chief of Staff in General Radetzky.

The entrance of Austria into the Allied camp seriously undermined Napoleon's strategic position, for the line of the Elbe could now be turned from the south by an army debouching from Bohemia through the passes of the Erzgebirge, directed on Leipzig and Dresden. This in fact was the plan of the Allies. Their forces were grouped in three armies: the Army of Silesia (95,000) under Blücher was to advance from Breslau on Görlitz to pin down the French right wing, while the Army of Bohemia (230,000) under Schwarzenberg would move north-west from Prague, cross the Erzgebirge and attack Dresden from the south. Meanwhile the Army of the North (110,000) under Prince Bernadotte, Napoleon's brother-in-law and now Crown Prince of Sweden, would threaten the French garrisons on the lower Elbe at Wittenberg, Magdeburg and Hamburg, and cover Berlin. The Allied forces available, Austrians, Prussians, Russians and Swedes, totalled 435,000, thus outnumbering Napoleon's striking force of 375,000.

As soon as hostilities were resumed on 17 August after the armistice, the Allies put their plan into execution. Napoleon was at first undecided how to meet the Allied offensive; he felt reasonably secure behind the line of the Elbe, and the bulk of his army was concentrated in advance of it, between Dresden and Görlitz. He had taken the precaution to construct a strongly entrenched camp at the southern exits of Dresden to form a secure fulcrum for offensive operations, but his policy was to wait and see how the Allied attack developed. Undoubtedly, he should have first overwhelmed Blücher with his whole striking force, and then should have turned south to deal with Schwarzenberg's Army of Bohemia as it emerged from the passes of the Erzgebirge. The Bonaparte of 1796 would have adopted such a plan and carried it out with lightning rapidity; the Napoleon of 1813 hesitated and was lost.

What he did was to form two detached armies: one, under Oudinot (not a very good choice), consisting of IV, VII and XII Corps and 3rd Cavalry Corps (72,000), was to concentrate at Luckau (65 miles north of Dresden) and to seize Berlin; the other under Macdonald (also an indifferent commander), consisting of III, V and XI Corps and 2nd Cavalry Corps (102,000), was to attack Blücher. This latter group was given the following directive:

The main object of this army is to hold in check the enemy's Army of Silesia, and prevent it from advancing, either on Zittau to cut my communications, or on Berlin to attack Oudinot. I want it to drive the enemy beyond Jauer, and then to hold the line of the Bober. (*Corr.* 20442)

Unfortunately, both of these detachments met with disaster. Oudinot penetrated to within 12 miles of Berlin, when he was vigorously attacked by the Prussians on 23 August at Gross-Beeren, and driven back to Luckau with the loss of 3000 men and 23 guns. Macdonald fared still worse; on 26 August he was completely routed by Blücher on the Katzbach (a tributary of the

Oder) and driven back in disorder, having lost 20,000 men and 103 guns. By sending off these two detachments on widely separate missions Napoleon had wasted six infantry and two cavalry corps at a critical juncture, reducing his own striking force to 201,000 men. He thus entirely surrendered the initiative which his concentration on interior lines could have ensured him.

The weakness of the Emperor's strategy in this campaign is confirmed by a note which he dictated to Berthier on 23 August:

Tell Macdonald that my G.H.Q. moves today to Görlitz; that my operations depend on those of the enemy; that if, on 23rd or 24th, the enemy definitely advances on Dresden, my intention is to leave the initiative to the enemy and to move at once to the entrenched camp at Dresden and there fight a pitched battle; in this case the enemy will have his back to the Rhine and we shall have ours to the Oder; so that if we do not win the battle I can withdraw into my entrenched camp; at the worst, I would cross to the right bank of the Elbe, I would maintain my communications by it, and I would act as circumstances dictate, by crossing either at Torgau, Wittenberg or Magdeburg. If the enemy makes no definite offensive move, either today or tomorrow, I shall probably make one myself, by marching on Prague. (*Corr.* 20443)

He was apparently gambling on Oudinot's successful capture of Berlin; in fact he uselessly sacrificed the detached armies of Oudinot and Macdonald to the tender mercies of Bernadotte and Blücher.

To begin with, Napoleon succeeded better than he deserved. Schwarzenberg's army of 230,000 men started their march across the Bohemian mountain range on 22 August. On the 26th, although not yet fully deployed, Schwarzenberg attacked the southern perimeter of Napoleon's entrenched camp at Dresden. The Emperor was far from satisfied with the state of the defences; on the 25th he admonished General Rogniat, his Chief Engineer, as follows:

The chess-board of the present war is complicated; the number of enemies whom I have to fight is formidable; if the three redoubts which you designed had been completed, if the street barricades had been finished, and if the Pirna ditch had been properly dug, I should have had greater confidence in the strength of Dresden, and I should have hoped to defend it for ten or twelve days; then I could have laughed at the enemy, and I would have marched into Bohemia. But, in the present state of the town, I cannot have the confidence in it that I should expect. (*Corr.* 20465)

Napoleon always liked to find a scapegoat when things were going wrong. However, the field fortifications served their purpose well enough. Schwarzenberg's attack was launched at 4 p.m. on the 26th; Russians on the right, Prussians in the centre and Austrians on the left; but cooperation between the Allies was weak and their attacks were delivered piecemeal. Strong counter-attacks were made by Saint-Cyr's corps and by the Guard under Ney and Mortier, and the enemy was repulsed at all points. On the 27th the battle was continued in drenching rain, after the arrival during the night of the corps of Victor and Marmont. Fierce fighting took place, but the Allies failed to penetrate the French defences, and in the late afternoon Schwarzenberg ordered a general retreat towards the Bohemian frontier. The Allies suffered about 38,000 casualties and they lost 26 guns; the French losses amounted to 10,000. The retreating enemy was not pursued vigorously. The Emperor, soaked to the skin, returned to the Royal Castle at Dresden at 6 p.m.; beyond ordering Murat, Marmont and Saint-Cyr to follow the enemy to the south-west and south, he seemed to lose interest in further active operations.

Napoleon's failure to pursue the enemy relentlessly as they withdrew to the mountain passes shows that his powers of leadership, as well as his strategic vitality, were on the wane. Had he not detached two out of his four cavalry corps with Oudinot and Macdonald, Schwarzenberg's army could have been completely destroyed before it reached the shelter of the mountains. The battle of Dresden was a victory, and indeed it was his last victory on foreign soil; but, like Bautzen, it was barren of strategic results.

Napoleon left his corps commanders to keep touch with the retreating enemy on their own initiative while he himself remained in Dresden. This led to another disaster. On 28 August Vandamme's I Corps, 30,000 strong, was ordered to 'penetrate into Bohemia' and crush the Russian corps which formed the right wing of Schwarzenberg's army; Vandamme, unsupported, proceeded on his mission, but on the morning of the 30th his corps was trapped in a defile of the Erzgebirge at Kulm (Chlumec) by Kleist's Prussian corps and was practically annihilated, losing all its guns and equipment. Vandamme was taken prisoner.

The successive disasters to Oudinot, Macdonald and Vandamme illustrate once more the complete break-down of the Napoleonic system of command when the Emperor himself was not in active control of the operation. His subordinates were trained to act as gear-wheels in a machine, and were consequently incapable of acting independently.

Two days before the battle of Dresden an incident occurred which shook Napoleon's faith in the reliability of his confederate German contingents. Two regiments of Westphalian hussars, sent by King Jérôme as a contribution to the *Grande Armée*, went over to the enemy with all their arms, horses and regimental transport. It was not in itself a military disaster, but it augured ominously the graver defections to come.

His failure to crush the armies arrayed against him at Dresden presented the Emperor with a strategic problem akin to that which confronted him after his retreat from Moscow. The summer was nearly gone, and every week that elapsed meant the arrival of fresh Russian reinforcements. His own man-power problem was serious; he had already called up the 1814 class of con-scripts, and the losses in men and guns suffered by Oudinot, Macdonald and Vandamme would be hard to replace. His only remaining formation in reserve was Augereau's IX Corps, which was guarding his lines of com-munications through Bavaria. On 30 August at Dresden he reviewed his strategic situation and dictated a long memorandum, parts of which have considerable interest in illustrating Napoleon's changed mentality:

I have the choice between two operational plans: The first is to advance on Prague, profiting by my successes against the Austrians. But firstly I could not get there before the enemy; it is a fortified town and I should not be able to capture it, and if Bohemia were to rise in revolt I should be in a difficult position. I should be holding the Elbe from Prague to the sea, but it is far too extended; if it were pierced at any point, it would open the way to Westphalia and might force me to withdraw into the weakest part of my States.

On the other hand, by marching on Berlin, I should at once achieve a great re-sult; I should protect my line from Hamburg to Dresden; I should be centrally placed; in five days I could reach either end of my line; I should relieve Stettin and Küstrin; I should at once separate the Russians from the Austrians; I should find plenty of food in Berlin, especially potatoes, and I should hold the war where it is now. My war against Austria would only mean keeping 120,000 men on the de-fensive between Dresden and Hof, which would give my troops a chance to reorgan-ize. (*Corr.* 20492)

This frank appreciation of the situation reveals a new train of thought in Napoleon's strategic conceptions: he is no longer intent on ruthlessly des-troying the enemy's forces in the manner of Montenotte, Jena, Friedland and Austerlitz; his mind is now obsessed with geographical objectives—Prague, Berlin. Worse still, in this campaign he had abandoned those cardinal prin-ciples of war which he had hitherto strictly obeyed, and which he had con-stantly impressed upon his subordinates: 'keep your forces concentrated'; 'do not squander them in little packets'; 'march in columns within mutual supporting distance'; 'pursue the enemy with your sword in his backside'. All these lessons had been neglected; Oudinot and Macdonald had been given objectives 120 miles apart; Vandamme had been sent into the Erzge-birge with his nearest supporting column (Mortier's) 20 miles in rear at Pirna. The magnificent conception of the *bataillon carré* had gone by the board.

Dissatisfied with Oudinot's discomfiture at Gross-Beeren, the Emperor

sent Ney to retrieve the situation and renew the attempt on Berlin. But
another catastrophe occurred; the French encountered the Prussian corps of
Bülow and Tauentzien on 6 September at the village of Dennewitz (four
miles south-west of Jüterbog). Ney made a tactical blunder and his force was
completely routed with the loss of 24,000 men and 80 guns. The Prussian
casualties were about 6000.

But the Emperor was still more angry at Macdonald's defeat by Blücher on
the Katzbach. After giving vent to an unseemly exhibition of temper, on
5 September he went up himself to Bautzen to take charge and restore the
situation with fresh troops. Blücher, however, cautiously withdrew, and
Napoleon returned to Dresden two days later. For the next few weeks the
Grande Armée remained on the defensive. In the plain between Dresden and
the Erzgebirge the two armies watched each other, each side sending out
strong reconnaissance patrols to ascertain the enemy's intentions. The
Emperor made a tour of inspection of the front and was far from satisfied
with the alertness of his troops. On 19 September he issued the following
Army Order:

His Majesty is displeased with the way in which the light cavalry regiments perform outpost duties. General Gobrecht, commanding the light cavalry of I Corps,
was covering the flank of the army without having posted pickets and with all his
horses unbridled. Under military law such negligence is punishable with death.

His Majesty found a corporal of the Guard Cavalry on outpost duty near Pirna
with his horse unbridled. His Majesty orders that this corporal be reduced to the
ranks.

Any cavalry General, stationed on the flank of the army, who neglects to put out
pickets in accordance with standing orders, and exposes the army to a surprise
attack, will be tried by court-martial and condemned to death. (*Corr.* 20595)

Napoleon was still undecided as to what he should do next, and during the
following weeks he ordered a number of troop movements and then cancelled
them. He began to realize that, although he had won three battles, he had
already lost the campaign. The initiative had passed to the Allies, whose
resources were greater than his. He could not make up his mind where he
should spend the winter; the Elbe would be frozen in January, and the
Cossacks and Uhlans would be able to cross anywhere; the French garrisons
at Hamburg, Magdeburg and Wittenberg would be cut off, as well as the
Oder bridgeheads at Stettin, Küstrin and Frankfurt. Supplies were running
short in the region east of Dresden; the daily ration of the troops was reduced
to eight ounces of bread, eight of meat and three of rice. On 23 September the
Emperor wrote to his chief administrative officer:

The army is no longer fed. It would be an illusion to see matters otherwise. (*Corr.*
20619)

These difficulties caused Napoleon to think about withdrawing from Dresden to Leipzig, where the supply situation would be easier, and he began to be worried about the security of his line of retreat. On 17 September he sent a cipher message by the hand of an officer to Augereau at Würzburg to bring his IX Corps forward at once by Coburg and Jena to cover the crossings of the Saale.

While the Emperor was vacillating between various courses of action, the Allies were mounting their offensive movement. Blücher, prompted by his able Chief of Staff Gneisenau, persuaded the three sovereigns that the moment had now come to launch a vast pincer operation to envelop the *Grande Armée*. He himself, with 65,000 men, would advance north-westwards parallel to the Elbe and, after crossing that river near Wittenberg, would turn south to Leipzig. On his right, Bernadotte would cross the river near Dessau and also move south, while Schwarzenberg, forming the southern jaw of the pincer, would debouch from the Erzgebirge and advance on Leipzig from the south-east. It was a sound plan, and Napoleonic in its conception.

Blücher began his move on 26 September; on 3 October he crossed the Elbe at Wartenburg (10 miles above Wittenberg) and drove back Bertrand's IV Corps, with considerable loss on both sides. Bernadotte with 70,000 crossed the Elbe farther down stream at Dessau unopposed. By the end of September Schwarzenberg had crossed the Erzgebirge with 130,000 men and advanced on Chemnitz.

Napoleon began to get wind of the Allied moves on 27 September and ordered strong reconnaissances to be sent out. He ordered the number of pillboxes (*blockhaus*) on the left bank to be doubled, so that between Pirna and Wittenberg there would be a pillbox every 2½ miles. He was too late; the Allies were already across the river. He was now living in a cloudy atmosphere of make-believe; as alarming rumours came in from all sides, he rebuked Berthier on 3 October:

One must not create alarm over trifles; one must not let oneself be scared by bogies; one must have more firmness and discernment. (*Corr.* 20676)

On 6 October the Emperor at last began to take things seriously and made a desperate effort to concentrate a striking force at Meissen, opposite which the enemy appeared to be massing and threatening his main line of retreat to Leipzig. On the following day he left Dresden and moved to Meissen himself, accompanied by the King and Queen of Saxony. He still refused to admit that he was abandoning the Saxon capital; he left Saint-Cyr with XIV Corps to hold the city, and from Meissen sent him the following rather incoherent instructions:

I hope to draw the enemy into a battle. Hold the positions in front of Pirna all day on the 8th. My ideas will be finally defined tomorrow and, if I have any hope of inducing the enemy to fight, my intention is to hold on to Dresden. Have bread baked; work on the entrenched camp, and evacuate all the wounded you can. The fruit-barrows in Dresden can be used to transport the wounded. Reassure the inhabitants; tell everyone that there is no question of evacuating Dresden and that you have 50,000 men to defend it. (*Corr.* 20719)

The Emperor then moved his headquarters back 40 miles to Wurzen on the road to Leipzig, and from there issued a number of conflicting orders to his troops. He never saw Dresden again.

On 10 October Napoleon moved his headquarters to Düben, 20 miles north of Leipzig, and announced his intention of crossing the Elbe at Wittenberg with the bulk of his forces to destroy Blücher's army. He even contemplated abandoning Leipzig and moving north towards Magdeburg and Berlin; but on the same day he told Murat that, after defeating the Army of Silesia, he would probably return to Leipzig on the 13th. His enemies were now closing in on him from three directions, even the hesitant Bernadotte having advanced cautiously from Dessau towards Halle, cutting him off from Magdeburg. On 12 October the Emperor at last decided that he must concentrate the whole of his army at Leipzig to fight a defensive battle; Murat was ordered to hold off Schwarzenberg on the hills south-east of the town, while Ney retired before Blücher to a position near Taucha on the north-east (p. 240). On the 14th the Emperor moved his own headquarters back from Düben to Reudnitz, a small village less than two miles north-east of Leipzig.

Napoleon could hardly have chosen a worse position to fight his last pitched battle on German soil; he was in fact driven into it because he persistently deluded himself that he could always defeat his enemies by a series of offensive blows. He might have done so two months earlier while the Allied armies were still widely separated, but now it was too late. His own army of 190,000, famished and fatigued by long marches, was being remorselessly hemmed into a narrow ring, with no space for manœuvre, by 300,000 Allied troops. Leipzig, then as now a busy commercial town, lay in the centre of a shallow marshy depression at the junction of the rivers Elster, Pleisse and Partha. Seven roads, all blocked by the Allies, converged on the town from the north, east and south. Only one escape route still lay open to the south-west, crossing the Elster marsh by a stone bridge, and leading by the upper Saale valley to Erfurt, Gotha and Mainz.

On 16 October the Allies launched their concentric attack, and the

Völkerschlacht—the 'Battle of the Nations'—began. Napoleon had drawn up the bulk of his army, consisting of the II, V, VIII, IX, XI and XII Corps, on a low ridge five miles south-east of Leipzig to meet the brunt of Schwarzenberg's attack. Behind these were the Imperial Guard and Murat's Cavalry Corps. On the north face of the perimeter, where Ney held the over-all command, Blücher had driven Marmont's VI Corps back to Möckern, within two miles of the town. On Marmont's right were Reynier (VII) and Souham (III). The all-important exit to the south-west was defended by Bertrand (IV) at the village of Lindenau, which was heavily attacked by Gyulay's Austrian division. It was a cold misty day with heavy showers. Schwarzenberg's attack on the south face at first made progress, and the French were driven out of the villages of Wachau and Mark-Kleeberg. Napoleon hastened to the spot and massed a huge concentration of artillery which shattered the Austrian columns. Murat then led a magnificent cavalry charge with 10,000 sabres. The French cavalry, however, lost cohesion and were driven back by counter-attacks. Heavy fighting also took place on the northern sector and Blücher drove Marmont out of Möckern, capturing 53 guns. The day ended in a drawn battle, each side having suffered some 20,000 casualties.

On the 17th both sides were licking their wounds. Napoleon sent over a request for an armistice, as a preliminary to discussing peace terms, but this produced no response as the Allies had had enough of the Emperor's diplomatic evasions. They were in no hurry to resume the fight, for Bennigsen was now arriving with a fresh Russian corps of 40,000; Colloredo's Austrian corps was also on the way, and the reluctant Bernadotte, now that the battle was nearly won, was at last deploying his army of 60,000 on the north-east of the town, at Taucha. Bernadotte's army was accompanied by a British unit, the Rocket Troop of the Royal Horse Artillery, armed with Congreve rockets.*

The battle was resumed on 18 October. Before dawn Napoleon was inspecting the various sectors of his battle front. The Allies opened their attack at 7 a.m. and the French, though resisting stubbornly, were gradually pressed back by sheer weight of numbers into the outskirts of Leipzig. During the afternoon the Saxon and Württemberg troops in Reynier's corps went over to the Allies. The French artillery had exhausted almost all its ammunition; during the day each side had lost some 25,000 men. At nightfall the Emperor gave in and ordered a retreat to the south-west. It was the first anniversary of his retreat from Moscow.

Fortunately Bertrand had been able to drive Gyulay away from Lindenau and had kept open the road through Lützen to Weissenfels and the valley of

---

* A Royal Artillery detachment had, for the first time in European land warfare, used rockets against Massena's Army of Portugal on the Tagus in November 1810.

the Saale. The *Grande Armée* began its retreat on the morning of the 19th, but disaster still dogged its steps. The narrow road was congested with traffic, and the bridge over the Elster, through the mistake of a sapper sub-altern, was blown up before the rearguard could cross. In the resulting confusion Prince Poniatowski, who had been created a Marshal of France two days earlier, was drowned in the river; two other corps commanders, Lauriston and Reynier, with 33,000 troops and 260 guns fell into the hands of the Allies. If Schwarzenberg, instead of leaving one Austrian division to block this exit, had directed the whole of Bennigsen's corps to Lindenau, the Emperor himself and the whole of his army would have been captured.

The remnant of Napoleon's army made its way back to the Rhine, not very actively harassed by the enemy. On 30 October, when approaching Frankfurt, Napoleon found his way blocked by 40,000 Bavarian troops under Wrede, the King of Bavaria having already transferred his allegiance to the Allies. Drouot brought 50 guns into action and blasted away the opposition. The Emperor reached Mainz on 2 November. Leaving Marmont with three corps to act as rearguard, he departed for Paris on the 7th.

Napoleon himself must be held responsible for the disaster of Leipzig. Because of his political craving to maintain the line of the Elbe as the eastern frontier of his Empire, he persistently shut his eyes to the military impossibility of holding it in face of the numerical superiority of the Allies. His chess-board had become too large and his mental agility was decaying. The distance from Hamburg to Dresden is 240 miles as the crow flies; the river line is considerably longer and could be crossed by a determined enemy at many points. Yet he left, locked up in Hamburg, 30,000 troops under his best corps commander, Davout. At the other extremity of the line, in Dresden, he left another 30,000 men under Saint-Cyr and Mouton. The addition of these 60,000 men under able commanders might well have given him the victory at Leipzig, had he occupied a suitable defensive position such as Wellington would have chosen. Instead, he allowed himself to be driven into a death-trap. Napoleon sacrificed his military genius on the altar of political ambition.

XVII

At Bay

1814

On returning to Paris after his defeat at Leipzig, Napoleon was faced with a Herculean task. He was determined not to make peace until he had gained a substantial victory, but this meant raising and equipping an entirely new army in order to meet the impending invasion of France by the Allied hosts. From Germany he had only managed to bring back 56,000 very tired men who had lost the greater part of their equipment, so he was in the same position as at the beginning of 1813 after the retreat from Moscow, except that this time he would be fighting on French soil. He had been forced to leave behind in Germany 100,000 men garrisoning the isolated fortresses on the Rhine, the Elbe and the Oder, and these were now beleaguered by the Allies, including Davout with 30,000 men in Hamburg. As he was still engaged in a war on two fronts, another 100,000 men were with Soult, facing Wellington in the valleys of Gascony, and with Suchet in Catalonia. The invading armies of Schwarzenberg, Blücher and Bernadotte would muster at least 350,000, although some months must elapse before these could all deploy on the French frontier.

By dint of combing the regimental depots and by calling up in advance the 1815 class, the Emperor had raised his field army to a strength of 100,000 by the beginning of January 1814, but of these only 12,000 were cavalry. His treasury was empty, and he found the Legislative Body uncooperative and reluctant to vote more funds. The French people were war-weary; he had to make great exertions to raise their morale and encourage them to continue the struggle.

The Allied advanced guards crossed the Rhine on 1 January. Leaving garrisons to hold Metz and the fortresses on the Meuse, Napoleon concentrated the bulk of his field army behind the bend of the Marne near Châlons; Victor's corps was pushed forward to hold Nancy. On 4 January he ordered a *levée en masse* throughout the twelve Departments adjacent to the eastern frontier, under which all able-bodied men were called up to act as partisans in order to harass the invaders with guerrilla warfare; he also gave orders for the fortification of Paris. Although the Empress Marie-Louise was nominally the Regent, the Emperor appointed his elder brother to act as his deputy in Paris, with the title of *le roi Joseph*.

The field army which the Emperor succeeded in collecting at Châlons-sur-Marne during January was organized as follows:

Old Guard (Mortier)	11,000
Young Guard (Ney)	16,000
II Corps (Victor)	12,000
V Corps (Macdonald)	8,000
VI Corps (Marmont)	14,000
VII Corps (Oudinot)	12,000
1st Cavalry Corps (Doumerc)	3,000
2nd Cavalry Corps (Exelmans)	2,000
3rd Cavalry Corps (Arrighi)	2,000
5th Cavalry Corps (Milhaud)	5,000
	85,000

In the north Maison (I Corps) with 16,000 men was rather feebly trying to hold up Bernadotte's advance through Belgium. On the south flank Augereau, with some 20,000 men, formed what was euphemistically called the *Armée de Lyon*. To obtain further reinforcements Napoleon ordered Soult to send two divisions from the Pyrenees front and Suchet to despatch 10,000 men from Catalonia.

Napoleon estimated that by mid-January the Allies could deploy against him:

20,000 under Bülow, advancing from Belgium.
60,000 under Blücher, advancing from Lorraine.
100,000 under Schwarzenberg, advancing from Alsace and Switzerland.

180,000

His only chance to deal with this numerical superiority was to defeat separately each of the hostile armies in turn before they could unite in a concentric drive on Paris.

CAMPAIGNS OF 1814-1815

On 17 January Blücher's advanced guard reached Nancy, and Victor, who was holding a forward position there, evacuated the town and retired to Saint-Dizier. He was severely reprimanded by Napoleon, who ordered him to be relieved of his command, but afterwards relented, as he was very short of commanders. In the north, Maison asked permission to withdraw from Antwerp to Lille, but was also reprimanded. By 23 January Schwarzenberg had occupied Langres, Chaumont and Châtillon-sur-Seine; two days later Napoleon left Paris to take over command of his army at Châlons-sur-Marne (p. 249).

On 26 January the first directive issued to Berthier was as follows:

It is annoying that Victor has evacuated Saint-Dizier; if he had been up there in person with his corps united, he could have held this important point. From Paris I ordered this place to be held, but one does not hold a place by leaving in it a rearguard, ready to quit.

My intention is to attack tomorrow. . . . Vitry is a walled town and will serve as a bridgehead. I must have information about the enemy at Saint-Dizier; who commands them and what is their strength. If there are only 25 to 30,000 men, we can beat them, and if this operation succeeds, the whole situation will be changed. . . . Requisition at Vitry 2 to 300,000 bottles of wine and brandy, to be issued to the army today and tomorrow. If there is no other wine than bottled champagne, take it all the same; it is better that we should take it than the enemy. (*Corr.* 21135)

The champagne ration was issued, but the attack did not materialize, for Blücher evaded it by moving south to gain touch with Schwarzenberg. Napoleon's first encounter with the enemy took place on ground familiar to him, at Brienne-le-Château, the scene of his early school days 35 years previously. He deployed Victor and Mortier on a ridge at La Rothière, four miles south-east of Brienne, with their right flank resting on the river Aube. Blücher, who had now joined hands with Schwarzenberg, attacked the French on 1 February with greatly superior numbers and drove them back, capturing 3000 prisoners and 73 guns; each side lost about 5000 killed and wounded. During the night Napoleon withdrew his left flank to Lesmont, behind the river Voire, and his right flank to Troyes. It was an inauspicious start to the campaign, but the enemy did not pursue.

Now, however, the Allies played into the Emperor's hands, for they decided to separate; Blücher was to advance north-westwards, directly on Paris, while Schwarzenberg was to march due west by Bar-sur-Seine and Sens, and then to follow the Seine valley to Paris by Fontainebleau. Napoleon was quick to take advantage of this division; he decided to strike first at Blücher, who was the more immediate threat to Paris. On 3 February he moved to Troyes and withdrew down the Seine valley to Nogent to collect reinforcements. Concentrating Mortier, Ney, Victor and Oudinot between Nogent and Provins, he ordered Marmont back to Sézanne, and on his left flank withdrew Macdonald down the Marne valley from Châlons to Épernay.

Meanwhile Blücher was advancing north-westward through Fère-Champenoise, midway between the Marne and the Seine. On 9 February his advanced guard, formed by Sacken's Russian corps, reached Montmirail, only 60 miles from Paris. Napoleon ordered Marmont to clear up the situation. Marmont reached Sézanne on the 8th and reported back that Sacken had passed through on the 6th, heading for Montmirail; strung out behind him were Olsúfiev's division and Kleist's corps, while further north Yorck had driven Macdonald down the Marne valley from Épernay to Château-Thierry.

Napoleon snatched at the opportunity; he was now midway between Schwarzenberg south of the Seine and Blücher between the Seine and the Marne. Leaving Victor and Oudinot to hold the line of the Seine between Bray and Nogent, facing Schwarzenberg, he moved rapidly north to Sézanne with Mortier, Ney and his cavalry to support Marmont. His striking force numbered 45,000. Early on the morning of 10 February he moved north from Sézanne with Marmont leading. At 9 a.m. the head of the French column reached Champaubert, 12 miles north of Sézanne, where they struck Olsúfiev's Russian division in flank and annihilated it. That night the Emperor reported to Joseph:

I attacked the enemy today at Champaubert. He had 12 regiments and 40 guns. The commander, General Olsufiev, was captured with all his Generals, Colonels, officers, guns, limbers and baggage. So far we have counted 6000 prisoners, 40 guns, 200 vehicles. This corps is entirely destroyed. We are marching to Montmirail, where we shall be tonight at 10 p.m. Tomorrow before daylight I shall be there in person to attack Sacken with 20,000 men. (*Corr.* 21229)

It was a complete victory, but the report is slightly exaggerated; Olsúfiev's division actually consisted of 4500 infantry and 24 guns.

At 5 a.m. on the following morning Napoleon turned to deal with Sacken's corps which was now completely isolated. Sacken had actually advanced as far west as La Ferté-sous-Jouarre, only 40 miles from Paris, but there he was held up at the Marne bridge by Macdonald's corps, which was on the right bank, so he turned back to Montmirail. Four miles west of the town he ran into Mortier's vanguard. A sanguinary battle took place, which lasted all the afternoon. Sacken was completely defeated and retired northwards to join Yorck's Prussian corps, which had been following Macdonald down the Marne valley and was now 15 miles to the north at Château-Thierry. Napoleon at once followed up his Montmirail victory and drove both Sacken and Yorck northward across the Marne with great loss. On 12 February he reported his treble victory to Joseph:

I am in the suburb of Château-Thierry. I have pursued the rearguard of the enemy army. Having cut his road to Châlons, his whole army has been forced to cross the Marne to reach the Soissons road. I have captured the whole of his rear-guard, consisting of four Russian battalions, three Prussian battalions and three guns, including the Russian General commanding it. Today we have taken 2000 prisoners. Marmont will move from Étoges on Épernay or Châlons. If Marshal Macdonald had, as I hoped, played his part on the right bank of the Marne, not a man would have escaped. However we have taken 8 to 10,000 prisoners, including five or six Generals, who will leave tomorrow for Paris. We have captured nearly all his artillery, all his transport, and killed a great number. This army, which numbered 35,000, certainly cannot have more than 12,000 left today. The enemy is in a horrible mess. (*Corr.* 21233)

The corps of Sacken and Yorck had indeed been practically annihilated; the remnants burnt the bridge at Château-Thierry and retreated northwards towards Soissons.

In the battles of Champaubert, Montmirail and Château-Thierry Napoleon had defeated the advanced guard and the flankguard of the Army of Silesia, but he still had to deal with Blücher's main body. Leaving Mortier to follow the retreat of Sacken and Yorck northward beyond the Marne, during the early hours of 14 February he marched to the support of Marmont, who had fallen back before Blücher to Vauchamps, four miles east of Montmirail. The weather had been appalling, and the roads were deep in mud and snow. Marmont was being hard pressed, but the Emperor arrived at 8 a.m. on the 14th and turned the tables on the enemy. Ordering Marmont to stand firm, at noon he attacked with the Guard under Friant and Curial; while Drouot brought all the guns of the Guard artillery into action, Grouchy's cavalry division was sent round to Champaubert and Étoges in order to cut off the enemy's retreat. Blücher's troops, however, hacked their way through and withdrew eastwards. That evening Napoleon described his victory to Joseph:

It is 9 p.m. I write a word to tell you the happy result of the battle of Vauchamps. Blücher, who was separated from his army and whose headquarters were at Vertus, had been joined by Kleist's corps of 24 battalions just arrived from Germany and a new Russian corps of 12 battalions, making in all 20,000 men. On the 13th he reached Étoges and Champaubert. Marmont, hearing of this movement, withdrew without getting engaged. I left Château-Thierry at 3 a.m. this morning and got to Montmirail when the enemy had nearly reached it. I deployed facing the enemy, who took up position at the village of Vauchamps. I defeated him, taking 8000 prisoners, three guns and 10 colours, and drove him back to Étoges. He must have lost more than 4000 killed and wounded; I have only lost 300. This great result is due to the fact that the enemy had no cavalry, while I had 6 to 8000 very good horsemen. . . . Throughout the day I pounded him with grape-shot from a hundred guns. (*Corr.* 21255)

This succession of brilliant victories between 10 and 14 February shows Napoleon at his best. He had recaptured the *élan* and vigour which the youthful Bonaparte had displayed in the earlier Italian campaigns, and there was none of the lethargy and hesitation which dulled his faculties at Borodinó, Bautzen and Dresden. It is also noteworthy that in these engagements round Montmirail he took personal command of the action. Although Ney, who was nominally in command of the Guard, was present, Napoleon gave all the orders directly to his divisional commanders.

Meanwhile in the south, where he had left Victor and Oudinot with 32,000 men and 90 guns to hold the Seine crossings against Schwarzenberg, things were not going so well. Urged forward by the Tsar, one of Schwarzenberg's columns had attacked Victor at Bray-sur-Seine and captured the bridge there. Victor retreated 15 miles northward to Nangis, thus leaving the road to Paris open. There was not a minute to lose; the Emperor had already despatched Macdonald's corps south to the Seine front; now, leaving Mortier and Marmont to watch Blücher, he hastened there himself with the Guard, moving by La Ferté-sous-Jouarre and Meaux. On the 16th he reached Guignes, where he expected to encounter the Austrians. He met them further south at Nangis, drove them back across the Seine and restored the situation. On the 19th he wrote from Montereau to Joseph, who was greatly alarmed by Schwarzenberg's approach to Paris down the Seine valley:

Yesterday I defeated two reserve divisions under the Austrian General Bianchi and the Württembergers; they have lost heavily. We have taken several colours and 3 to 4000 prisoners. What is best of all, I had the good fortune to capture the bridge before they could destroy it. I have dismissed Oudinot, as I am very displeased with his lethargy and negligence. (*Corr.* 21297)

Schwarzenberg, in despair at his failure to cross the lower Seine, retreated to Troyes and requested Napoleon for an armistice, which the Emperor rejected with scorn; he wrote to Joseph:

Schwarzenberg has just sent a *parlementaire* to ask for a suspension of hostilities. What a coward! . . . At the first reverse these miserable fellows fall on their knees! I shall grant no armistice until they have quitted my territory. (*Corr.* 21293)

The Emperor now thought that he had won the campaign, and followed his timid opponent up the Seine to Troyes, which he reached on 24 February. Schwarzenberg, although he had double the number of troops that Napoleon had, retired behind the Aube. But time was on the side of the Allies, not of the Emperor. Bülow, with three of Bernadotte's corps, commanded by Winzingerode, Vorónzov and Strogónov, was now approaching from the north, and these were assigned to Blücher's army. Before their arrival, however, Blücher had taken advantage of Napoleon's absence to advance between the Marne and the Seine towards Sézanne, threatening Paris. Napoleon at once sent Ney northwards to counter him, and he himself followed, reaching the Marne at La Ferté-sous-Jouarre on 2 March. He was beginning to realize that Blücher was by far his most dangerous enemy. Blücher evaded him by slipping across the Marne at La Ferté and destroying the bridge; Napoleon, having no bridging train, was held up for 36 hours.

Marching rapidly northwards, now that a frost had set in again, Blücher effected a junction with Bülow's fresh troops near Soissons, the French garrison of which had capitulated on 3 March, much to Napoleon's indignation. Blücher now had an army of over 100,000 men, but he continued his withdrawal northwards as far as Laon, which occupies a commanding position dominating the surrounding country. Napoleon left Oudinot and Gérard (who had taken over Victor's corps) on the Aube to contain Schwarzenberg, and with the rest of his army crossed the Marne and the Aisne, pushing north in pursuit of Blücher.

Nine miles south of Laon rises a remarkable hog's back, 20 miles in length, running east and west, parallel to the Aisne and four miles north of the river. This is the famous Chemin des Dames, the scene of fierce fighting in the First World War during 1917 and 1918. To hold this ridge Blücher had posted Vorónzov's Russian corps, with its left flank resting on the village of Craonne. On 7 March Ney, commanding the French advanced guard, made a frontal attack on this strong position, and one of the bloodiest battles of the campaign ensued. The struggle lasted all day, and only after Napoleon had brought up the cavalry and artillery of the Guard did the Russians fall back on an almost equally strong position at Laon. Each side suffered about 7000 casualties.

On the following day Napoleon advanced on the Laon position, hoping at last to crush Blücher with a decisive victory. He made, however, the tactical mistake of dividing his attacking force into two groups, advancing respectively on the roads from Soissons and from Reims, and separated by the wooded hills north of the Chemin des Dames. Ney on the left was to attack Laon by the Soissons road, while Marmont on the right advanced from the direction of Reims. Communication between the two wings was impossible as the intervening country was patrolled by Blücher's Cossacks. Ney's attack was held up south-west of Laon; on the right wing Marmont's corps was subjected to a surprise night attack by Yorck and Kleist; the French panicked and the whole corps was driven back to the Aisne with the loss of 2500 men and 45 guns. Napoleon's troops could no longer stand up to the intense strain and fatigue which they had undergone, and were beginning to crack. The Emperor wrote to Joseph:

I have reconnoitred the enemy's position at Laon. It was too strong to be attacked without incurring excessive casualties. I have therefore decided to return to Soissons. It is probable that the enemy would have evacuated Laon under the threat of being attacked, but for Marmont's stampede; he behaved like a Second Lieutenant. The enemy has suffered enormous losses; yesterday he attacked Clacy five times but was always repulsed.

The Young Guard is melting away like snow. The Old Guard holds on. My Guard Cavalry is also melting away. . . . You must give orders to start work on the redoubts at Montmarte. (*Corr.* 21461)

Blücher's tenacity was at last wearing Napoleon down. Bad news also arrived from the Seine front, 50 miles further south. Schwarzenberg had come to life again, and had driven Oudinot and Macdonald back from the Aube to the neighbourhood of Provins; Paris was again in danger. Napoleon made a quick dash eastward to Reims, where on 13 March he defeated St. Priest's Russian corps, but he was beginning to realize the hopelessness of his position. On 16 March he wrote from Reims to Joseph:

If the enemy were to advance on Paris in such force that all resistance becomes impossible, see that the Regent and my son, together with all the Court officials, are sent off in the direction of the Loire. Do not get separated from my son, and remember that I would rather see him drowned in the Seine than fall into the enemy's hands. (*Corr.* 21497)

On the following day, in an interesting memorandum, the Emperor reviewed the three strategic courses open to him:

(1) To march south to Arcis-sur-Aube and attack Schwarzenberg's right flank.
(2) To march south-west to Sézanne and Provins, thus placing himself between Blücher and Schwarzenberg.
(3) To fall back on Meaux in order to protect Paris from Blücher.

He decided to adopt the first plan, as the boldest and most likely to produce far-reaching results. He wrote to Joseph:

I expect great results from my move, which will throw the enemy's rear echelons and headquarters into great confusion and disorder, if he is still at Troyes. (*Corr.* 21508)

Leaving Mortier with 10,000 at Reims and Marmont with 7000 at Berry-au-Bac to hold Blücher in check, Napoleon moved southward on the 18th and two days later reached the Aube eight miles west of Arcis at Plancy, which was strongly held by the Austrians. But this time the enemy stood firm and desperate fighting took place for the possession of Arcis. After losing 4000 men, Napoleon withdrew his exhausted troops to Sézanne. Before doing so he dictated a message to Mortier and Marmont:

It is not possible that Blücher can make any offensive movement; if however he does so, Mortier and Marmont should retire on Châlons and Épernay, so that we are all concentrated, and cover the road to Paris with some cavalry detachments; in the present situation Blücher would be mad to attempt any serious move. (*Corr.* 21522)

This was wishful thinking, and Blücher was by no means mad; he and Schwarzenberg decided, now that Napoleon had divided his forces, to ignore his movements and to make a combined advance directly on Paris. It was Napoleon who at this critical juncture lost his mental balance; he conceived the desperate plan of advancing eastwards between the armies of Blücher and Schwarzenberg to reach the Meuse at Saint-Mihiel; he intended to relieve the beleaguered French garrisons at Metz and Pont-à-Mousson on the upper Moselle, and thus obtain fresh troops to reinforce his exhausted army. He would then be in a position, he thought, to threaten the Austrian line of communications and force the timid Schwarzenberg to retreat to the Rhine. It was a crazy project, which left Paris to be defended by Mortier and Marmont with 17,000 men against Blücher's 100,000.

In pursuance of this plan the Emperor marched eastward on 22 March. Finding Vitry-le-François strongly held by the Austrians, he crossed the Marne further south and continued eastward to Saint-Dizier. Unfortunately he had written a letter to the Empress Marie-Louise, giving an indication of his plans:

I have decided to march towards the Marne in order to drive the enemy's army further from Paris, and to draw near to my fortresses. This evening I shall be at Saint-Dizier. Adieu, my dear! A kiss for my son.

This letter was intercepted by Blücher's Cossacks and revealed the Emperor's plan to the Allies. They seized their opportunity and continued their joint drive on Paris. Leaving a cavalry corps of 8000 to contain Napoleon's eastern force of 40,000, Schwarzenberg advanced westward on 25 March. At Fère-Champenoise he encountered Mortier and Marmont and routed them with the serious loss of 9000 men and 50 guns, while Blücher moved south-westward unopposed. The Allies crossed the lower Marne at Meaux on the 27th. Joseph, accompanied by the Imperial family and the Court, fled to Rambouillet in accordance with Napoleon's previous orders.

The Allied armies were now approaching the suburbs of Paris in over-whelming force, and Marmont, with his shattered corps, had no option but to sign a capitulation on the 30th. The Allies entered Paris on the following day. The eldest surviving brother of Louis XVI, the Comte de Provence, was proclaimed King of France with the title of Louis XVIII. The 1814 campaign was at an end.

Meanwhile Napoleon, launched on his eastward adventure, learnt on the 29th of the disaster to Marmont and Mortier at Fère-Champenoise. Too late, he realized the terrible blunder he had made in leaving Paris inadequately covered. By a forced march through Troyes, on the night of the 30th he reached Juvisy,* 12 miles south of Paris. There he found that Paris had capitulated a few hours earlier; the Allies had forestalled him. Crushed and broken in spirit, he withdrew 30 miles southward to Fontainebleau. On 2 April the Senate and the Legislative Body in Paris decreed that the Emperor had ceased to reign.

Yet he would not give in; he still had his faithful Guard, nearly 9000 strong, though exhausted by long marches, and with them he proposed to march on Paris. But Caulaincourt and the Marshals (Berthier, Ney, Oudinot, Macdonald, Moncey and Lefebvre) pointed out to him firmly that this would only lead to a useless sacrifice of life. Napoleon finally gave way and made an offer to abdicate, provided that the Empress should act as Regent for his infant son. The Allies rejected this condition, and a final Act of Abdication omitting it was formally ratified on 11 April and confirmed by the Treaty of Fontainebleau. On the previous day Soult had capitulated to Wellington at Toulouse.

One cannot but admire Napoleon's courage and determination in resuming the uneven contest at the beginning of 1814. By scraping the barrel he could barely put 100,000 men into the field; by the first week of March, when Bülow had reinforced Blücher, the numerical odds against him were more than three to one. Like a desperate gambler, he hoped to gain such a decisive victory in the field that he would be able to dictate his own terms to the Allies. At any time during February he could have negotiated a reasonable peace settlement, and might possibly have retained his throne. A peace conference did in fact open at Châtillon-sur-Seine on 5 February and, with a week's suspension, remained in session until 19 March. Napoleon was represented there by an able and wise plenipotentiary, Caulaincourt, Duke of Vicenza, but whenever the latter approached a reasonable agreement with the Allied statesmen, Napoleon repudiated the terms. With each success in the field he became more unyielding, and insisted throughout that both Holland

* Juvisy is now a Parisian suburb, just south of Orly Airport.

and Italy were integral parts of France, which could not be alienated; naturally the Allies would not accept such extravagant claims.

From the military point of view the 1814 campaign was an amazing achievement. Napoleon's swift blows at Blücher's columns in the Montmirail region, while holding Schwarzenberg in check with Victor and Oudinot, were a strategic masterpiece. Owing to Victor's incompetence, however, he had to dash back to the lower Seine to restore the situation. A fortnight later, on the other hand, Napoleon's pursuit of Blücher as far north as Laon was a strategic error, for it left the road to Paris uncovered; he could not afford the losses sustained in his Pyrrhic victory at Craonne, whereas the Allies could. Napoleon's final gamble in attempting to join hands with the Meuse and Moselle garrisons was, of course, a fatal blunder which lost him the war and his throne.

One cannot say that Napoleon was well served by his Marshals in the 1814 campaign, but their inadequacy when given independent tasks was mainly due to his own method of treating and training them. Victor, Oudinot and Macdonald made blunder after blunder when left to themselves. As Napoleon wrote plaintively to Joseph on 6 March:

Nobody could be worse served than I am; at Troyes I left a fine army with fine cavalry, but the soul is lacking. . . . The worst thing of all is to have a commander who is sick. (*Corr.* 21449)

He was referring to Macdonald, whose health had broken down at a critical moment.

Ney and Mortier, commanding the Young and Old Guard, were working during most of the time under the eye of their chief, and so were given little chance to go wrong, but neither of them distinguished himself. Augereau, with an independent role in the Lyonnais, proved lethargic and unenterprising; Napoleon was deeply disappointed in him and on 19 February wrote to the War Minister:

Tell Augereau to forget his 56 years and to remember the splendid days of Castiglione. (*Corr.* 21314)

Except for Berthier, Augereau was the oldest of the active Marshals. Perhaps the most successful of them in this campaign was Marmont, the youngest. Unfortunately his corps panicked and ran away when surprised by a Prussian night attack, and Marmont seems to have lost all control of his troops. Then, at the end, he had the onus of signing the capitulation to the Allies on 30 March, for which Napoleon never forgave him and branded him as a traitor. This, however, was an unjust accusation, as Marmont had no other alternative.

Napoleon himself was the only outstanding leader on the French side. He was now 44 years old and becoming corpulent. Nevertheless, he displayed amazing vitality and powers of endurance. Only at the last, when he decided on his dash to the east, did his strategic sense fail. He certainly overstrained the endurance of his troops and in the end he was out-generalled by the Allies.

XVIII

Elba to Waterloo
1814-1815

Napoleon's abdication gave Europe less than a year of peace. On the following day he attempted to commit suicide, but the poison failed in its effect. By the Treaty of Fontainebleau the Emperor was allowed to retain his imperial title, but his place of residence and his sovereignty were restricted to the Island of Elba, lying a few miles off the coast of Tuscany, between the mainland of Italy and his native Corsica. The island had a population of 112,000 and was slightly smaller than the Isle of Wight.

On 20 April 1814 the dethroned Emperor bade a touching farewell to his Old Guard and travelled south by coach, accompanied by a small retinue and the Austrian, British, Prussian and Russian Commissioners, who were responsible for his safety. In Provence, where Bourbon loyalties were strong, he met with a hostile reception, and at one moment had to disguise himself in order to escape insult. On 28 April he embarked at Saint-Raphaël in a British frigate, H.M.S. *Undaunted*, and on 4 May landed at Porto-Ferraio, the capital of his island of exile. The Treaty of Fontainebleau allowed him an armed bodyguard of only 400 men, but many more of his Old Guard insisted on following him. Three weeks later, 700 of them, commanded by General Cambronne, after marching overland, joined him on Elba.

Napoleon threw himself with energy and enthusiasm into the administration of his tiny kingdom. He constructed roads, he encouraged agriculture, he introduced sanitation; he revived the languishing iron-ore industry, which had been the main source of the island's wealth since the days of the Etruscans. With his amazing capacity for attention to detail he completely regenerated the island's economy. To all appearances, he had no ambition to return to France, to lead armies in war, or to interfere in European politics.

Several factors, however, existed to upset this pacific disposition. In the first place, the Bourbon Government failed to pay him a single *sou* of the annual pension of two million francs guaranteed to him by the Treaty of Fontainebleau; nor did any of his family receive the pensions promised to them. In fact, the island budget had to be kept in balance by generous contributions from his mother and his sister, Princess Pauline Borghese, who came to live with him. His other great grievance was that the Empress Marie-Louise and his three-year-old son had been prevented by the Austrian Court from joining him; indeed the Empress's affections were soon to be diverted into another channel.

News also began to accumulate of the growing unpopularity of the Bourbon régime throughout France. Louis XVIII had pledged himself to rule in accordance with a democratic constitution, but failed to do so; the Old Guard was abolished and the *Maison Militaire du Roi* (a bodyguard corps of the old nobility) was reintroduced; the Marshals' wives were cold-shouldered at a Court which resumed the ostentatious extravagance of pre-Revolution days.

The smouldering fire of resentment in Napoleon's heart was fanned to a flame by a visit which he received on 13 February 1815. A young civil servant, named Fleury de Chaboulon, landed at Porto-Ferraio, disguised as an Italian sailor, and obtained an interview with the island's ruler. The visitor was the emissary of a group of Napoleon's supporters in France, including the devoted Hugues-Bernard Maret, Duke of Bassano. They wished to assure their old chief that the moment was now ripe for his return to France, where the whole nation would rise to overthrow the Bourbons. It so happened that Colonel Sir Neil Campbell,* the only Allied Commissioner acting as watchdog on the island, left Elba three days later for a fortnight's leave in Florence. Napoleon jumped at the opportunity and made a quick decision. After carefully concealed preparations, he embarked after dark on 26 February in his brig *l'Inconstant* and some smaller vessels, with Generals Bertrand, Drouot and Cambronne and 1050 officers and men.

The little flotilla eluded the British and French guard-ships, and on the afternoon of 1 March cast anchor in Golfe Juan, between Antibes and Cannes. Bertrand and Drouot had advised their chief to land at Toulon, but that was a defended port, and Napoleon was doubtful of the reception he

---

* Colonel Sir Neil Campbell (1776–1827) distinguished himself as a light infantry officer in the Peninsular War, and also when attached to the Russian army in the 1814 campaign. He was knighted on 2 October 1814.

would get there. The nearest coastal fort to his landing-place was Fort Carré at Antibes, only three miles away. Napoleon sent a platoon of Guardsmen under an officer to reconnoitre that place, but they were all taken prisoner. Marshal Massena was in command of the 8th Military District at Marseille, 100 miles away, but Napoleon was dubious as to how Massena would react to his arrival, as they had never been close friends. He decided, therefore, to strike inland from Cannes and cross the Basses Alpes by Grasse, Sisteron and Gap, to reach Grenoble in the Dauphiné where Bourbon sympathies were less strong than in the Midi. It was an astute move.

With his 800 Guardsmen and four field-guns Napoleon marched northward through the mountains unopposed until, on 7 March, he approached Grenoble, where General Marchand commanded the 7th Military District. Marchand sent a battalion of the 5th Infantry Regiment to halt the invader at the Laffrey Pass, 15 miles south of the town. It was one of the regiments which had fought in Bonaparte's early battles in Italy. The officers gave the order to fire on the advancing column, but Napoleon, dismounting from his horse, walked up to the levelled muskets and, opening his coat, shouted: 'Soldiers of the 5th, don't you recognize me?' The men lowered their weapons and replied with shouts of '*Vive l'Empereur!*'

From then on Napoleon's progress northward became a triumphal procession as the local garrisons threw away their white Bourbon cockades and swelled the ranks of his column. On the 10th he reached Lyon, where Marshal Macdonald and the Comte d'Artois took flight and left open the road to Paris. On the 18th he was joined at Auxerre by Marshal Ney, commanding the 6th Military District at Besançon; a week earlier Ney had promised King Louis that he would bring Napoleon back to Paris 'in an iron cage'. Ney had always been impetuous and unpredictable; now he was losing his mental balance.*

On the evening of 20 March Napoleon entered the Palace of the Tuileries in Paris, which had been evacuated the previous night by King Louis and his Court in their flight to Belgium. The Emperor had within three weeks fulfilled the prophecy made in his Proclamation to the Army, written during his passage from Elba: 'The eagle, with the national colours, will fly from steeple to steeple to the towers of Notre Dame.'

On reaching Paris Napoleon lost no time in re-establishing his position and the military power on which that depended. He was faced, for the third year in succession, with the recurrent problem of creating a field army at

---

* Marshal Ney was on 6 December 1815 convicted by the Chamber of Peers of High Treason and condemned to death (by 139 votes out of 161). On the following morning he was shot by a firing squad outside the Palais du Luxembourg.

short notice. During the ten months of the Bourbon régime the armed forces had been severely cut down on the score of economy; a large proportion of the officers had been placed on half-pay and many thousands of N.C.O.s and men had been demobilized. Louis XVIII had earned popularity by abolishing conscription, and Napoleon hesitated to introduce it for the same reason. He therefore could only replenish the cadres by recalling to the colours the discharged N.C.O.s and men, and returned prisoners-of-war, and by calling up the National Guard, which constitutionally could only be employed on home defence duties. His greatest shortage was in capable commanders. Nine Marshals, including Macdonald, Oudinot and Saint-Cyr, had refused to serve under him; on 10 April he ordered that the names of Berthier, Marmont, Victor, Pérignon, Augereau and Lefebvre should be struck off the list of Marshals. On the day after reaching Paris he appointed the faithful Davout to be his War Minister. Massena, commanding at Marseille, was 57 and unfit for active service; there only remained Soult, Ney, Mortier, Suchet and Brune available as commanders in the field.

On 15 April the Emperor awarded a Marshal's baton to General Emmanuel Grouchy, aged 48, a fine cavalry officer, who had distinguished himself in Russia and in the 1814 campaign. He was now suppressing the Royalist revolt in the south of France, and was only created a Marshal for having taken the surrender of the Duc d'Angoulême.

The stocks of arms and munitions had been allowed to run down by the Bourbon administration, so on 23 March Napoleon ordered the immediate manufacture of 150,000 muskets of the 1777 pattern; the output of the arms factories at Tulle and Versailles was to be trebled, and he even authorized the immediate purchase of 200,000 muskets 'either in England or in Switzerland'. At the end of March Davout was ordered to raise the cavalry establishment to 34,500.

On 30 April an Imperial Decree created four new armies (the North, Moselle, Rhine and Alps) and three 'observation corps' to guard the Jura, Var and Pyrenees frontiers. The *Armée du Nord* was the principal one and would be commanded by the Emperor in person; it was to consist of four corps (I, II, III and VI) and three cavalry divisions. On 1 May Davout was ordered to create a belt of fortifications round Paris; this may have been part of a deception plan, to impress on the world in general and on the French nation in particular that Napoleon's intentions were purely defensive.

The Emperor's strategic plan, however, was to take the offensive at the earliest possible moment. It was indeed essential that he should do so. On hearing of Napoleon's landing in France, the Allied statesmen in Vienna took immediate action. The news reached them on 7 March; on the 13th the eight Allied Powers, abandoning their internal squabbles over territorial claims, issued a joint Declaration proscribing Napoleon, 'the disturber of world repose', as an outlaw. Five days later the Treaty of Chaumont was reaffirmed and the four major Powers, Austria, Britain, Prussia and Russia, agreed that each should put 150,000 troops into the field to crush the usurper. On 4 April the Duke of Wellington arrived in Brussels from Vienna to assume command of the Anglo-Netherland army, which would be paid for by Britain.

Napoleon calculated that the Austrian and Russian contingents would not be able to cross the Rhine until the end of June. The nearest threat to Paris therefore came from Wellington's army in western Belgium and Blücher's Prussian army occupying the eastern part of that country. He was determined that this time he would not be forced to fight a defensive battle, with his back to the wall, as in 1814. He decided to strike first, and strike rapidly, alternate blows at his nearest two opponents, Blücher and Wellington; and a decisive victory had to be gained before the end of June, to enable him to deal with the Austrians and Russians.

On 21 May the Emperor appointed Marshal Soult as Chief of Staff of his *Armée du Nord*. It was an unfortunate choice. Soult was a capable commander who had played a distinguished part in the victory of Austerlitz, but he was lazy and unmethodical; he had twice been badly beaten by Wellington; as Chief of Staff he was a poor substitute for the meticulous Berthier, who had deserted his master after 18 years' service. Napoleon was short of senior officers, but he would have done better to appoint Davout, or Suchet, who was wasted in command of the Army of the Alps.

The Allied armies confronting the *Armée du Nord* were scattered, for subsistence purposes, over the whole of Belgium. Blücher's Army of the Lower Rhine, based on Maastricht and Aachen, occupied the eastern half of the country, while Wellington's Army of the Netherlands, based on Ostende, held the western part. They were divided by a line running north and south through Brussels and Charleroi (p. 266). Napoleon's strategic plan was simple: he would concentrate the *Armée du Nord* during the first week of June in the angle between the Sambre and the Meuse, just south of the Belgian frontier (which in 1815 ran east and west about ten miles south of Charleroi). He would cross the Sambre at Charleroi on 15 June, swing to the right and smash Blücher's army, driving it back to the Rhine; on the following day he would swing to the left and crush Wellington's army, driving it back from Brussels to Ostende; having driven a wedge between the two Allied armies, he would occupy Brussels on 17 June.

Napoleon might have adopted an alternative plan, namely to advance

27 *Napoleon landing at Golfe Juan from Elba, 1 March 1*
From a contemporary print. The Emperor was accompa
by only 800 Guards

28 *The Battle of Waterloo, 18 June 1815. After a painting by Carle Vernet (1758–1836). The artist does not seem to have visited the battlefield. The village far right appears to be Waterloo ; La Haye Sainte and Hougoumont are presumably obscured by smoke. Napoleon (near right) is giving the order to retreat after the failure of the Guard's final attack*

29 *The Grande Armée crossing the Danube, 5 July 1809*
After a painting by Jacques-François Swebach (1760–1823). The trestle bridges

directly through Maubeuge–Mons–Hal on Brussels, defeating Wellington's army first and then turning on Blücher, whose army was more widely dispersed; by this plan he would have cut Wellington's communications with his base, and he would have also mopped up Louis XVIII and his Court, who were sheltering at Ghent under Wellington's wing, but this course of action might have driven Wellington north-eastwards to join hands with Blücher; the two Allied armies together greatly outnumbered the *Armée du Nord*. Wellington believed that Napoleon would adopt this latter course, and he had disposed his troops accordingly, concentrating them in the area south-west of Brussels, centred on Enghien.

By the middle of June the opposing forces were organized as follows:

ARMÉE DU NORD	Infantry and field artillery	Cavalry and horse artillery	Guns
Imperial Guard (Drouot)	14,600	5,000	118
I Corps (Drouet, Count d'Erlon)	17,800	1,800	46
II Corps (Reille)	21,800	1,800	46
III Corps (Vandamme)	16,000	1,000	38
IV Corps (Gérard)	13,900	1,600	38
VI Corps (Mouton, Count Lobau)	10,100	—	32
1st Cavalry Corps (Pajol)	—	2,800	12
2nd Cavalry Corps (Exelmans)	—	3,300	12
3rd Cavalry Corps (Kellermann)	—	3,700	12
4th Cavalry Corps (Milhaud)	—	3,000	12
	94,200	24,000	366
Cavalry	24,000		
Engineers, etc.	2,000		
Grand total	120,200		

On 13 June Napoleon had secretly concentrated this force on a front of 15 miles between Philippeville and Beaumont, a few miles south of the Belgian frontier.

This sector of the frontier was held by the outposts of Blücher's Army of the Lower Rhine, which was disposed as follows:

	Infantry and field artillery	Cavalry and horse artillery	Guns	Location
I Corps (Zieten)	29,700	2,300	88	Charleroi
II Corps (Pirch)	27,500	4,900	80	Namur
III Corps (Thielmann)	22,700	2,500	48	Ciney
IV Corps (Bülow)	28,300	3,700	88	Liège
	108,200	13,400	304	

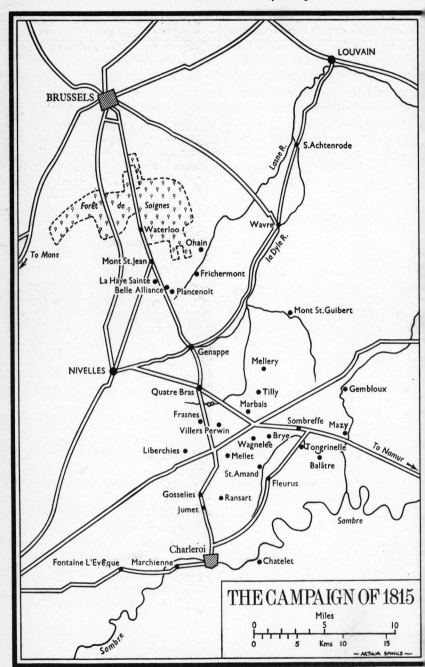

THE CAMPAIGN OF 1815

Miles

0 _____ 5 _____ 10

0 _____ 5 | Kms 10 | 15

~ ARTHUR BANKS ~

Thus Blücher's army of 121,000 was approximately equivalent to Napoleon's but, though stronger in infantry, was weaker in cavalry and artillery.

Wellington's army was inferior in numbers to either Blücher's or Napoleon's. It was organized in two corps and a cavalry corps, with a general reserve retained in the hands of the Duke.

ARMY OF THE NETHERLANDS

	Infantry and field artillery	Cavalry and horse artillery	Guns
I Corps (Prince of Orange)	28,000	3,400	66
II Corps (Lord Hill)	25,100	—	44
Reserve	23,000	1,200	28
Cavalry Corps (Lord Uxbridge)	—	12,000	36
	76,100	16,600	174
Cavalry	16,600		
Total	92,700		

Of Wellington's army, only about one-third of the units were British. The remainder consisted of a mixture of Hanoverians, Brunswickers, Nassauers and Dutch-Belgians, many of whom were raw recruits.

On 7 June the Emperor ordered Marshal Mortier to report at Soissons to take command of the Guard Cavalry; he never assumed his command, as he fell a victim of sciatica. On 11 June Napoleon gave Davout a somewhat peculiar order:

Send for Marshal Ney; if he wants to take part in the first battles, tell him to be at my headquarters at Avesnes on the 14th. (*Corr.* 22042)

This was a casual way of employing his senior surviving Marshal in the field. Napoleon knew that Ney's temperament was unstable and unreliable; he had displayed great personal courage at Ulm, Friedland and in Russia, but his rashness at Jena had nearly wrecked that battle, while his dilatory tactics at Bautzen had prevented the consummation of that victory; as an independent commander at Dennewitz he had been soundly thrashed by the Prussians. His performance during the Waterloo campaign was the prelude to disaster.

Napoleon left Paris at 4 a.m. on 12 June and spent the night at Laon, where he found Grouchy trying to organize his Cavalry Reserve. The Emperor was annoyed that the four cavalry corps were not already on the march to the frontier, but Soult had neglected to send them any orders. Napoleon reached Avesnes on the 13th and dictated preparatory orders for the advance to start on the 15th. The troops were to keep their bivouac fires well screened from the enemy's view. Each man was to carry 50 rounds of ammunition, four days' bread ration and half a pound of rice. The four cavalry corps were to march first and form the advanced guard.

On the 14th the Emperor moved up to Beaumont and issued detailed orders for each corps to march before dawn the following day and seize the Sambre bridges between Charleroi and Thuin. Reille (II) and d'Erlon (I) on the left were to cross at Marchienne and Thuin, while the remainder of the army, including the four cavalry corps, were to cross at Charleroi. 'The intention of His Majesty is to have crossed the Sambre before midday.'

But the operation took considerably longer; the Prussian outposts at the bridges were soon overwhelmed, but there was only one bridge at Charleroi, where the bulk of the army had to cross, and great congestion occurred in the early morning fog. Lobau's VI Corps, marching from Beaumont to Charleroi, ran into the bivouacs of Vandamme's III Corps, who were still asleep, having received no movement order. Further delay occurred with Gérard's IV Corps, as Lieutenant-General de Bourmont, commanding the 14th Division, deserted to the enemy with all his staff during the night. Eventually, at 12.30 p.m. the French sappers blew up the barricades which the Prussians had constructed on the bridge at Charleroi, and the army began to cross. At 3 p.m. the Emperor himself reached Charleroi and issued fresh orders. Reille (II), followed by d'Erlon (I), was to march north on Gosselies and attack any enemy there.

Meanwhile Zieten, commanding the Prussian corps holding the line of the Sambre, retired from Charleroi to Fleurus (p. 266), six miles to the north-east, leaving a brigade at Gosselies to cover the withdrawal of the outposts. As soon as Field-Marshal Blücher learnt that the French were crossing the Sambre, he ordered his whole army to concentrate at once at Sombreffe, 12 miles north-east of Charleroi. This was an easy matter for Zieten (I) and Pirch (II), as Sombreffe is equidistant (12 miles) from Charleroi and Namur; but Thielmann (III) at Ciney had 32 miles to march, while Bülow at Liège was 52 miles distant. Blücher reacted quickly to the French invasion, but to fix a concentration point for his scattered corps as far forward as Sombreffe was to invite disaster. He would have done better to have fixed it at Wavre, where he would have been in closer touch with Wellington; if the Prussians intended to fight so far forward, they should have held a properly prepared defensive position on the river Sambre, which flows through a deep and narrow gorge, forming a serious military obstacle.

Napoleon's brilliantly conceived concentration between Philippeville and Beaumont and his crossing of the Sambre at Charleroi completely 'hum-bugged' Wellington, as the Duke himself admitted, for he had expected the

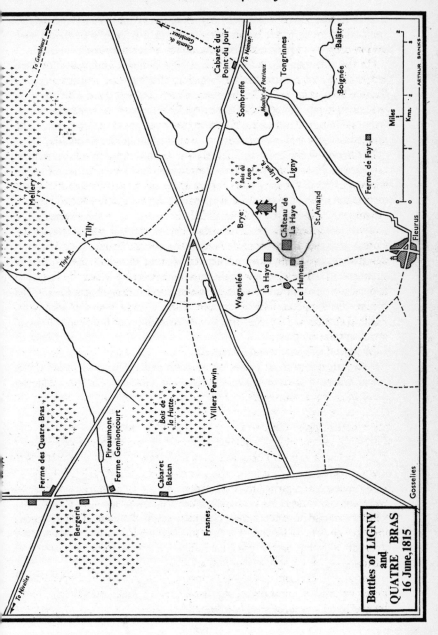

To Gembloux

Chemin de Gembloux

Cabaret du Point du Jour

To Namur

Sombreffe

Tongrinnes

Moulin de Potriaux

Boignée

Balâtre

Miles

Km.

ARTHUR BANKS

Ferme de Fayt.

Bois du Loup

La Ligne

Ligny

St.Amand

Mellery

Tilly

Brye.

Château de La Haye

Fleurus

Thyle R.

La Haye

Le Hameau

Wagnelée

Villers Perwin

Bois de la Hutte

Ferme des Quatre Bras

Pireaumont

Ferme Gemioncourt

Cabaret Balcan

Gosselies

Bergerie

Frasnes.

To Nivelles

**Battles of LIGNY and QUATRE BRAS
16 June, 1815**

French to advance on Brussels by Maubeuge and Mons. The Prussians also were taken by surprise; on 12 June Gneisenau, Blücher's Chief of Staff, wrote to the War Minister: 'The danger of an attack has almost vanished.'

On the afternoon of 15 June Marshal Ney, hitherto unemployed, arrived at Charleroi and reported to the Emperor, who had just woken up from a short nap, having been on his feet since 2 a.m. Napoleon then gave Ney verbal orders to take command of the left wing of the army and advance northward on Gosselies, to sweep aside the Prussian rearguard reported there. The order was vague and was not confirmed in writing till the next day. Ney at once carried out the order and advanced to Gosselies, the Prussians retiring eastward to Fleurus. Ney's cavalry then pushed northward through Frasnes to the Ferme des Quatre-Bras, where the road from Nivelles to Namur crosses the main highway from Charleroi to Brussels. They found Quatre-Bras occupied by a Nassau brigade, commanded by Prince Bernhard of Saxe-Weimar, belonging to Wellington's army. After a short skirmish the French cavalry withdrew to Frasnes, and Ney spent the night at Gosselies.

Napoleon had given similar orders to Marshal Grouchy, putting him in command of the right wing, consisting of Vandamme (III) and Gérard (IV) with a large force of cavalry. There was still considerable congestion at the Sambre bridges, but Grouchy's columns made progress to the north-east, Zieten's rearguards retiring through Fleurus. Blücher intended, however, after concentrating as much of his army as possible, to stand and fight at Ligny, between Fleurus and Sombreffe.

The Emperor rose at 4 a.m. on 16 June and confirmed in writing his verbal orders of the previous day to Ney and Grouchy. To the former he wrote:

I am directing Marshal Grouchy with III and IV Corps on Sombreffe. I am placing my Guard at Fleurus, and I shall be there before midday. I shall attack the enemy if I meet him, and I shall clear the road as far as Gembloux. There, according to what happens, I shall make my decision, perhaps at 3 p.m., perhaps this evening. My intention is that, immediately I have decided, you must be ready to march on Brussels. I shall support you with my Guard, which will be at Fleurus or Sombreffe and I should like to arrive in Brussels tomorrow morning. Your leading division should be five miles beyond Quatre-Bras, with six divisions round Quatre-Bras. . . . In this campaign I have adopted the general principle of dividing my army into two wings and a reserve. Your wing will consist of the four divisions of I Corps, the four divisions of II Corps, two light cavalry divisions and two divisions of Kellermann's cavalry corps. That should be not far short of 45 to 50,000 men. Marshal Grouchy will have nearly the same strength and will command the right wing. The Guard will form the reserve and I shall move to one wing or the other, according to circumstances. (*Corr.* 22058)

Similar instructions were sent by an A.D.C. to Grouchy. These instructions make Napoleon's plan quite clear. He imagined that Grouchy could drive the Prussians headlong to Maastricht, while he himself, with Ney as advanced guard, would march triumphantly to Brussels.

As these orders went off a report arrived from Grouchy, timed at 5 a.m., that strong enemy columns had arrived during the night by the road from Namur and were deploying near Ligny. A report also came from the left wing that the enemy were massing at Quatre-Bras. Napoleon at once sent an order to Ney to concentrate his two corps and his cavalry, and to attack and destroy any enemy encountered. He then rode forward to join Grouchy, reaching Fleurus at 11 a.m., and reconnoitred the enemy's position at Ligny. Thinking that he had only Zieten's corps in front of him, the Emperor decided to attack it. Vandamme (III) and Gérard (IV) had now arrived, together with Girard's division which had been detached from Reille's corps, so he was able to deploy 38,000 men and 84 guns. The attack was launched at 3 p.m. but the Prussians resisted strongly at all points and the French suffered heavily from the Prussian guns at close range. Blücher himself was in command, and he had now reinforced Zieten with Pirch (II) and Thielmann (III), so that he had concentrated 70,000 men on the battlefield. Napoleon soon realized that the Prussians were in far greater strength than he had supposed, so he sent several urgent messages to Ney to break away from Quatre-Bras and come in on the Prussian right flank. The afternoon wore on, but the French still failed to get further than the village of Ligny.

Napoleon still had in reserve Lobau's VI Corps, which was in the outskirts of Charleroi, eight miles away. Unaccountably and inexcusably he made no use of it, indeed he seems to have forgotten its existence. At last he brought up the Young Guard to reinforce his tired battalions, for there was no sign of help from Ney. Finally, at 7.30 p.m., a determined attack by the Young Guard broke the Prussian centre at Ligny. The Prussian cavalry, led by Blücher in person, made several desperate charges to restore the situation, but the troops were completely exhausted and, as night fell, they withdrew slowly from the field, having lost 16,000 men and 21 guns. The French casualties were also heavy, amounting to more than 11,000. A peculiar lassitude seems now to have overcome the Emperor; after dark he rode off the battlefield, leaving Grouchy with no instructions as to the pursuit of the beaten enemy.

Meanwhile, six miles to the north-west, the French left wing under Ney was also engaged in battle. That commander had been instructed verbally to brush aside any opposition at Quatre-Bras and advance on Brussels. Ney carried out this order in leisurely fashion and advanced three miles from

Gosselies to Frasnes, where he received at 11 a.m. the Emperor's lengthy written directive sent off at 6 a.m. (see p. 270). He then ordered Reille, his leading corps commander, to deploy and dislodge the enemy holding the Quatre-Bras crossroads. But it was already too late. During the previous evening and night reinforcements had been arriving to support Perponcher's Dutch-Belgian division, and Wellington himself had arrived from Brussels at 10 a.m. and had taken charge. Reille advanced cautiously and did not attack until 2 p.m., when he was already outnumbered. Ney sent back for d'Erlon's corps to reinforce Reille, but found to his indignation that d'Erlon had vanished. While his leading corps and his cavalry were trying in vain to break the British squares at Quatre-Bras, at 4.15 p.m. Ney received an order from Soult, despatched from Fleurus at 2 p.m.:

The Emperor instructs me to inform you that the enemy has concentrated his troops between Sombreffe and Brye, and that Marshal Grouchy will attack at 2.30 p.m. with III and IV Corps. His Majesty intends that you should attack whatever is in front of you and, after driving it back vigorously, that you should move to our support and help to envelop the enemy.

Ney was now both angry and perplexed. His leading corps was heavily engaged and could not be withdrawn; his reserve corps had disappeared. How could he obey the Emperor's orders? Apparently what had happened was that General La Bédoyère, one of Napoleon's A.D.C.s, had been sent with an order scribbled in pencil for d'Erlon's corps to move eastwards to outflank the Prussian position at Ligny; the A.D.C. had passed d'Erlon's corps on his way up, and had taken it on himself to divert the corps in the direction desired by the Emperor.

According to d'Erlon's Memoirs, La Bédoyère was the bearer of a scribbled 'pencil note' given him by Napoleon. It has been suggested that this note ordered d'Erlon's corps to march to *Wagnelée* (2 miles north-west of Ligny), where his corps would have turned the Prussian right flank. La Bédoyère may have read the name as *Wangenies* (a village 3 miles south of Wagnelée), which was in rear of Vandamme's corps. The note has disappeared and La Bédoyère was shot two months later, so d'Erlon's erratic movement remains a historical enigma.*

* The officer who conveyed this unfortunate message to d'Erlon's corps was never given an opportunity to explain his action. Colonel Charles de La Bédoyère (1786–1815) was in command of the 7th Infantry Regiment at Grenoble when Napoleon arrived there on 7 March after his landing from Elba. La Bédoyère was one of the first officers to desert the King's service and join Napoleon, who made him a General and one of his A.D.C.s. After Waterloo, La Bédoyère was arrested and convicted by Court-Martial of desertion and treason; he was shot on 19 August.

Ney now received a further order from Soult, despatched from Fleurus at 3.30 p.m.:

An hour ago I informed you that the Emperor would at 2.30 p.m. attack the enemy position between the villages of Saint-Amand and Brye; the battle is now in full swing. His Majesty instructs me to order you to move at once so as to envelop the enemy's right flank and make every effort to fall on his rear; his army is lost if you act vigorously; the fate of France is in your hands. So do not hesitate for a moment in carrying out the Emperor's orders, and advance on the high ground between Brye and Saint-Amand to take part in a decisive victory. The enemy has been caught in the very act of attempting to join forces with the British.

On reading this order, Ney completely lost control of himself, and at once sent an officer to recall d'Erlon to Frasnes. D'Erlon received Ney's order in the late afternoon as he was approaching the Ligny battlefield, where indeed the appearance of his corps in the distance created a panic among Vandamme's troops, who mistook them for Prussians. D'Erlon retraced his steps towards Quatre-Bras. His corps of 20,000 men and 46 guns had marched and counter-marched all the afternoon between the two battlefields, on either of which his intervention might have proved decisive. Napoleon's ability to direct a battle was evidently breaking down.

Night was approaching as d'Erlon returned to Ney's command, but it was now too late to renew the struggle. Wellington's reinforcements continued to arrive, and Ney was forced to retire to Frasnes after losing 4000 men; Wellington's casualties were slightly higher.

On the morning of 17 June Napoleon was in no hurry to bestir himself; in fact he was far from well. During the night Grouchy had sent Pajol's cavalry corps eastwards to keep touch with the retreating Prussians; at 4 a.m. he had reported back that the enemy were in full flight to Namur, and that he had caught up with their rearguard and captured eight guns. He was mistaken; the battery which fell into his hands had lost its way while trying to find its ammunition park. The whole Prussian army, apart from a few stragglers, was in fact heading northward through Gembloux to Wavre.

Pajol's report reached the Emperor at 7 a.m. as he was breakfasting at the Château de la Paix near Fleurus. It confirmed his opinion that Blücher was retreating through Namur and Liège to Maastricht and that Wellington's army was now at his mercy. He also received a report from Ney excusing his failure to occupy Quatre-Bras: 'A misunderstanding on the part of Count d'Erlon robbed me of the chance of a splendid victory.' To which Napoleon replied:

Your divisions acted piecemeal. If the corps of d'Erlon and Reille had been together, not an Englishman in the corps facing you would have escaped; if Count d'Erlon had carried out the movement on Saint-Amand ordered by the Emperor, the Prussian army would have been totally destroyed and we would have taken perhaps 30,000 prisoners. . . . The Emperor intends that you should move to Quatre-Bras.

At 9 a.m. Napoleon rode out to inspect the battlefield of Ligny; he visited the wounded in the dressing-stations and reviewed some of his troops. Then, rather late in the day, he gave Grouchy an operation order:

Proceed to Gembloux with General Pajol's cavalry corps, the light cavalry of IV Corps, General Exelmans' cavalry corps, General Teste's division (detached from VI Corps) and III and IV Corps. You will send reconnaissances towards Namur and Maastricht and pursue the enemy; find out the direction of his retreat and report his movements, so that I can guess his intentions. My headquarters are moving to Quatre-Bras, where the British were still in position this morning.

Napoleon here made the most disastrous strategic blunder of his whole career, and it led to his downfall. Although he was convinced that Blücher's army was finished and retreating to the Rhine, he sent, very tardily, on a purely reconnaissance mission, 33,000 men and 96 guns, nearly one-third of his available force. One cavalry corps, supported by an infantry division, should have been able to perform this task. The Emperor then left for Quatre-Bras; he never saw the unfortunate Grouchy again.

Napoleon's intention to pursue and destroy Wellington's army with his left wing was largely frustrated by Ney's culpable inactivity throughout the morning of 17 June. In spite of the fact that d'Erlon's corps had rejoined him, and notwithstanding the Emperor's orders to press on to Quatre-Bras, Ney's troops were still in their bivouacs near Frasnes when, about 2 p.m., Napoleon arrived within sight of Quatre-Bras. Ney and d'Erlon arrived a little later, and Ney excused himself for not being at Quatre-Bras 'because it was occupied by the whole of Wellington's army'. As a matter of fact Wellington, having at last heard of Blücher's defeat at Ligny, had at 10 a.m. ordered his infantry to withdraw to a defensive position which he had previously chosen, two miles south of Waterloo. The position at Quatre-Bras was now held only by a rear-guard consisting of Lord Uxbridge's six cavalry brigades, each with its attached Troop of Royal Horse Artillery.

Napoleon was furious when he saw that his prey had eluded him; throwing off all his lethargy of the morning, he set off in pursuit himself. Mounted on his fast grey Arab mare, Désirée, he put himself at the head of Milhaud's two cuirassier divisions and rode straight for Quatre-Bras. The nearest British battery ('G' Troop, R.H.A.) greeted him with a round of gun-fire, after which Uxbridge ordered his brigades to retire to Waterloo. At that moment an unusually severe thunder-storm burst on them, accompanied by torrential rain, and the ground became so water-logged that the pursuing cavalry were confined to the pavé roads. Three miles farther on, at Genappe where the Brussels chaussée crosses the little river Dyle, the British cavalry checked their pursuers with a rearguard action. The check was of short duration, and the chase continued for six more miles, when the French cavalry were finally halted by Wellington's guns in position on the ridge of Mont-Saint-Jean (see Map facing p. 272).

Napoleon spent the night at the farm of Le Caillou, two miles distant from Wellington's front line. His army, soaked to the skin and without rations, bivouacked by the roadside all the way back to Genappe; Soult had not issued any orders about billeting or bivouac areas. At 2 a.m. on the 18th an officer arrived at the Emperor's headquarters with a report from Grouchy, sent off from Gembloux four hours earlier:

The enemy, 30,000 strong, continues his retreat. . . . It appears that the Prussians have divided into two columns: one must have taken the Wavre road by Sart-à-Walhain, the other column appears to be directed on Perwez. One might infer from this that one portion will join Wellington, and that the centre, Blücher's army, will retire on Liège. After the battle of Fleurus, one Prussian column took the Namur road.

After a day's reconnaissance with two cavalry corps at his disposal, Grouchy's report was not very illuminating, but it did give a hint that at least part of Blücher's army might be trying to join Wellington. Although the messenger had been told to bring back an immediate reply with further instructions, Napoleon took no action for another eight hours, when Soult was told to send Grouchy the following directive:

The Emperor has received your first report sent from Gembloux. You only told His Majesty of two Prussian columns that passed through Sauvenières and Sart-à-Walhain; however, we have reports that a third, pretty strong column passed through Géry and Gentinnes in the direction of Wavre. The Emperor instructs me to inform you that he is now about to attack the British army which is in position at Waterloo, near the Forest of Soignes. His Majesty therefore wishes you to direct your movement on Wavre, in order to be nearer to us, to be in operational touch, and to link our communications, driving before you the corps of the Prussian army which has taken that direction and which may have halted at Wavre, which you should reach as soon as possible.

You will send some light detachments to pursue the enemy columns on your right, so as to observe their movements and pick up their stragglers.

This makes it clear that Napoleon did not require any reinforcement from Grouchy; he was convinced that the Prussians were on the run, and Grouchy's role was to get to Wavre and interpose himself between the Prussians and Waterloo.

The morning of 18 June was fine after the deluge of the day before. Napoleon went out before dawn with Soult to inspect the battlefield. He indicated the assembly positions for the corps in front line on the forward slope of the gentle rise at the Belle Alliance inn, parallel to Wellington's position and within 1400 yards of it—easy cannon range. He gave orders that the army should be ready to attack at 9 a.m. after the troops had breakfasted. It was a well-intentioned order, but very few units had any rations, as they had out-distanced their regimental transport.

At 8 a.m. the Emperor breakfasted with his staff at Le Caillou; he was optimistic, and particularly pleased that he had at last brought Wellington to battle. He told his staff: 'We have not less than ninety chances in our favour, and not ten against.' Soult, Reille and d'Erlon had all fought against Wellington in the Peninsula and were not so optimistic as their chief. Zero-hour for the attack was then postponed, as many of the troops were not yet deployed, and Drouot reported that the ground was too water-logged for the guns to get into position.

The Emperor had concentrated 72,000 men on the battlefield, supported by 270 guns; thus he had a distinct superiority, especially in artillery, over Wellington's 68,000 men and 154 guns. As an insurance premium, the Duke had detached a further force of 17,000 men and 20 guns to hold an alternative position south of Hal on the Mons–Brussels road, eight miles west of Waterloo, as he always suspected that Napoleon might attempt to turn his right flank and sever his communications with Ostende; General Fuller, a sound strategic authority, has condemned this dispersal of force as 'a blunder of the first magnitude' on the part of Wellington; the Duke, however, was perhaps wise to take this precaution against a commander of Napoleon's calibre; had the Emperor employed Grouchy's detachment of 33,000 men and 96 guns on the left wing instead of uselessly on the right, the result of the battle of Waterloo might have been different.

At 11 a.m. Napoleon issued his last operation order to his corps commanders:

As soon as the whole army is in order of battle about 1 p.m., when the Emperor gives the order to Marshal Ney, the attack will be launched to capture the village of Mont-Saint-Jean at the intersection of the roads. To support this, the 12-pounder batteries of II and VI Corps will be massed with that of I Corps. These 24 guns will open fire on the troops holding Mont-Saint-Jean, and Count d'Erlon will begin the attack with his left division leading, supported as necessary by the divisions of I Corps.

II Corps will advance on a level with Count d'Erlon's corps. The sapper companies of I Corps will be ready to fortify Mont-Saint-Jean immediately. (*Corr.* 22060)

There was no inspired manœuvre in this plan; it was a rigid tactical movement of medieval vintage, in order to break the enemy's centre with a massed phalanx. It might have succeeded against the Mamelukes; it was doomed to failure against unbroken squares of steady infantry supported by well-trained gunners. In his overweening contempt for the British troops and their commander, the Emperor was convinced that a preliminary bombardment by his favourite 12-pounders, followed by a wedge-shaped column advancing up the Brussels chaussée, would split Wellington's centre and demolish his army. The Emperor, accompanied by his Guard, would then have an easy 12-mile march to Brussels; the knapsacks of the Old Guard contained their parade uniforms for the occasion.

Wellington's position had been skilfully chosen. It extended for 4000 yards along a gentle crest, intersected near the centre by the Charleroi–Brussels chaussée. At a distance of 600 yards in advance of the right flank lay the château and farm of Hougoumont (Goumont on modern maps), surrounded by a rectangular walled orchard and copse; 300 yards in front of the centre of the position was the farmstead of La Haye-Sainte; both of these buildings had been put hastily into a state of defence, and were held as advanced posts.

The heterogeneous Allied units were judiciously intermingled along the whole front; the important right flank, north of Hougoumont, was allotted to Cooke's 1st Division, consisting of four battalions of British Foot Guards. The cavalry brigades were placed centrally in reserve between the front line and Mont-Saint-Jean, except for two British ones which formed the extreme left flank, where the ground was more level. The bulk of the 24 horse and field batteries occupied positions on the crest-line west of the Charleroi chaussée, from which they could sweep the glacis slope in front. The gunners were ordered by Wellington to ignore the enemy's batteries, and to concentrate their fire at close range on his infantry and cavalry.

Napoleon had deployed his army on the forward slope of the Belle Alliance ridge, facing Wellington's position; d'Erlon's I Corps extended eastwards from the Charleroi chaussée for 2000 yards, while on the left of that road Reille's II Corps occupied a similar frontage with its left flank south of Hougoumont. Behind d'Erlon was Milhaud's 4th Cavalry Corps, and supporting Reille was Kellermann's 3rd Cavalry Corps. Lobau's VI Corps, two cavalry divisions and the Imperial Guard were in central reserve behind La

Belle Alliance. The bulk of Napoleon's 36 batteries were sited on the crest-line running east and west of La Belle Alliance. His three 12-pounder batteries out-powered and out-ranged Wellington's 9-pounders and 6-pounders.

The battle began at 11.30 a.m. with a preliminary bombardment by 80 French guns, not only by the 24 12-pounders originally designated. The effect was not so terrific as Napoleon had expected; Wellington had followed his usual plan of making his infantry lie down behind the crest; a large proportion of the French round-shot, which on hard ground would have produced a devastating ricochet effect, plunged harmlessly into the rain-sodden forward slope.

Napoleon had a good view of the battlefield from the farm of Rossomme, 1400 yards in rear of La Belle Alliance. Strange to say, he handed over to Ney the whole conduct of the attack—a fatal error. Ney's gallantry in action was unchallenged, but he was headstrong and wayward, with little tactical sense. His blunders on the battlefield had led to unfortunate results at Jena, Bautzen and Dennewitz; on the previous day he had missed a great opportunity at Quatre-Bras. At this stage there was no reason why the Emperor should not have conducted the battle himself, without Ney's intervention; at Wagram he had personally controlled a battle-front five times as extensive as at Waterloo, and he had there handled twice the number of troops and guns than were now present. With blind intrepidity Ney repeatedly led the courageous French columns up that glacis slope against the British infantry squares and guns double-shotted with case and round-shot, only to recoil with heavy losses. Ney had had a similar experience five years earlier against Wellington's troops at Bussaco, but on this occasion it was Napoleon, not Massena, who had ordered the attack to be made frontally.

Napoleon had also been unwise in giving his youngest brother Jérôme command of the 6th Division in Reille's corps. Jérôme was a charming young man, 30 years of age, who had proved a complete failure as a naval officer, as King of Westphalia, and as a corps commander in the Russian campaign. His division now formed the left flank of Reille's corps; when the whole corps advanced, Jérôme, quite unnecessarily, launched his division in an all-out attack on the advanced post at Hougoumont, which he ought to have outflanked. Reille felt obliged to support Jérôme, so brigade after brigade were fruitlessly thrown in to capture this locality, which was never taken in spite of tremendous losses.

Meanwhile, to the east of the Brussels–Charleroi road, Ney was urging on d'Erlon's corps to capture the other key-point, La Haye-Sainte, which covered Wellington's centre. This assault was also made in massed columns, which suffered heavily and were charged successfully by two of Uxbridge's cavalry brigades.

Napoleon was now threatened with a new danger. The sturdy veteran Blücher, faithful to his promise, had urged his army westwards from Wavre over 12 miles of miry lanes to Wellington's succour. Leaving Thielmann's corps to hold Grouchy in check, 'Marshal *Vorwärts*' had brought up Bülow's fresh corps, followed by those of Pirch and Zieten. About 1 p.m. Napoleon's staff at Rossomme observed a distant column approaching from the wooded eastern horizon. It was believed at first to be Grouchy arriving, but half an hour later this wishful thinking was contradicted by the capture by a French cavalry patrol beyond Frischermont of a Prussian officer of Bülow's advanced guard. This officer carried a message from Blücher to Wellington announcing that he was on the way to join him. Soult despatched a second message to Grouchy:

At this moment we are engaged in battle near Waterloo, in front of the Forest of Soignes. The enemy's centre is at Mont-Saint-Jean. Therefore, move to join our right flank.

P.S. An intercepted letter shows that Bülow is going to attack our right flank. We think we can see this corps on the Saint-Lambert ridge; so do not lose a moment to close in on us and cooperate with us in crushing Bülow, whom you will catch in the very act.

An officer was sent off with this order about 2.15 p.m. Owing to the bad state of the roads he did not reach Grouchy's headquarters until 6 p.m., and arrived drunk.* Grouchy at that time was heavily engaged with Thielmann's corps and could not move.

Napoleon should now have called off his frontal attacks on Wellington's position and massed all his cavalry to cover his right flank and attack the heads of the Prussian columns. He did move towards Frischermont a part of his general reserve, consisting of Lobau's VI Corps and the light cavalry divisions of Domon and Subervie; Lobau only had two divisions (7000 men), for Napoleon had previously detached Teste's division to Grouchy's right wing. At about 4.30 p.m. Bülow's vanguard debouched from the woods beyond Plancenoit, so that Lobau was now faced by 30,000 men, backed by Pirch's corps with 25,000 more. Lobau was driven out of Plancenoit, only 1200 yards from Napoleon's command post. The Emperor threw in the Young Guard to support Lobau, and Plancenoit was recaptured.

* *Lachouque*, p. 236.

At this critical juncture Ney, without orders from Napoleon, placed himself at the head of Milhaud's cavalry corps and carried out a series of charges against the unbroken British squares between La Haye-Sainte and Hougoumont. The onset of these 5000 horsemen was irresistible; they actually penetrated between the squares and captured some of the gun-positions, but a counter-charge by Uxbridge's squadrons drove them back again in disorder. Kellermann's cavalry corps was then launched in support of Milhaud, but suffered the same fate. Ney had delivered his infantry and cavalry assaults independently, with no attempt at mutual cooperation between the two arms.

At 6 p.m. Napoleon gambled once more on breaking Wellington's front and ordered Ney to make another attempt to capture La Haye-Sainte. This was eventually achieved by two of d'Erlon's divisions, as the defenders had run out of ammunition, but Ney had exhausted all his cavalry and could not exploit the success.

At 7 p.m. the climax of the battle had come. The Prussians had built up their strength at Plancenoit and were threatening the Emperor's line of retreat. He now only had in reserve the battalions of the Old Guard. Sending two of them to throw the Prussians out of Plancenoit, he handed over eight battalions to Ney for a final effort to smash Wellington's line. Instead, however, of exploiting the gap at La Haye-Sainte, Ney led the Guard in two massed columns farther to the left against the sector held by the British Foot Guards. Though suffering heavy casualties from the French artillery, the British infantry stood firm; holding their fire until the enemy were within 20 yards, they met them with a shattering volley; the Guard recoiled, broken. Napoleon had expended his last reserve; it was his final gamble.

As the attack by the Imperial Guard melted away, the sun was sinking. Wellington gave the signal for the whole line to advance. Most of his own troops were too exhausted to continue, but the Prussians eagerly took up the pursuit. Napoleon's army abandoned the field; the Emperor himself rode off at 9 p.m. and reached Genappe at five o'clock the following morning. Three days later he abdicated.

It was the end of an era. Napoleon had attempted too much, and he was worn out in body and spirit. If he had been badly served, he was himself to blame; he was too confident in his own abilities and too contemptuous of others. During his meteoric career his military genius shone unrivalled, and the aura of his legend still glows.

Six years later, after Napoleon's death on St. Helena, the following pronouncement was made by Carl XIV Johan, King of Sweden, the former

Marshal Jean-Baptiste Bernadotte, who had fought both under and against the Emperor:

> Napoleon has not been conquered by men. He was greater than all of us. But God punished him because he relied on his own intelligence alone, until that prodigious instrument was strained to breaking point. Everything breaks in the end.*

It was a fitting epitaph.

* Léonce Pingaud, *Bernadotte, Bonaparte et les Bourbons*, 1901, p. 368.

Napoleon's Marshals

Created 19.5.1804

Berthier, Louis-Alexandre (1753-1815) *Prince of Neuchâtel and Wagram*
Moncey, Bon Adrien-Jannot (1754-1842) *Duke of Conegliano*
Augereau, Charles-Pierre-François (1757-1816) *Duke of Castiglione*
Massena, André (1758-1817) *Duke of Rivoli, Prince of Essling*
Jourdan, Jean-Baptiste (1762-1833) *Count*
Bernadotte, Jean-Baptiste-Jules (1763-1844) *Prince of Ponte-Corvo*
Brune, Guillaume-Marie-Anne (1763-1815)
Murat, Joachim (1767-1815) *Grand Duke (later King of Naples)*
Mortier, Adolphe-Édouard-Casimir-Joseph (1768-1835) *Duke of Treviso*
Bessières, Jean-Baptiste (1768-1813) *Duke of Istria*
Ney, Michel (1769-1815) *Duke of Elchingen, Prince of the Moskova*
Soult, Nicolas-Jean de Dieu (1769-1851) *Duke of Dalmatia*
Lannes, Jean (1769-1809) *Duke of Montebello*
Davout, Louis-Nicolas (1770-1823) *Duke of Auerstädt, Prince of Eckmühl*

(Honorary)

Kellermann, François-Christophe (1735-1820) *Duke of Valmy*
Serrurier (Sérurier), Jean-Mathieu-Philibert (1742-1819) *Count*
Pérignon, Catherine-Dominique (1754-1818) *Count*
Lefebvre, François-Joseph (1755-1820) *Duke of Danzig*

13.7.1807

Victor, Claude-Victor Perrin (1764-1841) *Duke of Belluno*

12.7.1809

Macdonald, Étienne-Jacques-Joseph-Alexandre (1765-1840) *Duke of Taranto*
Oudinot, Nicolas-Charles (1767-1847) *Duke of Reggio*
Marmont, Auguste-Frédéric-Louis Viesse de (1774-1852) *Duke of Ragusa*

8.7.1811

Suchet, Louis-Gabriel (1770-1826) *Duke of Albufera*

7.8.1812

Gouvion Saint-Cyr, Laurent (1764-1830) *Marquis*

16.10.1813

Poniatowski, Joseph-Antoine (1763-1813) *Prince (of Poland)*

15.4.1815

Grouchy, Emmanuel de (1766-1847) *Marquis (hereditary)*

Chronological Table

1763	10 February	Peace of Paris ends Seven Years' War.
1768	15 May	France acquires Corsica from Genoese Republic.
1769	29 April	Arthur Wellesley born (later 1st Duke of Wellington).
	9 May	Paoli defeated by French at Ponte Nuovo and driven out of Corsica.
	15 August	Napoleone Buonaparte born.
1774	10 May	Death of Louis XV and accession of Louis XVI.
1778	15 December	Napoleone Buonaparte leaves Corsica for France.
1779	1 January	Napoleone and his older brother Giuseppe enter religious school at Autun.
	15 May	Napoleone enters cadet school at Brienne.
1784	30 October	Napoleone enters École Militaire, Paris, as *cadet-gentilhomme*.
1785	24 February	Death of Napoleone's father, Carlo Buonaparte.
	1 September	Napoleone Buonaparte passes out of École Militaire as *lieutenant en second d'artillerie*.
	30 October	Buonaparte leaves Paris to join La Fère Artillery Regiment at Valence-sur-Rhône.
1786	1 September	Buonaparte goes to Corsica on long furlough till June 1788.
1788	June	Buonaparte rejoins his regiment at Auxonne, attached to School of Artillery.
1789	17 June	National Assembly assumes constitutional powers.
	14 July	Storming of the Bastille.
	16 August	La Fère Artillery Regiment mutinies.
	15 September	Buonaparte goes on leave to Corsica.
1790	13 February	Suppression of religious orders in France.
	14 July	Paoli returns from exile to Corsica; Buonaparte adheres to him.
1791	10 February	Buonaparte returns from Corsica to regimental duty at Auxonne.
	1 April	Buonaparte promoted *premier lieutenant*.

	20 June	Flight of Louis XVI to Varennes.
	6 July	Buonaparte takes oath of allegiance to National Assembly.
	1 September	Buonaparte's third furlough to Corsica.
1792	6 February	Buonaparte promoted *second capitaine* (antedated).
	1 April	Buonaparte elected Lieut.-Colonel, 2nd Battalion, Corsican Volunteers.
	8–12 April	Riot at Ajaccio.
	20 April	French Assembly declares war on Austria.
	29 April	Austrians defeat French Revolutionaries near Lille.
	15 May	French Assembly declares war on Kingdom of Sardinia.
	28 May	Buonaparte goes to Paris, instead of rejoining his regiment.
	10 August	Massacre of Swiss Guards at Tuileries by Paris mob.
	19 August	Prussians invade France.
	15 September	Buonaparte returns to Corsica with his sister Elisa.
	20 September	Prussians defeated at Valmy by Dumouriez and Kellermann.
	21 September	Establishment of National Convention.
	22 September	Abolition of French monarchy; proclamation of Republic; First day of Year I.
	28 September	D'Anselme invades and occupies Comté de Nice.
	6 November	Dumouriez defeats Austrians at Jemappes, near Mons.
1793	21 January	Execution of Louis XVI.
	1 February	French Convention declares war on Britain and Holland.
	20 February	French Convention calls up 300,000 conscripts.
	22–25 February	Failure of French landing on Maddalena Island.
	3 March	Buonaparte breaks with Paoli.
	9 March	French Convention declares war on Spain.
	18 March	Dumouriez defeated by Austrians at Neerwinden.
	5 April	Dumouriez defects to Allies.
	6 April	Establishment of Committee of Public Safety.
	31 May	Reign of Terror begins.
	2 June	Girondins overthrown by Jacobins.
	13 June	Buonaparte and family arrive at Toulon from Corsica.
	27 August	Toulon handed over to the British by Royalists.
	7 September	Carteaux and Lapoype invest Toulon.
	8 September	Houchard defeats Allies at Hondschoote.
	16 September	Buonaparte given command of artillery besieging Toulon.
	15–16 October	Jourdan and Carnot defeat Allies at Wattignies.
	16 October	Execution of Marie-Antoinette.
	18 October	Buonaparte promoted *chef de bataillon* (Major).
	17 November	Dugommier takes over command of troops besieging Toulon.
	17–19 December	French recapture Toulon from British and Royalists.

	22 December	Major Buonaparte promoted *général de brigade*.
1794	6 February	Buonaparte given command of artillery of Army of Italy.
	22 February	General Duteil guillotined.
	21 March	Dumerbion given command of Army of Italy.
	5 April	Execution of Danton.
	6 April	Dumerbion captures Onéglia (Buonaparte's plan).
	26 June	Jourdan defeats Allies at Fleurus.
	27 July	*Coup d'état* of 9 Thermidor, Year II.
	28 July	Execution of Maximilien and Augustin Robespierre. End of the Terror.
	9–20 August	Buonaparte imprisoned at Antibes, suspected of treachery.
	21 September	Dumerbion defeats Austrians at first battle of Dego.
	3 November	Schérer replaces Dumerbion in Army of Italy.
1795	3 March	Kellermann replaces Schérer in Army of Italy.
	11–15 March	Abortive French expedition to Corsica.
	5 April	Peace of Bâle between France and Prussia.
	2 May	Buonaparte leaves Army of Italy for Paris.
	18 May	*Coup d'état* of 1 Prairial, Year III, Revolt of Jacobins.
	8 June	Death of the Dauphin in Temple prison.
	24–27 June	Kellermann driven back by Austrians.
	4 July	France makes peace with Spain.
	22 July	Hoche defeats Royalists at Quiberon.
	21 August	Buonaparte appointed to *bureau topographique*.
	30 September	Schérer replaces Kellermann in Army of Italy.
	4–5 October	*Coup d'état* of 13 Vendémiaire, Year IV.
	16 October	Buonaparte promoted *général de division*.
	26 October	Buonaparte appointed to command *Armée de l'Intérieur*.
	30 October	Directory replaces the Convention.
	22–24 November	Massena (under Schérer) defeats Austrians at Loano.
1796	4 February	Schérer resigns command of Army of Italy.
	2 March	Bonaparte appointed to command Army of Italy.
	9 March	Bonaparte marries Marie-Joseph-Rose (Joséphine) de Beauharnais.
	11 March	Bonaparte leaves Paris to take up his appointment.
	26 March	Bonaparte assumes command of Army of Italy.
	12 April	Bonaparte defeats Austrians at Montenotte.
	13 April	Bonaparte defeats Sardinians at Millésimo.
	14–15 April	Bonaparte defeats Austrians at Dego.
	21 April	Bonaparte defeats Sardinians at Mondovi.
	28 April	Armistice of Cherasco with King of Sardinia.
	7 May	Bonaparte crosses the Po at Piacenza.
	10 May	Bonaparte defeats Austrians at Lodi. Suppression of Babeuf conspiracy in Paris.

	15 May	Bonaparte enters Milan.
	23 June	Armistice of Bologna with Papal delegates.
	29 July	Wurmser drives French from Rivoli plateau.
	2 August	Bonaparte defeats Austrians at Lonato.
	5 August	Bonaparte defeats Austrians at Castiglione.
	19 August	Treaty of San Ildefonso between France and Spain.
	8 September	Bonaparte defeats Austrians at Bassano.
	8 October	Spain declares war on Britain.
	15–17 November	Bonaparte defeats Austrians at Árcole.
	16 November	Death of Empress Catherine II; accession of Tsar Paul.
	16–30 December	Hoche's failure to land at Bantry Bay.
1797	12–14 January	Bonaparte defeats Allvintzy at Rivoli.
	16 January	Bonaparte defeats Provera outside Mantua.
	2 February	Wurmser capitulates at Mantua.
	14 February	Britain captures Trinidad from Spain.
	19 February	Bonaparte signs Treaty of Tolentino with the Pope.
	22–24 February	Failure of French landing at Fishguard, Pembroke.
	18 April	Preliminary Peace Treaty of Leoben with Austria.
		Hoche defeats Austrians at Neuwied.
	16 May	Bonaparte occupies Venice.
	28 June	French fleet occupies Ionian Islands (Venetian).
	8 August	Augereau to command Paris Military District.
	4 September	Coup d'état of 18 Fructidor, Year V; Barthélemy and Pichegru deported; Carnot escaped to Switzerland.
	15 September	Death of General Hoche.
	17 October	Peace Treaty of Campo-Formio between France and Austria.
	27 October	Bonaparte appointed to command Armée d'Angleterre.
	9 November	Berthier assumes command of Armée d'Italie.
	16 November	Accession of King Frederick-William III of Prussia.
	10 December	Bonaparte officially received by Directory in Paris.
	27 December	Riot outside French Embassy in Rome; Duphot killed.
1798	20 February	French arrest Pope Pius VI and deport him to France.
	23 February	Bonaparte advises against invasion of England.
	5 March	Directory abandons plan of invading England.
		French occupy Berne.
	12 April	Bonaparte appointed to command Armée d'Orient.
	26 April	France annexes Republic of Geneva and creates République Helvétique.
	19 May	Bonaparte's Armée d'Orient sails from Toulon.
	10–12 June	Bonaparte annexes Malta from the Knights of St. John.
	1 July	Armée d'Orient disembarks at Alexandria.
	13 July	Bonaparte defeats Mamelukes at Shubra Khît.
	21 July	Bonaparte defeats Mamelukes at Battle of Pyramids.
	1 August	Nelson destroys Brueys's squadron in Abu Qir Bay.

	2 September	Turkey declares war on France.
	5 September	France introduces conscription for all men aged 20–25.
	21 October	Revolt in Cairo against French occupation.
	29 December	Second Coalition formed against France.
1799	20 February	Bonaparte captures El Arish and invades Palestine.
	1 March	War breaks out between France and the Second Coalition.
	3 March	Russian fleet captures Corfu from French.
	7 March	Bonaparte captures Jaffa and massacres Turkish prisoners.
	18 March	Bonaparte commences siege of Acre.
	25 March	Archduke Charles defeats Jourdan at Stockach.
	16 April	Bonaparte defeats Turks at Mount Tabor.
	17 May	Bonaparte abandons siege of Acre and retreats to Egypt.
	4 June	Massena driven back to Zürich by Archduke Charles.
	14 June	Bonaparte returns to Cairo from expedition to Acre.
	18 June	*Coup d'état* of 30 Prairial, Year VII.
	17–19 June	Suvórov defeats Macdonald at the Trebbia.
	25 July	Bonaparte defeats Turkish landing at Abu Qir.
	30 July	French garrison of Mantua surrenders to Austrians.
	15 August	Suvórov defeats Joubert at Novi; Joubert killed.
	23 August	Bonaparte sails from Alexandria for France.
	27 August	Duke of York invades Holland with Anglo-Russian force.
	29 August	Death in exile of Pope Pius VI.
	25–30 September	Massena defeats Suvórov at second battle of Zürich.
	9 October	Bonaparte lands at St. Raphaël from Egypt.
	9–10 November	*Coup d'état* of 18 Brumaire, Year VIII. Directory abolished.
		Bonaparte, Sieyès and Ducos appointed Consuls.
	19 November	Duke of York's expeditionary force evacuates Holland.
	12 December	Constitution of Year VIII. Bonaparte appointed First Consul; Cambacérès and Lebrun, Second and Third Consuls.
1800	20 January	General Joachim Murat marries Caroline Bonaparte.
	24 January	Convention of El Arish (later repudiated).
	14 March	Pius VII elected Pope.
	20 March	Kléber defeats Turks at Heliopolis.
	5 April	Austrians attack Massena at Genoa.
	4 May	Moreau defeats Austrians at Stockach.
	15–20 May	Bonaparte's Reserve Army crosses the Great St. Bernard Pass.
	1 June	French capture Fort Bard.
	4 June	Massena capitulates at Genoa.
	9 June	Lannes defeats Austrians at Castéggio-Montebello.

	14 June	Bonaparte defeats Melas at Marengo. Death of Desaix. Kléber assassinated at Cairo.
	15 June	Convention of Alessándria.
	19 June	Moreau defeats Austrians at Höchstädt.
	15 July	Convention of Parsdorf.
	28 July	Preliminary peace between France and Austria.
	3 September	Admiral Lord Keith captures Malta from French.
	7 October	Secret treaty of San Ildefonso between France and Spain; Louisiana ceded to France.
	November	French expedition to Santo Domingo.
	5 November	Hostilities resumed between France and Austria.
	3 December	Moreau defeats Austrians at Hohenlinden.
	23 December	Armistice of Steyr.
	24 December	Bomb attempt on Bonaparte's life in Paris.
	December	Macdonald crosses the Splügen Pass.
1801	15 January	Armistice of Treviso.
	9 February	Peace of Lunéville between France and Austria.
	21 March	Abercromby defeats French at Alexandria.
	23 March	Assassination of Tsar Paul I. Accession of Tsar Alexander I.
	2 April	Nelson destroys Danish fleet at Copenhagen.
	April	Bonaparte establishes invasion camp at Boulogne.
	15 July	Pope Pius VII signs the Concordat.
	10 September	Bonaparte ratifies the Concordat.
	14 September	French finally evacuate Egypt.
	1 October	Preliminary peace treaty between France and Britain.
	13 December	French expedition sails from Brest to Santo Domingo.
1802	5 February	French expedition reaches Santo Domingo.
	25 March	Peace of Amiens between France and Britain.
	19 May	Institution of the Legion of Honour.
	2 August	Bonaparte proclaimed Consul for life. French annexation of Elba.
	2 September	French annexation of Piedmont.
	15 October	French invasion of Switzerland.
1803	19 February	Bonaparte's Act of Mediation in Switzerland.
	11 March	Bonaparte orders creation of two flotillas for the invasion of England.
	13 March	Bonaparte's stormy interview with British Ambassador.
	3 May	French sale of Louisiana to U.S.A. for 70 million francs.
	12 May	British Ambassador leaves Paris.
	16 May	Britain declares war on France.
	1 June	Mortier occupies Hanover and disarms Hanoverian Army.
	June–July	Five assembly camps formed for invasion of England and Ireland.

	23 August	Main invasion camps formed at St. Omer and Bruges; invasion flotillas concentrating at Ambleteuse, Wimereux, Boulogne and Étaples.
	9 October	Franco-Spanish treaty of alliance.
1804	13 February	Discovery of Royalist plot to kidnap Bonaparte.
	19 February	General Moreau arrested.
	28 February	General Pichegru arrested.
	9 March	Georges Cadoudal arrested.
	21 March	Duc d'Enghien kidnapped and executed.
	24 March	Promulgation of Code Civil (renamed Code Napoléon in 1807).
	15 April	Death in prison of General Pichegru.
	18 May	Bonaparte proclaimed Emperor of the French, Napoléon Ier.
	19 May	18 Generals created Marshals of the Empire.
	24 June	Execution of Georges Cadoudal; banishment of Moreau.
	2 December	Coronation of Napoleon I at Notre Dame, Paris.
	14 December	Spain declares war on Britain.
1805	11 April	Alliance between Britain and Russia.
	26 May	Napoleon crowns himself as King of Italy.
	4 June	Napoleon annexes Genoa.
	7 June	Prince Eugène Beauharnais appointed Viceroy of Italy.
	22 July	Villeneuve intercepted by Calder off Ferrol.
	3 August	Napoleon at Boulogne camp expecting to invade England.
	9 August	Austria joins Britain and Russia in Third Coalition.
	24 August	Boulogne camp broken up; *Grande Armée* starts its march.
	10 September	Austrians under Mack invade Bavaria.
	25 September	*Grande Armée* crosses the Rhine.
	7 October	French cavalry cross the Danube at Donauwörth.
	8 October	Murat defeats Austrians at Wertingen.
	14 October	Ney defeats Austrians at Elchingen.
	20 October	Mack surrenders at Ulm with 30,000 men and 60 guns.
	21 October	Nelson destroys Franco-Spanish fleet at Trafalgar.
	28–31 October	Drawn battle of Caldiero between Massena and Archduke Charles.
	14 November	Napoleon enters Vienna.
	2 December	Napoleon defeats Austro-Russian Army at Austerlitz.
	15 December	Convention of Schönbrunn between France and Prussia.
	27 December	Treaty of Pressburg between France and Austria.
1806	23 January	Death of William Pitt.
	15 February	Modification of Schönbrunn Convention between France and Prussia.

	1 April	Joseph Bonaparte created King of Naples.
		Joachim Murat created Grand Duke of Berg and Cleve.
	16 May	Britain declares blockade of French continental ports.
	20 June	Louis Bonaparte created King of Holland.
	4 July	British defeat Reynier at Maida.
	12 July	Confederation of the Rhine formed with Napoleon as Protector.
	18 July	Massena captures Gaeta from Neapolitans.
	20 July	Peace Treaty signed between France and Russia.
	6 August	Dissolution of German Empire; Francis becomes Emperor of Austria.
	9 August	Prussian army mobilizes.
	24 August	Tsar Alexander refuses to ratify Peace Treaty with France.
	1 October	Prussian ultimatum to Napoleon.
	7 October	Napoleon invades Prussia and Saxony.
	14 October	Napoleon defeats Prince Hohenlohe at Jena.
		Davout defeats Duke of Brunswick at Auerstedt.
	27 October	Napoleon enters Berlin.
	28 October	Prince Hohenlohe surrenders to Murat at Prenzlau.
	7 November	Blücher surrenders to Bernadotte and Soult near Lübeck.
	8 November	Kleist surrenders fortress of Magdeburg to Ney.
	10 December	Treaty of Posen; Saxony becomes ally of France and Elector created King.
	18 December	Napoleon enters Warsaw.
	26 December	Napoleon defeats Russians at Pultusk, north of Warsaw.
1807	1 January	Napoleon meets Countess Walewska in Warsaw.
	7 January	British Order in Council on carrying contraband to French ports.
	8 February	Indecisive battle of Eylau between Napoleon and Russians.
	19 February	Admiral Duckworth's squadron forces the Dardanelles.
	2 March	Admiral Duckworth withdraws from the Dardanelles.
	26 April	Convention of Bartenstein between Russia and Prussia.
	24 May	Kalckreuth surrenders Danzig to the French.
	14 June	Napoleon defeats Russians at Friedland.
	25 June	Conference between Napoleon and Tsar Alexander on Niemen raft.
	7–9 July	Treaties of Tilsit between France, Russia and Prussia.
	7 September	British capture Danish fleet at Copenhagen.
	27 October	Secret Treaty of Fontainebleau between Napoleon and Charles IV of Spain.
	7 November	Tsar Alexander breaks off relations with Britain.
	27 November	Prince Regent of Portugal sails for Brazil.

	30 November	General Junot occupies Lisbon.
1808	20 February	Prince Murat appointed the Emperor's deputy in Spain.
	March	12 Marshals and one General created Dukes.
	18 March	Spanish revolt at Aranjuez; Charles IV forced to abdicate and Ferdinand VII proclaimed King.
	24 March	Murat enters Madrid and suppresses rebellion.
	2 May	Spanish revolt at Madrid against French occupation.
	May	Napoleon at Bayonne forces Charles IV to abdicate.
	6 June	Napoleon proclaims Joseph Bonaparte King of Spain; Murat to succeed him as King of Naples.
	14 July	Bessières defeats Spaniards at Medina de Rioseco.
	20 July	General Dupont surrenders to Spaniards at Bailén.
	1 August	Sir Arthur Wellesley's expeditionary force lands at mouth of Rio Mondego in Portugal.
	17 August	Wellesley defeats Junot at Roliça.
	21 August	Wellesley defeats Junot at Vimeiro.
	30 August	'Convention of Cintra' under which French army evacuates Portugal in British transports.
	8 October	Convention of alliance between Napoleon and Tsar Alexander at Erfurt.
	15 October	Napoleon dissolves *Grande Armée* and creates the Army of the Rhine; three corps and three cavalry divisions transferred from Germany to Spain.
	27 October	Sir John Moore leaves Lisbon to invade Spain.
	5 November	Napoleon assumes personal command of the Army of Spain.
	23 November	Napoleon defeats Spaniards at Tudela.
	4 December	Napoleon enters Madrid.
	21 December	Moore's cavalry defeat Soult's cavalry at Sahagún.
	22 December	Napoleon crosses the Guadarrama in pursuit of Moore.
	24 December	Moore decides to retreat to Corunna and Vigo.
1809	1 January	Napoleon's decree limiting Prussian army to 42,000 men.
	16 January	Battle of Corunna (La Coruña); death of Sir John Moore.
	24 January	Napoleon leaves Valladolid for Paris.
	24 February	British capture Martinique from French.
	29 March	Soult captures Oporto.
	9 April	Archduke Charles invades Bavaria.
	20–23 April	Battle of Eckmühl.
	26 April	Wellesley lands at Lisbon with new British army.
	12 May	Wellesley defeats Soult at Oporto.
	13 May	Napoleon enters Vienna.
	17 May	Napoleon annexes the Papal States.
	20–23 May	Battle of Aspern-Essling.
	11 June	Pope Pius VII excommunicates Napoleon.
	5–6 July	Battle of Wagram.

	6 July	Pius VII arrested and removed to Savona.
	11 July	Armistice of Znaim.
	27–28 July	Battle of Talavera.
	29 July	British land at Walcheren, but evacuate in October.
	14 October	Treaty of Schönbrunn between France and Austria.
1810	2 April	Napoleon marries Archduchess Marie-Louise of Austria.
	17 April	Massena appointed to command Army of Portugal.
	9 July	Massena captures Ciudad Rodrigo.
		Napoleon annexes Holland as French territory.
	August	Napoleon annexes Westphalia as French territory.
	21 August	Prince Bernadotte elected Crown Prince of Sweden.
	27 August	Massena captures Almeida and invades Portugal.
	27 September	Wellington beats Massena at Bussaco, but retreats.
	10 October	Massena halted by Wellington's Lines of Torres Vedras.
	18/25 October	Napoleon issues Fontainebleau Decrees tightening blockade of British commerce.
	December	Napoleon annexes north-west Germany.
1811	January	Napoleon annexes Grand Duchy of Oldenburg.
	5 March	Massena commences retreat from Portugal.
	20 March	Birth of the King of Rome.
	3 April	Wellington defeats Massena at Sabugal.
	3–5 May	Wellington defeats Massena at Fuentes de Oñoro.
	10 May	Marmont takes over command of Army of Portugal.
	16 May	Beresford defeats Soult at Albuera.
	4 December	Napoleon starts preparations for Russian campaign.
1812	10 January	Napoleon occupies Swedish Pomerania.
	19 January	Wellington captures Ciudad Rodrigo.
	26 February	Treaty of Alliance between France and Prussia.
	March	Treaty of Alliance between France and Austria.
	24 March	Secret treaty between Russia and Sweden.
	6 April	Wellington captures Badajoz.
	24 April	Tsar's ultimatum to Napoleon to evacuate Prussia.
	28 May	Peace of Bucharest between Russia and Turkey.
	18 June	War declared between Britain and U.S.A.
	24 June	Napoleon crosses the Niemen and invades Russia.
	18 July	Treaty of Örebro between Britain and Russia.
	22 July	Wellington defeats Marmont at Salamanca.
	28 July	Napoleon reaches Vitebsk.
	17–18 August	Battle of Smolénsk.
	7 September	Battle of Borodinó.
	14 September	Napoleon enters Moscow.
	18 October	Battle of Tarútino.
	19 October	Napoleon evacuates Moscow.
	23 October	Malet conspiracy in Paris.
	24 October	Battle of Málo-Yaroslávets.

	17 November	Action at Krásnoye.
	26–28 November	*Grande Armée* crosses the Bereziná.
	5 December	Napoleon leaves the *Grande Armée*.
	14 December	Ney commands rearguard at the Niemen.
	18 December	Napoleon reaches Paris.
	30 December	Convention of Tauroggen between Prussian and Russian troops.
1813	25 January	Napoleon signs new Concordat with Pope Pius VII.
	26 February	Secret Treaty of Kalisz between Prussia and Russia.
	16 March	Prussia declares war on France.
	25 March	Death of Field-Marshal Kutúzov; replaced by Wittgenstein.
	25 April	Napoleon assumes command of *Grande Armée* at Erfurt.
	1 May	Marshal Bessières killed near Lützen.
	2 May	Battle of Lützen; Napoleon defeats Prussians and Russians.
	18 May	Bernadotte with Swedish corps lands at Stralsund to join Allies.
	20–21 May	Battle of Bautzen.
	26 May	Blücher defeats Ney at Haynau.
	4 June	Armistice of Pleischwitz between Napoleon and Allies.
	21 June	Wellington defeats French at Vitoria.
	27 June	Secret Treaty of Reichenbach between Austria and Allies.
	12 August	Austria declares war on France.
	17 August	Armistice of Pleischwitz ended: hostilities resumed.
	23 August	Prussians defeat Oudinot at Gross-Beeren.
	26 August	Blücher defeats Macdonald at the Katzbach.
	26–27 August	Battle of Dresden; Napoleon defeats Allies.
	30 August	Kleist defeats Vandamme at Kulm.
	31 August	Wellington storms San Sebastian.
	6 September	Prussians under Bernadotte defeat Ney at Dennewitz.
	3 October	Blücher defeats Bertrand at Wartenburg.
	7 October	Wellington crosses the Bidassoa and invades France.
	16–19 October	Battle of Leipzig; Allies defeat Napoleon.
	18 October	Bavaria and Saxony join Allies.
	30 October	French defeat Bavarians at Hanau.
	2 November	Napoleon retreats to Mainz from Leipzig.
	12 November	Wellington crosses the Nivelle.
	13 December	Wellington crosses the Nive.
1814	11 January	King Murat of Naples signs separate treaty with Austria.
	25 January	Napoleon leaves Paris for Châlons-sur-Marne.
	1 February	Blücher defeats Napoleon at La Rothière.
	5 February	Congress at Châtillon-sur-Seine opens.

10 February	Napoleon defeats Olsúfiev at Champaubert.	
	Châtillon conference suspended till 17 February.	
11 February	Napoleon defeats Sacken at Montmirail and Yorck at Château-Thierry.	
14 February	Napoleon defeats Blücher at Vauchamps.	
18 February	Napoleon defeats Schwarzenberg at Montereau.	
27 February	Wellington defeats Soult at Orthez.	
1 March	Treaty of Chaumont between Allies.	
7 March	Napoleon defeats Vorónzov at Craonne.	
9 March	Blücher defeats Marmont at Laon.	
12 March	Wellington enters Bordeaux.	
19 March	Congress at Châtillon-sur-Seine ends.	
25 March	Schwarzenberg defeats Marmont and Mortier at Fère-Champenoise.	
31 March	Allies enter Paris.	
2 April	French Senate declares that Napoleon has forfeited the throne.	
6 April	Abdication of Napoleon.	
10 April	Wellington defeats Soult at Toulouse.	
11 April	Allies ratify Napoleon's Act of Abdication; Treaty of Fontainebleau.	
26 April	Louis XVIII proclaimed King of France.	
28 April	Napoleon sails from Saint-Raphaël in H.M.S. *Undaunted*.	
3 May	Louis XVIII enters Paris.	
4 May	Napoleon lands at Porto-Ferraio, Isle of Elba.	
29 May	Death of Empress Joséphine at Malmaison.	
30 May	First Treaty of Paris.	
1 November	Congress of Vienna opens.	
24 December	Peace Treaty signed at Ghent between Britain and U.S.A.	
1815 26 February	Napoleon escapes from Elba.	
1 March	Napoleon lands at Golfe Juan near Cannes.	
13 March	Allies at Vienna outlaw Napoleon.	
18 March	Marshal Ney defects to Napoleon.	
20 March	Napoleon enters Paris.	
28 March	Allies renew Treaty of Chaumont.	
31 March	King Murat declares war on Austria.	
4 April	Wellington reaches Brussels from Vienna.	
3 May	King Murat defeated by Austrians at Tolentino.	
12 June	Napoleon leaves Paris for Belgian frontier.	
16 June	Battles of Ligny and Quatre-Bras.	
18 June	Battle of Waterloo.	
22 June	Napoleon's final abdication.	
3 July	Convention of Saint-Cloud regulating surrender of French army.	

	7 July	Allies enter Paris.
	15 July	Napoleon embarks at Rochefort in H.M.S. *Bellerophon* for Plymouth.
	7 August	Napoleon leaves Plymouth in H.M.S. *Northumberland* for St. Helena.
	13 October	Joachim Murat court-martialled and shot in Italy.
	17 October	Napoleon reaches St. Helena.
	20 November	Second Treaty of Paris; formation of Quadruple Alliance.
	7 December	Execution of Marshal Ney.
1821	5 May	Death of Napoleon on St. Helena.
1824	16 September	Death of Louis XVIII; Accession of Comte d'Artois as Charles X.
1840	15 December	Napoleon's body brought back from St. Helena and deposited at Hôtel des Invalides, Paris.

Bibliography

Correspondance de Napoléon Ier. (Paris, 1858–70), 32 vols.
Correspondance inédite de Napoléon Ier. (Paris, 1912–13), 3 vols.
Lettres inédites de Napoléon Ier, 1799–1815. (Paris, 1897), 3 vols.
Barras, Paul. *Mémoires de Barras,* ed. by G. Duruy. (Hachette, 1895), 4 vols.
Bonnal, Général H. *La manœuvre d'Iéna.* (Paris, 1904).
Bonnal, Général H. *La manœuvre de Landshut.* (Paris, 1905).
Bourrienne, Louis A. F. de. *Mémoires.* (Paris, 1829), 2 vols.
Chesney, Colonel Charles. *Waterloo Lectures.* (Longmans, Green, 1907).
Chuquet, Arthur. *La jeunesse de Napoléon.* (A. Colin, 1898), 3 vols.
Colin, Capitaine Jean. *L'éducation militaire de Napoléon.* (Paris, 1900).
Cugnac, Capitaine de. *Campagne de l'Armée de Réserve, 1800.* (Paris, 1901).
Debidour. *Recueil des actes du Directoire Exécutif.* (Paris), 2 vols.
Ferrero, Guglielmo. *The Gamble.* (G. Bell, 1961).
Foucart, P. *Campagne de Prusse (1806): Iéna.* (Paris, 1887).
Fuller, Major-General J. F. C. *Decisive Battles of the Western World.* Vol. II.
    (Eyre and Spottiswoode, 1955).
Geyl, Pieter. *Napoleon, for and against.* (Jonathan Cape, 1964).
Gourgaud, Gaspard. *Journal inédit de Sainte-Hélène.* (Flammarion, 1880), 2 vols.
Henderson, H. N. B. *A Dictionary of Napoleon and His Times.* (Cassell, 1920).
Herold, Christopher. *Bonaparte in Egypt.* (Hamish Hamilton, 1963).
Houssaye, Henri. *1815.* (Paris, 1905), 3 vols.
Jomini, Baron Antoine de. *Napoléon dans l'Autre Monde.* (Paris, 1827).
Kurtz, Harold. *The Trial of Marshal Ney.* (Hamish Hamilton, 1957).
Lachouque, Commandant Henry. *Le secret de Waterloo.* (Amiot-Dumont, 1952).
La Jonquière, C. de. *L'expédition d'Égypte, 1798–1801.* (Paris, 1899–1907), 5 vols.
Las Cases, Emmanuel de. *Le Mémorial de Sainte-Hélène.* (Paris, 1957).
Lettow-Vorbeck, Oberst Oscar von. *Der Krieg von 1806 und 1807.* (Berlin, 1891–
    96), 4 vols.
Liddell Hart, B. H. *The Ghost of Napoleon.* (Faber and Faber, 1933).
Ludwig, Emil. *Napoleon.* (Ernst Rowohlt Verlag, Berlin, 1927).
Madelin, Louis. *Le Consulat et l'Empire.* (Hachette, 1933).
Markham, Felix. *Napoleon.* (Weidenfeld & Nicolson, 1963).
Masson, Frédéric. *Napoléon inconnu.* (Paris, 1895), 2 vols.
Maude, Colonel F. N. *The Ulm Campaign, 1805.* (George Allen, 1912).

BIBLIOGRAPHY

Maude, Colonel F. N. *The Jena Campaign, 1806.* (Swan, Sonnenschein, 1909).
Maude, Colonel F. N. *The Leipzig Campaign, 1813.* (Swan, Sonnenschein, 1908).
Phipps, Colonel R. W. *The Armies of the First French Republic.* (O.U.P., 1926–39), 5 vols.
Quimby, Robert S. *The Background of Napoleonic Warfare.* (Columbia U.P., 1957).
Rose, J. Holland. *The Life of Napoleon I.* (George Bell, 1902), 2 vols.
Rose, J. Holland. *The Personality of Napoleon.* (George Bell, 1912).
Rovigo, Duc de. *History of the Emperor Napoleon.* (1828), 2 vols.
Saxe, Comte Maurice de. *Mes Rêveries.* (1757), 2 vols.
Ségur, Général Comte de. *An Aide-de-Camp of Napoleon.* (Hutchinson, 1895).
Six, Georges. *Dictionnaire biographique des Généraux et Amiraux français.* (Paris, 1934), 2 vols.
Thompson, J. M. *Napoleon Bonaparte: His Rise and Fall.* (Basil Blackwell, 1952).
Wartenburg, Count Yorck von. *Napoleon as a General.* (Kegan, Paul, Trench, 1902), 2 vols.
Wilkinson, Spenser. *The French Army before Napoleon.* (O.U.P., 1915).
Wilkinson, Spenser. *The Rise of General Bonaparte.* (Clarendon Press, 1930).

Index

The numerals in **heavy type** refer to the *figure numbers* of the illustrations

INDEX

Carteaux, General Jean-François, 36, 38–9
Carthage, 118
Casale, 195, 112
Cassel, 153, 192, 221
Cassina Grossa, 110, 112
Castaños, General Francesco, 185–6, 189
Castéggio, 106–7
Castel-Ceriolo, 107–10
Castelnuovo di Scrivia, 106
Castelnuovo (Veronese), 65–6, 70–1
Castiglione, 66, 69, 127, 258; 7
Castiglione, Duke of, *see* Augereau
Castille, 196
Catalonia, 183–4, 247–8
Cathcart, Lord, 182
Catherine, Grand Duchess of Russia, 218
Catherine, Princess of Württemberg, 151
Cato, 29
Caucasus, 81, 169
Caulaincourt, General Armand-Augustin, (Duke of Vicenza), 150, 219, 226, 257
Cavalry tactics, 25, 56, 112–13, 128, 142, 176
Cayenne, 77, 119, 133
Cervoni, General Jean-Baptiste, 51, 55
Ceva, 45, 48, 50, 52–4
Chabran, General Joseph, 98, 102–3, 111
Chalon-sur-Saône, 97
Châlons-sur-Marne, 248–52, 256
Chambarlhac, General Jacques-Antoine, 101–2, 106, 109
Chambéry, 102
Champagny, Jean-Baptiste Nompère de, 180, 182–3, 191
Champaubert, 249, 251–2
Charlemagne, 124, 179, 217
Charleroi, 264–5, 268, 270–1, 277–8
Charles, Archduke of Austria, 73, 114, 129–30, 138–40, 193–4, 198, 200–7, 209, 211–15
Charles IV, King of Spain, 169, 181–2, 184–5
Charles XII, King of Sweden, 219
Chasteler, General, 194
Château-Thierry, 249, 251–2
Chatham, 125
Châtillon-sur-Seine, 249–50, 257
Châtillon (Val d'Aosta), 103
Chaumont, 249–50, 264
Chemin des Dames, 254
Chemnitz, 243
Cherasco, Armistice of, 54, 58
Cherbourg, 117
Cherwell, Lord, 82
Chichágov, Admiral Pavel, 225–7
Chiese, 110
Chivasso, 104–5
Choiseul, Claude, Marquis de, 80

Churchill, Mr. Winston, 82
Ciney, 265, 268
Cintra, Convention of, 187
Cisalpine Republic, 79
Ciudad Rodrigo, 217
Cividale, 74
Civita Vecchia, 82
Clacy, 255
Clarke, General Henri-Jacques, (Duke of Feltre), 77, 151, 194, 205, 216–17
Clary, Désirée, (Princess of Ponte-Corvo), 166
Clary, Julie, (wife of Joseph Bonaparte), 166
Closewitz, 160, 163
Coalition, Second, 95, 115
Coalition, Third, 126, 128, 137, 145
Cobenzl, Count Ludwig von, 128–9
Coburg, 151, 153–5, 243
Colin, Captain Jean, 11, 24
Colle Ardente, 41, 45
Colle di Nava, 45
Colle di Tenda, 41, 45
Colli, General Michael von, 46, 50, 52–3, 70, 206
Colloredo, General Count Jerome von, 245
Colonna-Cesari, Colonel, 35
Committee of Public Safety, 38, 40–3, 183
Compiègne, 150
Concordat, Papal, 116
Condé, Prince Louis-Joseph de, 120
Cogliano, Duke of, *see* Moncey
Congreve, William, 26, 245
Constantine Pavlovich, Grand Duke, 144
Constantinople, 80, 121
Consular Guard, 62, 96, 107, 110
Consulate, 94–5, 110, 117
Continental System, 168, 178–9, 219
Cooke, Major-General George, 277
Copenhagen, 115
Corbett, Sir Julian, 126
Córdoba, 185
Corfu, 76, 87, 129
Cornwallis, Admiral Sir William, 119, 122, 124
Correggio, Antonio Allegri, 59
Corsaglia, 54, 57
Corsica, 13, 14, 16–23, 34–5, 42, 61, 82, 260,
Corte, 21–2
Corunna (La Coruña), 190–3
Cossacks, 142, 173, 220, 224–6, 229–30, 242, 254, 256
Cosseria, 53
Craonne, 249, 254, 258
Crema, 60
Cremona, 111
Cromwell, Oliver, 12, 95
Crusades, 80–1
Cuesta, General Gregorio de la, 185
Cúneo, 50, 58

Curial, General Philibert-Jean-Baptiste, 252
Custine, General Adam-Philippe, 40
Czartoryski, Prince Adam Casimir, 168

Dachau, 134
Dallemagne, General Claude, 59
Dalmatia, 76, 147, 179, 210–11
Dalmatia, Duke of, *see* Soult
Damanhur, 84–5
Damascus, 91
Damietta, 83–4, 87, 90
Danube, 67, 114–15, 129–40, 146, 169, 193–4, 195, 198–202, 204–9, 211–14, 216, 226; 26, 29
Danzig (Gdansk), 168, 171, 174–5, 178, 220
Danzig, Duke of, *see* Lefebvre
Daru, Pierre-Antoine, 169, 172, 242
Dauphiné, 262
David, Jacques-Louis, 103
Davidovich, General Paul von, 67–9
Davout, Marshal Louis-Nicolas, (Duke of Auerstädt, Prince of Eckmühl), 118–20, 125, 131, 134, 139–40, 142–5, 147, 149–51, 153, 155, 158–9, 161, 163–5, 168, 170–1, 173, 178, 180–1, 188, 191, 194–204, 209–10, 212, 214–15, 220–3, 225, 230–1, 237, 246–7, 263–4, 267, 282
Decrès, Admiral Denis, 117, 123–5, 133, 141, 151, 169
Dego, 42, 45, 47, 50, 52–3, 55, 57, 59, 60
Denmark, 182
Dennewitz, 242, 267, 278
Desaix, General Louis-Charles, 75, 79, 85, 87–9, 106–7, 109, 111–12
Desgenettes, Dr. René-Nicolas, 91
Despinois, General Hyacinthe, 66
Dessau, 243–4
Deutsch-Wagram, *see* Wagram
Dieppe, 119
Dijon, 97–9, 101
Dillingen, 134
Directory, 47–8, 51, 58–9, 61–4, 72–4, 76–7, 79–81, 91, 94, 96, 116
Discipline, 17, 22, 35, 57, 76, 92, 234
Dnepr, 221–2, 225
Dombrowski, General Jan Henryk, 170
Dominica, 123
Dommartin, Captain Elzéar-Auguste, 36, 38
Domon, General Jean-Simon, 279
Donauwörth, 132, 134, 195, 197–200
Donnaz, 103

INDEX

Dora Baltea, 103
Dornberg, 160
Dornburg, 159–60, 164, 166
Doumerc, General Jean-Pierre, 248
Dover Castle, 125
Dresden, 150–2, 155, 158, 194, 205, 220, 231–5, 237–44, 246, 253
Drissa, 221
Drouet, *see* Erlon
Drouot, General Antoine, 214, 233, 246, 252, 261, 265, 276
Düben, 244
Dublin, 23, 122
Ducos, Roger, 94–5
Duero (Douro), 190–1
Dugommier, General Jacques Coquille, 38–40, 47
Dugua, General Charles-François-Joseph, 85–7, 89
Duhesme, General Philibert-Guillaume, 102, 104, 106, 111, 183–5
Dumerbion, General Pierre Jadart, 40–2, 45, 47
Dunkirk, 117–18
Dupont, General Pierre-Antoine, 98, 100, 104, 183–7
Dürnstein (Danube), 139
Dürnstein (Styria), 74
Duroc, General Géralud-Christophe-Michel, (Duke of Friuli), 82, 130, 230
Duteil, General Baron Jean-Pierre, 17, 20, 30, 33, 40
Du Teil, General Jean, 30–1, 33, 35, 38–9, 52
Dvina, 221, 225
Dyle, 275

East Prussia, 168, 170, 172, 175, 220, 226, 229
Ebelsberg, 204–5
Ebersdorf, 155
Éblé, General Jean-Baptiste, 226
Ebro, 185, 187, 189, 237
Eckartsberga, 163
Eckmühl, battle of, 203–4, 216; 25
Eckmühl, Prince of, *see* Davout
École Militaire, 15–17, 22, 91
Eggmühl, 202–3
Egypt, 80–2, 88–91, 93–4, 96, 106, 114–15, 119, 121–2
Eisenach, 149, 153, 156
El Arish, 89
El Azhar, 89
Elba, 117, 260–2
Elbe, 149–50, 152, 157–9, 178–9, 229–31, 235, 237–9, 241–4, 246–7
Elbing (Elblag), 171, 175
Elchingen, 137–8, 196
Elchingen, Duke of, *see* Ney
El Dikheila, 83
El Rahmaniya, 84–6, 92
Elsnitz, General Anton von, 100, 105
Elster, 150–1, 153, 232, 244, 246
Enghien, 265

Enghien, Louis-Antoine de Bourbon Condé, Duc d', 14, 120
England, *see* Britain
English Channel, 80, 118–23, 125–6, 128, 130–1, 133; 14
Enns, 138–9
Épernay, 249, 251–2, 256
Erfurt, 149, 152–3, 157–9, 163, 188, 191, 232, 244
Ergolding, 203
Erlon, General Jean-Baptiste Drouet, Count d', 265, 268, 272–4, 276–8, 280
Erzgebirge, 149, 238, 240–3
Esdraelon, Plain of, 91
Esla, 191
Espagne, General, Jean-Louis, 176, 203
Essen, General, 173
Essling, 207–8, 210–11
Essling, Prince of, *see* Massena
Étaples, 118–19, 121, 125
Étoges, 252
Étroubles, 103
Etruscans, 260
Eugene, Prince of Savoy, 24
Eugène, General Prince, Viceroy of Italy, *see* Beauharnais
Europe, 92, 117, 124, 129, 145–6, 150, 179–80, 191, 220–1, 260–1
Exelmans, General Rémi-Joseph, 248, 265, 274
Extremadura, 185
Eylau (Bagrationovsk), 173–5, 178; 23, 24

Faenza, 73
Faypoult, Guillaume-Charles, 51
Feltre, 74
Feltre, Duke of, *see* Clarke
Ferdinand, Archduke of Austria, 62, 129–30, 134, 137, 140, 143, 194
Ferdinand VII, King of Spain, 181, 184
Fère-Champenoise, 249, 251, 256–7
Ferrara, 63, 73
Ferrol, 121, 123, 125–6, 128
Finckenstein, Schloss, 174
Finisterre, 125
Fischamend, 206
Fishguard, 80
Fleurus, 25, 270–3, 275
Fleury de Chaboulon, Pierre-Alexandre-Édouard, 261
Florence, 63, 261
Flushing, 119
Fontainebleau, 125, 182, 188, 249–50, 257, 260–1
Fontenoy, 27, 31
Forchheim, 151, 155–6
Fort Balaguier, 36–9
Fort Bard, 103, 105, 111
Fort de l'Éguillette, 36–9
Fort Mulgrave, 37–9
Fouché, Joseph, (Duke of Otranto), 94, 124
Fourès, Pauline, 88, 92

France, 19, 22, 24, 30, 79–80, 88, 94, 104, 115, 117, 130, 140, 143, 145–6, 149, 174, 181, 188–9, 210, 217, 228–9, 247, 258, 261, 263, 273
Franceschi, Major Jean-Baptiste, 101–2, 190
Francis I, Emperor of Austria, 46, 53, 74, 78, 93, 95, 140–2, 145, 192, 197, 206, 218, 237
Franconia, 230–1
Franken-Wald, 149, 153
Frankfurt am Main, 147, 150–1, 246
Frankfurt an der Oder, 242
Frasnes, 270, 272–4
Frederick the Great, 24, 27–8, 31, 148, 156, 165
Freiburg, 131
Freising, 200–2
French Revolution, 16, 18, 22–3, 29–30, 34, 116
Friant, General Louis, 164, 252
Friedland (Pravdinsk), 175–8, 180, 215, 234, 241, 267
Frischermont, 279
Friuli, Duke of, *see* Duroc
Fructidor *coup d'état*, 77, 98, 119
Fuentes de Oñoro, 218
Fulda, 152–3, 156
Fuller, Major-General J.F.C., 276

Galicia (Austria), 194, 219
Galicia (Spain), 185, 189, 192, 196
Ganteaume, Admiral Honoré-Joseph, 92, 119, 122–5, 128
Gap, 262
Garda, Lake of, 64–6, 69–71
Gardanne, General Gaspard-Amédée, 105–7, 109
Garéssio, 52, 55
Garnier, General Pierre-Dominique, 50
Garran de Coulon, Jean Philippe, 61
Gascony, 247
Gasparin, T. A. de, 38
Gaza, 90
Gazan, General Honoré-Théodore, 160
Geisenfeld, 200
Geisenhausen, 203
Gembloux, 270, 273–5
Gemona, 74
Genappe, 275, 280
Geneva, 99–102
Geneva, Lake of, 98–100
Genoa, 13, 42, 46, 50–1, 55, 61, 63, 82, 97, 99–102, 104–7, 111, 113, 124
Gentinnes, 275
George III, King of Great Britain, 95
Gera, 150, 153, 158–9, 163
Gérard, General Étienne-Maurice, 254, 265, 268, 270–1
Germany, 126, 133, 146–7, 149, 151, 174, 187–8, 194, 230, 237, 247, 252

302

INDEX

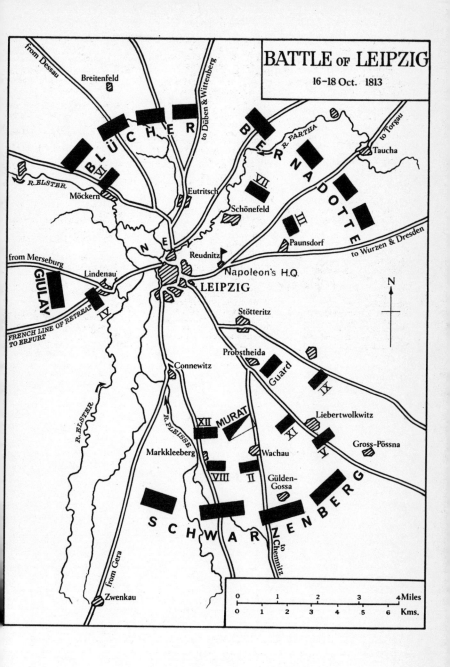

BATTLE OF LEIPZIG
16–18 Oct. 1813

from Dessau

Breitenfeld

BLÜCHER

IV

R. ELSTER

Möckern

BERNADOTTE

R. PARTHA

to Düben & Wittenberg

to Torgau

Taucha

Eutritsch

VII

Schönefeld

III

Paunsdorf

to Wurzen & Dresden

Reudnitz

Napoleon's H.Q.

from Merseburg

GIULAY

Lindenau

NE

LEIPZIG

IV

FRENCH LINE OF RETREAT
TO ERFURT

Stötteritz

Probstheida

Connewitz

Guard

IX

R. ELSTER

R. PLEISSE

Liebertwolkwitz

MURAT

XII

XI

V

Gross-Pössna

Markkleeberg

Wachau

Gülden-Gossa

VIII

II

SCHWARZENBERG

to Chemnitz

from Gera

Zwenkau

N

| 0 | 1 | 2 | 3 | 4 Miles |
| 0 | 1 | 2 | 3 | 4 | 5 | 6 | Kms. |

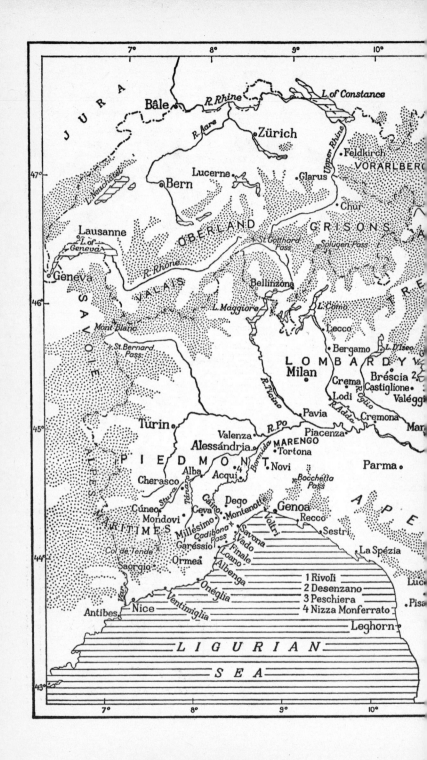

JURA

Bâle

R. Rhine

L. of Constance

R. Aare

Zürich

Feldkirch

VORARLBERG

47°

Lucerne

Glarus

L. Neuchâtel

Bern

Chur

Lausanne

OBERLAND

GRISONS

L. of Geneva

St. Gotthard Pass

Splugen Pass

Geneva

VALAIS

Bellinzona

46°

L. Maggiore

L. Como

Mont Blanc

Lecco

St. Bernard Pass

Bergamo

L. D'Iseo

SAVOIE

LOMBARDY

Milan

Bréscia

Crema

Castiglione

R. Ticino

Lodi

Valéggi

R. Oglio

R. Adda

Pavia

Cremona

45°

Turin

R. Po

Piacenza

Valenza

MARENGO

ALPES

Alessándria

Tortona

Parma

Bormida

Novi

PIEDMONT

Bocchetta Pass

Cherasco

Alba

Acqui

Stura

Caino

Dego

Cúneo

Ceva

Montenotte

Genoa

Mondovi

Millésimo

Cadibona Pass

Recco

MARITIMES

Garéssio

Vado

Sestri

Col de Tende

Ormea

Loano

Voltri

Savona

La Spézia

44°

Finale

Saorgio

Albenga

1 Rivoli

Var

Onéglia

2 Desenzano

3 Peschiera

Antibes

Nice

Ventimiglia

4 Nizza Monferrato

Luc

Leghorn

Pisa

LIGURIAN

SEA

43°

APE

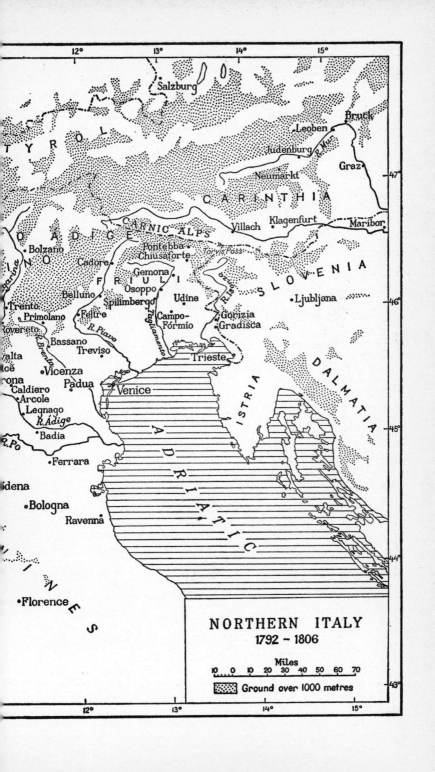

NORTHERN ITALY
1792 – 1806

Miles
10 0 10 20 30 40 50 60 70

Ground over 1000 metres

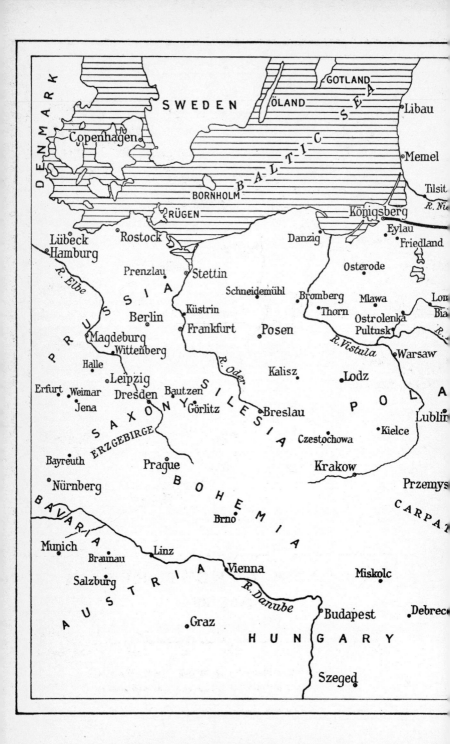

POLAND & WEST RUSSIA
1806-1813

Napoleon's invasion of Russia............
Napoleon's retreat............

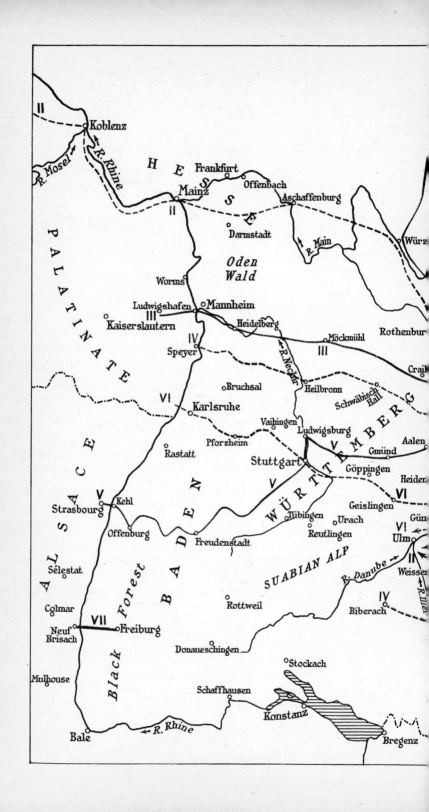

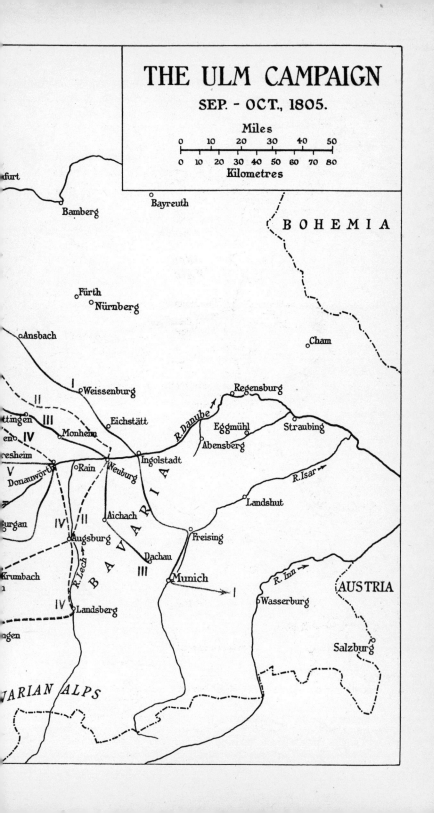

THE ULM CAMPAIGN
SEP. - OCT., 1805.

Miles
0   10   20   30   40   50

0   10   20   30   40   50   60   70   80
Kilometres

B O H E M I A

afurt

Bamberg

Bayreuth

Fürth
Nürnberg

Ansbach

Cham

I   Weissenburg

Regensburg

II

ttingen   III

Eichstätt

R. Danube

Eggmühl

Straubing

en   IV

Monheim

Abensberg

resheim

Ingolstadt

V   Donauwörth

Rain   Neuburg

B A V A R I A

R. Isar

urgan

IV   II

Aichach

Landshut

Augsburg

Freising

R. Lech

Dachau

III

Krumbach

Munich

R. Inn

AUSTRIA

IV   Landsberg

Wasserburg

ngen

Salzburg

VARIAN ALPS

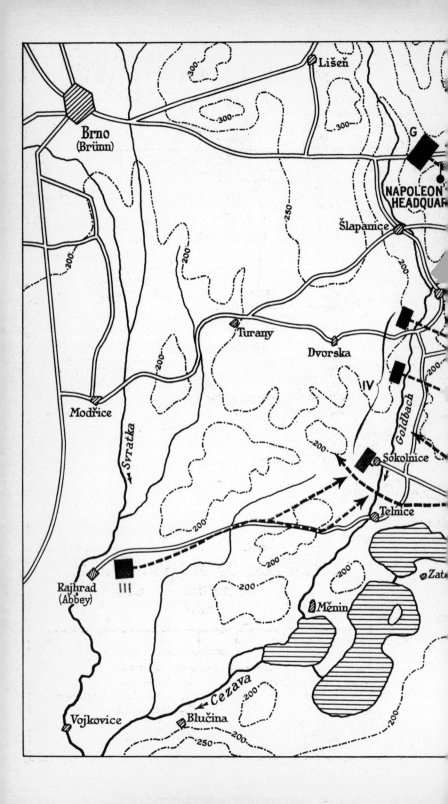

BATTLE OF AUSTERLITZ

2 DECEMBER, 1805

Miles

Kilometres

Contours at 50-metre intervals

I	Bernadotte	Ba	Bagratión
III	Davout	Co	Grand Duke Constantine
IV	Soult	Li	Liechtenstein
V	Lannes	Ko	Kolowrat
G	Guard	Bu	Buxhövden
M	Murat		

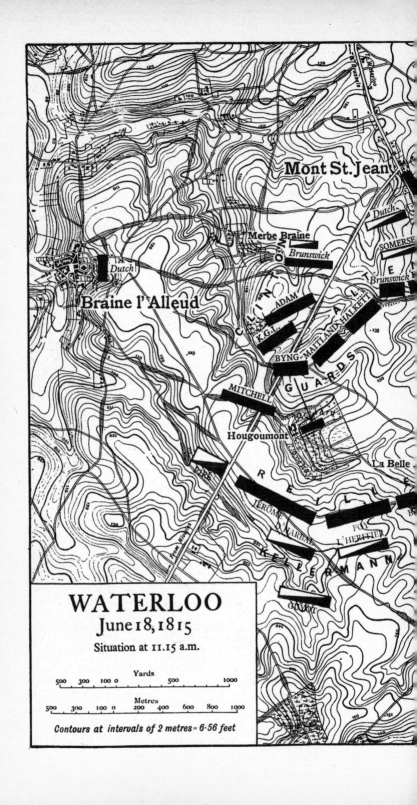

WATERLOO
June 18, 1815

Situation at 11.15 a.m.

Yards
500 300 100 0   500   1000

Metres
500 300 100 0   200 400 600 800 1000

Contours at intervals of 2 metres = 6·56 feet

Mont St. Jean

Dutch

SOMERSE

Brunswick

Brunswick

Merbe Braine

Dutch

Braine l'Alleud

C L I N T O N

ADAM

K.G.L.

MAITLAND

HALKETT

A

BYNG

GUARDS

MITCHELL

Hougoumont

La Belle

R E

JÉRÔME

L'HÉRITIER

BACHELU

FO

KELLERMANN

GUYOT

From Nivelles

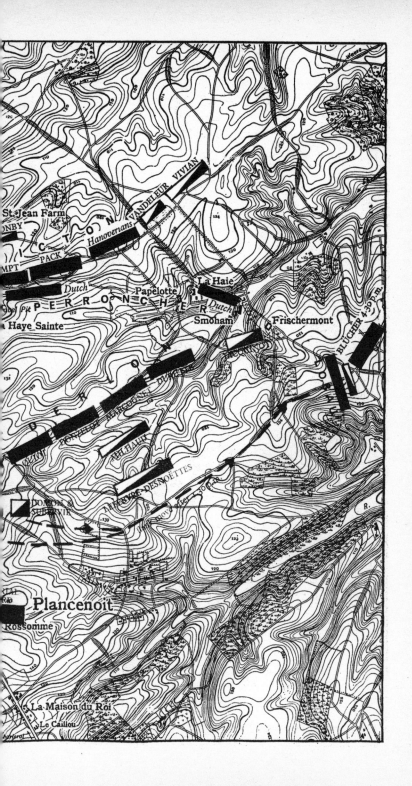

PENGUIN ONLINE

READ MORE IN PENGUIN

In every corner of the world, on every subject under the sun, Penguin represents quality and variety – the very best in publishing today.

For complete information about books available from Penguin – including Puffins, Penguin Classics and Arkana – and how to order them, write to us at the appropriate address below. Please note that for copyright reasons the selection of books varies from country to country.

In the United Kingdom: Please write to *Dept. EP, Penguin Books Ltd, Bath Road, Harmondsworth, West Drayton, Middlesex UB7 ODA*

In the United States: Please write to *Consumer Sales, Penguin Putnam Inc., P.O. Box 12289 Dept. B, Newark, New Jersey 07101-5289.* VISA and MasterCard holders call 1-800-788-6262 to order Penguin titles

In Canada: Please write to *Penguin Books Canada Ltd, 10 Alcorn Avenue, Suite 300, Toronto, Ontario M4V 3B2*

In Australia: Please write to *Penguin Books Australia Ltd, P.O. Box 257, Ringwood, Victoria 3134*

In New Zealand: Please write to *Penguin Books (NZ) Ltd, Private Bag 102902, North Shore Mail Centre, Auckland 10*

In India: Please write to *Penguin Books India Pvt Ltd, 11 Community Centre, Panchsheel Park, New Delhi 110017*

In the Netherlands: Please write to *Penguin Books Netherlands bv, Postbus 3507, NL-1001 AH Amsterdam*

In Germany: Please write to *Penguin Books Deutschland GmbH, Metzlerstrasse 26, 60594 Frankfurt am Main*

In Spain: Please write to *Penguin Books S. A., Bravo Murillo 19, 1° B, 28015 Madrid*

In Italy: Please write to *Penguin Italia s.r.l., Via Benedetto Croce 2, 20094 Corsico, Milano*

In France: Please write to *Penguin France, Le Carré Wilson, 62 rue Benjamin Baillaud, 31500 Toulouse*

In Japan: Please write to *Penguin Books Japan Ltd, Kaneko Building, 2-3-25 Koraku, Bunkyo-Ku, Tokyo 112*

In South Africa: Please write to *Penguin Books South Africa (Pty) Ltd, Private Bag X14, Parkview, 2122 Johannesburg*

INSPECTION COPY REQUESTS

Lecturers in the United Kingdom and Ireland wishing to apply for inspection copies of Classic Penguin titles for student group adoptions are invited to apply to:

Inspection Copy Department
Penguin Press Marketing
80 Strand
LONDON
WC2R 0RL

Fax: 020 7010 6701

E-mail: academic@penguin.co.uk

Inspection copies may also be requested via our website at:
www.penguinclassics.com

Please include in your request the author, title and the ISBN of the book(s) in which you are interested, the name of the course on which the books will be used and the expected student numbers.

It is essential that you include with your request your title, first name, surname, position, department name, college or university address, telephone and fax numbers and your e-mail address.

Lecturers outside the United Kingdom and Ireland should address their applications to their local Penguin office.

Inspection copies are supplied at the discretion of Penguin Books

READ MORE IN PENGUIN

PENGUIN CLASSIC HISTORY

Well written narrative history from leading historians such as Paul Kennedy, Alan Moorehead, J. B. Priestley, A. L. Rowse and G. M. Trevelyan. From the Ancient World to the decline of British naval mastery, from twelfth-century France to the Victorian Underworld, the series captures the great turning points in history and chronicles the lives of ordinary people at different times. Penguin Classic History will be enjoyed and valued by everyone who loves the past.

Published or forthcoming:

Leslie Alcock	**Arthur's Britain**
John Belchem/Richard Price	**A Dictionary of 19th-Century History**
Jeremy Black/Roy Porter	**A Dictionary of 18th-Century History**
Ernle Bradford	**The Mediterranean**
Anthony Burton	**Remains of a Revolution**
Robert Darnton	**The Great Cat Massacre**
Jean Froissart	**Froissart's Chronicles**
Johan Huizinga	**The Waning of the Middle Ages**
Aldous Huxley	**The Devils of Loudun**
Paul M. Kennedy	**The Rise and Fall of British Naval Mastery**
Margaret Wade Labarge	**Women in Medieval Life**
Alan Moorehead	**Fatal Impact**
Samuel Pepys	**Illustrated Pepys**
J. H. Plumb	**The First Four Georges**
J. B. Priestley	**The Edwardians**
Philippa Pullar	**Consuming Passions**
A. L. Rowse	**The Elizabethan Renaissance**
John Ruskin	**The Stones of Venice**
G. M. Trevelyan	**English Social History**
Philip Warner	**The Medieval Castle**
T. H. White	**The Age of Scandal**
Lawrence Wright	**Clean and Decent**
Hans Zinsser	**Rats, Lice and History**

READ MORE IN PENGUIN

PENGUIN CLASSIC MILITARY HISTORY

This series acknowledges the profound and enduring interest in military history, and the causes and consequences of human conflict. Penguin Classic Military History covers warfare from the earliest times to the age of electronics and encompasses subjects as diverse as classic examples of grand strategy and the precision tactics of Britain's crack SAS Regiment. The series will be enjoyed and valued by students of military history and all who hope to learn from the often disturbing lessons of the past.

Published or forthcoming:

Correlli Barnett	**Engage the Enemy More Closely**
	The Great War
David G. Chandler	**The Art of Warfare on Land**
	Marlborough as Military Commander
William Craig	**Enemy at the Gates**
Carlo D'Este	**Decision in Normandy**
Michael Glover	**The Peninsular War**
	Wellington as Military Commander
Winston Graham	**The Spanish Armadas**
Heinz Guderian	**Panzer Leader**
Christopher Hibbert	**Redcoats and Rebels**
Heinz Höhne	**The Order of the Death's Head**
Anthony Kemp	**The SAS at War**
Ronald Lewin	**Ultra Goes to War**
Martin Middlebrook	**The Falklands War**
	The First Day on the Somme
	The Kaiser's Battle
Desmond Seward	**Henry V**
John Toland	**Infamy**
Philip Warner	**Sieges of the Middle Ages**
Leon Wolff	**In Flanders Fields**
Cecil Woodham-Smith	**The Reason Why**